WOMANPR

MW00813863

CATHOLIC PRACTICE IN NORTH AMERICA

Series Editor:

John C. Seitz, Associate Professor, Theology Department,
Fordham University; Associate Director for Lincoln Center,
Curran Center for American Catholic Studies

———————————————

This series aims to contribute to the growing field of Catholic studies
through the publication of books devoted to the historical and cultural study
of Catholic practice in North America, from the colonial period to the present.
As the term "practice" suggests, the series springs from a pressing need in the
study of American Catholicism for empirical investigations and creative
explorations and analyses of the contours of Catholic experience. In seeking to
provide more comprehensive maps of Catholic practice, this series is committed
to publishing works from diverse American locales, including urban, suburban,
and rural settings; ethnic, postethnic, and transnational contexts; private and
public sites; and seats of power as well as the margins.

Series advisory board:
Emma Anderson, Ottawa University

Paul Contino, Pepperdine University

Kathleen Sprows Cummings, University of Notre Dame

James T. Fisher, Fordham University (Emeritus)

Paul Mariani, Boston College

Thomas A. Tweed, University of Notre Dame

Womanpriest

*Tradition and Transgression
in the Contemporary Roman Catholic Church*

Jill Peterfeso

FORDHAM UNIVERSITY PRESS

NEW YORK 2020

FRONTISPIECE: Chava Redonnet and Theresa Novak Chabot distribute
Communion at their ordination at Spiritus Christi in Rochester, New York,
in May 2010. (Photograph by Judith Levitt.)

Fordham University Press has no responsibility for the persistence
or accuracy of URLs for external or third-party Internet websites referred
to in this publication and does not guarantee that any content on such websites is,
or will remain, accurate or appropriate.

Fordham University Press also publishes its books in a variety of electronic formats.
Some content that appears in print may not be available in electronic books.
Visit us online at www.fordhampress.com.

Library of Congress Cataloging-in-Publication Data available online
at https://catalog.loc.gov.

For today's Catholics,
especially those who seek answers yet cling to mystery

CONTENTS

Introduction

St. Louis, Missouri
December 27, 2009

T HE FEAST OF THE Holy Family in December 2009, mere days after Christmas, was not my first experience with the Roman Catholic Womenpriests (RCWP) movement. Yet it was early enough in my research that I could not decide what to make of the womanpriest-led Mass at Therese of Divine Peace Inclusive Roman Catholic Community. Did this service remind me of the thousands of Catholic services I had attended throughout my life, or did it unsettle me because it was unlike the Catholicism I knew?

About twenty congregants had gathered on that Sunday evening. It was one of those cold winter days when a cloudless sky yields vibrant yellows, oranges, and reds as the sun sets. Inside the Hope Chapel of the First Unitarian Church in downtown St. Louis, Missouri, womanpriest Marybeth McBryan prepared to baptize her granddaughter, Chloe. RCWP had ordained McBryan to priesthood on November 1, All Saints Day, nearly two months earlier. Chloe, a spirited child with blond curls and a dark-green velvet dress, had just turned three on December 6. Chloe was the center of attention. Restless and curious, she often squirmed away from adult arms to explore the worship space in sparkling silver Mary Jane shoes.[1]

Much like any other assembled community of Roman Catholics on this feast day, we sang seasonal songs like "The First Noel" and "Silent Night." We heard readings from Sirach and Colossians, books in the Bible's Old and New Testaments. We listened to the story from Luke's Gospel about twelve-year-old Jesus teaching in the temple and becoming separated from his panicked parents. We offered prayers of the faithful, shared the sign of peace, and received the consecrated host and wine. These elements felt familiar to me.

Yet significant differences signaled that I was in new territory. The presiders were not iconic "Fathers" but rather three women: Elsie McGrath, Rose Marie Hudson, and McBryan. The small chapel's circular arrangement of chairs offered intimacy but didn't have the fixed wooden pews, statues, tabernacle, elevated altar, or large crucifix that typically signal Catholic space. The womenpriests had modified familiar prayers to be gender inclusive. For example, the Our Father began "Our Mother, Our Father, who are in heaven, hallowed is your name." Throughout this communal prayer, the word "kingdom" became "kin-dom," removing images of male monarchical dominion. During the liturgy of the Eucharist, the congregants and womenpriests together held the power to consecrate bread and wine into body and blood. As such, instead of intoning, "May the Lord accept the sacrifice at your hands, for the praise and glory of his name, for our good and the good of all his church," these worshippers said, "May God accept these gifts from our hands, for the praise and glory of God's name, for our good and the good of all the church." Not only did this prayer over the gifts turn male language of "Lord" and "his" to the neutral "God," but the sacrifice of bread and wine was at *our* hands, the community's, and not just the priest's.

"A baby changes everything!" Hudson's homily began. Congregants chuckled and nodded, and Chloe, as if on cue, walked about, touching chairs and altar pieces, noticing the worshippers as they noticed her. Hudson's reflections affirmed the challenges and rewards of parenting. She suggested that Mary and Joseph must have felt this way, too, as they watched Jesus grow. At age three, Chloe could watch, wonder, and wiggle. During the baptismal rite, McBryan whispered gently to her granddaughter, holding her hands while showing her the water, the baptismal font, and the oil of catechumens. McBryan's emotion was palpable. At one point, as she prayed over Chloe, she began to cry, and she had to pause to collect herself. Moments later, she tenderly marked Chloe's forehead with the sign of the cross, pushed the child's curly bangs back from her face while she poured the water, and prayed the ages-old words of baptism.

Meanwhile, I could not stop the questions coming to mind. Would Chloe, unlike billions of Catholics throughout the world and across time, grow up without equating priests with men? Would her grandmother's modeling suggest to her another way of envisioning Catholic authority? Could a celibate priest without children have spoken about parenthood with the same gravitas I felt in Hudson's homily, as she drew upon her personal experiences as a wife, mother, and grandmother? Was Chloe's baptism offering a different kind of sacrament because a grandmother-priest welcomed her flesh and blood into the church? What might be lost if a ritual becomes a family affair rather than a way of connecting a child to a broader religious community?

More questions arose during the distribution of the Eucharist. McBryan guided Chloe through the Communion line where McGrath distributed the hosts. McBryan received the Eucharist, and as she and Chloe turned toward the wine, Chloe began to fuss. McGrath interpreted Chloe's displeasure as I did: the child wanted Communion. Without missing a beat, McGrath broke off a small part of the host. She tapped McBryan and handed it to her to give to Chloe. Chloe took the Eucharist from her grandmother and placed it in her mouth, and her fussing subsided. Had Chloe just celebrated her first Communion? I thought back to a Mass at Therese in July 2008, when Hudson had prefaced the serving of Communion with this announcement: *"All* are welcome at this table."[2] I had taken Hudson to mean that at Therese, all people gathered could take the Eucharist, even if they were not Roman Catholic by baptism. I had not anticipated, however, a three-year-old receiving Communion, since Catholic children do not traditionally receive their first Communion until age seven or eight. Spontaneous maternal instinct, it seemed, had won out over Catholic custom.[3]

Did the womenpriests concern themselves at all with the church's typical practices around first Communion? After all, the Roman Catholic Church had already excommunicated these three women: a May 2008 decree, issued by the Congregation for the Doctrine of the Faith (CDF), stated that all women who "attempted to receive Holy Orders" were excommunicated *latae sententiae* (automatically). The CDF argued that the women had excommunicated themselves by pursuing ordination.[4] Even before that, McGrath and Hudson had been singled out and excommunicated *ferendae sententiae* (upon official notice) by then St. Louis archbishop Raymond Burke.[5] According to Roman officials, everything womenpriests did sacramentally was invalid, a blasphemous "simulation of a sacrament."[6] If McGrath, McBryan, and Hudson were not "real" priests, then Chloe's was not a "real" baptism, and the technicalities of her impromptu first Communion were moot because it was not a "real" Eucharist. Or, conversely, were the womenpriests "real," as they and allies saw it, because they were ordained as priests, operated as priests, and were recognized by congregants as priests? It was early in my nearly ten years spent in the company of Roman Catholic womenpriests, and I could not stop the questions from coming to mind.

I knew some things already. I knew that many of the womenpriests' most progressive liturgical and sacramental actions did not originate with RCWP, and I knew that other Catholic—but not "Roman Catholic"—groups ordained women. In fact, such practices had been in play for years in Europe and the United States. Intentional Eucharistic Communities (IECs), the Ecumenical

Catholic Communion (ECC), and some independent Catholic groups retain key elements of Catholic tradition and ordain women but are not in communion with Rome.[7] Communities of women religious—or "nuns," as they are often called—have long covertly celebrated the Eucharist without male priests. And I knew about Mary Ramerman, a Roman Catholic woman in Rochester, New York, who was ordained a priest in 2001.[8] After her illegal ordination, Ramerman's church, Spiritus Christi, left the Roman Catholic communion and became an independent Catholic church.

I also knew, however, that RCWP was doing something distinctive. I knew that RCWP's public ordinations of women, combined with the womenpriests' active ministries, all provocatively under the name "Roman Catholic," invited a reexamination of contemporary Catholicism and questions about women in religious authority. This was a group I needed to study further.

RCWP Emerges *Contra Legem*

The group that became known as Roman Catholic Womenpriests started in Europe in 2002. Its first public ordination took place on June 29, 2002, on a rented ship sailing the Danube River, when two male bishops ordained seven women to the priesthood.[9] The movement came to North America on July 25, 2005, when three womanbishops ordained nine women on a boat on the St. Lawrence Seaway, four as priests and five as deacons. The first ordination within US boundaries occurred on July 31, 2006, when three womanbishops ordained twelve women, eight as priests and four as deacons, on the riverboat *Majestic* in Pittsburgh. Holding these early ordinations on rivers and waterways allowed the movement to control attendance and avoid diocesan jurisdiction.

All of the womanpriest ordinations were, in terms of Roman Catholic canon law, *contra legem*, "against the law." Specifically, womenpriests violated canon 1024, which reads, "Only a baptized man can validly receive sacred ordination."[10] RCWP uses the same canon law to different, dissident ends. The movement acknowledges that it ordains women *contra legem* but defends doing so on the basis that canon 1024 is unjust. RCWP argues that when laws are unjust and contradict God's calling of women to the priesthood, it is morally just to oppose such laws.

RCWP's ordinations have continued in locations across the world, and the organization now comprises a number of branches and subgroups, including in regions of the United States, Canada, and Europe, and has ordained women in South America, South Africa, and (as of 2017) Taiwan. The Association of

Roman Catholic Women Priests (ARCWP) is a branch of the RCWP tree that formed a separate organization in 2010 and spans regional and international boundaries. In 2019, the entirety of the international womanpriest movement (including ARCWP and regions abroad) included 229 ordained individuals worldwide, most living in the United States and Canada.[11] RCWP describes itself as a Roman Catholic reform movement that seeks to change Roman Catholicism from within, and their mission statement promises "a new model of ordained ministry in a renewed Roman Catholic Church."[12]

Women's ordination activists have been asking for ordination since the last worldwide meeting of bishops in the Roman communion, known as the Second Vatican Council or Vatican II, which was held from 1962 to 1965 and resulted in a broad *aggiornamento* (updating) of church customs and theology for the modern world. This activism through formal channels has never been successful. Popes John Paul II, Benedict XVI, and Francis all have said that women's ordination is not open to discussion and have further contended that women have never been ordained in Catholicism's two-thousand-year history, a stance that many historians of Western Christianity find questionable. In 2016 Pope Francis created a papal commission to study the possibility of women joining the diaconate. The office of deacon is an ordained role preceding the office of priest; some deacons—aptly called "transitional deacons"—go on to become priests, while those who are members of the "permanent diaconate" can marry/be married. Yet Francis repeated his predecessors' claims that only men could be ordained priests (even if women could be deacons) and added "that door is closed" to the question of including women in priesthood. Some have heard Francis as saying that the ban on women priests will stand "forever."[13]

Within the last half century, the ban on women priests (and most clerical marriage) has become more glaring partly because of the massive drop in numbers of US priests since Vatican II. In the US, there were 58,632 priests in 1965 but only 39,600 in 2013.[14] The post–Vatican II decline creates ministerial challenges because there are fewer priests to pastor parishes and provide sacraments. Vocations are actually increasing in Africa and Asia, however, so to counter this distinctly Western problem, priests from non-English-speaking countries serve many North American Catholic parishes.[15] American bishops have employed laypeople—including laywomen—as parish administrators for priestless parishes; they do many of the pastoral and administrative tasks of an ordained priest but not the sacramental work.[16] Thus, Catholic officials are working to alleviate the declining vocations in North America and Europe and are willing to use women administratively, even though they will not entertain the idea of ordaining women to priesthood.

Exacerbating the issue in the Western church are majorities of Roman Catholics who support the idea of ordaining women as priests. A 2015 Pew study on American Catholics and family life revealed that 59 percent of Catholics, 77 percent of cultural Catholics, and 66 percent of ex-Catholics support allowing women to be priests.[17] These figures coincide with the 2015–2016 Gender and Religious Representation Survey, which found that 69.5 percent of surveyed American Catholics supported women's ordination.[18] A 2014 Univision survey, conducted by Bendixen & Amandi International, sampled Roman Catholics in the US, Mexico, Colombia, Brazil, Argentina, France, Spain, Italy, Poland, the Philippines, Uganda, and Congo. In France, Spain, Argentina, Italy, Brazil, and (again) the United States, the majority of respondents showed a willingness to ordain women as priests. The divide between Europe and the Americas on the one hand and Africa and Asia on the other—on this issue and many others, including married priests and Communion for divorced Catholics—helps illustrate the challenges of a universal Catholicism when opinions diverge so widely around the world.[19]

Into this contentious context steps Roman Catholic Womenpriests. RCWP agitates for women's ordination and stands out from its activist predecessors: womenpriests do not ask for permission to become priests; they just do it. RCWP disagrees with Roman authorities both historically and pragmatically: the group invokes scholarship attesting to women's ordination in early Christendom and argues that a return to ordained female leadership (and married clergy) is a commonsense way of addressing the current problem of declining vocations. Womenpriests believe that they must defy the official Catholic teaching that only men can be priests in order to restore and redeem the Roman Catholic Church. Womenpriests' actions are designed to be controversial because they are constructing a new model of priesthood that invites new models for being Roman Catholic. The group's very existence is an ongoing protest against official Catholic doctrine and offers an alternative Roman Catholic Church in the bodies of womenpriests.

Adding to the controversy, womenpriests assert that, despite their *contra legem* ordinations and official excommunications, they are still validly ordained. While they cannot study for priesthood in Roman Catholic seminaries, they take part in an RCWP-designed preparation program that requires a master of divinity degree or its equivalent. To ensure canonical validity, RCWP conducts ordinations "in the line of apostolic succession," which Catholics understand as an unbroken chain of ordination going back to Jesus's apostles and which determines Catholic ordinations as ritually effective or "valid." Womenpriests agree that their ordinations are illegal because they break canon law but argue that they are valid because they are in the line of apostolic succession. In Catholic theological and catechumenal discussions, this difference between valid and legal ordination basically means that, while everyone agrees that the Roman Catholic Church did not sanction the RCWP ordinations, there is more ambiguity about whether womenpriests have the ritual power to celebrate the sacraments on Roman terms.

Roman Catholic leadership says womenpriests definitely do not have the ritual power to celebrate sacraments. In fact, Rome's official stance holds that even a valid ordination will not "work" on a woman because woman are not biologically male and only males can stand *in persona Christi*, that is, in the place of Christ as a sacramental minister of the church.[20] Following John Paul II's 1994 *Ordinatio Sacerdotalis*, Rome contends that it has "no authority whatsoever" to confer ordination on a woman, since it is Christ's will and Roman Catholic tradition that priesthood be reserved for men alone.[21] Rome holds that the matter is "definitively" and "authoritatively settled" and has condemned the women's actions as heretical and schismatic.[22]

But womenpriests' actual congregations get past technical concerns around official status fairly quickly, as do many of RCWP's allies across the Catholic world, including the historic Women's Ordination Conference (founded in 1975), the leadership of the twenty-five-thousand-member lay organization Call to Action, the editorial staff of the *National Catholic Reporter* (an influential, liberal-leaning newspaper), and numerous other progressive Roman Catholic organizations. Like RCWP, these allies find the ban on women's ordination unjust. They also recognize, very pragmatically, that womenpriests act as male priests do. They pray familiar prayers; they lead worship communities and perform sacraments; they minister to the oppressed and marginalized.

Womenpriests also act as male priests do not. They use gender-inclusive language. They reject clerical celibacy and preside over democratized communities. They embrace sexual diversity and therefore perform sacraments more widely than officially ordained priests, including officiating same-sex weddings.[23] They do not pledge obedience to a bishop, nor do higher-ranking clerics determine their ministerial assignments. The movement does not pay its priests, nor can it afford to, and thus the women are "worker priests" who carve space for their priesthoods out of their existing lives and careers. The womenpriests wear vestments that are far simpler than those worn by male Roman Catholic priests.

Many womenpriests are married, some are lesbians, and most—like McBryan, McGrath, and Hudson—are mothers and grandmothers. All of this, they say, is part of enacting the changes that the Roman church desperately needs to preserve what is rich, true, and holy about Catholicism in contemporary times. These stances, too, give the RCWP movement admirers and points of connection with their congregations and allies.

Womenpriests do what they do because they hold two separate and seemingly opposing beliefs. While they believe that Roman Catholic traditions are too precious to lose, they also believe that Catholic women deserve the opportunity to serve the church through the ministerial priesthood. By getting ordained illegally and disobeying Vatican teachings, womenpriests are declaring that sacraments are important, priesthood is important, and the Roman Catholic faith is important. Quite simply, the RCWP movement believes that positive change for Roman Catholicism demands the inclusion of women in the priestly office.

As ordained women who see the official church rejecting their calls and claims to priesthood, womenpriests carry in their bodies, their histories, their educations, their ministries, and their sacramental actions a multitude of tensions confronting the contemporary Roman church. Whereas tens of thousands of American Catholics who want gender reform have left the Roman Catholic Church altogether, RCWP's women have stayed. Whereas tens of thousands of Roman Catholics horrified by the sex-abuse crisis and frustrated by Rome's slow pace of change have turned to Protestant Christianity, womenpriests have doubled down on the value of Roman Catholicism. Whereas older generations of Catholics are some of the most conservative in the US church, these female (mostly) baby boomers are outspoken agitators working to change their church. Whereas other Catholic feminists have used academic and theological arguments to challenge Roman authority, RCWP's women have put protest action front and center. In short, womenpriests are distinctive, and they offer a window onto the most fraught discussions within Western Roman Catholicism today.

Indeed, one is not excommunicated unless one has provoked authority at the deepest level, pushing boundaries deemed too dangerous to cross. Though a small movement, RCWP joins the multitudes of liberal Catholics who have claimed since Vatican II that the church is not limited to its clerical leaders but rather is made up of the whole "people of God."[24] Using their claimed authority as "people of God," the RCWP movement has ordained women separate from Roman leaders' approval—and Rome has pushed back. For that reason, even though Roman power is vast and RCWP is tiny, these two entities exist in a symbiotic relationship: like a small moon orbiting a larger planet, RCWP exerts force on Rome just as Rome exerts force on RCWP, with both bodies pushing and pulling. To understand either, you have to understand the mutual force between them.

For nearly ten years, I studied the Roman Catholic Womenpriest movement and its congregations in order to understand how and why this push and pull is unfolding now, in the third millennium of Western Roman Catholicism. This book attempts to answer the questions that started when I witnessed young Chloe's baptism and first Communion at an RCWP Mass. *Womanpriest* is my journey of discovery about a movement that uniquely illuminates contemporary Roman Catholicism as a whole.

Three main questions came to shape my research. First, why do womenpriests want to be ordained? Certainly, Roman Catholic priesthood today is a vocation under siege, largely because of the sex-abuse crisis and the hierarchical power malfeasance the crisis has laid bare. The title alone of a 2013 book by former Jesuit seminarian Garry Wills—*Why Priests? A Failed Tradition*—shows present-day suspicion of priesthood.[25] This does not stop womenpriests, however; in fact, it invigorates them. I argue that womenpriests want to be ordained to save their relationship with their church, with their idea of Catholicism, and with their God. Although decades of Catholic feminists have tried other strategies—including lay ministries, experimenting with Protestantism, becoming women religious (that is, sisters or "nuns"), or working with Women's Ordination Conference (WOC) and other Catholic reform groups—none of these options gave RCWP's women the spiritual, religious, and social justice sustenance that they believe priesthood does. Womenpriests' Catholic identity comes through a participatory—and often fraught—performance of female-embodied priesthood.

Second, what can womenpriests' actions as creative agitators reveal about contemporary Roman Catholicism? Opponents of women's ordination might dismiss RCWP as anathema, but my research shows that womenpriests display deference for much of Catholic tradition. RCWP retains Catholic rituals, Catholic sacraments, a ministerial priesthood, and the priest's ability to stand *in persona Christi*, all while calling upon institutional Roman Catholicism to minister differently, imagine differently, and be, in the womenpriests' view, more prepared to survive the current challenges to its reputation and membership. RCWP's reimagined Catholicism requires us to take a new look at contemporary Catholicism's ways of negotiating authority.

Finally, how can womenpriests' form of protest (specifically, *contra legem* ordinations resulting in excommunication) illuminate the challenges surrounding religious change in and beyond Roman Catholicism? Certainly, religious innovation is commonplace today: if someone does not like the options before them, they can look elsewhere or even create something new. RCWP's women are a splinter group that wants to remain connected to the original; with their *contra legem* actions, womenpriests telegraph a desire to remain part inside and part outside, standing at a transition between what was and what is still being imagined. In doing so, they must navigate a myriad of challenges: organizational, structural, interpersonal, theological, sacramental. Womenpriests' struggles illustrate the messy discursive practices of "doing" religious change, in Roman Catholicism and beyond.

As I argue throughout this book, RCWP straddles transgression and tradition, sometimes strategically, sometimes unintentionally. By ordaining women as priests, the group defiantly transgresses canon law and Roman Catholic tradition; yet *as* priests, transgressively ordained, the women enact many traditional elements of Catholic worship. RCWP picks and chooses which elements of their faith tradition to emphasize and which to jettison. Of course, *all* Catholics (and all religious people) do this, too, whether they recognize it or not; womenpriests are significant because they do this as priestly leaders of their vision for Roman Catholicism. This dialectic of the traditional and the transgressive marks RCWP's complicated relationship with the Roman Catholic Church, but it also makes RCWP an invaluable case study for how all people of faith navigate vast, internally diverse traditions and handle religious change, particularly when they are in some way marginalized within their faith communities.[26]

Spending Time with Womenpriests

Womanpriest is an ethnography of the RCWP movement, meaning my main approach to learning about womenpriests involved listening to their stories, participating in their liturgies, and reading their literature. In this book, I focus mainly on American and Canadian womenpriests during the group's first decade in North America. I look at the ways RCWP inhabits tensions around gender, priesthood authority, and religious change, and I analyze the actions and explanations of these women who defied canon law to become ordained priests. This project is not a work of theology, and yet I watched and analyzed womenpriests' theologies, including the embodied theologies womenpriests live out through their priesthoods.[27]

As I spent time with womenpriests and their congregations, I realized that I would learn the most in a dialogical relationship between researcher and subject.[28] Because as a researcher I would interpret findings and influence readers,

I hoped all the more to allow each subject to become an evolving presence of her own. RCWP's women do not speak with one voice—in fact, they differ in their theology, activism, and motivations—so I hoped to make room for all these differences, as messy as that might make my conclusions. And *Womanpriest*'s conclusions inevitably reflect my presence as ethnographer: on more than one occasion, women would report to me that a question I asked during the interview had moved them to reconsider an idea or practice. Rather than pretending that either my outsider expertise or their insider experience was sufficient, with this dialogue model I aimed to blend both perspectives for a richer account.[29]

Staying aware of my own position as an ethnographer seemed all the more important to me because the first RCWP news story I encountered touched me so personally. I began studying Roman Catholic Womenpriests in the fall of 2007 when Elsie McGrath and Rose Marie Hudson's actions captured my attention. As a native St. Louisan and "cradle Catholic" with seven years of education in Catholic schools, I learned from family and friends in my hometown about the controversy surrounding McGrath and Hudson's November 2007 ordination to priesthood. The story dominated local television and newspapers, and although I was in graduate school some eight hundred miles away, it seemed a story worth following. As the ordination date approached, St. Louis's archbishop, Raymond Burke, threatened to excommunicate McGrath, Hudson, and the ordaining womanbishop, Patricia Fresen.[30] Burke was none too popular with progressive Catholics in the area, and the RCWP ordination offered some Catholics a sense of schadenfreude at Burke's expense. Then, as the story spread beyond the Catholic community, a local reform Jewish synagogue, Central Reform Congregation (CRC), offered to host the illicit ordination (because no Catholic church could). Some of my relatives were active CRC members, and I knew of and respected Rabbi Susan Talve immensely. Archbishop Burke publicly chastised Rabbi Talve and insisted that her openness to RCWP would harm Jewish-Catholic relations throughout St. Louis. This contention amid interfaith cooperation, dramatically taking place between two religious communities to which I felt connected, drew me in.

Honoring the women's stories and spiritual disclosures while balancing my own position became one of this project's greatest challenges—but also an exhilarating dance. So much of what RCWP's women described was familiar to me as a Catholic progressive and a woman. Yet nearly every womanpriest I spoke to was one or two generations older than I, and they'd been struggling creatively with their Catholicism since long before I was born. Unlike these women, I had never experienced a call to the priesthood. I did not risk excommunication,

familial ire, or loss of my home parish to pursue my scholarship.[31] The fact that
I have spent years studying this group suggests correctly that I sympathize with
a feminist vision for the Roman Catholic Church, but I have long thought there
are myriad ways for the church to become more progressive, the ordination of
women being only one of them. As a scholar of religion, I tend to sight everything critically, including my own and others' personal experiences, so I contin-
uously kept in mind how struggles against sexism and patriarchy had shaped
the individuals I studied. Although most (though not all) womenpriests so far
are white, middle-class women with at least a master's degree, and as such are
privileged in certain ways, I also knew that their *contra legem* ordinations were a
concerted response to the authoritative forces that shaped their Catholic lives.[32]
And because critics often dismissed womenpriests before even hearing them out,
I knew that listening and understanding would be my first job if I wanted to tell
a full story.

Interviews made up the backbone of my research. I interviewed thirty-five
individuals between 2009 and 2014. Of these, thirty were women ordained
through RCWP and belonged to RCWP-USA, ARCWP, RCWP-Canada, or
RCWP in Europe. Interviews that took place in person or over the phone typically lasted anywhere from one to two and a half hours. Some were conducted in
writing (e.g., via email) if that was what the interviewee preferred. For all interviews, my questions offered only a starting point, and I encouraged respondents
to take the interview where their ideas pulled them. A full list of interviews and
the initial interview questions can be found in this book's appendices.

As part of my fieldwork, I attended RCWP services and sacraments whenever
possible, taking notes on what I observed and reflecting on my role as an ethnographic presence and participant. I attended four ordinations between 2009
and 2013, Chloe's baptism in 2009, and Masses in seven different RCWP communities in different parts of the United States. Because womenpriests cannot
celebrate Mass in Roman Catholic churches, they create worship spaces in living
rooms or non-Catholic churches and chapels. I often helped the women set up
for liturgy, placing candles and altar cloths, laying out worship aids and music
books. At Mass's end, I helped in the disassembly. When asked, I read inter-
cessory prayers at Mass or carried offertory gifts. I joined in the concelebration
of the Eucharist with all congregants. I welcomed the women's prayers for my
work; likewise, at their request, I prayed for them and their ministries. I invited
friends and family to attend RCWP Masses with me. I gratefully accepted womenpriests' help finding lodging when I traveled for research. I shared meals with
the women. I spent nights in their homes.

In order to connect with womenpriests I had not interviewed, as well as re-visit past interviewees, I conducted two online surveys in the summer of 2014. The first was designed for women ordained through RCWP and ARCWP. Thirty-five people filled this out. The second survey aimed to collect stories and experiences from womenpriests' congregants. Thirty people answered this survey. The questions I asked in these surveys can be found in appendices B and C, respectively.

I also found other ways to capture the voices of womenpriests, their communities, and their critics. The single most invaluable resource aside from my interviews was the more than one hundred hours of footage that went into the making of *Pink Smoke over the Vatican*, a 2011 documentary by filmmaker Jules Hart. This raw footage included thirty-two interviews with twenty-seven different people, including womenpriests and candidates for ordination, spouses and supporters, critics and congregants. I got access to *Pink Smoke*'s raw footage from Hart herself, who sent a box of video cassettes to my home. In addition, the 2008 book *Women Find a Way* offered personal stories and testimonies from twenty-five ordained women during a time when the nascent movement was beginning to explode with new members, creating questions about identity and objectives. The 2014 RCWP-published booklet *Here I Am. I Am Ready: A New Model of Ordained Ministry* combined photographs with a history and timeline.

Other primary and secondary sources enriched my research. When I attended RCWP's Masses, I collected worship aids and bulletins; I noted liturgical changes and modified song lyrics and prayer language; I recorded homilies and community announcements. Some worship communities invited me to join their listservs, and there I "overheard" conversations on topics ranging from next week's liturgical assignments to potluck preparations to prayer requests for sick members. One of the womenpriests shared with me her program of preparation for ordination, the RCWP educational curriculum that she was using as she moved into the diaconate and then the priesthood.[33] Many womenpriests sent me—often over email—items like homilies, personal mission statements, photographs, and local news articles.

The movement has a vast online presence. RCWP's website and, later, ARCWP's offered valuable starting places with biographies of the ordained women, footage from ordination ceremonies, news reports on RCWP ordinations, and promotional videos. A by-product of diverse opinions about the movement's direction, RCWP's document titled "Constitution and Operating Structures" was often amended during my research, but the website typically contained the latest available version.[34] Additionally, RCWP strategically uses online video to make visible womenpriests' existence, and I was able to watch several liturgies and ordinations online. ARCWP created a Facebook page, and I followed its regular posts starting in 2011; RCWP-USA followed suit a few years later. These social media and public relations efforts show how women-priests seek to direct discourse about their movement.

Criticism of RCWP was also essential to my research. Some progressive Catholics have criticized RCWP for conservatively upholding the priesthood or not fully crediting past Catholic feminist activism, and so I situated RCWP amid these intellectual, theological, and activist histories. Some conservative Catholics have criticized RCWP for transgressing church law and tradition, and so I immersed myself in official Roman Catholic teachings on the ministerial priesthood and theological anthropologies of gender. Copies of the *Catechism of the Catholic Church* and *The Code of Canon Law* were always close at hand during my analysis, as were papal encyclicals and decrees from the CDF. Whenever possible, I sought to hear the voices arguing against women's ordination and RCWP's validity. This meant, for instance, learning about the Roman church's stance on women's ordination not just from progressive women like Deborah Halter, author of *The Papal "No"* and a former president of the Women's Ordination Conference, but also from conservative women like Sister Sara Butler, author of *The Catholic Priesthood and Women: A Guide to the Teaching of the Church* and a theology professor at St. Joseph's Seminary in New York City.

Yet actual interviews with conservative Catholic critics proved difficult to come by.[35] This is understandable. If John Paul II's 1994 *Ordinatio Sacerdotalis* is to be the definitive word on women's ordination, and if the May 2008 general decree deepened the finality of the hierarchy's "no" to ordaining women, then it makes sense that Roman leaders would feel they could say little in public beyond reiterating the church's stance. But while this limited my possible ethnographic subjects, criticism from church leaders abounds throughout this study, found in print sources (e.g., diocesan newspapers, letters to the diocese and local churches), online sources (e.g., priests' blogs), and interviews (e.g., *Pink Smoke* documentary footage with ordained men).

A Word on Terminology

I am calling RCWP-ordained women "womenpriests," but RCWP does not have formal terms, and even the womenpriests themselves vary in self-naming. Consider Elsie McGrath's definition from 2011: "[Rose Marie Hudson and I] call ourselves priests. When using the proper title, it is Roman Catholic womenpriests because we were ordained through the Roman Catholic Women-priests initiative. When speaking in general, we are women priests because we are priests and we are women."[36] McGrath's response shows that the women are thoughtful about their titles; it does not show that all women are in agreement.

Throughout this book, I use *womanpriest* and *womenpriests*—without the space between words—to describe the ordained women because the primary North American movement is called Roman Catholic Womenpriests, and because a majority of the women call themselves "womenpriests." Moreover, *womanpriest* offers specificity that terms *priest* and *woman priest* do not, because *priest* includes ordained men and *woman priest* includes women who are ordained as priests in other Christian traditions, such as Episcopalian and Lutheran. As RCWP does, I sometimes use *womenpriests* as a catchall term to describe all of the women in the movement, some of whom are priests but others of whom are deacons or bishops.[37]

There are more disclaimers. First, there are men in RCWP, if relatively few (six in early 2019).[38] From the start of RCWP's time in North America, spokespersons often talked about ordaining those Roman Catholic men who, like called women, could not be ordained: this included men who were openly gay or married.[39] Second, the first openly transgender, nonbinary priest was ordained through RCWP in February 2020. Although this incredibly significant development happened long after my research ended, we must acknowledge that the RCWP movement is now growing in this direction and will continue to challenge familiar terminology around gender and priesthood.[40] Third, the RCWP-ARCWP split in 2010 also complicates naming, since ARCWP tends to make the term two words (*woman priest*). ARCWP and RCWP remain informally connected and largely amicable, but there are differences I explore later in more detail.[41] Throughout this book, when I use *RCWP* to refer to the entirety of the Roman Catholic womenpriests' movement around the world, I am to some extent eliding womenpriests and men, RCWP and ARCWP, but I do make the distinction when it's relevant to my analysis. With some misgivings, I decided that using *womenpriests* and *RCWP* as shorthand for everyone was warranted because Roman Catholic womenpriests who are women still comprise the majority of the international movement that started on the Danube River in 2002.

Roman Catholic is also a complicated term. In fact, the complexity and contestation of that term lies at the heart of this book, because the RCWP movement reimagines Roman Catholicism as it reimagines Catholic priesthood. Womenpriests provocatively understand themselves as standing in the *Roman* Catholic tradition, and they have named their movement accordingly. The RCWP movement deliberately positions itself against the canonical Roman Catholic Church and all the popes, cardinals, archbishops, bishops, and priests that uphold it—all the while claiming to be part of that same faith system. Indeed, the womenpriests' own rhetoric creates a particular idea of "the church," just as the womenpriests are cast as heretics, schismatics, and excommunicants in critics' pronouncements. Of course, the "Roman Catholic Church" is not just one monolithic thing, nor does the "Roman Catholic Church" *do* things; rather, the pope, the curia (administrators who assist in church governance), the magisterium (the church's teaching authority), ecumenical councils (international meetings between the pope and bishops), and so on do things. These entities speak *for* the Roman Catholic Church and sometimes claim to be speaking *as* the Roman Catholic Church. Sociologists recognize this as the micro-macro problem, where institutional structures are anthropomorphized and take human verbs.

This poses research challenges, as most scholars of contemporary Catholicism—myself included—would prefer to uphold the diversity of opinions in Catholicism today, among both leaders and laity. As illuminating recent studies like Julie Byrne's on Independent Catholics have shown us, Roman Catholics are only one type of Catholic—there exist numerous groups that resemble Roman Catholicism and use the name *Catholic* but who claim (or want) no connection to Rome.[42] And still, the church in Rome often seeks to speak and act as a monolith with a unified voice—over and above the multiplicity of Catholic perspectives. It is all the more important, then, that I am clear at the outset about what I, as author, mean by *Roman Catholic*.

For my part, I often streamline my prose by using "Roman Catholic Church," "institutional church," "Roman church," "church official(s)," "Vatican," and "Rome" as umbrella terms that capture the actions and utterances of the Roman Catholic Church's governing structures. These words describe the Catholic tradition that traces itself through the papal line. This authorial choice shows my attempt to name concisely the colossal entity that boasts over one billion members and claims a two-thousand-year history. But let the objection be noted: discussing the "Roman Catholic Church" can be problematic, not least of all because one of the primary challenges in today's Roman Catholic world is finding suitable answers to the question, "Who is the church?" Vatican officials will publicly contend that "the true church" comprises faithful members who regularly receive the sacraments and honor Rome's teaching authority, doctrines, and decrees. Women who claim to be ordained Catholic priests break this mold, all the while claiming to be a faithful part of Roman Catholicism. The back-and-forth continues, with no clean answers.

Book Chapters

In Chapter 1, "Called," I use three womenpriests' call-to-priesthood narratives to analyze the rhetorical moves RCWP's members make in interviews and personal reflections. In telling these stories, womenpriests make God a main character and place divine wisdom over and against Vatican authority in knowing the women's suitability for priesthood. Call stories introduce the womenpriests, their understanding of God, and their multilayered relationships with Catholicism.

Chapters 2 and 3 work in tandem to lay the contextual foundations and ongoing challenges for the RCWP movement. In Chapter 2, "Rome's Mixed Messages," I show that, when placed in context, Rome's insistence on a male-only priesthood did not come about in a straightforward fashion. The late twentieth century, in fact, featured much back-and-forth between feminist activists and Roman leadership, and women demanding ordination sought to situate their faith within rapidly shifting social and theological contexts. I argue here that RCWP emerged in part from feminist Catholics' frustrations surrounding their church leaders' ambiguous words and actions.

Chapter 3, "Conflict and Creativity," locates RCWP within contemporary Catholic struggles (primarily in North America and Europe) that convinced RCWP's founders and members that Roman Catholicism needs women as priests, immediately. With American Catholic demographic trends in view, this chapter examines womenpriests' appeal to disgruntled Catholics and unpacks the specific challenges facing the RCWP movement. These conflicts highlight successes as well as fractures in RCWP and present questions about Roman Catholic identity in the early twenty-first century.

Chapter 4, "Ordination," uses the performative complexity layered in RCWP's ordination ceremonies to analyze how RCWP understands itself as a reform movement and what transformations it envisions for Roman Catholicism. There is more than apostolic succession at stake here, and ordinations put womenpriests in tension with the Vatican, with feminist theologians who claim that "ordination is subordination,"[43] and with the contentious history of women's ordination throughout Christendom. As I argue in Chapter 4, RCWP uses *contra legem* ordination to ordain women as priests and, perhaps even more significantly, to position the movement publicly and provocatively within debates about women and church authority.

Chapter 5, "Sacraments," explores the shifting meaning of sacraments in the hands of womenpriests and their worship communities. By eschewing a strict lay-clergy divide, womenpriests try to shift the traditional Catholic sacramental economy toward the community gathered—and not toward the ordained womanpriest. This chapter also analyzes a tension around sacramental efficacy within RCWP's own membership: some women believe wholly in mystery and ontological change through the apostolic line, while others believe that sacramental power comes from a worship community's intent and faithfulness. As dispensers of grace, then, RCWP's sacraments give what womenpriests and their congregants want and need—not necessarily what Rome would dictate.

Chapter 6, "Ministries on the Margins," analyzes RCWP's ministerial actions and language of marginality in order to highlight both challenges and opportunities for womenpriests. I examine how womenpriests have carved out ministerial lives as "worker priests," and I show how RCWP's perceived marginalization has led womenpriests to forge links and build relationships with Protestants and male Catholic priests. Thus, RCWP's language of marginalization is simultaneously empowering and obfuscating.

Bodies and embodied performances of priesthood feature throughout the book, but Chapter 7 specifically analyzes the implications of womenpriests' bodies as symbols for social justice and resisting sexism. "Bodies *in Persona Christi*" considers the distrust facing Catholic priests' bodies today—specifically because of the sex-abuse crisis—alongside womenpriests' potential as female-bodied priests to reposition the gendered, sexual, and sacred natures of Catholic priesthood. Yet tension exists here as well: while the womenpriests seek to overcome Roman prohibitions on women's ordination, which are primarily located in Catholic theological anthropology, womenpriests often use gender complementarity and essentialism as proof that the church needs ordained women. And so, I argue, while Catholic womenpriests may ultimately have the potential to generate new discourse on priesthood and gendered authority (that is, to "queer" priesthood), RCWP's women currently fall short of fully dismantling associations between priesthood and gender. Where womenpriests do succeed is in modeling new theological images and changing congregants' experiences of priesthood.

By focusing sequentially on womenpriests' calls to priesthood, RCWP's emergence and struggles, ordination ceremonies, the movement's sacramental actions and ministerial endeavors, and the embodiment of priesthood, *Womanpriest* places RCWP in ever-widening concentric circles that demonstrate the movement's significance for the women themselves, for twenty-first-century Catholicism, and for patterns of religious change. In these early years of the movement's existence, RCWP's ordained are struggling to discover what it means to be female Catholic priests. In embarking on this theological and sacramental social justice experiment, they navigate the pressing issues facing contemporary Catholics: conflicting understandings of Catholic tradition, the place of sacred mystery, the role of sacraments in Catholic life, the way priests can best minister to suffering Catholics, and women's leadership in Catholic traditions. However controversial their journey, womenpriests believe this is what God is calling them to do.

CHAPTER I

Called

W HEN SHE WAS A child, Victoria Rue played priest. Growing up as the oldest of eight in a "good Catholic family" in Downey, California, the young Rue distributed Necco Wafers to neighborhood children. She would place the chalky candy discs upon her playmates' tongues in imitation of the pre–Vatican II practice of the time. As an adult, Rue recalls this practice with much animation and vocal inflection—she is, after all, according to her partner Kathryn Poethig, a "theater person." Rue believes this childhood game was an early sign of God calling her to priestly ministry.[1]

Other Roman Catholic Womenpriests (RCWP) women tell similar stories. When she was six years old, Juanita Cordero also reenacted the Communion ritual with Necco Wafers. When she was five years old, Gabriella Velardi Ward played Mass and told family members that she would be a priest when she grew up. Mary Grace Crowley-Koch led fellow preschoolers in Eucharistic celebrations at age four. Kathleen Kunster was not raised Catholic, but as a child she learned about Roman Catholicism during her school's required religious education lessons. She played Mass with the young boy next door, who wore his brother's cassock and informed Kathleen she could never be a priest. Her solution: she would play the Virgin Mary. In retrieving their girlhood memories, these women weave narratives of call and use their childhood behavior to help explain why they disobeyed canon law and became ordained through the RCWP movement.[2]

This book begins with call narratives, where so many womenpriests start their stories. In conducting interviews and reading womenpriests' autobiographies, I quickly found that women loved talking about their journeys to RCWP. I also found that, despite initial appearances, these stories are not simple feel-good reflections. Instead, they are deeply layered accounts that serve to argue for women's ordination.

With their passion for telling their call narratives, womenpriests show not only that they believe God has summoned them to *contra legem* ordination but also that they trust the rhetorical power these stories can have on an audience. As this chapter will show, call narratives do many things. Telling stories of God's call empowers the women to control their own stories, counters Rome's refusal to accept that women can be called to priesthood, minimizes womenpriests' reputation as lawbreakers, and casts them as obedient to God's voice and not to man-made rules.

Honoring the Call, Not the Church

Victoria Rue's journey from child priest distributing wafer candies to womanpriest celebrating Eucharist was not without detours. As a young woman, she entered the Sisters of the Holy Names, a teaching order of women religious, but departed after a year. Thereafter, the theater became her congregation and the women's movement became her church. These passions carried her to Nicaragua, where she experienced Catholic social teaching and liberation theology in action. She went on to study liberation and feminist theologies at Union Theological Seminary in New York City. After then Cardinal Joseph Ratzinger issued the "Letter to the Bishops of the Catholic Church on the Pastoral Care of Homosexual Persons" in October 1986, which called homosexuality a "moral disorder," Rue got involved in liturgical protests with the lesbian and gay community. She pursued a doctorate at the University of California, Berkeley, where her work merged theology, theory, feminism, and her artistic endeavors. In the Bay Area, she cofounded A Critical Mass: Women Celebrating the Eucharist, a group that gathered monthly in a public park to feed the homeless and celebrate a feminist-inspired liturgy.

In summer 2002, Rue learned of the womanpriest developments in Europe, where seven women had been ordained by male bishops on the Danube River. Knowing this option was now available to her, Rue began a discernment process. She concluded that she was being called, and a *contra legem* ordination followed. She was ordained a deacon in summer 2004 and a priest in summer 2005.[3] Why be ordained? Rue told me, "It was an opportunity to claim what I had already been living and [was] called forth to be."[4]

Honoring the call came with challenges. As for all of RCWP's ordained, no Roman Catholic parish awaited Rue's sacramental ministry, so Rue had to be creative: she had to identify need, offer her services, and hope a community formed. In February 2006, she began a weekly Eucharist at the nondenominational chapel at San Jose State University, where she taught classes in gender and religion. She often celebrated these Masses with others, including Don

Cordero (a married Catholic priest who was her ordination mentor), Juanita
Cordero (Don's wife and a womanpriest), and Kathleen Kunster (another womanpriest). The liturgy attracted students from SJSU as well as nearby Santa Clara
University, a Jesuit institution that would not have permitted Rue to celebrate
on campus.

Despite (or maybe because of) Rue's energy and enthusiasm, problems began.
Signs advertising Rue's weekly services were defaced or torn down. New signs
appeared, condemning Rue's actions. The Diocese of San Jose instructed local
parishes to publish warnings in weekly bulletins, informing parishioners that
Rue's liturgies were invalid and must be avoided. When Rue sought an audience
with the bishop, she was told there were "no grounds for dialogue" so long as she
continued to call herself a Roman Catholic priest. Rue's excommunication from
the institutional church became finalized in May 2008, when the Congregation
for the Doctrine of the Faith's general decree announced that RCWP's womenpriests had all excommunicated themselves by attempting to become priests.[5]

Young girls who play with these rituals show how readily Catholic ideas and
images take hold. Adult women who perform sacraments, however, defy Catholic dogma. As the girls become women, play becomes protest—and the stakes get
higher. Of all of her faith-centered actions, from studying feminist theology to
working with gay and lesbian Catholics to starting a liturgical community in an
Oakland park, it was Rue's priesthood ordination and sacramental ministry that
riled the Roman Catholic hierarchy. Rue's story reveals how seriously the Vatican takes an adult woman's seeking illicit ordination and calling herself a priest.

This is because the Roman Catholic Church teaches not only that men alone
can be priests but that men alone are called to priesthood. In 1976, *Inter Insigniores* addressed the issue of women feeling called to priesthood: "Women
who express a desire for the ministerial priesthood are doubtless motivated by
the desire to serve Christ and the Church." Furthermore,

> it is sometimes said and written in books and periodicals that some women
> feel they have a vocation to the priesthood. Such an attraction, however
> noble and understandable, still does not suffice for a genuine vocation. In
> fact a vocation cannot be reduced to a mere personal attraction, which can
> remain purely subjective.[6]

Honoring a vocational call to the priesthood is fundamental for womenpriests,
who have felt pain from Rome rejecting their call's authenticity. The *Catechism*
states that "*Church authority alone* has the responsibility and right to call someone to receive the sacrament of Holy Orders" (emphasis mine).

In telling their call stories, womenpriests claim that only God has the authority to determine their suitability for priesthood, subverting Roman authority in the process. These stories also construct an essentialist narrative by arguing that these women had, from childhood, an innate, God-directed pull toward the church, the sacraments, and ministerial priesthood. This counters the gender essentialism in Roman Catholic theology, which says only men have the intrinsic characteristics needed for the priestly role. In telling their stories now, as illicitly ordained womenpriests, these women cast off Roman Catholic rules about an all-male priesthood and instead cast their lot with God: God has called them, loud and clear. To deny God's call—to not become priests, as God has summoned them to—would be the true crime. Breaking canon law and being excommunicated are secondary.

Embodying Tradition and Transgression

It was January 17, 1998, and Janice Sevre-Duszynska's forty-eighth birthday. Believing herself called to Catholic priesthood, Sevre-Duszynska readied her body. She put on an alb and cincture that she had ordered from a Protestant supply store. She covered herself in a coat. She went to Christ the King Cathedral in her hometown of Lexington, Kentucky, where an ordination was taking place. She sat in a pew. And when the presiding bishop asked the candidates for ordination to come forward, Sevre-Duszynska took off her coat and walked to the altar. She said, "Bishop Williams, I'm called by the Holy Spirit to present myself for ordination. My name is Janice. I ask this for myself and for all women." She then prostrated herself.

She knelt "for a minute or so," she recalled when she told her story. When she stood, she spoke again: "I am all the oppressed women of the Bible. I am Sarah, I am Elizabeth, I am the woman who touched the hem of Jesus's garment, I am the woman who poured the oil over Jesus's head, I am Veronica. I came here today with the help of my patron saint, St. Joan of Arc, hoping that you would ordain me. Would you ordain me?"[7]

Sevre-Duszynska remembered the bishop growling at her in a voice that reminded her of Darth Vader. She was instructed to return to her seat and stop disrupting the service. She remembered a cadre of ordained men surrounding her, ready to escort her back to her seat—with force, perhaps, if necessary. After her speech—her sermon, her declaration, her petition—she returned to her space in the pew. During the sign of peace, many moments later, the same bishop approached her and hugged her, and she hugged him in return. It was, it seems, a brief moment of reconciliation between two representatives of Catholic calls to priesthood: the patriarchal male gatekeeper and the aspirational activist.

At this ceremony, Sevre-Duszynska showed her reverence for the tradition of sacramental ordination as well as her willingness to transgress institutional teaching. Acknowledging ordination's power to transform laypeople into priests, she selected this sacred occasion to petition Roman Catholic leaders and protest the all-male priesthood. Sevre-Duszynska's "gentle action" in Lexington, as she called it, was neither her first nor her last. She also witnessed at annual meetings for bishops, calling out to the men as they moved between sessions, "Bishops, remember to speak out for us women! Remember that Christ calls both men and women to the priesthood!"

She also recalled a time when Cardinal George of Chicago said to her, "Janice, you are not a Catholic," to which she replied, "I think Jesus would be doing this, too." Sevre-Duszynska explained that her history of activism stemmed from her understanding of Jesus and the incarnation. Her Jesus became human, took on a flesh-and-blood body, and had to accept the bodily consequences of his actions. It followed, then, that she saw priesthood as laying down one's body, one's life, for one another, as Christ did. Sevre-Duszynska has said of the Roman Catholic Church and its ministry, "It's not just statements and encyclicals. It's putting your bodies on the line."[8] She has done just that: put her body on the line to protest the Roman Catholic Church's refusal to ordain women.

In 2008, ten years after Lexington, Sevre-Duszynska became one of RCWP's illegally ordained womenpriests. My interviews and research around Sevre-Duszynska revealed how her lifelong Catholicism drew her to such dramatic action. She described feeling called to priesthood from an early age. Growing up on Milwaukee's south side during the 1950s, she longed to be an altar server. But that role was strictly reserved for boys, and women were forbidden from the altar during the liturgy. Instead, Janice routinely helped Sister DePaul clean the sacristy, a room located off the altar that holds vestments and ecclesiastical vessels. Sometimes young Janice would go to the altar and make believe she was celebrating Mass: she would pantomime lifting the Eucharist and the wine; she would bless the congregation; she would sit in the priest's chair. She believed there was a place for women on the altar.

Sevre-Duszynska's call story suggests that her activism and desire for Catholic reform found its realization in *contra legem* ordination through RCWP. Now a priest, she celebrates sacraments, ministers to the marginalized, and offers a new model of priesthood through her peace activism. Her call story, combined with her ongoing activism, invites a reexamination—theologically, culturally, biologically, and ecclesiologically—of what it means to be a faithful Catholic and what it looks like to stand *in persona Christi*. Sevre-Duszynska and other womenpriests are paradoxically attempting to save their relationship with God and Roman Catholic tradition by breaking institutional rules and revisioning and reconstituting what it means to be a Roman Catholic priest. Telling call narratives becomes an act of performance that helps them rhetorically bridge the gap between their obedience and their disobedience.

An Alternative to Male Priests and a Chance at Healing

Long before her RCWP ordination, Marie Bouclin built a ministry around her experiences counseling women who had been abused by ordained Catholic men. Her growing expertise led her to write *Seeking Wholeness: Women Dealing with Abuse of Power in the Catholic Church*.[9] Describing her call to ordination in RCWP's collection of testimonies, *Women Find a Way*, Bouclin wrote, "Women who have suffered violence at the hands of a priest know full well that as long as there are no women standing 'in loco Christi' at the altar, all women are at risk of being raped and exploited and harassed with impunity."[10]

Bouclin had observed a common pattern for adult female victims: a priest (usually a pastor or spiritual director) would persuade a vulnerable woman (suffering perhaps from the death of a spouse, problems in her marriage, or a history of abusive intimate relationships) to begin a sexual relationship with him. The priest would tell this woman that he needed her, that he alone knew and loved her, that his vow of celibacy did not prohibit sexual relations, that her soul would benefit from being with him. When he later ended the relationship, she would be left emotionally and spiritually bereft, for a man she loved—who stood in the place of God as a conduit of grace—had used and abandoned her.

Women tend to blame themselves entirely for this form of clerical abuse, Bouclin wrote.

> These women were taught to believe that priests do not lie. Priests are invested with Holy Orders; they are therefore holy men. These women were taught that priests speak for God and act in God's name, and that only priests—always male—have been entrusted with the most sacred source of grace, the Eucharist. These women were taught that faith in God means unquestioning intellectual assent to unchallengeable beliefs, and that salvation hinges on obeying the teachings of the Church as transmitted by the priest.[11]

In the wake of the Catholic sex-abuse crisis, in which over ten thousand victims alleged abuse by over four thousand priests in the United States alone, Bouclin's observations resonate in the testimonies of women and children alike.[12] Victims and their families echo Bouclin's words: the priest is the closest thing on earth to God; he cannot do wrong, cannot be anything but trustworthy. The power differential heightens the potential for abuse. Because priests are dispensers of sacramental grace, a layperson's relationship to a priest is inherently fraught on social and spiritual levels, impacting both body and soul.

Roman Catholicism has fallen under intense scrutiny since sex-abuse revelations emerged. All the more damning has been news of institutional obstruction that protected priests at the expense of civil justice and children's safety. A Pew Research Center study revealed that 27 percent of former US Catholics who are now religiously unaffiliated left as a result of the sex-abuse scandals, while 21 percent of Catholics-turned-Protestant name the crisis for their decision.[13] The abuse crisis has rendered church finances precarious, and devastating parish closures have become a common solution.[14]

The vast majority of Catholic priests are not abusers, of course, but it is relevant to womenpriests like Bouclin that the face and the body of the Catholic sex-abuse crisis is a male priest. Abusive priests and the superiors who protected them were all men. When only men are ordained, abusive Catholic priests are all male.[15] As a result of the crisis, many Catholics and non-Catholics no longer see priests, bishops, or even popes as gentle, pastoral patriarchs; instead, these men are more likely viewed as possible villains capable of anything from protecting pedophile priests to abusing children themselves. The bodies of men at the altar may never be perceived the same way again.

Bouclin has argued that male priests can reinforce female powerlessness or remind women of their abuser. Women cannot *be* priests; women must *obey* priests. As priests, men make decisions, stand in for Christ, and enact God's will on earth. Without the possibility of ordination, women—like children—lack power and thus protection within the Catholic hierarchy. Like child victims of sexual abuse, laypersons develop "uncritical reverence" for ordained men.[16] They cannot expect support from the institutional church because women who accuse priests of abuse are less likely to be believed—quite possibly because there are no women in the Roman hierarchy.[17] Victims are ashamed and guilt-ridden, and the abuse cuts to the heart of one's Catholic identity.

This also connects to the maleness of Jesus: Bouclin found that the person of Jesus Christ can be frightening for wounded women, and thus an exclusively male body at the Eucharistic table can prevent victims' healing and reconciliation.[18] Which makes it all the more important, in Bouclin's view, that women like herself seek ordination.

When she discerned a call to priesthood, Bouclin believed God wanted her to minister to vulnerable women who had been abused or exploited by ordained men.[19] She asked herself, "Can I possibly model a different kind of priestly, Christlike presence?"[20] In her mind, it is imperative that she can. Historically in Catholic law and teaching, women lack agency because their bodies bear the symbolic weight of feminized Catholic virtues.[21] RCWP upends this formation because womenpriests take on the gestures, dress, and authority of priests. As womenpriests—notably, not as Catholic women—RCWP's ordained women become symbols of both Christ and a reframed relationship between women and their church. Bouclin and other womenpriests see this symbol shift as a positive step toward rectifying the Catholic sex-abuse crisis, perpetuated overwhelmingly by ordained men.

Many womenpriests have come to understand their calls in light of the abuses and missteps of the institutional church. Their discernment processes often take into consideration the ways womenpriests can bring sacraments and healing to individuals previously harmed by Roman Catholic clergy. Bouclin described a woman who traveled a long distance to have Bouclin hear her confession.[22] Womanpriest Eleonora Marinaro also described the conciliatory power of RCWP sacraments, saying, "Reconciliation with the Roman Catholic Church after years of estrangement is a prime feature of our ministry."[23] What male priests cannot offer, womenpriests can: they are an alternative embodiment of priesthood, proffering a chance for healing.

From Call to Discernment and Formation

As I was doing my research, once I recognized how much womenpriests wanted to talk about their calls to priesthood, I modified my interview questions to give them this opportunity. For most womenpriests, the call is their starting point. But what moves the women from inception to action? What besides God's summons is motivating their call? What compels the women to proceed when Rome strictly forbids it?

When I asked womenpriests in interviews or surveys, "Why be ordained?" nearly every woman indicated she was honoring a call to priesthood. But I noticed other common responses as well. Some said they were resisting the all-male clergy. Others said social justice concerns compelled them and they wanted to work for equality in the Roman Catholic Church. Many wanted to be a role model for women and girls, and many wanted to stand within a lineage of activist Christian women. Others reported specifically wanting to be role models for their daughters and granddaughters. Canadian womanpriest Monica Kilburn-Smith wrote, "I am also doing this for my daughters, and for the women in the world, to be a small part of helping women feel empowered and value their wholeness, their blessedness, as people of God, as beloveds of God."[24]

One anonymous respondent indicated that she became ordained for a myriad of reasons, but to her list she added, "I was asked to [seek ordination] by others. Clergy from other denominations and laypeople asked me. Then there was God hounding me in my dreams and in my prayer life. The hounding ended when I was accepted into the RCWP program." Gabriella Velardi Ward also used the word *hound* in describing her call, saying she became ordained "to fulfill that to which God, the Hound of Heaven, has been calling me."[25] Both women evoked the nineteenth-century poem that describes God as a "Hound of Heaven" who pursues—or "hounds"—the souls that God most desires.[26]

The pull of Catholic visual imagery and sacramental experiences also motivates womenpriests, who feel called to a kind of Catholic priesthood that resembles what they have watched, worked with, and prayed alongside throughout their lives as Catholics. Womenpriests live in twenty-first-century social and political contexts where religious identity is a choice: they could leave Roman Catholicism altogether for a different religion. And indeed, some have tried—but have come back to their Catholic roots. The womenpriests' self-understanding is unequivocally Roman Catholic. They believe they should not have to abandon their faith tradition in order to live in a right and robust relationship with God and their Roman Catholic faith. "It's my church. [It] does not belong to the hierarchy," wrote Victoria Rue. Another woman explained, "Catholicism is my religious heritage; it is a vital part of who I am." Monica Kilburn-Smith's response was more legalistic: "Once you are baptized, the only way not to be Catholic is to deny one's baptism, which I won't do." For Christine Fahrenbach, not just God but the Catholic tradition "calls me deeply. I believe the [Roman Catholic] church carries the mystery of [Christian tradition] authentically."[27]

Roman Catholic memory runs deep, as does the Catholic attraction to liturgical forms and sacramental gestures. This is the powerful pull of the Catholic imagination, indicating how the sacred should look, feel, and even smell. The womenpriests want to change priesthood and Roman Catholicism, but they do not want to let either go.

Indeed, imagery has inspired womenpriests to hear the call and imagine the possibilities within priesthood ministry. Ironically, much of this visual inspiration has come from Episcopalian and Protestant women. Womenpriests report that the seemingly simple act of *seeing* a woman minister has inspired cradle Catholics who never imagined such a role to be possible for women. This is especially true of Episcopal services, as these most closely resemble Catholicism's "high church" flavor. Juanita Cordero, ordained through RCWP in 2007, recalled a 2003 Episcopal liturgy in Chicago where she first saw a woman priest. The experience stirred her own call to priesthood. Not long after, she saw another Episcopalian woman priest presiding at Eucharist; she joined this woman's community and started pursuing her own journey toward ordination.[28]

Younger Catholics report similar experiences. "Lauren," a young woman in her early twenties who participated in local RCWP Masses and was discerning a call to ordination when we spoke, vividly described the first time she saw a woman priest. She was in El Salvador, attending a liturgy led by an Episcopalian woman: "The idea a woman could be a priest never even entered my consciousness until I saw...this woman celebrating this Mass very similar to a Catholic Mass....That led to this whole new series of questions, like 'What role *do* women have in the church?' and 'How have women been excluded and oppressed?'" The experience, which she described as "beautiful," left Lauren feeling "overwhelmed," "shocked," and "in awe." Thereafter, she felt a "strong call" to study feminist theology.[29] The visual of a woman at the altar, presiding over Communion, led Lauren and Cordero to discern a call to priesthood. The Episcopal example of what was possible enabled them to imagine Roman Catholic priesthood anew. Now, RCWP's ordained women are doing the same for others, normalizing the image of an ordained, vested Catholic woman.

And yet most of RCWP's womenpriests modify the image of a typical priest by shaking up the traditional ages and backgrounds for Roman Catholic candidates for ordination. The typical womanpriest is in her fifties, sixties, or seventies, is or has been married, has or had a career, and has been performing service work (or charity, volunteer, or social justice work) for decades. Honoring her call to priesthood and getting illegally ordained severs her relationship with the Roman Catholic Church. The quintessential seminarian, in contrast, is a high school– or college-aged male who commits himself to a diocese or religious order that subsequently funds all or part of his education, pastoral training, and living expenses. After what may be a decade or more of preparation, candidates take vows, first as deacons and later as priests. Ordination signals male Roman Catholic priests' deepening obligation to and integration in the hierarchical church.

RCWP has no institutional oversight directing priesthood formation, no seminaries, and no requisite vows of obedience. No two womenpriests prepare and train for ordained ministry in the same way: RCWP understands priesthood formation as stemming from a woman's extensive personal and educational history. Instead of joining a Catholic seminary to train for priesthood, RCWP's cooperatively designed formation program integrates a candidate's educational and professional background with ordination-specific requirements.

RCWP's program of preparation for ordination builds on candidates' previous work and blends educational-degree seeking, distance learning, and hands-on training. Applicants submit recommendation letters, undergo criminal background checks and psychological evaluations, and sit for interviews. They present résumés, baptismal and confirmation certificates, and college transcripts. Some applicants have already completed the required theological work, whereas others augment their existing degrees once RCWP accepts them. Officially, applicants under age fifty-five need a master of divinity, master of theology, or equivalent; applicants over fifty-five need a bachelor of theology or equivalent. The program encourages applicants to complete a unit of clinical pastoral education. In addition, applicants complete writing- and activity-intensive program units, with each unit focusing on a different aspect of RCWP's approach to ordained service.[30] During this phase, which can take upward of a year, candidates write essays and homilies, design rituals and compose liturgies, and receive experiential training in sacraments. All steps are considered part of the discernment process, for ordination is not guaranteed—though nearly all of RCWP's applicants have moved on to the deaconate and priesthood.

Without an RCWP seminary, candidates do not live and study together as male seminarians do.[31] As a result, the women do not share foundations in personal experience, theology, religious studies, or pastoral studies, nor does RCWP instill in its ordinands a distinctively RCWP theology or ideology. This leads to challenges within the movement: for example, some womenpriests believe RCWP's formation program should include more deliberate and rigorous feminist theological education. Several womenpriests expressed to me great frustration at their ordained colleagues' lack of a foundation in feminist and intersectional thought. These women believe that RCWP can only lead twenty-first-century reforms if its womenpriests understand the ways gender and sexual orientation, as well as race, ethnicity, class, and ability, affect society's marginalized people.[32]

RCWP strives to show that the womenpriests are equipped for priesthood and ministerially capable. Without seminaries, womenpriests must be educated before entering the program. The movement then frames a woman's past education as laying a path to priesthood. The movement's websites, RCWP-edited books like *Women Find a Way*, and press releases for upcoming ordinations list the women's educational information and past service (most often to and for Catholic parishes, dioceses, and organizations), characterizing these details in a way that justifies the women's claims to a ministerial priesthood. Critics who claim the women are ill-prepared for priesthood are confronted with biographical evidence suggesting otherwise. This is strategic: *Inter Insigniores* may deny that the women have a "genuine vocation" to priesthood, but the Vatican cannot deny the existence of educational degrees. Critics can reject the notion that God has called the women to priesthood, and skeptics can point out that the women have been ordained outside of the church and trained outside its seminaries, but the RCWP movement intends for the womenpriests' professional histories to argue for their suitability for priesthood. And RCWP is thus far an education-focused movement, akin to Roman Catholic teaching orders like the Jesuits or Sisters of Loretto. RCWP requires its women to be educated, and the type of woman drawn to RCWP is well educated before joining the movement.[33]

RCWP's women did not prepare for priesthood decades ago when they pursued educational degrees and started jobs and careers—given Rome's firm no to ordained women, why would they have? But now, using websites, publications, press releases, and interviews, RCWP argues that its women have, in fact, spent years working toward honoring their call to priesthood. Rhetorically, these public displays engage and extend the discourse on true and legitimate priesthood and let RCWP argue that the model priest is experienced, educated, prepared, and well connected—even without Rome's blessing. With its priestly lineup of mature, ministerial, and highly motivated women, RCWP invites audiences to reconsider what kind of person is called to ordination.

RCWP argues for the womenpriests' legitimacy as priests by communicating their personal histories serving the Roman Catholic Church, as women religious, diocesan or parish employees, and lay ministers and volunteers.[34] In spite of Rome's rejection of their calling, womenpriests remained part of the institutional church for decades, often faithfully and dutifully carrying out consecrated service or lay ministries. RCWP's women worked within the Roman Catholic system, but either in spite or because of this proximity, they felt they could not reach a full ministerial calling. Ultimately, a *contra legem* ordination became a welcome alternative to unordained service.

Conclusion

Womenpriests' call narratives are an essential, performative starting point for understanding their *contra legem* actions. I want to highlight four characteristics of womenpriests' self-disclosures around call. First, telling call narratives allows women to craft their own stories. Women like RCWP's, who step into the limelight with illegal ordination, are readily constructed as either heroes or villains by the media, the Roman Catholic Church, critics, family, friends, and parishioners. Telling call narratives lets womenpriests take back control of their own stories and cast themselves in a positive light. Moreover, the deeply personal nature of call stories makes them difficult to dispute.

Second, call narratives give womenpriests tools to respond to Rome. The Roman church relies heavily on the language of "call" and "vocation" to describe its male-only priesthood and to argue that women are not and cannot be called to priesthood. In delivering deeply reflective call narratives of their own—and showing how the "Hound of Heaven" hounds them, too—womenpriests give themselves the "called" background that Rome reserves for men and, as such, attempt to negate Rome's chastisement.

Third, call narratives allow womenpriests to talk about their relationship with God, their understanding of Jesus, and their communion with the Holy Spirit. Many conservative Catholic clerics dismiss womenpriests' calls as inauthentic and "not of God." In talking boldly about their vocational calls, then, womenpriests underscore their faith and spirituality, arguing that their illegal actions come from a place of sincere belief.

Fourth, and perhaps most important, call narratives suggest that womenpriests are obedient—to God's voice, if not to Vatican mandates. In following a call, womenpriests are able to create themselves as passive receptors of God's word and counter their critics' accusation that they are activist agitators. Stories of calls help audiences see womenpriests as multidimensional, faithful, theologically reflective women who, in order to truly obey God, must disobey a patriarchal institutional that claims two thousand years of authority.

CHAPTER 2

Rome's Mixed Messages

IN 2004, TWO YEARS after the first RCWP ordination on the Danube
River and one year before the first North American RCWP ordination,
Reverend Michael G. Murtha of Havertown, Pennsylvania, wrote to the
Southeastern Pennsylvania branch of the Women's Ordination Conference,
deriding their activism for women's ordination. Father Murtha declared, "Some
of your members dare to say they have been called to the priesthood! Such a
judgment can only be made under the careful scrutiny of the church." Intimating that WOC's members were worse than Protestants, Murtha said that when
Martin Luther protested Roman Catholic teachings, he at least had the "courage
of his convictions" to no longer call himself Roman Catholic. He concluded,
"Dissenting Catholics are not truly Catholic—they dissent from the teachings
and practices of the Catholic church. One cannot speak with arrogance, disrespect, and disobedience toward the Holy Father—as your organization does so
frequently—and still hold to the theory that he is a 'Roman Catholic priest.'"[1] In
Murtha's understanding, WOC members could not call themselves true Roman
Catholics because they dissented from church teachings, disagreed with papal
leadership, and disrespected the Roman authority they should submit to.

In contrast with Murtha, RCWP's ordained women argue that it is *because*
they dissent, challenge authority, and understand themselves as distinct from
Protestant Christians that they deserve to call themselves Roman Catholic. For
example, Minnesotan womanpriest Mary Frances Smith looked into joining the
Episcopal church but realized, "I am Roman Catholic on a deep level, and that
is where I choose to stay. At this point in my life, I do not believe that I should
have to abdicate my Catholicism just because the men in the Vatican say that I
should. I am Roman Catholic, and I belong in the Church as much as anyone."[2]
Womanpriest Monique Venne, also of Minnesota, once resolved to leave the
church, even going so far as to enter a United Church of Christ ecumenical seminary, but she discovered that "I was Catholic to my bones!" She felt it would be

33

"dishonest" to join another denomination in order to be ordained, and she stays Catholic because of the "optimistic anthropology, the rituals, the sacraments, the history, and Vatican II."[3] Eileen DiFranco, a womanpriest living in Philadelphia, said, "My family has been Catholic since the time of St. Patrick and . . . I should not have to leave my faith."[4] My interviews with RCWP's women consistently revealed that they believe their commitment to Roman Catholicism can change the church for the better, especially during what many womenpriests see as a transitional time of great need in Western Catholicism.

Womenpriests fight to preserve a Roman Catholic identity while struggling with the elements they find irreconcilable with their own personal faith. RCWP's members are not alone in this struggle, and much of the contextual background in this chapter is history RCWP shares with a number of reform groups, particularly the WOC and Women's Ordination Worldwide (WOW), and also Call to Action (CTA) and CORPUS. Especially since the late twentieth century, individuals and groups have refused to abandon Catholicism and have instead tried to make the faith work for them.[5]

Even though Rome has laid out reasons for the all-male priesthood, proponents of women's ordination see mixed messages in late-twentieth-century Catholic doctrine. Womenpriests pursue ordination because they believe it is correctly Roman Catholic to do so, because it allows them to work within the tradition, retain sacramental and ministerial elements, and follow their Catholic conscience (and thus retain their Catholic identity) by transgressing unjust laws that the Vatican will not change. Critics view womenpriests as disruptively disobeying church laws. But the more nuanced history explored in this chapter reveals Rome's ambiguity on the subject of women's ordination. While Rome positions itself as speaking clearly with one voice, in fact the institution's mixed messages have shaped the work of women's ordination activists from the 1960s to today. Sometimes the church's own teachings inspire activism, and sometimes the church's recalcitrance helps women forge activist communities. In other words, the church has provided women with hope for ordination.

This chapter presents the theological and feminist Roman Catholic forces that gave way to RCWP's formation.[6] Drawing on recent Catholic history, interviews, surveys, and Vatican statements about women's ordination, I show how RCWP inhabits and exacerbates the struggles of post–Vatican II Catholic feminisms. For womenpriests, struggle is a sign of faithful engagement with Catholicism. RCWP has struggled with the church, with conservative Catholics, and with members of their own RCWP movement. Conflict inspired the movement and continues to mark it in nurturing ways.

Arguing from "Conscience" as the "People of God": Vatican II, the Catholic Sixties, and the Growth of Faithful Disobedience

When womenpriests break canon 1024, they break a law they see as unjust, and they argue that they obey God and their consciences when disobeying the church. Despite their excommunication, womenpriests do not accept the church's determination that RCWP's actions are criminal. Womanpriest Judith McKloskey, for instance, invoked "conscience" when comparing the womenpriests' excommunication to the church's treatment of sexually abusive priests (not one of whom has been excommunicated): "Pedophilia is a crime; covering up pedophilia is a crime; stealing from the Church is a crime. Responding to a call from the depths of one's conscience is not a crime."[7] Vatican II, more formally known as the Second Vatican Council, brought the word *conscience* into the contemporary Catholic vernacular, and RCWP uses it to defend its actions.

Vatican II documents also popularized the language of "the Church as the people of God," which RCWP draws upon. Indeed, the "people of God" refrain recurred throughout conciliar documents and appeared more than forty times in *Lumen Gentium* (Light of the Nations), one of the main documents coming out of Vatican II.[8] Now sacrosanct in progressive Catholic circles, *Lumen Gentium* empowered the laity to see themselves as invaluable, contributing members of the church.[9] In 2013, responding to Pope Francis's comments about women in the church, RCWP called for a "consultation with the total people of God on these deep questions [to] reveal a more comprehensive understanding."[10] ARCWP's mission statement reads, "We prepare and ordain qualified women to serve the people of God as priests."[11] RCWP and ARCWP see themselves as *composed* of the people of God, able to make much-needed reforms; at the same time, they view themselves as *serving* the people of God, for whom a sacramental ministry should take precedence over strict obedience to the Vatican.

The language of "conscience" and "people of God" received life during Vatican II. From 1962 to 1965, approximately 2,600 Catholic bishops from all over the world descended on Vatican City to take part in a series of meetings aimed at reorienting the church to the modern era. Vatican II documents and themes have fueled activists' fire for decades.[12] As Mary J. Henold shows in her book *Catholic and Feminist*, Catholicism did not transplant Catholic feminism from the secular culture. Instead, Catholics feminism emerged within the Catholic tradition. Henold writes that "the immediate catalyst for the emerging [Catholic feminist] movement . . . belongs to the institutional Catholic Church, which itself must take credit for both provoking and inspiring Catholic feminism in the early sixties through the Second Vatican Council."[13] Looking to their church for inspiration, many women found it in Vatican II documents, where they interpreted certain statements as gender progressive. Specifically, the Vatican II documents *Lumen Gentium* and *Gaudium et Spes* (Latin for "joy and hope") as well as the papal encyclical *Pacem in Terris* (Peace on Earth) captured reformers' attention.[14] In speaking about conscience and the people of God, these Vatican II documents inadvertently encouraged progressive Catholics to follow their own theological values—even when these differed from those of the institutional church.

Although Vatican II did not discuss women's ordination, the council became an ideological and theological foundation for movements like RCWP. For example, two of RCWP's founding mothers, Iris Müller and Ida Raming, entreated the council to take up the issue of ordaining women, submitting questions to the council fathers that were published in a 1964 book.[15] The voices of these young German theologians went unheeded, and perhaps even unheard, but in the absence of direct statements about feminism or women's ordination, Catholic women like Müller and Raming took Vatican II as permission to dream progressively.[16] In challenging the church, calling for reforms, and using Vatican II themes and documents selectively, post–Vatican II activists could locate themselves as faithful, insider agitators—not antagonists hostile to Roman Catholic teachings.

American Catholics' need to sometimes obey personal conscience and disobey the Roman church escalated three years after Vatican II's conclusion, with Pope Paul VI's encyclical *Humanae Vitae* (Of Human Life). Although the overwhelming majority of American Catholic bishops voted to allow married couples to use contraception, *Humanae Vitae* reaffirmed the church's long-held position that artificial birth control offended God's moral law. Millions of Catholics who had applauded some Vatican II reforms now found themselves at odds with the Vatican over *Humanae Vitae* and decided to disobey patriarchal authority for the good of their family. New questions emerged. Was the church out of touch with modern times, even in the wake of a council that had aimed to bring the church in line with the modern world? Was church authority waning amid late-twentieth-century challenges? Catholic scholar Peter Steinfels wrote, "The papacy's stand on contraception appeared to do much more than leave huge percentages of Catholics unconvinced. It opened up all sorts of questions . . . about the church's whole approach to morals, and about church authority generally."[17] *Humanae Vitae* had opened the door for outright disagreement between Catholics and those with hierarchical authority.[18]

In the following years, Catholic activists concluded that they could not accept Vatican pronouncements wholesale. They decided to pick and choose when carving out their Catholic identity. In one tumultuous decade, Catholics hoping to see ordained women had found reason both to applaud and to bemoan Vatican declarations. This ambiguity proved both frustrating and encouraging for women attempting to forge a new place for themselves in Catholic life.

Vatican II made certain rhetorical positions possible for progressive Catholics like those in the RCWP movement. In their online biographies, press releases, and the surveys and interviews I conducted, womenpriests invoked Vatican II as justification for their *contra legem* ordinations. They stated that today's Roman Catholicism faces real problems, which the spirit and teachings of Vatican II could correct. For instance, womanpriest Ann Harrington's comments to me on what the institutional church needs to change reflected the tumult of 1960s Catholic teachings: "empowering the laity, following Vatican II teachings, [having a] healthy understanding of human sexuality." Womanpriest Rosa Manriquez critiqued the church for "resisting the revelation of the Holy Spirit through Vatican II." Womanpriest Ann Penick wanted the church to do what it did after Vatican II—specifically, "meeting people where they are and allowing them to grow and become people of God."[19] With the Second Vatican Council as their inspirational starting point, many womenpriests position themselves as being on the right side of history by embracing certain Vatican II changes. Womanpriest Alice Iaquinta stated this directly in her online biography: "My ordination is an act of surrender to the Spirit and obedience to God, not an act of defiance of the church. I love the Roman Catholic Church and want to see the reforms of the Vatican II Council fulfilled."[20]

More than fifty years after the council, RCWP is forging an ongoing relationship with Vatican II: claiming obedience (to conscience), disputing the idea of defiance, proclaiming love for the church, and calling for the realization of Vatican II reforms.

Standing *in Persona Christi*: Barring Women's Ordination

RCWP positions itself against an all-male priesthood tradition that is ostensibly two thousand years old. Rome has long barred women from ordination but has done so more formally since the late twentieth century, largely as a reaction to feminist trends in Western culture and post–Vatican II Catholicism.

The Roman Catholic Church's first public statement of the modern era insisting women cannot and can never be priests came in 1976s *Inter Insigniores* (or "Declaration on the Question of the Admission of Women to the Ministerial Priesthood"), authored by the Congregation for the Doctrine of the Faith (CDF) and released in English in January 1977. The CDF argued that a priest must be able to stand *in persona Christi*—"in the person of Christ"—so the faithful will recognize Jesus and sacraments will work effectively. Phrased differently: because Jesus himself was male, a priest must be male, lest it become "difficult [for the faithful] to see in the minister the image of Christ." Womenpriests thus cannot be effective priests because they cannot emulate Christ's maleness. Moreover, sacraments include significant indicators—like the priest's gender—that point the way to Christ.[21]

The CDF added to these theological and Christological reasons a historical argument from the New Testament: that Jesus chose twelve male apostles shows that God wants men—and not women—to lead the church. As further evidence, the CDF cited the fact that Jesus did not select Mary, his most holy mother, for apostleship. The all-male priesthood, then, is an expression of Christ's will for the church.[22]

Women's ordination activists, of course, did not see these arguments as legitimate. And yet, in 1994, Pope John Paul II upped the ante with the apostolic letter *Ordinatio Sacerdotalis*, which upheld the church's ban on women priests and sought to end the debate altogether. The pontiff wrote, "I declare that the Church has no authority whatsoever to confer priestly ordination on women and that this judgment is to be definitively held by all the Church's faithful."[23] In other words, it was not in the Vatican's power to ordain women, and even the pope himself could not change church tradition and ordain women. Debate continues today about whether *Ordinatio Sacerdotalis* is an infallible teaching. RCWP's members and ordination activists say no, but Pope Benedict XVI and Pope Francis have said yes, thereby treating this apostolic letter as the final word on women's ordination.[24]

Catholic women who want ordination are up against documents like *Inter Insigniores* and *Ordinatio Sacerdotalis* but also, and in some ways more powerfully, Catholic theological anthropology. From here arise Catholic teachings on gender complementarity, a term describing the interdependent relationship between the sexes. Complementarity is not just biological but essential. In his 1995 "Letter to Women," John Paul II wrote, "Womanhood and manhood are complementary *not only from the physical and psychological points of view*, but also from the *ontological*. It is only through the duality of the 'masculine' and the 'feminine' that the 'human' finds full realization" (italics in the original).[25] God, in this view, ordered creation so that men and women have different abilities; going against this divinely ordained system offends human dignity.[26] The church often equates womanhood with the vocational roles of virgin, wife, and mother, and as such, Mary is women's ultimate role model.[27] But Mary was not—as noted above—a priest.

What is more, Catholic theology genders the church as a female wife and bride, linked in a complementary relationship with Christ, the faithful bridegroom. This bride-bridegroom analogy comes from a reading of the Hebrew Bible's Song of Songs (started by antiquity's rabbis and later taken up by early Christians) in which a loyal bridegroom declares his faithfulness to the bride in spite of her infidelities. *Inter Insigniores* draws upon this symbolism in arguing for the all-male priesthood: Christ was male, and the bride-bridegroom symbolism would crumble should a woman attempt to stand in Christ's place at the altar.[28]

In sum, the all-male Catholic priesthood aligns with Rome's view of men and women's God-given, complementary, non-interchangeable roles. Cultural changes (e.g., feminism, the gay rights movement) do not sway the church because the church stands outside of culture. No matter that women are working toward greater equality in society and culture, that the church opposes discrimination on the basis of sex, or that Protestant denominations ordain women: the CDF argued in *Inter Insigniores* that the Roman Catholic Church is *different*. The CDF conceded that its position would "perhaps cause pain" but claimed that, ultimately, it would positively help the faithful appreciate the distinctive roles that men and women must play, both in the life of the church and in the world.[29] Rome's statements failed to quell the debate, however, and organized Catholic feminist groups emerged in the 1970s to challenge the Vatican's authority within the post–Vatican II idiom.

Organizing for Women's Ordination: The Emergence of the Women's Ordination Conference

RCWP's activist foremothers owe a genealogical nod to watershed sociopolitical events like 1954s *Brown v. the Board of Education*, Dr. Martin Luther King Jr.'s national crusade, and Betty Friedan's 1963 book *The Feminine Mystique*. The civil rights movement and the rise of second-wave feminism invited Americans—including Catholics—to think differently about race, gender, and equality. Mary Henold pointed to the Grail Movement, the Christian Family

Movement, and the "new nuns" as evidence of an emergent socially progressive ethos in mid-twentieth-century Catholicism. Also significant was the Sister Formation Conference, which implemented a program of personal, professional, and spiritual development for women religious.[30] A new breed of Catholic feminist thinker emerged, armed with burgeoning Catholic feminism, cultural changes around secular feminism and civil rights, Vatican II documents like *Gaudium et Spes* and *Pacem in Terris*, and an invigorated interest in studying theology.

Yet the rise of women intellectual authorities who could talk theology with Roman patriarchs generated more conflicts than compromises. While women now could speak Catholicism's theological language, most male clerics were woefully uneducated in feminist thought. Feminist theology was, after all, an emerging field, and few ordained men had had the opportunity—or the incentive—to study it. Discussions between these theologically trained women and male clerics often ended with neither side feeling heard or understood.

Difficulties convincing Rome to adopt or even acknowledge new feminist ideas did not stop women from coming together to envision a different kind of Catholic priesthood. Within a decade of Vatican II, new movements started arguing for women's ordination from ministerial, theological, and civil rights perspectives. Catholic feminist ideas and women's ordination movements combined, resulting in calls for Catholic women priests. Ida Raming's 1970 dissertation, titled "The Exclusion of Women from Priesthood: Divine Law or Gender Discrimination?," helped establish the movement's intellectual foundation.[31] In the early 1970s, the Deaconess Movement (DM) took shape as a support network for Catholic women wanting to be ordained. Vatican II had turned the diaconate into a terminal stage of ministry (meaning it was no longer necessarily a step toward priesthood but could be an end unto itself), and some DM members envisioned themselves as deacons; still others wanted to become priests. DM leader Mary Lynch organized a 1975 Detroit meeting titled "Women in Future Priesthood Now: A Call to Action." When hundreds more people sought to attend the conference than the venue could accommodate, movement leaders decided to turn the Women's Ordination Conference (WOC) into a permanent organization. Today, WOC is the world's largest organization dedicated to Catholic women's ordination, and many of RCWP's ordained members participated in WOC in the years and decades before the 2002 Danube ordination.[32]

In its early years, WOC sought dialogue with church leaders and found both hope and frustration. In fact, the productive foundation laid by some Catholic feminists and some Catholic authorities in the 1970s only exacerbated the feelings of confusion and ambiguity among women's ordination activists. For example, in 1975, as the organization that would grow into WOC planned its first meeting, Archbishop Joseph Bernardin of Cincinnati, then president of the National Conference of Catholic Bishops (NCCB), issued a letter reminding the Catholic faithful that the church did not ordain women.[33] Ordination activists interpreted Bernardin's letter in different ways. Some viewed it as a veiled threat against the upcoming WOC meeting, a wielding of patriarchal power.

But some WOC members read Bernardin as taking a nonthreatening stance. Patricia Hughes, WOC's one-time national media spokesperson, told me in 2009 about her experiences working with Bernardin in 1975. In his letter, Hughes read Bernardin as trying to tread gently and articulate the Vatican's position without closing the door on future discussions. Encouraged, she called Bernardin to discuss the letter. That he even took her call, she believed, signaled mutual respect and a potential cooperation between WOC and the NCCB. She recalled their conversation: "And I said [to him], 'As I read [that letter], Archbishop, it seemed the equivalent of saying, "I am seated, and I'll remain seated until and unless I stand up."' And I will never ever forget the laughter I heard on the other end of the line. He said, 'Patricia, it took me so long to craft that. I was trying to get a snapshot of where we are now, in the history of the church!'"[34]

In Hughes' view, Bernardin was not saying "never" to women's ordination; instead, he was pointing out it had not ever been done. Rome would have to address questions about Catholic theology and tradition before making such a significant change.

Hughes told Bernardin that WOC wanted to work with him on laying the necessary groundwork. Hughes—then a prominent member of WOC's organizational committee—came away feeling that Bernardin's tone was light, positive, and pastoral, in contrast to most feminists' interpretations of his letter. When she hung up the phone, she felt hopeful: "There was a door open!" Hughes's optimism increased in February 1976 when Thomas Kelly, a Dominican priest and general secretary of the NCCB, approached her about appointing a permanent WOC liaison to the annual bishops' conference in March 1976. Hughes told me, "This was rather extraordinary, in my judgment; I thought it was phenomenal. . . . The bishops wanted to have an ongoing dialogue!"[35] Just ten years after Vatican II and the rush of Catholic feminist hope, it seemed to Hughes that high-ranking American bishops were willing to discuss women's ordination.

Unfortunately, Hughes explained, WOC leadership could not agree on the terms for this liaison. Should this individual agree to meet the bishops on their turf? Should WOC request a different setting altogether? Was it even the right time to establish a liaison? Without unified WOC support, Hughes

backpedaled with Kelly and suggested that March 1977 would be a better time
to move forward. By then, WOC would have had time to elect leadership and
determine a unified position.

But *Inter Insigniores* intervened and shifted the rules of the game, closing
the door on activists' hope that women's ordination could come from the Vatican. It was also now impossible for WOC to establish a permanent liaison to
the NCCB, because any bishops engaging in such a dialogue would be disobeying a Vatican declaration. In other words, *Inter Insigniores*, coming from the
CDF in Rome, seriously derailed real hope for American dialogue on women's
ordination.

Hughes's story, recounted to me more than thirty years later, raises important
historical questions: If WOC had established a liaison in 1976, would American bishops now have in place a theological framework for women priests?[36]
Would the arguments of *Inter Insigniores* have unraveled before landing on the
worldwide church? Would RCWP's twenty-first-century *contra legem* actions be
moot, because the church would have already allowed the ordination of women
deacons and even priests? None of these what-ifs came to pass, of course, and
instead, the debate over women priests grew more deeply entrenched as a matter
of male versus female, clergy versus laity.[37]

Hughes's recollection is not just about what might have been; it's about what
was: disputes within WOC escalated as the leadership tried to articulate a unified voice. Before these activist women had achieved their priesthood goals,
they began to disagree on their vision for a future church. How would WOC
relate to the NCCB? Should women be ordained into the church as it currently
stood? Was women's ordination primarily about pastoral care or equality of the
sexes? For her part, Hughes reported that some of her fellow activists accused
her of being "co-opted by the male bishops." Others disdained her because she
expressed genuine interest in being ordained in the church as it was then, in the
late 1970s. The conflicts Hughes describes—infighting, disagreements around
leadership and theology, questions about relationships with male clergy—continued through the 1980s and 1990s. RCWP, too—with over 200 strong-willed
women activists, many connected to this WOC history—struggles to speak
with one voice today, as I will show later in this chapter.

Ludmilla Javorova: Twentieth-Century Woman Priest

Ludmilla Javorova bears the distinction of being the first woman known
to have been ordained a Roman Catholic priest in the modern era. Born in

Czechoslovakia in 1932, Javorova grew up in a devout Catholic family and dreamed of becoming a religious sister. Geopolitics intervened. Nazis occupied Czechoslovakia during World War II, and Soviets ruled the country after the war. The Soviet Communist regime silenced churches and eliminated religious influences by confiscating church property and imprisoning thousands of Catholic priests and nuns in concentration camps.[38]

In order to preserve and protect Roman Catholicism, an underground resistance movement emerged. Javorova joined Koinotes, a community that met secretly for prayer, instruction, and spiritual reflection. Felix Maria Davidek, a childhood friend of Javorova's, became one of the group's leaders. Davidek was a Roman Catholic priest and former political prisoner. He had been secretly ordained a bishop and charged with helping keep Czechoslovakian Catholicism alive. This hidden church ordained hundreds of men. Davidek also authorized the ordination of married men—including Javorova's younger brother.[39]

But the situation remained grave. Catholic women in Communist Czechoslovakia had difficulty accessing sacraments and pastoral care—especially women in prison, who could only receive female visitors. Davidek began pressuring Javorova to accept ordination. Called by her bishop, she obeyed, even when men within the group questioned Davidek's decision. In a move that would be significant for RCWP decades later, Davidek used the standard ordination ritual to ordain Javorova; he did not revise the sacrament for a female ordinand, and he laid hands on her as he did male candidates for ordination. Javorova became a deacon first and later a priest. For over twenty years, the covertly ordained Javorova performed sacramental ministries and sustained Czechoslovakia's Catholic faithful.[40]

After Communism fell in 1989, stories of these irregular ordinations came to light. Rome now had to assess the validity of the underground church. In addition to Javorova and scores of married men, seven other women had been ordained as deacons and priests. As the Vatican deliberated its next steps, it excluded the ordained women from formal talks. Meanwhile, the women's male-priest colleagues distanced themselves from the women. Davidek had died in 1988, leaving Javorova and others without his crucial support. The Vatican forbade Javorova from speaking in her own defense, and no one else spoke for her. The Vatican ruled that validly ordained unmarried men could continue serving as priests; that validly ordained married men had to stop serving as priests, though their past sacramental actions were valid; and that the women were not and had never been validly ordained, and their past priestly ministries were not valid.[41]

To date, Javorova has obeyed Vatican prohibitions against serving as a priest, but she refuses to deny the fact of her priesthood. In 1995, she broke the silence the Vatican required from her, and she has since become a reluctant cause célèbre for women's ordination activists. RCWP uses Javorova's example in their website's FAQs to illustrate that a woman has been ordained a Roman Catholic priest in the twentieth century.[42] Javorova's experiences simultaneously inspire and incense supporters of women's ordination: inspiring that a male bishop ordained her to priesthood within the apostolic line but incensing that Rome denies any such thing truly, validly occurred.

The Pontifical Biblical Commission: The New Testament and Women's Ordination

Like Ludmilla Javorova's ordination, the Pontifical Biblical Commission (PBC) is another little-known church action. In 1975 and 1976, the PBC met to apply a scriptural lens to the question of women's ordination. This group of seventeen male, Vatican-appointed, Catholic biblical scholars reached three significant conclusions. First, the commission voted unanimously that the New Testament does not settle whether women can become priests. Second, the commission voted 12–5 in favor of the view that scriptural grounds alone are not enough to exclude women from the possibility of ordination. Third, the commission voted 12–5 that Christ's plan for the church and for humanity would not be transgressed if women were ordained and able to offer sacraments (specifically the Eucharist and reconciliation). The PBC's report ended with the following: "It does not seem that the New Testament by itself alone will permit us to settle in a clear way and once and for all the problem of the possible accession of women to the presbyterate."[43]

Striking here are the differences between the PBC's conclusions and those of *Inter Insigniores*, issued the very same year. *Inter Insigniores* cited New Testament examples in explaining Christ's will for a male-only priesthood—yet the PBC had reached different conclusions only months earlier. In short, the church held contradictory views on the issue of women's ordination within the same calendar year. Any Catholic agitating for women priests had reason to be confused.

These agitators might also have been angry: Rome did not have to reconcile the disparities between *Inter Insigniores* and the PBC report because the latter was never published or made official.[44] The commission's conclusions became known only because someone leaked them, and then scholars Leonard and Arlene Swidler exposed the commission's full report. Today, there is no mention

of the commission's report in official Vatican documents or on Vatican websites. Instead, women's ordination activists (such as the Wijngaards Institute
for Catholic Research, the Women's Ordination Conference, and RCWP) have
preserved and publicized the document. For over forty years, the commission's
unofficial report has intensified activists' beliefs that Roman Catholic tradition
need not oppose women priests and that certain male prelates have been acting
as gatekeepers and preventing the change.

The Philadelphia Eleven: Inspiration from Episcopal Women

RCWP's 2002 Danube Seven drew inspiration from the Philadelphia Eleven, a
group of Episcopal women who were validly but illegally ordained in 1974. Of
the many groups to emerge from the sixteenth-century Reformations (Protestant and English), the Anglican tradition is the most like Roman Catholicism
in its sacramentalism and ritual, its institutional and hierarchical structure,
and the importance placed on apostolic succession.[45] It is no coincidence that
Roman Catholic women modeled their *contra legem* actions on those of Episcopal activists.

In 1970, the General Convention of the Episcopal Church USA opened the
diaconate, but not the priesthood, to women. Like Roman Catholic deacons,
these women could preach the gospel, deliver homilies, and assist with holy
Communion, but they could not celebrate Eucharist or absolve sins. Episcopal
women continued pressing for priesthood ordination, and at a 1973 convention,
US Episcopal leaders took up the question of ordaining women as priests. After
much heated debate—which saw female deacons sitting silently while male
decision-makers discussed their fate—the General Convention rejected the motion to ordain women as priests.[46]

Within months, a group of eleven female deacons began planning an "irregular" (that is, illegal or unauthorized) ordination to priesthood. The women
found retired bishops in good standing to lay hands on them: this way, the ordination's validity could not be questioned, the women could claim to stand in the
line of apostolic succession, and the bishops would not risk their careers by participating. The ordination took place in 1974 at North Philadelphia's Church of
the Advocate, a community well known for its diversity and civil rights activism.
The Eleven faced a frenzy of flashbulbs and TV cameras; they were simultaneously applauded and reviled.[47] In 1976, the Episcopal Church legalized wom-
en's ordination and made valid the Philadelphia Eleven's "invalid" ordinations.
Debate continues about whether the Episcopal Church would have legalized

women's ordination in 1976 without the Eleven's much-publicized protest in 1974. Activists argue, however, that the Philadelphia Eleven provided the push to allow ordained women.[48]

This Episcopal case study and the subsequent policy change inspired Catholic ordination advocates—and enraged the Vatican. By the 1970s, many American Protestant denominations had started ordaining women (including large groups like the Presbyterians and Methodists, both in 1956, and the Lutherans, in 1970). But no ordination of Protestant women elicited a Vatican response quite like these Episcopal ordinations. Rome decried the change, first in the US Episcopal Church in 1976 and later in the Church of England in 1992. Pope John Paul II and Archbishop of Canterbury Richard Runcie exchanged letters on the issue in 1984. Both acknowledged the negative impact that the issue of women's ordination could have on the Anglican–Roman Catholic relationship. John Paul II wrote that women's ordination was "an increasingly serious obstacle" to reconciliation between the two churches.[49] Yet Runcie would not budge on the correctness of women's ordination, arguing that scripture and tradition do not fundamentally bar women from ministerial priesthood. Runcie further argued (now writing to Roman Catholic Cardinal Jan Willebrands) that divine law cannot be shown to be against women's ordination and that since Jesus became human for *all* people, women should be able to become priests so as to "more perfectly represent Christ's inclusive High Priesthood."[50] Rome disagreed. These two religious institutions, which had been at an impasse for over four centuries, saw tensions deepen over the question of women's ordination.

Catholicism and Anglicanism were interpreting and arguing from similar history, scripture, and tradition but in vastly different ways. Runcie's arguments in 1986 contradicted *Inter Insigniores*'s arguments in 1976. Rome saw Anglican actions as shortsighted. Anglicans bristled at what they viewed as Rome's overreach. When Vatican observer Peter Hebblethwaite labeled 1994's *Ordinatio Sacerdotalis* an "act of authority born of irritation," he was describing how this conflict between Rome and the Anglican Church propelled John Paul II's apostolic letter.[51] When papal authority did not convince the Anglican brethren, the pope redoubled efforts to influence the Catholic communion. Hundreds of women had been ordained Episcopal priests at the time of *Ordinatio Sacerdotalis*'s release, and viewed within this interreligious context, Anglican actions look like as much an inciting factor for the encyclical as Catholic women's continued calls for ordination.

RCWP's founders (and members of WOC and WOW before them) noted the Philadelphia Eleven's strategies and successes. Women's gains toward ordination in most Protestant traditions made little difference for Catholic discourse on women priests because those churches were too unlike Catholicism in terms of tradition, sacraments, and theology. The Episcopal example, however, changed everything. Here was a ministerial priesthood with sacramental power and an apostolic lineage, about as close to Roman Catholicism as a non-Catholic church could get. The Episcopal women did not achieve their goal by petitioning bishops or soliciting the General Convention; they had to act "irregularly." The Philadelphia Eleven applied pressure internally and externally: by using legitimate bishops in an authorized ceremony, the women worked within the system; by capturing media attention and inciting debate in the press, they reinforced external pressure. After decades of raising theological arguments for women's ordination, and after decades of the Vatican's "no," the Danube Seven (who would give rise to RCWP) drew upon a framework with seemingly proven results: if women would not be ordained legally with hierarchical approval, they would attempt ordination without it.

Conclusion

This chapter has demonstrated the ways in which Rome simultaneously encouraged and thwarted women's ordination activists throughout the late twentieth century. Recent Roman Catholic history has inspired RCWP's women and convinced them that they can demand and claim priesthood ordination, even if illegally. With the foundations offered by Vatican II and WOC, conflicting conclusions in *Inter Insigniores* and the Pontifical Biblical Commission report, the Philadelphia Eleven's irregular ordinations, and Ludmilla Javorova's underground ordination, activists have had reason to look skeptically on statements barring women from ordination. Without a definitive and cohesive message from church leaders, feminist reformers filled twentieth-century Catholicism's intellectual gaps with their own academic and theological ideas. When popes and prelates failed to modify or explain modern Catholicism in ways that made sense to these educated and socially engaged feminists, they crafted ways to make Catholicism work. When the Roman Catholic Church ceased to offer some women a way to understand themselves as women and as Catholics in the late twentieth century, they took to social movements that provided them community, spiritual sustenance, and a framework for resistance.

The majority of RCWP's women were born in the 1930s, '40s, and '50s, saw Vatican II changes happen, lived through massive shifts in Catholic culture, and felt optimism from these religiously and culturally driven transformations.

RCWP's women knew their church could change—they had seen it happen before, to a tremendous magnitude. Now, having become illegally ordained women caught up in debates about women's ordination, they looked to their church's teachings to defend their *contra legem* defiance.

CHAPTER 3

Conflict and Creativity

RCWP HAS TAKEN SHAPE at a time when the Roman Catholic Church is struggling to retain its former prominence in the United States, Canada, and Western Europe. The sex-abuse crisis has only exacerbated the issue. In a 2003 study, Peter Steinfels wrote, "American Catholicism, to put it bluntly, is in trouble. Absent an energetic response by Catholic leadership, a soft slide into a kind of nominal Catholicism is quite foreseeable."[1] RCWP has bought into rhetoric like Steinfels's, seeing the Western church in a transitional place of crisis and calling out for dramatic change. To be sure, in some ways the data calls for a more measured read of Roman Catholicism: numbers remain more or less steady in the US (thanks largely to Latin American immigration), and membership is climbing in many places worldwide. Yet womenpriests, along with a myriad of Catholic progressive groups, see the Roman Catholic Church as failing to meet many faithful Catholics' pastoral needs.

What are these important lapses in ministry? Womenpriests' survey responses to this question circle around themes of unchecked power and oppression of laity. The Roman Catholic Church is failing to "[meet] people where they are [and allow] them to grow and become people of God." Rome is "out of touch with reality." The Roman church is not "relevant to our times" and will not be until it includes the "voice of non-ordained people in decision-making" and recognizes women and LGBTQ people "as equals within the church."[2] As one would assume, issues of gender feature prominently in womenpriests' critiques of Rome, though perhaps Elsie McGrath put it most colorfully: the biggest problem in today's Roman Catholic Church, she said, is "the 2,000-year-old subjugation of over half the world's human population because of the hierarchy's tunnel vision and morbid preoccupation with issues of genitalia."[3] Womenpriests see the Roman church declining in relevance and increasing in power abuses, and so they seek to change the church into what matters to Catholics like themselves.

The RCWP movement and womenpriests' worship communities say that the "energetic response" Steinfels mentioned has already arrived, though it comes not from church leadership but from illegally ordained womenpriests. Like other progressive Catholics in the first decade of the twenty-first century, the young RCWP movement often repeated the statistic that *former* Catholics were the United States' second-largest religious group—behind Catholics.[4] If "American Catholicism must be seen as entering a crucial window of opportunity," as Steinfels stated, womenpriests are figuratively waving their hands in the air, calling upon others to see how they are seizing this opportunity and offering a distinct Catholic future.[5]

Whereas the previous chapter contextualized RCWP's activism and theological understanding with mixed messages from late-twentieth-century church statements and actions, this chapter examines RCWP's creative responses to contemporary conflicts. I look at challenges that have shaped the RCWP movement and consider the ways RCWP relies on struggles within contemporary Catholic life—both structural and theological—to create itself as an alternative to the institutional church. In creating the Roman Catholic Church that womenpriests long for, RCWP reveals the conflicts within contemporary Western Roman Catholicism, specifically around demographic changes, reform strategies, decision-making structures, and the parameters of a Roman Catholic identity.

Roman Catholic Identity amid Demographic Shifts

Globally, the Roman Catholic Church remains the world's single largest Christian body, with an estimated 1.15 billion adherents. The demographic and geographic makeup of these Catholics, however, is changing. According to a 2013 Pew study, in the past one hundred years alone, the percentage of Catholics in Europe relative to the global Catholic population has dropped from 65 percent to 25 percent, while Latin America has increased from 24 percent to 29 percent, Asia-Pacific has increased from 5 percent to 12 percent, and sub-Saharan Africa has increased from less than 1 percent to 16 percent. North America is more or less holding steady, growing from 5 percent to 8 percent.[6] In the United States, Catholics of European descent are leaving the church in droves, and Catholics of Latin American descent are filling the vacancies. What is more, some surveys show a stunning decline in numbers of American Catholics: the 2014 Religious Landscape Study from Pew found 20.8 percent of Americans are Catholic, down from 23.9 in 2007.[7] Put simply and somewhat cynically: Catholicism is on the decline among white, Western people, and some believe this to be a bad thing.[8]

Why are Western, white, "Global North" Catholics cutting ties with the church? Some defections connect to disparities between the personal convictions of many American Catholics and the Vatican's long-held teachings on gender, sex, and sexuality. Studies affirm this gap: Rome opposes gay marriage, but 54 percent of US Catholics support it; Rome affirms clerical celibacy, but 61 percent of US Catholics believe priests should be able to marry; Rome does not allow divorce and remarriage, and many priests will deny the Eucharist to divorced or remarried Catholics, but 60 percent of US Catholics believe that divorced and divorced-and-remarried Catholics should be welcomed as full members of the faith; Rome refuses to consider the ordination of women, but 59 percent of US Catholics think women should be allowed to be priests.[9] European Catholics align with American Catholics on several of these issues, but Catholics in places like Africa and the Philippines—also known as the "Global South," a term that replaces the more pejorative "Third World"—adhere strictly to church teachings on these hot-button issues.

In short, the global church is a divided church, and issues that RCWP stands for—like women's ordination, the end of clerical celibacy, and hospitality for gay couples—are not issues, per se, for all Catholics worldwide. And yet, for those Catholics who do focus on such topics, these can be the make-or-break reasons for staying Catholic or leaving the church.[10] Particularly for progressive Catholics, the declining numbers in the Global North bolster their call to change the church—namely, by allowing more of the progressive changes favored by financially secure, white, educated Western Catholics.

Younger Catholics also struggle with the Roman church's socially conservative elements. Writing about Roman Catholicism's difficulty retaining Catholic millennials, Kaya Oakes cited a 2015 survey that found only 16 percent of American millennials identify as Catholic. Oakes concluded that "the more young Catholics start to embrace marriage equality, safe and legal abortion, access to contraception, and the liberal side on many other issues in the culture wars, the more of those same Catholics will also drift away from a church they perceive as incapable of change."[11] Younger generations of Catholics—Generation Z, millennials, and some Generation Xers —have not seen their church keeping pace with modernizing changes, and this has impacted their commitment to Roman Catholicism.

Enter RCWP, part of a much larger network of present-day reform movements seeking to revive the church in these challenging times. In her study of what she calls present-day Catholicism's "underground church," Kathleen Kautzer situates RCWP among this large family of post–Vatican II Catholic reform groups and worship communities that "favor full equality for women and gays and lesbians in the church, an end to mandatory celibacy, approval of most forms of contraception, and a greater role for laity in decision making."[12] Kautzer's wide swath of reform-driven subjects are, like most RCWP members, "highly educated, middle-class Catholics" who are "intent on creating an alternative model of church that exemplifies Vatican II's open, receptive attitude toward the modern world."[13] RCWP fits within this family, sharing goals and often members with groups such as Women's Ordination Conference (WOC) and Women's Ordination Worldwide (WOW), Call to Action (CTA), Voice of the Faithful (VOTF), the Ecumenical Catholic Communion (ECC), FutureChurch, and CORPUS (a group of former priests calling for married *and* single male *and* female priests). RCWP's women often partner with these organizations, and some womenpriests learned about RCWP through other reform groups.

In this way, RCWP stands on the shoulders of what came before and shares goals with many contemporaneous movements. Several of RCWP's women have been members or leaders of WOC, WOW, and RAPPORT (formed in 1985, a group of women within WOC who wanted women's ordination to be an immediate reality).[14] When RCWP's liturgies use gender-inclusive language, they replicate feminist-inspired choices that are happening and have happened in progressive-and reform-minded groups for decades. When RCWP's women criticize male prelates for being obtuse or power-hungry, they join the chorus of organizations that locate Rome's problems in the (all-male) hierarchy. When they propose allowing clergy to marry, they echo an idea voiced previously by other reform groups. Like other Catholic feminist reform organizations, RCWP seeks to retain an essential "Catholic-ness" amid a renewing spirit.

RCWP stands out in this cadre of reformers for its desire to address the Roman church's contemporary problems by retaining the word *Roman* in its name and for illegally creating women clergy through the line of apostolic succession. There are, of course, other groups that support women's ordination and even ordain women as priests: they call themselves "Catholic" and retain liturgy and sacraments. They are not in communion with Rome, either by choice or as a result of excommunication. One example is the Ecumenical Catholic Communion, which describes itself as "a community of communities which are ecumenical and catholic."[15] The small-*c* "catholic" here simply means "universal" and indicates separation from Rome. Additionally, the Catholic Diocese of One Spirit uses a "fully Catholic model of Christianity as practiced by the early Christians" and eschews creeds, dogmas, and any "institutionalizing" impulse.[16] When these groups leave the word *Roman* behind, they signal that—unlike RCWP—they are willing to leave the Roman Catholic institution behind.

In spite of RCWP's insistence on a *Roman* Catholic identity, scholars like Kathleen Kautzer and Julie Byrne have classified RCWP as or alongside "independent" Catholics — that is to say, not Roman.[17] RCWP does closely resemble these groups: ordaining women, celebrating liturgy and Eucharist, combating Vatican decrees, placing new emphasis on lay involvement. Yet in keeping and emphasizing the "Roman" adjective in their name, RCWP signals its desire to be viewed differently from independent, catholic, and reform groups. As one womanpriest described in an email, "We have not walked away [from Rome] because *walking away from* the established Roman Catholic Church *allows it* to continue as the world's dominating bastion of male influence, power, money, and misogyny. . . . We offer a new model of ordained ministry in a renewed Roman Catholic Church" (italics in original).[18] She makes clear in her statement that, without the activism that aims to make women equal to men through priesthood, RCWP wouldn't be the reform movement it purports to be.

This is one of RCWP's recurring conflicts, both internal and external: the movement wants Rome to acknowledge its validity and emulate its egalitarianism, but it critiques Rome and distances itself from many Vatican habits and teachings. RCWP claims a Roman identity but admits—proudly, even—that it's not part of the institution. When I inquired during interviews, "If the pope said, 'You win; come join us!' what would you do?" nearly all the women replied they would not join the Vatican without major reforms within the church. "You come join *us*!" many women said. In other words, the women do not see themselves auditioning for a job as a "real priest" if and when the ban on women's ordination ever changes; instead, they see themselves as modeling and living out an entirely new priesthood, a whole new way of being priests. They believe the Roman church needs dramatic change, and they believe they are embodying that change.

RCWP views itself as remaining connected to Rome and offering a model church structure that can fix contemporary problems and honor Christ's vision for the church. What remains uncertain is whether RCWP's ordained believe that positive changes can happen within institutional structures or believe that the root of Roman Catholicism's patriarchal problems lie in institutional power. In RCWP's collective mind, can women as priests alleviate power abuses, or would women replicate them?

"Roman" and "Roaming" Catholics:
Womenpriests in the Eyes of Their Communities

Amid this context of contemporary Catholic history, American Catholic demographic shifts, and Catholic feminist reform movements, womenpriests serve
worship communities that embrace the idea of ordained Catholic women. Womenpriests' communities view womenpriests as offering a Catholic style and tone
that meet their own spiritual and religious aims. The following information on
RCWP's community members comes from my electronic survey of RCWP and
ARCWP community members and ethnographic data from two academic theses (one undergraduate, one master's) focused on specific RCWP communities
(Therese of Divine Peace in St. Louis, Missouri, and Sophia Inclusive Catholic
Community in Sussex County, New Jersey).

The majority of RCWP's community members tend to resemble the womenpriests themselves: older, well educated, white, and female. Perhaps the best
conclusion to draw here is the simplest one: just as women's ordination activists
have been arguing for decades, people want priests who look like them.[19]

RCWP's parishioners overwhelmingly identify as Catholic.[20] By "parishioners" I mean the individuals who regularly attend RCWP Masses and make
up the womenpriests' worship communities. Surveys revealed parishioners to
be religiously invested and engaged people: many reported attending other
churches in addition to the womanpriest-led ones, including Lutheran, United
Church of Christ (UCC), Mennonite, Episcopal, Presbyterian, and (in Vancouver, British Columbia) Anglican churches. Faith mixing is not unusual—a
2009 Pew Research Center poll on religion and public life found that just over
one-third of all Americans attend religious services at more than one place, and
nearly one-quarter of all Americans attend services that are not in their own
faith tradition[21]—but the practice is slightly less common among Catholics, so
its prominence among RCWP communities is noteworthy.

Because so many of RCWP's parishioners embrace theological variability,
many attend both RCWP services and Roman Catholic services. Why not
choose just one? For starters, many love being part of a large parish where they
have decades-long histories, longtime friends, responsibilities, and a familiar
community, often in a local neighborhood. They love the music and perhaps
participate in the choir. These characteristics of the parish experience are not
readily available in RCWP's small communities.

Some worshippers supplement RCWP liturgies with other services because
few womenpriests offer weekly Masses and none offer a daily Mass. Some do

Womanpriest Eileen DiFranco and members of her worship community,
St. Mary Magdalene in suburban Philadelphia, join hands for the Lord's Prayer.
Instead of saying, "Our Father, who art in heaven," the gatherers say, "Our God,
who art in heaven." (Photograph by Judith Levitt.)

not wish to abandon their parishes because they believe their home pastors and communities are welcoming and liberal, and they find spiritual sustenance there. These RCWP community members do not see a disconnect—theologically, doctrinally, or socially—between their presence at RCWP Masses and their presence at "valid and licit" Roman Catholic parishes. A cradle Catholic in Ohio said simply, "I believe in the validity of both."[22] Only a few respondents worried that worshipping with RCWP could jeopardize their relationship with their (arch)diocesan parishes.

A notable percentage of RCWP parishioners, however, feel that they cannot in good conscience attend both, and RCWP provides these individuals what the institutional church will not: a sense of belonging in a Catholic faith community. Consider this statement from "Rachel," a twenty-two-year-old queer woman who attended Therese of Divine Peace: "I really wanted to go to church. I just didn't want to go to church and feel like a pariah. I really value being Catholic. I really value the Mass, and I don't think I can practice my faith by myself, though I've tried. And so I feel like [Therese is] a community that I feel good being a part of, and I don't feel like I have to be someone different than who I am."[23] Rachel was not alone in pointing to this truism for RCWP communities: *belonging* is key.[24] Therese attendee Katie joked, "I call [Therese] St. Squarepegs. . . . It's like the Land of Misfit Toys. It's a bunch of people, just for whatever reason, they didn't fit in somewhere and everyone was brought here."[25] One person wrote of Sophia Inclusive Catholic Community, "I feel much more comfortable at Sophia because it's a lot of people who think the same as I do," while another said, at Sophia, "I can come together with people that think and feel like me, and it gives me a jolt to go through the next six days."[26] ARCWP priest Dorothy Shugrue expressed a familiar sentiment when she told me she wished Rome would recognize and "support that many [Roman Catholics] are returning to the faith because of us."[27] RCWP appeals to disillusioned Roman Catholics because it provides connection within a spiritually familiar package while letting participants feel that they belong.

Womenpriests are not simply bait for disillusioned Catholics. Parishioners value RCWP worship communities because they offer inclusivity, open table Communion (i.e., non-Catholics are welcome to share the Eucharist), spiritual empowerment, and a community of like-minded individuals. It is true that the provocative, illegal ordination of a woman to the priesthood initially draws curious observers, but it is the form of liturgy, the shared sacramental authority, the community, and the theological underpinnings that make worshippers stay. In parishioners' eyes, RCWP and its womenpriests symbolize the changing, accepting, progressive church that they have long awaited. Many community members said that their RCWP community—and not the institutional church—brings Jesus's message to a twenty-first-century world.

As excommunicated womenpriests, RCWP can position themselves as part of the solution while decidedly *not* part of the problem. Community members make a similar move: they take the Catholic history, tradition, and sacramental beauty that fuel them spiritually and jettison the elements they find toxic, unjust, or antiquated. I must be very clear: it is highly significant that parishioners view RCWP as a suitable alternative to the Roman Catholic status quo. This acceptance suggests that RCWP is Catholic enough—in the eyes of parishioners—to be authentic. They do not think they have left Catholicism; they believe they have moved on to its better, fuller, truer expression. They are still Catholic, but on social and theological terms to which they can readily acquiesce. Even better for these Catholics pained by contemporary church problems is the fact that RCWP is not one with Rome. To modify a popular Christian expression: these worshippers see themselves as *in* the church but not *of* the church. Instead of looking to the Roman church for guidance, they believe the Roman church should look to them: *they* are practicing the ideal, viable Roman Catholicism for the twenty-first century and beyond.

In this newfound Catholic space where womenpriests remake Roman Catholicism, parishioners make new discoveries: about priesthood, Roman Catholicism, the sacraments, and Jesus. Women see their priests as peers and not as "an elite separate role."[28] Their womenpriests are role models who "demonstrate what servant leadership is."[29] Many now appreciate Roman Catholicism more deeply and intimately because they feel engaged with liturgy, tradition, and sacraments in ways they never had before. A woman in Kentucky has found a new, feminine image for the Eucharist: "a mother carrying a child in her womb [with] the umbilical cord from mom to baby . . . feeding the child."[30] Several described how sacraments are more deeply, profoundly experienced, both individually and within community. One respondent in Orinda, California, delighted in how "we share equally in consecrating the host at communion [and] use inclusive language in all the sacraments. There is a freedom to be with my God/myself. It is refreshing to know I am not alone in my theology and thinking."[31] A parishioner from St. Louis said that participating in Eucharist at Therese of Divine Peace helped her see that "while the priest is the presider, we are all celebrants of the sacraments."[32] Having a woman in the role of priest also offers new images and ideas for Jesus. "He is our brother, not our Lord," one respondent succinctly stated.[33] Another elaborated: "I'm thinking even more of [the] feminine image of Jesus. Just being in service with womenpriests and women deacons and people supporting them gives me a deeper sense of Scriptures and parent and child and the love between them being the Spirit. I experience Jesus as sister as well as brother and mother."[34]

Taken together, the comments reveal how RCWP community members are finding new ways to understand themselves as spiritual beings and Roman Catholics. Furthermore, they see womenpriests as mapmakers for this journey. A cradle Catholic from Ohio praised her womanpriest, who "has facilitated a couple of book discussions and [led] some profound discussions on Who Jesus was and our concept of God. I think it has helped me form a faith that's more realistic, that takes into account modern science and generally makes more sense to me. It also challenges me in new ways to be more aware of the Divine Presence within myself and others, as well as our connectedness to all creation."[35]

As community members tell it, the RCWP experience offers space to explore untested theological ideas. Sometimes these ideas include open defiance of Rome. One Sophia Inclusive Catholic Community member reported, "We don't belong to the Roman Catholic Church R-O-M-A-N. This group belongs to the roaming R-O-A-M-I-N-G. . . . Everybody is searching, you know?"[36] A respondent from Covington, Kentucky, demonstrated some rebelliousness when she wrote, "I feel excited and energized to go to the womanpriest masses. It feels like we are saying to the CHURCH You can't stop us! So just get out of the way here we come."[37] These emerging religious identities are not about doctrinal certainty or rote answers to Christianity's big questions. Searching together, in community, with one foot planted safely in their notion of "Roman Catholic" and another foot stretching to the spiritual unknown, RCWP offers parishioners room for experimentation.

Although womenpriests and parishioners share demographic data, regional identities, and love for Roman Catholicism, as well as serious reservations about Rome as an institution, the two groups have important differences. First, unlike womenpriests, most (though not all) community members fly under the radar of disciplinarian prelates and can choose to be simultaneously members of licit Roman Catholic parishes and illicit RCWP communities. Second, and more important, womenpriests have followed their vocational calls to the point of excommunication. They are public figures whose *contra legem* actions are publicly known. While RCWP community members enjoy involvement in readings, shared homilies, concelebration, and home Masses, they do not aspire to sacramental priesthood. They do not feel called to leadership, to sacramental facilitation, to starting new worship communities. Priesthood is not their vocation.[38]

The distinction underscores the crucial vocational dimensions of RCWP priesthood. My interviews, surveys, and primary-source readings revealed that RCWP is not merely a club for people disillusioned with the Roman church, created by women angry at the Roman church. Womenpriests show a discrete way of being Roman Catholic in the twenty-first century: they do not join other Protestant or non–Roman Catholic communities but instead build from their Roman Catholic foundation. RCWP aims to practice the "discipleship of equals" ideal and as such break down the lay-clergy divide while answering a call that leads to an ordained state that differentiates them from laity.[39] Theirs is a "both/and" approach that works for their parishioners, who feel both shepherded by a role-model priest and included fully in their community's operations, both practical and sacramental. Though RCWP's numbers remain relatively small, survey responses suggest that womenpriests provide parishioners with a much-desired spiritual path. For some, this is a path they did not even know they wanted, paved with theological ideas they did not even know existed.

Organizational Questions and Conflicts

As RCWP settles into its second decade, a major concern for the group involves organization. RCWP aims to avoid the power structures that it criticizes in the institutional church. Specifically, and following the conclusions of many Catholic progressives, many womenpriests decry clericalism and hierarchy as synonymous with abuses of power. They see church bishops as out of touch with the laity and structurally emboldened to remain aloof, yet influential. All womenpriests hold some criticisms of the hierarchical bureaucracy, but RCWP is divided over the best way to rectify these challenges—within both RCWP and a reimagined Roman Catholic Church.

RCWP can be seen as analogous to early Christian communities in the first and second centuries—and, not surprisingly, this is a comparison the movement embraces. Like those intentional, worshipful communities in the wake of Jesus's death, RCWP is a faith-based, grassroots organization. Like RCWP, early Christ-following groups were small and intimate, and the men and women gathered for worship shared authority. Women had a voice and position in many of these communities owing to their cultural role within the home.[40] As early Christian groups evolved, there emerged a (perceived) need to organize and formalize. Leadership roles became more prescribed; titles like deacon, presbyter, and bishop gained authoritative weight; and men stepped into the positions of power.[41] Like the early Christians, RCWP found it necessary to develop more formal administrative structures than were first envisioned following the 2002 Danube ordination. As it grew, RCWP organized into geographic divisions (West, Midwest, Great Waters, South, and East Regions in the United States; West and East Regions in Canada), largely for practical reasons: women wanting to gather for meetings or retreats did not have ample resources to travel across the country or cross international borders, and the regions wanted to remain small enough to hear one another's voices and personally guide ordinands in their preparation programs.

While RCWP's current organization structure is largely pragmatic, the American movement's 2010 divide into RCWP-USA and the Association of Roman Catholic Women Priests (ARCWP) arose from disagreements about governance. Specifically, RCWP's South Region separated from RCWP and later formed ARCWP. As a researcher, I found it incredibly difficult to get information about the RCWP-ARCWP split. The women involved were reluctant to divulge specifics or speak ill of one another. Many concluded that disagreements are bound to arise out of a group of strong-willed women who have spent decades struggling against injustice—a conclusion I tend to agree with but find too simplistic. I finally got a sense of the conflict when one of the womenpriests shared with me a series of emails from 2010, leading up to the RCWP-ARCWP split.

At its core, the 2010 split was over dissenting opinions on how to avoid abusive power structures within RCWP. Generally speaking, womenpriests believe Catholic clerics often wield power dangerously but do not agree on ways ordained women might avoid replicating those problems. Much of the 2010 conflict was specific to the United States because it concerned questions about tax exemption and nonprofit status.

Several factors exacerbated the dispute. First, that most of the exchanges occurred over email worsened the disagreements. One gets the sense that face-to-face meetings would have led to, if not a different outcome, a more amicable split. But in-person meetings were and remain challenging for unpaid womenpriests, who might have to travel hundreds or thousands of miles to conference with other ordained women. Thus, womenpriests found themselves with principled differences of opinion and no easy way to connect in person and communicate in a straightforward fashion.

Second, some members felt railroaded. These parties believed themselves a minority who that could not convince the majority. Those holding a minority view had become distrustful that RCWP's Leadership Council (LC) could truly represent all perspectives. They called for a consensus model for decision-making, having come to view RCWP's democratic system cynically. In contrast, other members felt stymied. They trusted the LC's efforts to hear and accommodate all voices, and so they interpreted the minority as obstructionist. Frustration abounded and anger escalated.

Third, nonprofit status was an issue for the organization. In 2005, when the name "Roman Catholic Womenpriests" became formalized, some lawyer friends of the ordained women helped RCWP become a nonprofit corporation that could receive donations. Lawyers recommended that RCWP set up a limited liability company to better collect and manage money the organization collected. None of this impacted Canadian womenpriests, who fell under different laws, so RCWP-USA split from the Canadian groups solely for the purpose of gaining legal nonprofit status, not because of any ideological dispute. Unexpectedly, the nonprofit status and the way it was set up—long before many of RCWP's womenpriests were candidates or ordinands—aggravated the problems in the United States. As was required of LLCs and nonprofit organizations, RCWP put bylaws in place. But some of RCWP's women questioned whether these bylaws should be modified to be in more in line with documents outlining RCWP's ministerial aims and structures.

In other words, RCWP's need to become a nonprofit, within an American system that has certain legal and definitional requirements of nonprofits, led to heated debates about RCWP's mission, vision, and leadership. The very idea of "corporate" influences within RCWP—even if they served the purpose of soliciting donations—riled some women who felt called to a nonhierarchical church. Other womenpriests were more amenable to the changes, trusting that RCWP could and would avoid hierarchical power abuses in spite of increasingly formalized structures. Those who had an urgent need to address discrepancies felt silenced; those who had different priorities felt the other side was creating unnecessary conflict.

As a result of irreconcilable differences, in October 2010, RCWP's South Region decided to, in their words, "regionalize effective immediately." They likened their newly imagined relationship with RCWP-USA as being akin to Canada's and Europe's: "one with you yet on a parallel but unique road." They wanted to continue participating in nationwide meetings and retreats; they would also form their own 501(c)(3)—that is, a tax-exempt charitable organization—and develop their own decision-making processes. The now-independent South Region came to form ARCWP.

What differentiates RCWP and ARCWP? At the national level, RCWP-USA is guided by a board of directors. RCWP-USA aspires to make decisions based on consensus, but its constitution allows for a democratic majority vote when consensus cannot be reached.[42] In comparison, ARCWP has an operating structure with no boards or administrators, and its constitution emphasizes "circular leadership" and a vision "to live as a community of equals in decision making."[43] ARCWP is not organized by regions and includes members from across the United States, Canada, and South America.

What do womenpriests say are the differences? A few patterns emerged in the 2014 survey I conducted. First, several ARCWP women used words like "collaborative," "egalitarian," and "circle leadership" to highlight what they view as important about ARCWP's governing structure.[44] ARCWP's Diane Dougherty disliked that RCWP uses "decision-making boards" and championed ARCWP's efforts "for full participation" and for "finding ways to . . . be accountable to each other." Dougherty saw board-driven leadership as a structure given to problems of "hierarchical malfeasance."

Second, womenpriests focused on the speed of and preparation for ordination—namely, as RCWP womanpriest Ruth Broeski put it, that ARCWP "ordains women more readily and in greater numbers relative to geography than RCWP." One of RCWP's women wrote that "the process for preparing for ordination within ARCWP seems to take much less time." ARCWP bishop Bridget Mary Meehan framed this particular difference positively: "We also are flexible about our preparation program and allow equivalences by providing custom design certificates to prepare candidates and provide ongoing education for our ordained members." Tied to what Meehan called "flexibility" was the observation from both groups' women that ARCWP makes "more exceptions to the rules" or, phrased slightly differently, is "less attached to rules and regulations."[45]

I must note, though, that a number of respondents minimized any differences. Some women said they choose not to focus on differences; others said there were no important differences to report. Others understood differences—between ARCWP and RCWP and among all the RCWP regions worldwide—as a necessary part of growth. While some thought the division unfortunate, others framed it as understandable, even favorable. Womanpriest Gabriella Velardi Ward explained, "This movement allows for cultural differences and different ways of being [a] church." Womanpriest Victoria Marie of Canada West wrote, "I think we are all striving for the same thing but we have not set out to be a monolithic organization, it's more like a federation that can accommodate different regional needs."[46]

Clearly, the international RCWP movement strives to make room for differences of opinion. Variations exist, as do different branches and regions with similar but distinctive practices and tones. By forgoing a strong institutional core, RCWP gives up the power of exclusivity that characterizes the Roman Catholic hierarchy. But this does not mean that womenpriests do not worry about becoming hierarchical. My research has shown that womenpriests constantly try to keep themselves in check; they know they cannot complete their mission of reforming a troubled church if they replicate the very problems they denounce.

This struggle between organization and opposition to hierarchy continues to dog RCWP's heels. Is there a way for reform movements based in and seeking to reform an institutional model to truly practice a "discipleship of equals"? Will womenpriests find a way to lead their communities and organize themselves on national and international levels without linking this leadership and organization to power and authority? And how can RCWP avoid the problematic mixed messages that characterized the late-twentieth-century Roman Catholic Church, even to the point of inspiriting resistance movements like RCWP? RCWP is the test case for these questions. The ideal model may not yet exist, and to succeed, the movement may have to do something creative.

Protestantism and the Pull of a Catholic Identity

A familiar refrain in criticisms of RCWP is that it has crossed the line between Roman Catholicism and Protestantism. Some critics suggest, often snidely, that if the women really want the power and prestige of ordination, plenty of Protestant groups will take them. Much vitriol plays out online anonymously, as shown in this sampling of comments on a YouTube video from an RCWP ordination in Chicago:

Response #1
As a catholic woman I totally disagree with woman priests. However, if I felt like you, I would leave the catholic church and join one of the thousands of protestant churches that allow women ministers! Whats wrong?? are these churches not good enough for you??? Leave the catholic church_ to those that believe in it!!!

Response #2
Heresy. Gnosticism. Neo-Pagan. Disobedience to_ the_ Vatican. Liberalism, relativism, progressivism. They want same sex marriage, pro-choice ideology. Total wickedness. Excommunication

Response #3
stop trying to_ ruin the true Church.

Response #4
Women priests!!?lol What next..male nuns??? LOL. Heretics . . . thanks Vatican_ 2! You all opened up the floodgates for heretics such as these so called womenpriests to run absolutely rampant! Anyway. They arent accepted by the rock of st peter the popecand holy mother church..so lol you are never allowed to go to confession or any of the sacraments as they are al..EXCOMMUNICATED . . . THEY BROUGHT IT UPON THEMSELVES!

Response #5
This is the most BLASPHEMOUS video Ive seen to date concerning the Catholic church . . . we should pray for these poor lost unfortunate souls, and the souls that they deceive.[47]

These criticisms show how RCWP finds itself amid conflicting ideas of what Catholicism is and requires. The discourse of Protestantization removes womenpriests and their followers from the soteriological surety of the One True

Church. Additionally, this kind of labeling insults RCWP as well as Protestants, who get looped in with excommunicated women as removed from the graces of Roman Catholicism.

These are familiar moves in denominational boundary making. Christianity has a long history of establishing and enforcing religious categories as a way of carving out diverse Christian identities. This grouping separates members of the same religious affiliation by political affiliation, obedience to authority, and eternal destination. It is all too easy to define dissenting Christian groups—"heretics"—out of existence; Christians have been doing it for two thousand years.

Womenpriests are resolutely Catholic. Being Catholic is a tightly held, constitutive identity for womenpriests; to remove themselves from Catholicism would be disingenuous and a betrayal of conscience. Glossing over the ways womenpriests claim a Roman Catholic identity robs us as scholars of the chance to parse the many varieties of twenty-first-century Catholicism. As author and women's ordination activist Angela Bonavoglia quipped in response to the suggestion that Roman Catholicism would become something altogether different if women were priests, "I hardly think the hallmark of Roman Catholicism is discrimination against women!"[48]

For womenpriests, sacraments are the hallmark of Roman Catholicism, and their attachment to sacramental priesthood distinguishes womenpriests from Protestants. Womanpriest Mary Grace Crowley-Koch echoed other womenpriests when she merged call, community, and sacrament:

> I feel like I am now doing what I was called to do many years ago. I feel validated and affirmed by the people of God in my inner core. One of my greatest experiences was to celebrate a wedding with my husband (a married [Roman Catholic] priest), an Episcopal priest, and myself. A great balance and I knew in my heart and being this is what the Spirit wants for the [Roman Catholic] church.[49]

Womenpriests consistently name the sacraments as their primary reason for keeping a Catholic identity, even when other Protestant denominations would allow them to pursue ordained ministry.

Many of RCWP's ordained women tried to leave Catholicism for Protestantism but returned. Their online biographies and conversations with me attested to these patterns. Womanpriest Mary Kay Kusner's website biography testified to her own discernment, saying that many of her colleagues in Boston College's master of public ministry program left the Roman Catholic Church to get ordained.[50] She told me more about this in our interview. Her husband left the church because of the sex-abuse scandal, and so she tried to become an Episcopalian. Yet she realized that she did not "know how to be other than a Catholic." She sometimes wished that she could "switch to another tradition"—but she could not do so authentically. She felt she was "putting on a costume or mask" when she experimented with the Episcopal Church.[51] Catholicism was the only religious tradition that worked for her. She found in her relationship with the Episcopalians a dual confirmation of identity: one, she was truly called to ordained ministry; and two, she was a Catholic only and could not be anything else. She said of her decision to stay Roman Catholic, "I want my presence to speak louder than my absence."[52]

Womanpriest Beverly Bingle had a similar story. While in seminary, three non-Catholic traditions asked her to be ordained with them. "The impact of being asked was that it became very very clear to me that I could not be anything but Catholic."[53] The Danube Seven's Dagmar Celeste credited two Methodist women to "opening her eyes" to the call when they invited her—an unordained Catholic woman—to be their pastor. Denominational differences did not stop the women from selecting Celeste as their minister or seeing her ministerial potential.[54] Womanpriest Kathy Vandenberg admitted to a Lutheran minister that, if she could do anything, she would be ordained. In turn, he encouraged her, saying she reminded him of Lutheran women called to ministry.[55] Womanpriest Diane Dougherty wrote, "Almost everyone that recognizes my gifts and calls me forth to exercise and practice my priestly role are Christians from other traditions—ex-Catholics, non practicing Christians [and] non-Christians."[56] A womanpriest who did not recognize her call until she was sixty years old said, "[An] Episcopal priest called me a priest before I had recognized my calling."[57] Womanpriest Ann Penick, a convert to Catholicism, received discernment help from non-Catholic family members: her stepdaughter, who is a United Church of Christ minister, and her Jewish cousins affirmed her call and her plans for *contra legem* ordination.[58]

In spite of these personal explanations, critics find it easy to dismiss womenpriests as a disagreeable and contemptuous "other"—or as Protestant. This language of forced conversion, whereby critics unmake womenpriests as Catholics and remake them as Protestants, denies the women the right to name their own religious identity and disparages their intent to change their church. When used in this way, the myopic "Protestant" label condescends to a female-led movement that very deliberately uses "Roman Catholic" in its very title.

Instead, I suggest we look at the manner in which RCWP raises pressing questions about "real" Catholicism. Facets of RCWP may not seem Roman

Catholic, but undoubtedly Roman Catholics around the world understand their faith tradition and religious identity very differently. Moreover, women-priests argue passionately that their actions, their motivations, and their entire self-understanding are strongly and powerfully *Catholic*. Just as Catholic femi-nist women in the 1960s and '70s declared, "We are feminists BECAUSE we are catholic,"[59] womenpriests are saying with their actions, "We are priests because we are Catholic."

What they are *not* saying is, "We are priests because the institution says so"— and yet for some womenpriests, the Roman Catholic Church's pull is too great. Take the story of former womanpriest Norma Jean Coon, a wife, a mother, and the first (and so far only) RCWP woman to renounce her ordination. Made a deacon through RCWP in 2007, Coon renounced her ordination and her affiliation with RCWP and publicly sought full reconciliation with the Roman church on February 8, 2011. She created a website (deactivated shortly thereafter) on which she announced, "I wish to renounce an alleged ordination and publicly state that I did not act as a deacon as a part of this group except on two occasions, when I read the Gospel once at Mass and distributed Communion once at this same Mass." She went on to seek formal reinstatement and vowed obedience to Roman church teachings: "I confess the authority of the Holy Father on these issues of ordination and recognize that Christ founded the ordination only for men." She separated herself from RCWP, writing, "Formally, I relinquish all connection to the program of Roman Catholic Womenpriests and I disclaim the alleged ordination publicly with apologies to those whose lives I have offended or scandalized by my actions."[60]

RCWP let Coon go quietly. Administrator and womanpriest Suzanne Thiel announced that Coon was no longer a member and no longer affiliated with RCWP. The group knows that *contra legem* ordination and *latae senten-tiae* excommunication are not for the faint of heart: illegally ordained women risk losing family, friends, and their faith community.[61] Coon wanted recon-ciliation with the institutional church; leaving RCWP was the sole way this could happen.

Coon's story underscores the seriousness of RCWP's attempt to relocate Roman Catholicism out of institutional Catholicism. Coon's personal struggles around family and health propelled her to seek reinstatement with the Roman church. In the face of grave pressure and uncertainty, she felt the institutional church's lingering pull and returned to the Catholic fold. In so doing, Coon affirmed for herself Rome's authority to make rules for her salvation.

Coon's struggle reveals yet another conflict for the young RCWP movement: convincing others (and sometimes, as in Coon's case, womenpriests themselves) that people can be fully Roman Catholic while criticizing the institutional church they seek to reform. Womenpriests must further acknowledge their excommunications in order to argue—counter to Roman Catholic teaching— that one can stand outside the institutional church and find eternal life, because "real" Catholicism, as the movement understands it, has to do with sacraments, ministry, certain elements of church history, and following one's conscience. In RCWP's ministerial hands, Catholicism is not synonymous with Rome's institutional power.

And yet, because the movement thwarts institutional mandates, RCWP is readily condemned by certain critics as "Protestant." Many critics refuse to engage the reimagined relationship between Catholicism and the Vatican that RCWP has embarked on, instead painting womenpriests with the broad brush of Protestantism, reserved for Catholic renegades since the sixteenth century. Is RCWP "going Protestant" as it "goes rogue," or—as the group would argue—is RCWP opening eyes and doors to new ways of being Catholic?

Conclusion

RCWP's members have taken the Vatican messages that resonate with them most and brought them to bear on current challenges in the Western European and North American church. They believe that obedience to essential Roman Catholic issues (as they understand them) demands disobedience to certain authoritative decrees. Womenpriests look at the contemporary Catholic context—the declining numbers of self-identified Catholics in the Global North, the decades-old drop in vocations, the difficulty many Catholics face in receiving sacraments, and the toxic sex-abuse crisis—and believe ordained women can help change a struggling church for the better. They see themselves as truly, authentically Roman Catholic, obedient to the faith if not to the patriarchy, and able to help guide the church and its disillusioned members through twenty-first-century challenges.

But a problem remains for RCWP. A hallmark of Roman Catholicism is its highly structured, nondemocratic centralization. In spite of the theological and doctrinal ammunition the church gives RCWP, Rome offers RCWP no model for egalitarian decision-making. If womenpriests' fear of replicating clerical structures is at the heart of their movement, they need to discover new forms of priestly leadership. At some point, therefore, RCWP may have to relinquish its claims to the "Roman" adjective, considering the movement aspires to organizational structures the church does not follow. Or, not unlike the early Christians, RCWP may discover that hierarchical rigidity is necessary for strength and unity. If, somehow, RCWP finds a creative structural solution that incorporates movement-wide unity and rebukes hierarchy, the group may force us to reconsider what makes Catholicism "Roman" after all.

CHAPTER 4

Ordination

RCWP'S ORDINATIONS ARE, PARADOXICALLY, the group's most transgressive *and* most traditional acts. Ordination signals the women's ultimate disobedience to Rome's authority, and since May 2008, *latae sententiae* (automatic) excommunication has occurred at the moment of ordination. But RCWP also retains the Roman Catholic ordination ritual and works to ensure apostolic succession, signaling the group's desire to remain within the Roman Catholic lineage. RCWP's ordinations have long been a dance between polarities: the women break canon law while taking steps to guarantee they remain within the Catholic tradition. They ironically show their love for the Roman church as they rebuke it.

Being ordained allows womenpriests to honor a call, obey Christ and their conscience, and become the priests they have longed to be. Yet my research shows that, for womenpriests, ordination is far more than a personal journey: in RCWP's hands, ordination is corrective justice, historical reclamation, and an opportunity to steer public discourse. Ordinations seek a *contra legem* resolution to the many debates surrounding women's ordination. This chapter analyzes RCWP's ordinations as protest actions, personal transformations, and public displays whereby RCWP announces its existence and negotiates its identity. In referring to RCWP's ordinations as protests, I extend scholar Mary Fainsod Katzenstein's observations about "faithful and fearless" feminists protesting inside institutions—a change from earlier feminist protest models that took place "in the streets."[1] Because the women use Roman Catholic sacramental frameworks to become illegally ordained priests, their actions provoke the institutional church more than they would if, for instance, RCWP jettisoned "Roman" from their name or eschewed apostolic succession and the laying on of hands. RCWP's politics of protest are calculated to be disruptive and transformative—that is, they transform women into priests while transforming the church through the provocative reimagination of Roman Catholicism as a tradition that includes women in ordained authority.[2] Furthermore, in protesting through ordination, womenpriests position themselves outside some of the Catholic, feminist, theological aims of the 1980s and '90s, as *contra legem* ordination of women is not an agreed-upon strategy for all Catholic activists.

Thus, through *contra legem* ordination, RCWP situates itself uncomfortably within a Catholic feminist lineage, uses media to garner public support, and reframes women's ordination as a reclamation of a lost Roman Catholic history. In doing this, RCWP maneuvers in and around the future, present, and past of women's ordination and Roman Catholicism as it fractures the feminist vision for the future church, publicly asserts the present-day existence of womenpriests, and reasserts women's ordained roles in the Catholic past. Like the waters on the St. Lawrence Seaway on a hot July afternoon in 2005, during an RCWP ordination ceremony that I explore below, all of these temporal and discursive streams flow together in RCWP's carefully considered ordination activities.

Common Themes in RCWP Ordination Ceremonies

RCWP ordination ceremonies display the movement's goal of showing that womenpriests are faithful Catholics who use Roman Catholic idioms to protest the hierarchical church. Under the enthusiastic eyes of friends and family and the media's watchful attention, RCWP members use ordination ceremonies to perform what they see as a more progressive, spiritually expansive, and egalitarian Roman Catholicism. At the outset of this chapter on the relationship between RCWP and ordination, let us observe closely the themes at work on July 25, 2005, in the first public ordination of nine women in North America.

First: location. On a hot, sun-drenched afternoon, a chartered ship left Gananoque, Ontario, and sailed along the St. Lawrence Seaway, an international waterway between Canada and the United States. As with the Danube ordination three years prior, organizers avoided the jurisdictional watch of any one diocese with this waterway location.

Next: audience. Scores of family and friends crammed onto the boat, squirmed on sticky, hard, white plastic seats, fanned themselves with worship aids, chugged bottled water, and strained their necks to see the ceremony. The boat could not accommodate all who wanted to attend, and so tickets for the boat excursion were expensive. The press—yet another prominent character in these ordinations—jockeyed for position from the rear of the makeshift liturgical space.

RCWP ordinations often include the womenpriests' own notions of socially aware, spiritually progressive elements. Before the St. Lawrence ordination, for instance, an Algonquin woman led a call-and-response, beating a drum to keep time. Then, during the entrance processional, Americans Jane Via (an RCWP deacon) and Charles Nicolosi (husband of Regina Nicolosi, one of the ordinands) carried a cross to the makeshift altar. As an ordained priest himself, Charles Nicolosi's participation communicated a message that contradicted Rome's ban on women priests (as well as married priests). The cross Nicolosi and Via carried sat atop a wooden "raft" that stabilized the structure and echoed the day's water vessel motif.[3] Made of twigs and branches, the simple cross suggested humility, a contrast to the cathedrals that host valid and licit Catholic ordinations.

Like many ordinations—RCWP and otherwise—the ceremony involved three clerical ranks: deacons, priests, and bishops. On this July day, five women were being ordained to the diaconate. Four women, already deacons, were being ordained to the priesthood. Three women presided as bishops. Gisela Forster of Germany and Christine Mayr-Lumetzberger of Austria had been consecrated bishops shortly after their 2002 ordination to priesthood, and Patricia Fresen of South Africa had been made a bishop in January 2005. Missing from these bishops' bodies were the miter (the tall, traditional hat that bishops wear during formal ceremonies) and cope (an ornamental cloak typically accompanying the miter at high liturgical functions); the women also did not carry crosiers (the bishop's staff).[4] Instead, they wore white albs covered by red-and-coral-colored chasubles made of gently flowing material that easily caught the wind. Greek crosses with four arms of equal length hung around their necks. They stood out as distinctive even without the traditional episcopal dress.

Like many ordinations, particularly early in the movement, the St. Lawrence ceremony coincided with other Catholic activist events. Women's Ordination Worldwide (WOW) hosted a conference in Ottawa during the three days (July 22–24) leading up to the ordination. Some conference-goers had taken a "Witness Wagon" pilgrimage a week earlier, visiting landmarks from American women's history and celebrating suffragists like Elizabeth Cady Stanton and Susan B. Anthony. Before crossing the border into Canada, a large group from WOW and RCWP took part in Mass at Spiritus Christi, an independent Catholic church in Rochester, New York, with two female (but not RCWP) priests.[5] Organizationally, the St. Lawrence ordination became the centerpiece of the week's events focused on Catholic women's activism.

RCWP ceremonies find opportunities for creative ritual play and nonpatriarchal God language, despite the required formalities of Catholic ordinations. After the St. Lawrence entrance procession, Bishop Patricia Fresen evoked the divine feminine to introduce a water ritual in which the ordinands and ordaining bishops poured water from their hometowns and home countries into a clear glass bowl: "Today we give honor to our Mother God, that birthed us from the waters of creation and into life in this world. Just as the waters broke in the wombs of our mothers, so we break open the waters of Mother Church and welcome the birthing of her daughters into equality." Twelve women then came forward and poured their small vials of water into the communal bowl. Lake, river, and ocean water from such diverse places as Boston and Plymouth Harbors, the Mississippi River, the Sacramento River in California, and the Pacific Ocean mingled with water from the Isar River in Munich, a pond in the Austrian Alps, and the Danube River. The symbolism was multifaceted: the bowl of water represented the womenpriests' growing community, their desire to be unified as one in Jesus, the fusing of European and North American activism, and the female body's ability to bring forth new life.[6]

Ordination ceremonies also give womenpriests a stage from which to criticize what they see as Rome's sexism. On the St. Lawrence, the bishops' shared homily used nautical metaphors to criticize the Vatican, champion their own *contra legem* activism, and present a future-focused vision. Speaking English with a strong German accent, Mayr-Lumetzberger conflated the rented boat with the women's ordination movement when she preached, "A flowing, moving, sailing ship...full of thinking and feeling people, a living ship full of power and hope. . . . The ship as a symbol of movement...does not rest in stagnant water but is full of life and presence." Forster, also with German rhythms coloring her English, then contrasted this living, moving ship with the Vatican:

> The ship of the Vatican hierarchy has been lying at anchor in the harbor for many centuries. A ship filled with sleeping sailors squeezed into their self-made nets so that they cannot move. Sailors who are often unwilling to do the necessary work to keep the ship moving on the high seas but who are content to sleep on, sleep in the harbor, year after year, century after century. We are now boarding the ship, and we are saying—in a friendly way, we are saying—the sleep of the Roman Catholic hierarchy must end and the Vatican sailors must be awakened! We have to sing and shout so loudly that they will be awakened. . . . Women are ready...to guide the ship through dangerous water. We women are ready!

The audience laughed and applauded Forster's assessment of Vatican stagnation. Then Fresen, in her South African accent, acknowledged that the ordination movement's metaphorical ship would sail through many storms, "but the captain of our ship is the Holy Spirit." Paraphrasing woman's suffragist Susan B. Anthony, Fresen concluded, "Failure is impossible!" Attendees joined her in crying out a final time, "Failure is impossible!"

At its ordination ceremonies, RCWP's rhetoric points to the movement's understanding of the past, present, and future of the Roman Catholic Church. Womenpriests draw on past feminist activism while seeking to overturn past injustices against women; they bemoan the present-day struggles of the Roman Catholic Church while heralding their own presence as priests, today, as a remedy; they promise a future that will overcome challenges as it embraces women in ministry. With words and ceremony, the women braid together different temporal strands motivating their *contra legem* actions.

Amid these thematic refrains—and along with the media flashbulbs, the non-Catholic location, the creative symbolism and ritual, and the critique of Rome's patriarchs—womenpriests use apostolic succession, the ordination rite, and the bishops' authority to lay on hands to claim for themselves the identity of Roman Catholic priests. To do so, they must hold the transgressive and traditional in creative tension, embodying what the ideal Roman Catholic Church should look like, which Roman Catholic elements should stay and which should go. From its formation to the present, RCWP has navigated impulses that creatively complement each other in its quest for reform: valid and illicit, conservative and controversial, traditional and transgressive.

Rocking the Boat: The Danube River Ordination of 2002

RCWP's founding mothers believed their goal of empowering women with the sacred responsibilities of priesthood could come only through ordination into the existing sacramental system, with or without Rome's approval. How and by whom the women were ordained, with what authority and legitimacy, preoccupied the ordinands in the days, months, and even years leading up to RCWP's first public ordination, on the Danube River in 2002.[7] Ida Raming, a Catholic theologian and one of the Danube Seven, explained weeks before her ordination: "Women who feel called to the priestly ministry and who would like to live their call, thus find themselves in a serious conflict of conscience. On the one side they encounter the resolute position of the official leadership of the Church, on the other side God calls them to the priestly ministry in the Church. 'The love of Christ urges' them! The women who are concerned live in an intolerable tension and therefore seek a way out."[8]

Ordination admits women to the priesthood but also places womenpriests in larger discursive streams, allowing them to apply pressure on the Catholic hierarchy. In this way, the Danube ordination marked a tactical departure from past decades of women's ordination activism. No longer asking the Vatican for women's ordination nor writing feminist theological arguments against an all-male priesthood, the Danube Seven's actions announced that women would no longer wait for the Vatican to allow women's ordination. Women were now storming the castle walls.

Preparation for the 2002 Danube ordination started years before. In 1998 and 2001, Christine Mayr-Lumetzberger announced to WOW members that she had designed a three-year priesthood preparation program, and a local branch of an international Catholic reform group (We Are Church—Austria) had approved it. Knowing that ordination into the existing Roman Catholic institution was not a goal for all Catholic feminists, Mayr-Lumetzberger defended her decision: "I had the feeling that the groundwork on women in the church had reached a level on which a practical approach had to follow. I decided not to join into the discussion on women's ordination, but to take a practical step."[9] Theologians Ida Raming and Iris Müller, who had been making academic arguments in favor of women's priesthood since Vatican II, joined Mayr-Lumetzberger's group, which called itself the Danube Ordination Movement.[10] As ordinands in 2002, Raming and Müller wrote a public statement explaining the group's motives and approach:

> Since continuing discussion [of women's ordination] does not produce any prospect, as experience has shown, the women have decided to opt for an ordination *contra legem* (against the law; c. 1024 CIC). For a change in the juridical position of women in the Roman Catholic Church cannot be expected in the foreseeable future. As is known, in a General Church Council that could decide about the admission of women to the ministries, only bishops (therefore exclusively men!) would have voting rights, and bishops have shown themselves in the past as conformists to what the Pope and teaching authority want.[11]

Raming and Müller went on to use legal and theological tools to pick apart Rome's position, which they provocatively labeled a "heresy." They wrote, "The women...understand their action as a clear prophetic sign of protest, a protest against doctrine and Church law that discriminates against women." Given these conditions, if women were to obey their conscience and answer their calls, ordination-as-protest was the only possible solution.[12] To underscore this point:

RCWP's founding mothers concluded that action had to take precedent over discussion. Though Mayr-Lumetzberger, Ida Raming, and Iris Müller had participated in intellectual debates in the past, they now desired an action-oriented approach.[13]

Early on, leaders of the Danube Ordination Movement insisted that women be ordained by validly ordained male bishops in the line of apostolic succession. During the Roman Catholic ordination ceremony's most sacred moment, the laying on of hands, the bishop—whom Catholics believe is in the apostolic line by virtue of his own ordination—is said to pass the Holy Spirit to a candidate through his hands, making the ordinand ready and able to perform sacramental ministries. The Vatican's teaching on apostolic succession claims that twenty-first-century Catholic clergy can trace a line of sacred authority back two thousand years to the apostles, who are understood to have been ordained by Jesus himself, who was God in the flesh. At ordination, then, the bishop acts as a mediator who brings both God's Spirit and ordained legitimacy upon a candidate. If the Danube Ordination Movement was to follow the church's rules and claim valid priesthood, they needed a valid bishop—one willing to risk Vatican reprisal and perhaps even the end of his career.

Finding ordaining bishops proved challenging. Raming described one German bishop who was willing to speak against the Vatican's position, but he was not willing to act against canon law. Doing so, he believed, would create a scandal and harm the women's cause.[14] Eventually, the women found bishops committed to the ordination of women. Romulo Braschi of Argentina and Ferdinand Rafael Regelsberger of Austria were the two ordaining bishops at the 2002 Danube ceremony. Neither man was in communion with Rome at the time. Braschi, a validly ordained priest, broke from the Roman church in the 1970s over what he saw as the church's apathy during Argentina's Dirty War. He married and joined a charismatic Catholic group.[15] He had already left the institutional church when he was consecrated a bishop in 1998; he was remade a bishop, by a different ordaining authority, in 1999.

Braschi's episcopal lineage impacts Regelsberger's because Braschi ordained him a bishop a month before the Danube ordination so that he could be the Danube women's local bishop. Surely knowing his legitimacy as a bishop would be in question, at a press conference preceding the Danube ordination, Braschi produced a notarized document from an Argentine lawyer testifying to his validity.[16] Technically, an individual can be a validly ordained priest and not be in communion with Rome, but Braschi's situation raised further questions about an ordination already destined for heightened scrutiny.[17]

The Danube Ordination Movement knew that Braschi's and Regelsberger's apostolic lineages would cause problems, and so they planned for one more
bishop to lay hands on the ordinands. Juanita Cordero and Suzanne Avison
Thiel's book *Here I Am, I Am Ready*, published by RCWP, refers to this
third man as "Bishop X."[18] He had previously joined Braschi in ordaining the
six women as deacons on Palm Sunday, 2002, and would consecrate Fresen a
bishop in 2005.[19] But Bishop X did not attend the June 2002 Danube ceremony
as planned: at the last minute, he failed to appear. Some news reports stated
he was delayed by traffic. Ida Raming confirmed for me that the third bishop
"was indeed prevented from coming to the Danube ceremony," but she did not
know exactly what had happened. Gisela Forster claimed that the local monas-
tic community hosting Bishop X had locked him in his room, detaining him
indefinitely.[20] Stories surrounding this man's absence mirror the intrigue of his
top-secret identity.

The ceremony proceeded without Bishop X—but not without liturgical disruptions. The Danube Seven had designed the program with German-speaking
Bishop X in mind as the principal celebrant; Braschi, who spoke only Spanish,
kept the translator struggling to convey the details and nuances of his speech.
Braschi also had other ideas about how the ritual should proceed, and the worship aid became difficult to follow because Braschi went off script. Perhaps most
distressing to the organizers, who were fighting rigorously to remain within the
Roman Catholic tradition, Braschi publicly denied having any Roman authority
and reportedly told the gathered crowd, "I am catholic but not Roman, [and] I
am not working in the name of the Roman Catholic Church."[21]

Still, Braschi kept to the formal ritual and used the Roman rite—to the
point of swiftly silencing an enthusiastic attendee who called out "And *her-
manas*" ("sisters") when Braschi read the word *hermanos* ("brothers") from the
sacramentary.[22] Following Roman Catholic form, the candidates stood before
the bishops in the presentation of candidates; the ordinands prostrated themselves on the floor during the singing of the litany of the saints; the bishops laid
hands on the women, passing on apostolic succession; during the investiture, the
women were dressed in stoles signaling their priestly identities; and one of the
bishops anointed the new priests' hands with oil and presented them with their
chalices and patens.[23]

Despite his failure to appear on the Danube, Bishop X's work with the Danube Seven had not ended. Mayr-Lumetzberger told the *National Catholic Reporter* that the Seven planned to ask the absentee third bishop to ordain them

later, *sub conditione* ("subject to condition" or "conditionally"). In other words, if the Danube ordination was for some reason invalid, Bishop X's later sacramental gestures would ensure a valid ordination. If, however, the Danube ordination *was* valid, Bishop X's ordination would be unnecessary and ineffectual.[24] Here the women worked to prevent questions about their legitimacy. While they were ready to disobey the church's teaching on women's ordination, they were unwilling to go without apostolic succession.[25]

Critics have seized upon inconsistencies in the ceremony and dismissed the women's priesthood outright. For its part, RCWP remains confident in the womenpriests' apostolic authenticity. There existed (and may still exist) European male bishops in good standing with the church who, along with Braschi and Regelsberger, mentored and ordained the women.[26] Because Roman Catholic priests could be punished for supporting women's ordination, they have chosen to remain anonymous. Most of RCWP's women, and certainly the majority I interviewed in North America, do not know details about these behind-the-scenes bishops who supported the early movement. RCWP women who *do* know the men's identities show little interest in telling anyone. I have read and heard countless times that the unnamed bishops are validly and legitimately ordained and were in good standing with Rome at the time of the ordinations, and that notarized documents attesting to the ordained women's place within apostolic succession are being held in a European safe-deposit box, to be revealed after the bishops die.[27]

Relying exclusively on male bishops posed strategic difficulties. First, when Braschi improvised liturgical changes and disregarded the prepared remarks at the 2002 Danube ceremony, he ironically removed decision-making authority from the seven ordinands, who had taken great care in planning their ordination ritual. The Danube Seven's need for male bishops put power in male hands and made the movement subject to patriarchal forces. Second, anonymous male bishops lacked the freedom and flexibility to meet the needs of the growing womanpriest movement. Their obligations to Rome prevented them from focusing exclusively on ordaining women *contra legem*.

Thus, the young womanpriest movement cultivated its own female bishops. Once women bishops could ordain other women, the movement could expand freely. Of course, these women would also need to claim and prove the legitimacy of apostolic succession. Mayr-Lumetzberger and Forster became the movement's first bishops. Because organizers worried for the group's longevity even in these early days, an unnamed woman was also consecrated as a bishop to ensure the apostolic line could continue should anything happen to Mayr-Lumetzberger or Forster.

Fresen was the fourth bishop to be ordained. As she tells the story, Bishop X had to persuade her. He argued that, because Fresen's native language was English, and because most of the women preparing for ordination were North Americans, an English-speaking bishop was necessary. Even more pressing, Bishop X believed that the Vatican was onto him and that it could soon be impossible for him to ordain more women. Fresen recalled him telling her, "If we ordain you a bishop, it is not for you. It is for the women whom you will lay hands on. It was passed on to me. It goes back through the centuries in apostolic succession. It was given to me not for me. And I want to pass it on to you, and it is not for you. And you will lay your hands on others."[28] Confident she was proceeding with legitimacy, she became a bishop, seeing the role as a position of service to the women's ordination movement and not a position of power.[29]

More bishops came about in subsequent years: Ida Raming in 2006; Dana Reynolds, the first American bishop, in 2008; and Marie Bouclin, the first Canadian bishop, in 2011. The RCWP movement currently has thirteen active and six retired bishops. The group concedes that bishops are an essential if initially unforeseen part of RCWP's activism and longevity. Womenbishops empower RCWP to grow without male's sacramental authority. But bishops also, problematically, undermine the group's commitment to omitting Roman Catholicism's lay-clergy divide. Bishops have become for RCWP a necessary evil.

In staging ordinations as protests, RCWP draws its own line between what the Roman Catholic Church can and cannot do. For RCWP, the church cannot decree women incapable of receiving ordained authority. The church has dismissed womenpriests as "invalid and illicit," but while RCWP allows the "illicit" descriptor—they admit they are, after all, breaking canon law—it renounces any rejection of validity. RCWP grants Rome the authority to establish a theological framework and sacramental system that creates deacons, priests, and bishops through apostolic succession and the laying on of hands. God can and does work through these ritual transactions. Through their actions, the Danube Seven and ensuing RCWP movement have declared simultaneously their outright dismissal of particular church laws as well as their willingness to embrace traditions they deem viable for a reformed, egalitarian future church.

Capitulating to Kyriarchy? Fragmenting the Catholic Feminist Vision for the Future

Whereas Rome has dismissed RCWP's actions as gravely transgressive, certain Catholic feminists have dismissed RCWP as dangerously *regressive*. The RCWP movement spends little energy engaging the scholarship of Catholic feminists in interviews or public discourse. RCWP founding mother Christine Mayr-Lumetzberger accepts her own philosophical and strategic disagreements with certain academics, largely because she believes women will find justice only when women are ordained just as men are. For Mayr-Lumetzberger, ordaining women is not about hierarchy but equality.[30] Of a similar mind, Patricia Fresen wrote, "Women have the right, not only to be ordained to the diaconate, priesthood and episcopacy, but to be ordained in the same way, in the same tradition, as men."[31] In short, RCWP's ordinations reflect a new way for Catholic feminists to *act* (i.e., in a *contra legem* ceremony) but do not offer any new ways to *argue*. RCWP aims to reform the Roman church, not Catholic feminist discourse.

Many but not all of RCWP's members are well read in Catholic feminist theology and third-wave feminist discourse. RCWP's ability to embrace a noncelibate priesthood and lesbian priests shows RCWP's blending of second-wave and third-wave activism, yet because it emphasizes equality with men first and foremost, some Catholic feminist theologians have accused RCWP of returning to second-wave feminism, rehashing old debates and offering little that's new.[32] Others disagree with RCWP's very premise, that women should be ordained Roman Catholic priests—let alone bishops—at all. At stake are disagreements around power and privilege, justice and vision. With ordination and, even more so, the consecration of bishops, RCWP has created a clerically empowered type of Roman Catholic woman, which many of the most vocal Catholic feminist scholars have decried.

Decades before the 2002 Danube ordination, feminist-leaning women were more unified. During Vatican II, feminist theologians like Iris Müller and Ida Raming issued strong calls for women in the priesthood. As the name suggests, the Women's Ordination Conference (WOC) held the goal of ordaining women in the 1970s. Women's Ordination Worldwide (WOW) created a global community aiming to ordain women starting in 1996.

Yet cracks in Catholic feminist collegiality became glaringly apparent at the November 1995 WOC meeting in Arlington, Virginia—the first such meeting since 1985 and one that commemorated WOC's twentieth anniversary.[33] There, Elisabeth Schüssler Fiorenza famously declared that "ordination is subordination." Instead of aspiring to ordain women, Schüssler Fiorenza's proposed an idea that echoed the title of her 1993 book, *Discipleship of Equals*:

> What is the dream that still needs to be realized? Is it that women in the Roman Catholic Church finally will be able to call themselves "Reverend," to wear the clerical collar, to don clerical vestments or to receive clerical privileges, to receive the indelible mark of essential difference, the promotion to upper-class status, not only in the church but also in heaven? Is it a dream to get a piece of the clerical pie even if we choke on it . . . or is it a dream to create a different ministry and church, a dream to transform kyriarchical church and society into the discipleship of equals?[34]

Catholic feminism and Catholic priesthood cannot coexist, Schüssler Fiorenza argued: the former's commitment to equality and justice would disappear in the latter's kyriarchical structures. By "kyriarchical," Schüssler Fiorenza referred to intersecting systems that suppress and dominate. Criticisms of kyriarchy indict structures that enable sexism, racism, heterosexism, classism, and any institutionally enabled oppression. In Schüssler Fiorenza's view, feminist reformers must create something entirely different than the institutional church.

Not everyone at the 1995 conference agreed with Schüssler Fiorenza. Some conference attendees expressed disappointment that the actual ordination of women no longer seemed to top WOC's agenda. Progressive Loretto sister and WOC officer Maureen Fiedler said, "I love the ideal of a discipleship of equals, but if it means we don't seek ordination in the Roman Catholic Church, I don't buy one syllable of it."[35] Other attendees felt frustrated that those who advocated positions like Schüssler Fiorenza's did not offer steps WOC could take to make the discipleship of equals a reality. One of the most strident critics of the "ordination is subordination" claim was Ida Raming, who wrote a preconference letter to WOC organizers in which she underscored the need for women's ordination. Raming argued that it was "treachery" to shift focus away from the ordination of women. Doing so, she said, handed the Vatican a victory and betrayed women who felt called to ordained service within the Roman Catholic Church.[36]

Ten years later, the 2005 WOW conference saw Catholic feminist scholars arguing about the church's future. Keynote speakers and Catholic theological foremothers Schüssler Fiorenza, Mary Hunt, and Rosemary Radford Ruether championed feminist ministries and the dismantling of kyriarchical structures. Once again, their visions did not include womenpriests. Showing they remained committed to the antiordination positions advanced at WOC in 1995, they took subtle and not-so-subtle jabs at RCWP. They criticized RCWP's methods and warned the group against falling into "traditional" quicksand.

Ordination was sexy, appealing, and an easy magnet for drawing in activists, they admitted. But, Hunt argued, asking for ordination was "still a defensive—not offensive—move...a reaction—not a construction."[37] Radford Ruether argued that clericalism is "incompatible" with a "liberative understanding of church and ministry."[38] Schüssler Fiorenza warned that the "Women's Ordination Movement"—which surely included Roman Catholic Womenpriests, though they weren't mentioned by name—must not fixate on "wo/men's exclusion from the 'sacred power of domination,'" because doing so could construct "an anti-hierarchy of wo/men which is still a hierarchy." She proposed another option: all Catholics could claim priesthood. The goal must be "a radical democratic church" and not simple acceptance into hierarchy and domination.[39] At the heart of this proposal was the idea that Catholic feminists should have more to offer Roman Catholicism than women's stepping into centuries-old clerical structures like priesthood.

With these competing visions, WOC was caught between the proverbial rock and hard place when RCWP emerged on the scene. Some WOC members applauded what they saw as radical feminist action that decried the goal of women's ordination; other members celebrated RCWP's *contra legem* ordinations; still others were unsatisfied. Women who had long wanted ordination only with Rome's blessing were shaken by these RCWP-proclaimed "valid but illicit" ordinations, which resulted in formal excommunications. Other WOC members bristled at womenpriests who looked and acted too much like the Catholic patriarchy. After all, the majority of women's ordination activists wanted much more than "adding women and stirring": they wanted a complete reimagining of sacramental ministry and lay involvement.[40]

Laura Singer, who was president of WOC's board when she and I spoke in 2010, confirmed these internal debates. In July 2002, WOC issued a formal statement supporting the Danube ordination, calling the action "another important step in the struggle for women's equality in the church."[41] WOC's choice of words is significant here: the group did not see the ordinations as the definitive step. What would be WOC's role be now that RCWP existed? Singer described a "pendulum shift" from the early years, when WOC's majority wanted to wait for Rome to welcome womenpriests with open arms, to the later years, when WOC's members resisted RCWP's actions because they too closely imitated the institutional church.[42]

The current tenor is more conciliatory than contentious, which shows how quickly the discourse has evolved since RCWP's formation. Rosemary Radford Ruether softened on RCWP somewhat in a 2011 article, acknowledging the benefits of different approaches to church reform. Still, she remained concerned about possible power issues in RCWP: "I am inclined to think that Roman Catholic Womenpriests needs to keep a critical albeit caring eye on the Roman Catholic Womenpriests movement and help keep them honest in their intention of being a movement of prophetic obedience to the Spirit that avoids power roles of some over others. Once one starts calling oneself a priest or a bishop, the temptation to drift into thinking of oneself as holier than others and empowered to dominate them is seductive."[43]

In 2015, speaking at the Women's Ordination Worldwide conference in Philadelphia, Mary Hunt applauded the global Catholic women's movement, saying, "We have avoided being co-opted." Striking a different tone about RCWP's ordained than she had a decade earlier in Ottawa, Hunt said, "For some people, seeing women ministers, indeed women priests, in action, especially but not only in sacramental ministry, is a catalyst for moving beyond kyriarchy."[44] In other words, the *contra legem* ordinations of women need not automatically lead—and in fact has not led—to a reinscription of patriarchy/kyriarchy. Feminist theologians are not giving RCWP a pass: the movement still is pushed to consider the ramifications of its actions and its public ministries. But if there's a villain in the women's ordination world today, it is a reluctant, kyriarchical Rome—not fellow advocates of greater women's leadership in contemporary Catholicism.[45]

Maximizing Media Attention: Ordinations as Staged Protests

Nothing brings RCWP media attention quite like an ordination ceremony. A quick sampling of local, national, and international headlines shows the news media's excitement over the women's illegal actions: "Catholic Women Priests Ordain Six in Emotional Ceremony Despite Church's Stance," "For Women Priests, a Moment of Justice—And Excommunication," "Female Priests Defy Catholic Church at the Altar," "Kentucky Woman Goes against Roman Catholic Law; Ordained as Priest," "Catholic Church Advises Parishioners in Kalamazoo to Avoid Ordination of Female Priest," "Woman Priest Defies Catholic Diocese."[46]

Ever since the media seized upon the 2002 Danube ordination, RCWP has benefited from media attention. Sociologist Doug McAdam has argued that scholars should attend to both the strategic use of media to accompany social movement tactics (he calls this "strategic dramaturgy") and the media-related processes though which many social movements succeed. As part of the framing process in social movements' early stages, groups consciously and strategically "fashion meaningful accounts of themselves and the issues at hand in order to motivate and legitimate their efforts."[47] RCWP has used ordination ceremonies to articulate its theological positions, announce its existence, and garner support, both ideological and financial.

Media attention and RCWP ordinations go hand in hand. In 2007, then public relations director (and now ARCWP bishop) Bridget Mary Meehan explained, "Media is very important in spreading the word to a larger community. If people see womenpriests in action, then they realize that there is hope for change in the church since womenpriests are now a reality. We get inquiries from people all over the country as to when and where they can find a womanpriest-led liturgy. Some are more than ready now."[48] While ordinations can happen privately and even secretly (in what are known as "catacomb ordinations"), media publicity allows RCWP to reach audiences who would otherwise know nothing about the *contra legem* ordination of women. Some individuals will never support RCWP's actions, of course, and media attention just enrages them; others, however, respond to womenpriests with curiosity or approval, and RCWP benefits most when media stories reach this audience. Ordinations are RCWP's best chance for capturing media attention; once the womenpriests settle into their ministries, media eyes turn elsewhere.

The relationship between the media and movements is crucial. By ensuring that information flows easily to reporters, movements can develop a positive working relationship with the media; in turn, the media can shape a movement's message and introduce its activists as "real people." Movements can stage newsworthy disruptions that capture media attention—and even better if organizers can guarantee the media a "show" worth watching.[49] Consider as an example the November 11, 2007, priesthood ordinations of Rose Marie Hudson and Elsie Hainz McGrath in St. Louis, Missouri. Hudson, then sixty-seven years old, had long been active in parish life and prison ministries. McGrath, then sixty-nine, had worked for the St. Louis archdiocese and St. Louis University's theology department. Both had been ordained deacons in a small, private ceremony in August that same year. A confluence of forces—ranging from RCWP's media strategies to the ceremony's location (a Reform Jewish synagogue) to the reaction (prolonged, emphatically critical, and condemnatory) of strongly conservative archbishop Raymond Burke—ensured a frenzied level of controversy that kept RCWP in the spotlight for weeks.

A full month before the ordination, Meehan issued a press release, tempting the media with a juicy story: two local women would be ordained Roman Catholic priests in a "historic ceremony" held, not at a Catholic church, but at the Central Reform Congregation (CRC), a Reform Jewish community well known throughout St. Louis for its social justice activism and prominent female rabbi, Susan Talve. When the women had approached Talve about using the CRC for the ordination, she had agreed immediately.[50] Talve had taken the unusual request to the CRC board, and they'd unanimously approved. Because of the CRC's involvement, the ordination dramatically became an interfaith affair. The press release quoted Talve as saying, "Our building was built to be a Sukkat Shalom—a shelter of peace—for those who need it."[51]

Over a third of the press release outlined opportunities for the media to view the ceremony and speak with the ordinands. RCWP invited reporters and photographers to a briefing with representative from both RCWP and WOC. RCWP welcomed cameras at the ceremony, setting aside a section of the sanctuary for journalists' use and making a back-door exit available to any reporter unable to stay for the entire service. Working cooperatively with the media, RCWP asked journalists to secure permission before publishing any photo in which an ordination-goer's face was visible, since participants and attendees had been threatened with excommunication. RCWP partnered with the media (by giving them journalistic opportunities and special ceremony seating), retained the sacred nature of ordination ceremonies (by keeping media movement to a minimum), and brought invested individuals to the ordination ceremonies while protecting them from potential fallout.

Meehan's press release allowed RCWP to set the initial tone for how Hudson and McGrath would be described and ultimately judged. Strategically casting the ordinands as sympathetic and relatable, Meehan emphasized that neither RCWP nor Hudson and McGrath wanted to separate from the church; instead, they wished to create "a renewed model of priesthood for a renewed church." The press release read, in part: "Rose Marie and Elsie have both earned graduate degrees in theology and ministry, and have been engaged in active ministry for many years. Rose Marie is a retired school teacher, a wife, mother, and grandmother. Elsie is a retired editor, a widow, mother, grandmother, and great-grandmother. Prophetic obedience, a hallmark of the RCWP movement, led them to make this life-altering commitment and 'walk the talk' of clerical reform in the Roman Catholic Church. As priests, they will continue to exercise a variety of volunteer ministries."[52] The press release humanized the women by using their first names and avoiding "deacon" as an honorary title. Sharing the women's ministerial and educational backgrounds communicated that the women were prepared for priesthood. In contrast with the St. Louis archdiocese's characterization of the women as schismatics, the press release depicted the women as obedient to a higher power.

In the weeks surrounding the ordination, local media repeated the ordinands' favorable characteristics. Most articles gave the women's ages, described their roles as mothers, grandmothers, and spouses, and remarked upon their years of service to the St. Louis archdiocese.[53] Thanks to this framing, Hudson and McGrath were not simply faceless figures disobeying the Roman Catholic hierarchy; rather, they were individuals with families, service backgrounds, and a commitment to Catholicism. They were longtime St. Louisans seeking to serve local residents. They were women people might know or encounter on any given day in St. Louis.

What elevated this ordination from back-page blurb to front-page news story, however, was the swift and unequivocal reaction of the St. Louis archbishop, Raymond Burke. In the archdiocesan newspaper days before the ordination, Burke wrote that the proposed event "imperils the eternal salvation of the women seeking the attempted ordination and the woman, claiming to be a Roman Catholic bishop, who proposes to attempt the ordination." Furthermore, "it generates confusion among the faithful and others who are not Catholic regarding an infallible teaching of the Catholic faith." He threatened excommunication if the women continued with their plan. He also criticized Rabbi Talve and denounced the CRC's role in hosting, saying it "constitutes a grave violation of the mutual respect which should mark the relationship between the Jewish faith and the Roman Catholic faith."[54] All of this contention played out in the local news media, which became the locus of debates about women's ordination and Jewish-Catholic interfaith cooperation. In many ways, the ordination was no longer about two retired women answering a vocational call: it was now a politicized event where, in the media's telling, powerful Catholic patriarchs were fighting to stop a small reform movement of retired women.

Burke played the ideal antagonist in this scenario. As a well-known public figure, Burke's reputation had long been marred by controversy. Since becoming archbishop in 2004, he had made many contentious decisions. Many observers saw Burke as more concerned with canon law than with pastoral care. The RCWP ordination was not the first time Burke appeared angry, unrelenting, and out of touch in local media—which only helped Hudson and McGrath.[55]

As Burke proclaimed the Catholic position to be eternally right and RCWP to be dangerously wrong, the media reimplemented his black-and-white casting—and flipped the roles. By and large, the media portrayed RCWP favorably and the archbishop unfavorably. The media helped create characters—if not caricatures—out of the main players: On one side were four women (Hudson, McGrath, Bishop Fresen, and Rabbi Talve) trying to do God's work. On the other side was an angry man trying to stop it.

As the ordination day neared, Burke's rhetoric intensified. He wrote in the *St. Louis Review*, "What is most painful about the proposed attempted ordinations is the calculated and grave offense they will offer to our Lord Jesus Christ and His Church. . . . There is no doubt that our Lord Jesus Christ chosen only men for the Holy Priesthood, even as He, at the Last Supper, consecrated only men for the priestly office and ministry." Father Vincent A. Heier, the archdiocese's director of ecumenical and interreligious affairs, went after the CRC, intimating that the Jewish community's decision could irrevocably harm Jewish-Catholic relations in St. Louis. Heier contacted St. Louis's Jewish Community Relations Council, hoping they would stop Talve's synagogue from hosting. The council instead took a neutral position and defended CRC's autonomy in such matters.[56]

McGrath and Hudson admitted to me that they had been worried at first about how the media would slant their story. Two years later, though, during a lunch interview, they agreed that the coverage had been "wonderful" and "very, very supportive." They marveled at the media's dogged interest in their ordination ceremony. McGrath recalled a local television station calling her at four thirty in the afternoon, hoping to get an interview for the six o'clock news. When she told them she had plans, the news cameras showed up at the restaurant where she was meeting friends.[57] Hudson recounted, "The week or two before our ordination, Elsie and I ran our legs off. We were called by every radio station and television station."[58] Both women said they were interviewed at least three times in McGrath's home. St. Louis's media storm went national, and the *National Catholic Reporter* published several related stories.[59]

The women had known Burke would react forcefully to their ordination, but they hadn't anticipated his condemnation of Talve and the CRC. McGrath expressed surprise at Burke's belief that he could "go outside of his Catholic realm and tell everybody else what they can and cannot do. It was as if he were excommunicating Susan Talve and the whole CRC congregation because they refused to back away." McGrath and Hudson acknowledged that the heightened controversy helped bring attention to RCWP. "We had a tremendous controversy,"

Hudson told me, laughing at the memory. McGrath chimed in that their ordination was distinctive "because of our archbishop, obviously, who was the greatest PR person anyone could've gotten a hold of." Then she added, with a smile and a glint in her eyes, "And it didn't cost us anything."[60]

Despite archdiocesan attempts to halt the ceremony, the ordination took place as scheduled. An interfaith, standing-room-only crowd of nearly six hundred people watched Fresen ordain Hudson and McGrath to priesthood. In the following weeks, video footage from the ceremony became an additional part of RCWP's media strategy. Meehan turned the two-hour ritual into a ten-minute video and placed it on Google Videos. Subtitles named the different parts of the ritual; the song selection (which included the familiar Catholic songs "The Summons" and "All Are Welcome") highlighted themes of inclusivity and welcome; Rabbi Talve's introductory words and yarmulke-wearing supporters reflected RCWP's interfaith aspirations. Meehan told me, "[People] who are not quite sure [about the idea of womenpriests] can get used to the symbol shift by seeing women in videos online. . . . I have worked hard to get our videos up on Google and YouTube."[61] Videos helped continue the conversation about women's ordination well beyond the event itself.

Honoring his promise, Burke formally excommunicated Fresen, Hudson, and McGrath on March 12, 2008. He published the excommunication decree in the archdiocesan newspaper and declared that the women had committed "the most grave delict of schism [and had] lost membership in, good standing in, and full communion with the Roman Catholic Church."[62] This was RCWP's first excommunication since the Danube Seven. Although more than two dozen women had been already ordained in the US and Canada and others had been threatened with excommunication, Burke was the first to follow through. This would also be RCWP's last *ferendae sententiae* ("imposed by a church authority") excommunication, because starting in late May 2008, all ordained women would be excommunicated *latae sententiae* ("automatically"), without the need for a formal declaration.

RCWP's relationship with the media suggests, as Doug McAdam wrote of social movements' early phases, that "actions *do* speak louder than words."[63] Decades of feminist theological discourse petitioning the Vatican to discuss women's ordination yielded few concrete results. In contrast, RCWP's ordination ceremonies moved the debate into the court of public opinion. Reactions like Burke's helped. He inadvertently empowered RCWP by engaging them. In subsequent years, patriarchal leaders still dutifully warned local Catholics of possible excommunication for participating in RCWP ordinations and sacraments, but overall they seemed to have learned that the louder they yelled, the more attention RCWP received. The St. Louis archdiocese, for its part, took a different approach to RCWP ordinations just two years later: in 2009, St. Louisan Marybeth McBryan was ordained to priesthood. McBryan's ordination drew fewer than one hundred attendees, and there was no media storm. By this time, Burke had departed St. Louis for a position in Rome, and his successor, Robert Carlson, ignored the ordination. In addition, perhaps local media found a second RCWP ordination far less enticing a spectacle than St. Louis's historic first. California-based womanpriest Victoria Rue reflected, "The Vatican saw that if they made us a cause célèbre, people would gather around us. If they didn't give us publicity, then people wouldn't know that womenpriests exist."[64] Rome's May 2008 *latae sententiae* decree also changed the rules of engagement: now, local dioceses do not need to involve themselves with disciplining womenpriests because such discipline is automatic and needs no explanation.

Media attention brings RCWP curious observers and one-time donations but does not guarantee future congregants or success in reforming the church. Roman prelates will not revisit the male-only priesthood because local newspapers or Protestant and Jewish supporters advocate for women's ordination. If sociologist Mark Chaves is correct, no degree of liberal or secular bias will help the women; in *Ordaining Women*, he wrote that sacramental traditions like Roman Catholicism hold fast to an all-male priesthood in part because it allows the church "to carve out and sustain religious worlds that are not liberal. [Roman Catholicism's] strong resistance to women's ordination is part of their broader anti-liberal identity."[65] If Chaves is right, Rome will not capitulate to outside pressure, and the more pressure secular forces exert on Rome, the more entrenched Rome will become in its traditional position.

RCWP longs to succeed in the "court of public opinion," yet approval in the minds of some Catholic and non-Catholic observers has, to date, done little to reform the church. The reverse may even be true. But RCWP does not argue that a media storm will change the church; if anything, the media attention is one step in a long journey. What the media can do is broadcast the present-day existence of womenpriests and allow RCWP some control over discourse from which women are typically absent.

Reclaiming and Reframing Ordained
Traditions in Roman Catholic History

RCWP ordinations appeal to a largely unknown history of women's ordained ministry. Ordinations give womenpriests the opportunity to embody what they see as a correction to two thousand years of Catholic history and give audiences a new way of appreciating Catholic women in antiquity.

RCWP's practice of using illicit ordinations to reclaim a lost Christian tradition is a strategic theological choice. Scholarly debate about women's ordination in the early church tends to fall into three camps. Some, like RCWP, argue that women were ordained in the past and so should be ordained in the present. Some, like Rome, argue that women were not ordained in the past and thus should never and can never be ordained, now or in the future. A third group argues that women were not ordained in the past because the early church was misogynist, but that that should not preclude women's ordination today or tomorrow. These debates primarily dispute what it meant to be "ordained" throughout Christian history and which, if any, clerical offices women held. This is the real issue. The first few centuries of Christianity were not models for twenty-first-century notions of gender equality, and yet early Christian women did things that, to modern eyes, appear to be sacramental and priestly. What those gestures and actions meant has long been a source of contention, primarily between Rome and women's ordination advocates.

RCWP's ordination ceremonies attempt to take control of this historical narrative. For example, organizers of the May 1, 2010, RCWP ordination in Rochester, New York, framed the ceremony with the history of women's ordination. Before the entrance processional, participants adorned the altar with four large banners. Each banner was a different color: royal blue, olive green, dark blue, and dark red. Each bore an illustrated picture of a female leader in the early church; these were identified as "Mary Magdalene, Apostle," "Junia, Leader," "Theodora, Bishop," and "Phoebe, Deacon." Each banner proclaimed, above the pictures, the words "Nothing New!" in all capital letters. Beneath the pictures, each banner read, again in caps, "Women Re-Claiming Priesthood." The banners remained on the altar throughout the nearly three-hour-long ceremony, suggesting that these ancient Christian women participated in the day's events as approving foremothers.[66]

Before the ordination began, womenpriests Jean Marchant and Eileen Di-Franco stepped to the podium and explained that RCWP's lineage was "nothing new" and could be traced back to early Christianity. Marchant said, "Historical and archaeological evidence reveals that women served as deacons, priests, and bishops from the second to the sixth centuries. . . . In the outer room at Pentecost, God called the followers of Jesus, men and women whose hearts were open and who were ready for the coming of God's spirit as promised by Jesus for all humankind, for all time. All those served as leaders in the first years of building the Christian community." Focusing on history, archaeology, and theology, Marchant invoked the language of call, saying that men *and* women were summoned to fill Christ's promise and lead the nascent Christian community.

DiFranco then connected RCWP's actions with Jesus's mission: "Today, in the ordination of deacons and priests, we continue in the renewal of our very first Christian traditions, and we celebrate the fact that Jesus invited women as well as men to become leaders in building the kin-dom that we desire. . . . And just as Jesus promised, he is still with us, and will continue to send spirit, Wisdom Sophia, to dwell in us, and lead us forward, in being church, in a way that is faithful to the original intent of our brother Jesus." Notably, DiFranco evoked early Christian traditions, used the term *kindom* (as opposed to the masculine *kingdom*), and referred to the Holy Spirit as the feminine Wisdom Sophia. She thus located RCWP within a feminine-inspired, early Christian narrative.

Christian feminists have not always known what to do with Jesus, a male savior. For instance, Rosemary Radford Ruether provocatively asked, "Can a Male Savior Save Women?" in a chapter from her 1983 book *Sexism and God Talk*. She concluded that a male savior could save women—but only if we acknowledge that "the maleness of Jesus has no ultimate significance." For Ruether, Jesus is and must be viewed as a "liberator" who "calls for a renunciation" of systems of patriarchal dominance.[67] In a more extreme position, British theologian Daphne Hampson argued that "there can be no Christology which is compatible with feminism" because any soteriological Christian message comes back to Jesus, who was male.[68] Ambivalence about Jesus's role is not just an academic debate: reporting at the 1995 WOC national meeting, *National Catholic Reporter*'s Pamela Schaeffer noted that "explicit mention of Jesus or of Christ was rare in liturgies."[69]

Using Jesus to argue for women's ordination, then, is a deliberate rhetorical move for RCWP, not least of all because Rome's arguments against women's ordination begin with Jesus—specifically his maleness and his selection of twelve male apostles. RCWP gives Jesus a central position in its ordination rhetoric as a way of promoting its own conclusions about Jesus's acceptance of women's ordination. RCWP draws on theology and activism that supports the idea of Christ

Chava Redonnet (left) and Theresa Novak Chabot (right) celebrate their ordinations to the priesthood with RCWP bishop Andrea Johnson (center) at Spiritus Christi in Rochester, New York, on May 1, 2010. (Photograph by Judith Levitt.)

as liberator of the oppressed.[70] RCWP believes that womenpriests embody the church that Jesus himself envisioned, no matter what Rome says.

In contrast to Rome, which argues that Jesus willed only men to become priests, RCWP draws on scholarship that argues that Jesus never ordained anyone, that he was not ordained himself, and that ordination is a post-resurrection, man-made construct. While Rome claims that women have never been ordained at any time in Christian history, RCWP contends that women enjoyed ordination (albeit a later Christian construct) for approximately one thousand years, until a dramatic change took place. A 2008 book by historian Gary Macy, *The Hidden History of Women's Ordination*, tackled this change. *Hidden History* examined when, why, and how women came to be seen as incapable of ordination. Macy also investigated whether the definition of *ordination* changed over time so that it only later came to exclude women.[71] Macy's approach was strictly historical, and he carefully avoided wading into theological waters.[72] His extensive research (showcasing nearly 120 pages of appendices, endnotes, and bibliographic material) led him to conclude that women *were* ordained through the early Middle Ages. He wrote, "According to the understanding of ordination held by themselves and their contemporaries, they were just as truly ordained as any bishop, priest, or deacon."[73] He continued, with words that critique anyone who suggests that women have never held ordained authority, "To argue that these ordinations were not 'true' ordinations since they were not ordination to service at the altar, or because they did not always involve the laying on of hands or lead inexorably to the ministry of priesthood, would be at best a theological judgment based on the standing these women would now have in some Christian communities (if they were alive), and is anachronistic."[74]

RCWP used Macy's scholarship to bolster its claims to ordination.[75] The movement's website has promoted Macy's title along with other studies looking anew at the history of women's ordination.[76] ARCWP bishop Bridget Mary Meehan wrote an essay titled "There Have Always Been Women Priests," which argued that the movement's women were "reclaiming the ancient heritage of ordained ministry in the Catholic Church." Using scholarship like Macy's, Meehan wrote, "Although the Roman Catholic leadership has been all-male for the past 900 years, Christianity's first millennium saw numerous women serving with distinction as deacons, priests and bishops."[77]

Meehan cited the work of Dr. Dorothy Irvin, a biblical archaeologist who interpreted the titles of engravings, women's clothing, and women's gestures and actions in catacomb frescoes and sarcophagi, in Rome, Egypt, and the Middle East. Irvin has concluded that women were ordained in the first millennium of Christianity in many parts of the ancient world. Her archaeological photographs and artwork have been featured at receptions following RCWP and ARCWP ordinations. At a 2009 ordination in Minneapolis, for example, Irvin set up a table where she displayed and sold images of ancient frescoes and mosaics depicting women acting in religiously authoritative ways. I purchased a collection of note cards reproducing authentic ancient images and artifacts, such as a painting of women celebrating the Eucharist (from the Catacomb of Priscilla in Rome, dated 100–125 CE), a mosaic covering Julia Runa's tomb (from the Cathedral of Annaba in Algeria) that identified her as a *presbyterissa* ("priest"), and the tombstone of a woman said to be *Bishop* Aleksandra (from Rome). Irvin does not label Catholic women's desire for ordination as "reclaiming": she has said that women who want ordination have a "genetic memory of women's equality" and know, on some level, that women are and have always been capable of ordination. For Irvin, it is important for today's women to feel connected to ancient women like Phoebe, because RCWP is reenacting the early church—not going against the church.[78]

Rome dismisses these historical and archaeological findings in two ways: One, when Roman leaders concede that some women were ordained, they argue this happened only in heretical groups that had separated from the one true church. Two, when confronted with examples of ancient women with titles like *deaconess* or *presbytera*, leaders say these women were not themselves ordained but rather were the wives or widows of ordained men (as celibacy was not mandatory until the Second Lateran Council in 1139). Take, for example, Theodora, a revered holy woman whose ninth-century mosaic image, found in the Basilica of Saint Praxedes in Rome, once made up the banner on RCWP's website. The mosaic labels Theodora *episcopa*, interpreted as a feminized version of *episkopos*— "bishop." Irvin, feminist archaeologists, and RCWP herald Theodora as one example of a medieval female bishop. The church, however, argues that Theodora received this honorific not because she was ordained a bishop but because she was the mother of Pope Paschal I. Irvin has pushed back against the Vatican's conclusions, pointing out, for example, that many of these women were buried with parents and not with husbands, suggesting they were unmarried.[79] This debate has no easy resolution.

My ethnographic work at RCWP ordinations shows how RCWP uses ordination to enact the history the movement deems correct—that is, that women were validly ordained in the first millennium. With this historical framework as a starting point, RCWP's actions look like reclamation of a lost heritage of Christian women's authority, not the schismatic act that Rome disavows. By positioning themselves in a lineage of ancient ordained women, RCWP tries to shift the discourse surrounding their actions. Thanks to work like Macy's and Irvin's, RCWP can go on the offensive with its arguments for ordination: they rhetorically place the burden of proof on Catholic leaders who argue that the Roman church has never and will never confer ordination on a woman. Ordination's fraught history intersects with education and interpretation, and both RCWP and Rome want their version of events to win out. One cannot neatly argue from historical tradition when there is no agreement on what that tradition is.[80]

Conclusion: Tensions around Ordained Authority

There remains a historical tension in RCWP's ordinations that we must explore: RCWP's approach to ordination conflicts with its stated desire to stand with the early Christianity's female leaders. The terms of this conflict are neatly captured

in a welcome paragraph taken from the worship aid of the August 2009 ordination of four women in Minneapolis:

> Since the ordinations of the Danube Seven in 2002, we stand with our fore-
> mothers and forefathers validly ordained in Apostolic Succession through
> anointing and laying on of hands. . . . We stand, too, as women and men of
> the long view. Historical and archaeological evidence reveals that women
> served as deacons, priests and bishops from the 2nd to the 6th centuries
> AD: Deacons Phoebe, Sophia and Maria; Priests Leta and Vitalia; and
> Bishops Theodora and Alexandra. Before that, in the Upper Room on
> Pentecost, God surprised the followers of Jesus, women and men whose
> hearts were open and who were ready for the coming of God's Spirit prom-
> ised by Jesus for all humankind, for all time.[81]

The movement celebrates female leaders in Christianity's first millennium—
women like the historical actors featured on ordination banners, and women
ordained in the early Middle Ages, as Macy described. Yet RCWP's ordinations
retain the sacramental gestures, rituals, and performances of priesthood that
emerged in Christianity's second millennium, after women were defined out of
ordination. Womenpriests are not becoming deacons, priests, or bishops in the
way ancient women (and men) did but rather in a later Middle Ages, post-Refor-
mation, and contemporary fashion that makes sacramental power and hierarchical position ordination's defining characteristics. Although historians like Gary
Macy have denied the idea that Catholic ordination has been the same throughout Christendom, and although RCWP champions Macy's work, RCWP steps
into a present-day understanding of ordination while claiming connections to
ordained early Christian women. In doing so, RCWP raises questions about
which past they embody today and envision for the future.

I offer two readings of this tension. First, as a resistance movement focused
almost exclusively on women's ordination, RCWP makes every possible argument to justify women's right to valid ordination—even when those arguments
conflict with the history they use to support their claims. Rather than creating
an all-new Roman Catholicism, RCWP covers its bases by holding ordinations
that look, sound, and feel like "legal," present-day ordinations—ordinations that
mirror those that men go through. For good measure, RCWP adds the argument that their right to ordination comes from Jesus and the early Christians.
RCWP's priesthood ordinations thus become a hodgepodge of two thousand
years of ordination practices. For RCWP, it is important to perform a persuasive
ordination.

A second, alternative interpretation places the womenpriests in a broader Roman Catholic context. RCWP's path to ordained priesthood may seem historically and rhetorically convoluted, but, following Macy, no less so are the Roman church's requirements for male priests. What, after all, *is* this ordination tradition? I have already outlined academic debates about the history of Catholic ordination. Disagreements further exist among Christian groups: while the Vatican holds firm to a sacramental priesthood located in Jesus's New Testament actions, Protestant denominations use the same New Testament but understand ordination very differently. Moreover, Catholic tradition holds different histories around apostolic succession—specifically, what it means and who lays hands on an ordinand.[82] If RCWP seems to pick and choose arguments, statements, and scriptures that suit their goals, they proceed no differently than the Roman Catholic Church, which RCWP claims to remain part of. Just as Rome derives its understanding of tradition from its particular theological interpretation of select histories and scriptures, so too do the womenpriests.

Using language of reform and reclamation, RCWP is forging its path to priesthood. Womenpriests have sought to retain Catholic traditional visuals: the bodies moving in procession, the rhythm of ritual and recitation of prayer, the vestments and stoles, and the historical significance of authentication coming from the laying on of hands. This claim to apostolic succession chafes feminist scholars and historians—who see it as ahistorical at best, kyriarchical at worst—and yet allows RCWP to trace their priesthoods back nearly two thousand years to an early church where women were allowed remarkable degrees of leadership for the time period.

Because of ordination, now women have the power and authority to act sacramentally. But *power* and *authority* are words around which RCWP treads carefully. Nevertheless, womenpriests' actions reveal that they believe they cannot begin to re-create the church in a reformed idiom without that power—that is, without the sacramental, Spirit-infused, sacred presence that comes upon a candidate at ordination. Ordination is about that moment, and RCWP must assert that transformational power—especially during ordinations, the public ceremony where others are watching and during which the women, by their actions, "excommunicate themselves" from their church.

To be a true reform movement, however, and to show they heed their radical feminist colleagues' concerns, RCWP cannot keep that power for itself. The inward change that happens to the women at ordination through sacred mystery cannot remain with the women alone. If it did, this would erect a high wall between clergy and laity, echoing the existing Roman church and failing to create reform. So once the womenpriests obtain grace through the laying on of hands, and once they are ministering to others and serving their worship communities, they share their newfound sacramental power and authority with others. After obtaining power during ordination, the women attempt to gift that power to the laity in the form of sacraments.

CHAPTER 5

Sacraments

C HAVA REDONNET WAS CONFLICTED—BUT comfortably so. This single working mother of three grown children had been a womanpriest for just over seven months when I asked her during a phone interview, "Why be ordained?" After all, she was already doing pastoral ministry as a chaplain before her *contra legem* ordination. Chava responded immediately, echoing many womenpriests when she said, "The sacraments," specifically the Eucharist. As a priest, she could now celebrate Communion every week for Oscar Romero, the worship community she'd started at a nearby Catholic Worker house, St. Joseph's House of Hospitality, and out of which she had been called to priesthood. She could also now consecrate the Eucharist at the nursing home where she worked. Redonnet described her theology of the Eucharist as being "as holy as it can get," with God "totally, truly present" in the Eucharist and in the people gathered. Being an intimate part of that sacrament made ordination make sense.[1]

Then she paused and reflected. "I'm inconsistent," she admitted. She explained that what she thought happens at Communion is not a change in bread and wine—because "the holiness is already there"—but rather "a change in *us*" that allows the assembled community to focus their holiness. "We just take the veil away," she said. She knew that this meant she was not fully on board with the Roman Catholic teaching on transubstantiation, the idea that the substance of bread and wine is transformed into the body and blood of Jesus at consecration. But for Redonnet, sacraments were no less holy because their meaning and mechanism shifted toward the people. Like all of RCWP's ordained women, Redonnet reframed the relationship between sacraments, Catholic priesthood, and Catholic worshippers.

To be a Roman Catholic priest is to be a conduit for the sacraments. As Catholics understand it, the priest performs the "visible rites" that make "present the graces proper to each sacrament."[2] The *Catechism of the Catholic Church* defines *sacraments* as "efficacious signs of grace, instituted by Christ and entrusted to the Church, by which divine life is dispensed to us."[3] The sacraments are "necessary for salvation," for only through the sacraments can the Holy Spirit bestow the "sacramental grace" that provides healing, transformation, and unity with Jesus Christ.[4] In Roman Catholic theology, the sacraments have the power to *do* things spiritually, religiously, and soteriologically, as well as communally, individually, and ecclesiastically. Roman Catholics understand the sacraments to confer grace from the Holy Spirit to the believer; to allow recipients to grow closer to God in faith; to help communities embody and express their faith; and to enable the ecclesiastical communion to strengthen and manifest itself.[5]

Since the early third century, Catholic life has involved seven sacraments, and today the Roman church and RCWP celebrate seven sacraments. Baptism, confirmation, and the Eucharist are the sacraments of Christian initiation; penance (or reconciliation) and anointing of the sick are the sacraments of healing; holy orders (ordination) and matrimony are sacraments of service. The Catholic sacramental tradition marks the Catholic sacred experience as distinct from other Christian traditions. On this Rome and RCWP would emphatically agree.

But womenpriests step away from Roman Catholic teaching in their attempts to remodel and reframe the Catholic sacramental economy. The *Catechism* defines *sacramental economy* as the way Christ acts through the sacraments in the present age, bestowing upon Catholics those blessings that arose as a result of his passion, death, and resurrection.[6] RCWP's sacraments aim to do that and more. As I argue in this chapter, RCWP's sacramental economy offers three ways of reimagining sacraments:

1. RCWP's sacraments place the nexus of sacramental authority in the community gathered, not strictly in the hands of the ordained womenpriests.
2. RCWP aims to create a radical inclusivity whereby all people present—Catholics, non-Catholics, and Catholics in poor standing with the Roman church—can receive the sacraments and facilitate sacramental grace.
3. By inserting womenpriests into a Roman Catholic liturgical and sacramental framework, and by making women visible *as* priests, RCWP modifies traditional ideas about who can and does image Christ.

In RCWP's sacramental theology, anyone who reaches out for sacraments and salvation can receive it—regardless of their standing in the institutional church. RCWP retains yet relocates the performance of sacraments, the theological heft of sacraments, and the grace of sacraments. In RCWP's hands, the Vatican is no longer the soteriological arbiter: rather, the people and the sacraments themselves, working in tandem, provide salvation.

Sacraments, Priesthood, and RCWP's Theological Tension

What most stood out to me when I attended the RCWP Rochester ordination in May 2010 was the way so many different people—female and male, clergy and laity, Catholic and non-Catholic—participated in the act of ordaining. Let me again take Chava Redonnet as an example. As she knelt in front of the altar at Spiritus Christi, RCWP womanbishop Andrea Johnson laid her hands on Redonnet's head, in standard Roman Catholic practice. But then, in a departure from tradition, unordained individuals that the ordinands had preselected came forward and also solemnly laid hands on the candidates for priesthood. Meanwhile, all of us in the pews extended our hands outward toward the candidates in a sign of prayer and support.

The ordinands' family members played active roles in the Rochester ceremony, and I remembered vividly Chava's investiture, when her vestments changed from those of a deacon to those of a priest. Four young women came up to the altar and helped Redonnet with her stole and chasuble: her three daughters, Clare, Bridget, and Emily, and her oldest daughter's partner, Katie. The sight was a stirring reversal of the typical mother-child relationship. Instead of the mother dressing and tending to the daughter's body, here the children dressed the mother, physically creating her as a priest. Redonnet's status as a single mother heightened the moments of investiture, for she had struggled with poverty as she'd fought to raise her daughters and earn an education. Now, on this May day, these four young women helped Redonnet remove her red deacon's stole. They helped place the chasuble over her head. They helped situate the red priest's stole around her neck. They fretted over her, gently adjusting the garments and lovingly touching her body. When she was fully vested, Redonnet enveloped her daughters and daughter-in-law in giant bear hugs. This family of five women, standing on the altar, investing a newly made womanpriest, signaled lay women's authority and ability in the sacred ordination process. Redonnet now embodied the iconic Catholic priest and was therefore, in Roman Catholic parlance, imaging Christ—and her daughters had helped make that iconic change possible.

The performances surrounding Redonnet's ordination were striking in their reimagining of women's relationships to sacramental power. Roman Catholicism's sacramental economy requires women to be excluded from the priesthood role that facilitates sacramental grace. *Inter Insigniores* argued that women are not suitable "signs" and "symbols" for Christ and sacramental efficacy:

It must not be forgotten that the sacramental signs are not conventional ones. Not only is it true that, in many respects, they are natural signs because they respond to the deep symbolism of actions and things, but they are more than this: they are principally meant to link the person of every period to the supreme Event of the history of salvation, in order to enable that person to understand, through all the Bible's wealth of pedagogy and symbolism, what grace they signify and produce. For example, the sacrament of the Eucharist is not only a fraternal meal, but at the same time the memorial which makes present and actual Christ's sacrifice and his offering by the Church.[7]

The document says that only men are suitable signs for Christ because, as males, they carry a "natural resemblance" to Christ. Faithful Catholics would have difficulty seeing Christ in the priest if this natural resemblance were not retained, "for Christ himself was and remains a man."[8] For Rome today as for *Inter Insigniores* in 1976, Christ's incarnation in a male body is "indeed a question of fact" that "cannot be disassociated from the economy of salvation: it is indeed in harmony with the entirety of God's plan."[9]

For RCWP, in contrast, the centrality of sacraments for salvation is precisely why women must have the equal opportunity to honor calls to priesthood and become these agents of grace. And all the more reason, then, that the RCWP movement believes that everyone should be invited to receive the sacraments. Hence RCWP's most frequent refrain: "All are welcome" to the sacramental table. At Redonnet's ordination and at every RCWP ordination I attended, women, lay people, and non-Catholics participated in sacraments as receivers and facilitators.

I would describe Redonnet's personal sacramental theology as comfortably conflicted: like so many of RCWP's ordained women, she unapologetically holds in theological tension both the traditional importance of sacraments and a transgressive revisioning of sacramental authority. Redonnet's understanding of Catholic sacraments puts greater emphasis on transformation through community than transformation through ordained authority. She pursued ordination to priesthood because she was called—not by the institutional church but by God and by the Catholic Worker community she served. She found the laying on of hands at her ordination to be powerful, not merely because the RCWP bishop bestowed her with the Holy Spirit, but because a church full of supporters blessed her. The Eucharist is holy not because of Chava's new power, stemming from an ontological transformation at ordination, but because of the holy intentionality of the gathered faithful. In Redonnet's hands, the sacraments are about service, community, and family. They are about the community's ability to interpret sacramental meaning, facilitate sacramental grace, and share in sacramental power.

Notably, in stepping away from the institutional church's authority to regulate economies both sacramental and salvific, neither Redonnet nor RCWP eschew the power and mystery of Catholic sacraments. That known but unknown, describable but indescribable *something* remains. That numinous experience of encountering the divine, which theologian Rudolf Otto called *mysterium tremendum*, is every bit a part of RCWP's worship practices. This may be how best to understand Redonnet's "inconsistency," or the comfortable conflict in her understanding of sacramental power and authority, of who has it and who generates it: "inconsistency" is an indication of Redonnet's and RCWP's location within the seemingly impenetrable, ineffable mystery of the Catholic sacramental imagination. For RCWP's womenpriests, Catholic holiness continues to permeate the world in inexplicable but fundamental ways. Now, however, ordained women and laypeople are conduits of that mysterious sacramental grace.

RCWP, Baptism, and the Importance of Sacramental Access

Baptism is the church's first sacrament and one that womenpriests perform regularly. The *Catechism of the Catholic Church* states, "The Lord himself affirms that Baptism is necessary for salvation."[10] The Catholic tradition of baptizing children at a very early age (i.e., infancy) serves to free them from original sin and bring them into communion with Christ and the Roman Catholic Church. The "ordinary ministers of baptism" are deacons, priests, and bishops—though the *Catechism* makes clear that "in case of necessity, anyone, even a non-baptized person, with the required intention, can baptize," so great is the need for baptism.[11] Believing themselves to stand in an apostolic line with ordained legitimacy, the womenpriests proceed with what they understand to be the holy act of celebrating sacraments like baptism. They adopt and adapt the Roman Catholic sacramental framework—with the significant difference of allowing women to act *in persona Christi*. Within sacramental performances, the womenpriests strike poses that male priests strike; they echo Christ's biblical words, as male priests do; they move, dress, and gesture in ways familiar to those who have watched male priests in action.

Rome, of course, says that womenpriests' sacraments are ineffectual and even dangerous. Because Rome does not entertain the notion that the women's illicit ordinations might also be valid, RCWP's sacraments do not count in Vatican minds. In the month leading up to the 2002 Danube Seven ordination, the Congregation for the Doctrine of the Faith (CDF) issued a "warning" on the "attempted" ordination of women, labeling it the "simulation of a sacrament."[12] The CDF dismissed the upcoming Danube ordination as an invalid reenactment, devoid of soteriological merit, and contended that any sacraments performed by women would also be invalid and inefficacious. In addition, local church officials have censured womenpriests individually. Womanpriest Theresa Novak Chabot, for example, received an official letter from her bishop, the bishop of Manchester (New Hampshire), John McCormack, who wrote that, because Chabot had "separated herself from the Church," she was "not permitted to celebrate or receive the sacraments" or participate at Mass. He requested that she not "simulate the celebration of a sacrament nor imply that [she] act in the name of the Roman Catholic Church." Doing so, he said, would imperil her salvation and that of others.[13]

RCWP disagrees with Rome and proceeds with sacraments, largely because womenpriests agree with the importance Rome places on sacraments and understand that some people who desire the sacraments will not or cannot receive them through the institutional church. Take baptism, for example. Leaving a child unbaptized can bring great anxiety to some Roman Catholics, and such was the case for the Wood family. On September 11, 2010, Theresa Chabot baptized Kira, Jolene, and Ryan Wood, ages nine, eight, and five. Kira, the oldest, was nervous about the baptism; she feared she was going to be publicly submerged in a small pool, like a character she had seen in *My Big Fat Greek Wedding*. Happily for Kira, Chabot used a bowl, baptizing the girls, who stood in front of her, just as she would an infant held in its parents' arms, by pouring small amounts of water over their heads and then anointing them with oil. Rachel Wood, the girls' mother, described the baptism as a "happy occasion." A sizable crowd came to Chabot's community, Church of the Holy Spirit, to join in the celebration. In the years following the baptism, the Wood family continued to join Chabot's community for Mass. Kira and Jolene became altar servers. They wore white robes, held the missal for Chabot, and assisted at the altar. "They enjoy going to church. They enjoy helping," Wood explained to me.[14]

Only a womanpriest could have made that particular baptism possible. Raised in very Catholic families, Rachel and Clayton Wood married in the Roman Catholic Church in 1975 but left shortly after because of Rome's position on women's ordination. As Rachel explained to me, the couple tried other Christian denominations but realized none was a suitable fit, as they were "pretty much

Catholics" only. They were still not practicing Catholicism when they adopted three daughters from China. While Rachel was comfortable not baptizing her daughters—"My kids were still blessed" without the formality, she said—her ailing parents were not. They fervidly wanted their granddaughters baptized into the Catholic Church. So Rachel made two promises, one to her father on his deathbed and one to her mother on hers, that when a woman could say Mass, the Woods would baptize their children. At times Rachel feared she would not be able to keep her promise. Then she learned about Roman Catholic Womenpriests and heard that Chabot, a woman in nearby New Hampshire, was preparing for ordination. Rachel met with Chabot and later said of the womanpriest, "I feel—I truly feel—that she was called back in 1970s" and that the only thing stopping Chabot from being ordained within the Roman church was her gender. As soon as "Reverend Theresa" (as Rachel called her) was ordained, the Woods scheduled the baptism. For Rachel, having the girls baptized by an ordained woman who claimed the validity of the Roman Catholic apostolic line "meant everything to me. I wouldn't have done it otherwise." Rachel kept deathbed promises to her parents and at long last saw a woman exercising "equal opportunity" in the church, celebrating Catholic sacraments.[15]

The Woods had no plans to raise their daughters in institutional Catholicism, but this did not prevent Chabot from baptizing their children. Chabot was an illegally ordained, excommunicated womanpriest, but this did not stop the Woods from recognizing her sacramental authority. Together with the children, the adults created a personalized experience that brought the girls into the Christian community. Sacramental efficacy came not through institutionally mandated power but through a sacramental authority shared among consenting parties.

Rachel Wood was not deluded about the diocesan response to her daughters' baptisms: "Of course . . . we are all excommunicated," she said matter-of-factly.[16] She believed that the certificate of baptism that Chabot provided the girls would not hold weight in the institutional church. Because Rome sees RCWP's sacraments as invalid, most of RCWP's American women certify their sacraments— specifically baptism and marriage—through the Federation of Christian Ministries (FCM), as do other independent Catholic groups not recognized by Roman officials.[17] Still, womenpriests understand that the children they baptize may be viewed as unbaptized in local Catholic parishes. Womenpriests' sacramental gestures might even be dismissed as dangerous. This happened to Chabot when her New Hampshire diocese issued the following warning about her in parish bulletins:

A member of the organization "Roman Catholic Womenpriests," has attempted ordination to the priesthood and has been presenting herself as available to offer "Catholic" ministry, including celebrating Mass and performing baptisms and other sacraments. This statement is to clarify that neither she nor the members and supporters of Roman Catholic Womenpriests act in keeping with Catholic Church teaching and practice. . . . Please be aware that Catholics who participate in the simulation of a Mass or other sacraments by a "Roman Catholic Womanpriest," also separate themselves from the Church. They are not permitted to celebrate and receive the sacraments or exercise a ministry within the church. (c.f., Canon 1378, § 2,3).[18]

Entanglements with local diocesan officials around sacramental legitimacy have become routine for RCWP's ordained. After all, in Rome's framing, some sacraments (those performed by Roman Catholic priests) are valid and true, while others (those performed by non–Roman Catholic groups or what some dioceses characterize as schismatic sects) cannot be.

RCWP occupies an interpretive space where sacramental validity is not black-and-white, and the movement has drawn male priests and practitioners alike into this gray area. Not all local priests and bishops respond with the heavy hand of Vatican law, and some privately record the names of children that womenpriests baptize in church records.[19] As I mentioned above, the Roman church does allow laypersons to baptize in certain circumstances, and so some priests' acceptance of RCWP-performed baptisms does not necessarily suggest silent support for womenpriests. And yet, several womenpriests I have spoken to see this as a small victory. If these children are in church records, they can perhaps make their first Communion or be confirmed in the diocese.

In a European example of local priests upholding womenpriests' authority, Austrian womanbishop and RCWP founding member Christine Mayr-Lumetzberger has presided at funerals alongside Catholic male priests. The men are "very respectful" of her position as bishop, she reported during an interview with the online British newspaper *The Independent*. She said that the male prelates demonstrate their deference to her episcopal position by, for instance, following in proper processional form when she leads the service. She explained that these male priests treat her like a validly ordained woman, as do the people she serves: "These priests, they accept me as a priest and let me officiate in their churches. And these people, they accept me as a priest and ask for me to officiate."[20] Bridget Mary Meehan also reported this on her blog in

Womanpriest Eileen DiFranco baptizes her grandnephew, Gavin. The baptism took place in DiFranco's sister's home in 2010. (Photograph by Judith Levitt.)

2010 and included a photograph of Mayr-Lumetzberger in her vestments. Meehan noted that some of the male priests protested Mayr-Lumetzberger's role, but in the case of a funeral, "the wishes of the relatives of the deceased took precedence."[21] Mayr-Lumetzberger seemed to delight in this story because the approval was coming from the people, not Roman church leaders. This acceptance from "the people in the pews" is crucial within the RCWP movement, and it appears again and again in womenpriests' communities. So often, RCWP's legitimacy and sacramental offerings matter largely because of what they mean in the hands and hearts of those who join in the liturgy and receive the sacraments. RCWP does not have the institutional backing to uphold the merits of their sacraments; instead, RCWP's congregations decide on the efficacy of womenpriests' sacraments.

What is the line between Roman-mandated efficacy and space for creative (re)expression? For the individuals who make up RCWP, that depends. Take, for example, womenpriests' different practices with the baptismal formula. Traditionally, the baptismal rite's necessary form (i.e., the words used to baptize) requires baptism "in the name of the Father, and of the Son, and of the Holy

Spirit," echoing the words that accompany the sign of the cross.[22] In 2008, the CDF issued a statement responding to questions about different baptismal formulas—specifically "Creator, Redeemer, and Sanctifier" and "Creator, Liberator, and Sustainer," which had become popular in feminist and gender-inclusive liturgies—and asserted that any baptism performed with words other than "Father, Son, and Holy Spirit" was invalid. An individual baptized with these erroneous words must be baptized again.[23]

A tension arises here because RCWP is committed to both gender-inclusive language *and* sacramental authenticity. Indeed, womenpriests do modify the language they use when making the sign of the cross to be less androcentric. Some extend that language to baptism, and some do not. At the mass I attended at Therese of Divine Peace in 2009, womanpriest Marybeth McBryan baptized her granddaughter Chloe "in the name of the Creator, and of the Redeemer, and of the Life-Giving Spirit."[24] But womanpriest Marie David, though willing to modify the sign of the cross to "Creator, Redeemer, and Sustainer," has made certain to use "Father, Son, and Holy Spirit" when performing baptisms.[25] Womanpriest Gloria Carpeneto resides somewhere in between: she uses "Father, Son, and Holy Spirit" at baptisms but adds nuanced and gender-inclusive language. She explained that she "retains the formula for authenticity but modifies it for understanding."[26] Because the RCWP movement does not mandate baptismal language, womenpriests speak and act in the ways that feel most true to them.

Sometimes, though, traditional formulas are nonnegotiable for RCWP's women, such as those at the ordination ceremony, which borrows extensively from the Roman Catholic rite. As I explored in the previous chapter, RCWP believes this form to be crucial. RCWP's ordinations follow the order of the ordination liturgy, including requisite parts such as the calling, presentation, and election of the candidates for the diaconate; the examination of the priest ordinands; the litany of the saints, sung while the candidates lie prostrate; and the laying on of hands. Newly made deacons are invested with a stole and receive a Bible; newly made priests are invested with stole and chasuble, have their hands anointed with oil, and receive a paten and chalice.[27]

Chava Redonnet commented that RCWP's emphasis on correct form means that ordinands cannot "get creative" with their ordination ceremonies, and although she found this "disappointing," she understood why: she saw it as having to do with RCWP getting Rome's attention and being taken seriously. Redonnet had a close-up view for comparison: for years she had been a member of Spiritus Christi, an independent Catholic church in Rochester, New York, that is, as she put it, "off the map" and therefore "completely ignored" by Rome. In

contrast, Redonnet believed, because RCWP deliberately uses the same ceremo-
nial form while only altering the candidates' gender, "we can know that Rome
is taking us seriously."[28] In RCWP's calculus, staying true to Roman Catholic
form ensures equality for women, the authenticity of their ordination, and—not
insignificantly—Rome's discomfort.

Sacramental Transformation? Making and Remaking Mystery

As an immediate result of her 2004 ordination to the diaconate, womanpriest
Victoria Rue said she saw the sky differently, felt her feet on the ground differently. She described her ordination as leaving her feeling "cellularly rearranged,"
a comment suggesting some kind of essential transformation. A year later she
was ordained to priesthood on the St. Lawrence Seaway. Again she felt a deep
change, but this time she attributed the change not to the bishops' laying on of
hands, as previously, but to the blessings and prayers from all of the ordination
attendees who'd laid hands on her. Rue recalled that she and the other ordinands
had been on their knees for forty-five minutes as family, friends, and supporters
came forward, filing by, laying hands on the candidates just as the bishops had
done. "What an extraordinary moment!" Rue recalled. After this laying on of
hands, she needed help standing. Truly, "the Spirit was at work."[29]

What happens to ordinands at ordination, and why? Roman Catholic teaching is clear on this point: "The sacrament of Holy Orders . . . confers an indelible spiritual character" upon a candidate that changes ordained individuals on
an "ontological" level.[30] Deacons, priests, and bishops are, therefore, essentially
different from unordained laypeople. The Vatican has further clarified its position on the priesthood for post–Vatican II Catholicism: "The consecration
which [ordained individuals] receive inserts them into the mystery of the apostolic succession and brings about in them a change in being."[31] In sum, Rome
teaches that Roman authority alone, exercised by a bishop through the laying on
of hands, brings about permanent ontological transformation in candidates for
ordination. As indelibly initiated members of the centuries-old apostolic line,
the ordained (men) can facilitate sacramental mysteries.

Chava Redonnet does not agree, at least not with the way the *Catechism*
describes it. In our interview, she said that she did "not believe in that whole
ontological change thing, but . . . " Here she paused again. Finally she admitted that *something* had happened at her ordination, and she had been forever
transformed. Being ordained was, she said, "the most empowering thing in the
world," and having "all of those people pray" for her was "so empowering." "I

feel like I'm not afraid of anything," she added. In sum, Redonnet—like many womenpriests—claims some kind of change took place as a result of sacramental ordination, but she is careful about claiming an ontological distinction or clerical power.[32]

Unlike Rome's clergy, RCWP's women hold no unified position on ontological change. Womenpriests come to the movement and to ordination with different views on this transformation, owing to their personal experiences and individual theologies. Many women are sure something—again, that mysterious, sacramental "something"—happened at their ordination; they are just careful about how they describe it. Rue's language of "cellular rearrangement" indicated a sacredness that impacted her deeply—but the word "rearrangement" implies a shifting of what is already there rather than an infusion of newfound holiness. Like Rue, who said she needed help standing after the laying on of hands at her priesthood ordination, womanpriest Rose Marie Hudson described a "heaviness" upon her back as she prostrated herself before God during her ordination. Later, a male priest friend interpreted this heaviness as the Holy Spirit and told Hudson the same thing had happened to him. "What a tremendous confirmation of ordination," Hudson wrote, viewing her experience as proof that her ordination really, truly happened.[33]

Was this male priest reassuring Hudson that she, too, was indelibly marked? Did Hudson believe she had been forever changed? Hudson's story—which she told in the 2008 book, *Women Find a Way*—made the case that womenpriests have as much legitimacy through the Holy Spirit as male priests. Womanpriest Kathy Vandenberg also addressed the change in *Women Find a Way*, though she did not know quite how to categorize it: "Even now I am still trying to understand what it means to be a priest. I look into a mirror and I look the same as I did before I was ordained. I know I am the same—but also different."[34] Womanpriest Mary Frances Smith was even more certain that something has changed in her life since ordination, but she described this not as an indelible change but as a transformation that came from finally honoring a lifelong call: "All my life, it seemed that I was searching for something. This was my experience for so many years that it seemed this urgent feeling was something that I would just always feel. After ordination, I suddenly realized that I felt as if I finally had crawled into my own skin. I felt congruent, inside and out. My entire life made sense. That pressured urgency was finally gone! Now I am working harder than I have ever worked in my life, and I am indeed exhausted. But I am very happy."[35] As Smith's story shows, women who spent years, sometimes decades, longing to serve as priests feel deeply the momentous occasion of receiving sacramental priesthood.

At the same time, womenpriests know they must tread gently when describing what happened to them at ordination: if they claim an indelible, essential transformation, they fall into the clerical power trap they seek to avoid; if they do not claim a transformation, they may lose some of their ordained authenticity. This mystery of holy orders creates tension for a reform movement seeking to change the Roman Catholic Church while remaining part of it. For those who have feared that RCWP is simply inserting women into a broken hierarchical system, sacraments problematically undercut the "discipleship of equals" ideal. Many womenpriests understand critics' concerns about power abuses that can arise from the Rome's "indelibly marked" sacramental system, and while they claim ordained legitimacy, they simultaneously argue for an altogether reconstituted system.

Part of that entails calling out "ontological change" as harmful and problematic. Trained in a Lutheran seminary, womanpriest Eileen DiFranco credited Protestant theology with showing her that "no special privileges were conferred by celibacy, no 'ontological' change occurred with ordination."[36] Similarly, womanpriest Kathleen Kunster wrote, "While I'm not at all sure that I would say there is an 'ontological' change at ordination, it is clear to me that God has been more present in my life since I said 'Yes' to being ordained. And it seems to be clear to other people as well."[37] Womanpriest Monique Venne was more direct: "There needs to be a wholesale revamping of the theology of the priesthood—no more ontological difference, no more mandatory celibacy, no more promise of obedience to the bishop, no more *in persona Christi*, no more description of the current hierarchy of the church as divinely ordained."[38] Because RCWP aims to dissolve the boundary between clergy and laity, womenpriests cannot simply uphold their own ontological specialness if they wish to empower the laity.

Here again, RCWP finds itself in a contentious place: Why does RCWP insist upon apostolic succession and sacramental priesthood if it wants to limit priesthood power and return the Roman Catholic Church to the laity as the "people of God"? When I asked her this question outright, Canadian womanpriest Monica Kilburn-Smith showed some exasperation: "We've explained that up the yin-yang!" She explained that you have to start with what people know, with what they already understand. For Kilburn-Smith, RCWP must start with that familiarity before diversifying into other ways of being.[39] Womanpriest Roberta Meehan would agree. "[Apostolic succession] is important—not for us but for people who hear about us. One of the things the church stresses is apostolic succession." So even though Meehan does not personally believe there is any such thing as apostolic succession, and even though she explained to me that Jesus never ordained anyone, she sees RCWP's claims to apostolic succession as necessary at this time. People who emphasize the apostolic lineage cannot deny RCWP's priesthood on the basis that it lacks apostolic succession. "They have to find another reason," Meehan added, a hint of challenge in her statement.[40]

RCWP offers what I call the "sacramental mystery of a middle way." Considering that RCWP insists on apostolic succession and the sacredness of the sacraments, all the while trying to distance themselves from a kind of priesthood authority distinct from the laity's relationship with God, RCWP is forging a path midway between two visions of Catholic sacraments. In spite of certain feminist theologians' call for Catholics to eschew sacramental specialness altogether, RCWP retains it as a way of sustaining an argument with Rome about womenpriests' validity. In spite of Rome's rigidity around sacraments, RCWP leaves room for interpretation. By emulating the centuries-old Roman church while injecting female-led innovation into it, RCWP extends to women the kind of sacramental authority that historically has been reserved for men—and then extends that authority still further, to congregants.

For RCWP, the Eucharist also takes this middle way. Canon law deems the Eucharist "the summit and the source of all worship and Christian life."[41] Catholics view the consecrated bread and wine as not symbols of Christ's body and blood but the actual body and blood of Christ. In celebrating the Eucharist, "Christ is thus really and mysteriously made *present*" (emphasis in original) through the process of transubstantiation, which only a validly ordained priest acting *in persona Christi* can facilitate.[42] Yet RCWP eschews the idea that the priest alone has power to make Christ present in the Eucharist, dismissing it as a mark of clericalism taken to a harmful extreme. Instead, womenpriests use a priesthood model whereby they take their own ordained authority—given to them through holy orders and the tradition of apostolic succession—and gift this power and authority to their communities, sharing the ability to consecrate with everyone gathered. Attempting to avoid a hierarchical structure, RCWP instead emphasizes communitarian inclusivity.

RCWP's communities retain the Roman Catholic rite but innovate within that formula, changing Christological emphases and communities' roles. Take, for example, the modifications to the Eucharistic prayer at womanpriest Eileen DiFranco's Community of St. Mary Magdalene in suburban Philadelphia. In Roman Catholic tradition, the Eucharistic prayer is the heart of the Mass.

During the prayer's many parts, such as the thanksgiving, the acclamation, the epiclesis, the institution narrative and consecration, the anamnesis, the offering, and the intercessions, Christ becomes present in bread and wine.[43] Whereas the Roman church dictates that priests alone extend their hands over the gifts during the epiclesis, DiFranco offers a different practice: two lay community members stand with her at the altar throughout the Eucharist, and they extend their hands over the gifts, calling forth the Holy Spirit. Moments later, everyone gathered for Mass says the words of institution, making Christ "sacramentally present."[44] The Eucharistic ministers standing at the altar then pray the offering.[45] This way of sharing consecrating authority happens at all of RCWP's communities. The community gathered does not passively experience the Eucharist; instead, the womenpriests invite the community to make Christ present in the Eucharist.

Sacred space comes into play here as well. In RCWP's sacramental economy, Christ can be made present in the Eucharist in small house churches, not just in formal church buildings. Womenpriests cannot use Roman Catholic Church buildings for liturgy, and so scores of RCWP communities meet in house churches. In the movement's early years, the Mary, Mother of Jesus House Church met on Saturday evenings in an intimate home setting in Sarasota, Florida. Womanpriest (and later ARCWP bishop) Bridget Mary Meehan saw this as a return to early Christians' house church model; church members agreed. One congregant, Jack Duffy, understood the community as emulating the early church, saying, "In this small, intimate, friendly, around-the-table setting, the worship was deep, spiritual, holy. We could all really sense that Jesus was there with us. This is the way early Christians celebrated the Lord's supper, during the time of the Acts of the Apostles, and for the first 200 to 300 years, before we became encumbered with big buildings." As Meehan emphasized, this community prayed together, announced the words of consecration together, and celebrated together the mysteries of the faith as present in the Eucharist.[46] RCWP's expulsion from formal church buildings became a reason for celebration because it invited a kind of authenticity missing in the formal church. Furthermore, these house churches help eliminate the clergy-lay divide when, for example, there is no altar around which to gather. This was the case when I visited the St. Praxedis Catholic Community in New York City in February 2010. The faithful sat not in pews but on sofas, armchairs, kitchen chairs, and even piano benches. In womanpriest Gabriella Valenti Ward's cozy Brooklyn living room, I felt the Mass's focus shift from the priest's actions to the intimate familiarity of sharing bread and wine blessed and passed among community members.[47]

Womanpriest Gabriella Velardi Ward celebrates Mass at St. Praxedis, the worship community she leads, which meets at her home on Staten Island. This Mass took place in May 2011, when RCWP bishop Patricia Fresen (far left) was visiting New York City on a speaking tour. RCWP bishop Andrea Johnson is also pictured, at left, wearing a stole. (Photograph by Judith Levitt.)

In this way, RCWP changes the physical relationship between priest and laity. In the typical Roman Catholic Mass, particularly those held in traditional churches, the priest stands at an altar, set apart from and often higher than the lay congregants. This layout conveys a symbolic message about the priest's importance. This is neither desirable nor possible for RCWP's communities. At the smaller services at Therese of Divine Peace in St. Louis, ten to twenty people gather in the Unitarian Universalist chapel stand and encircle the altar during the Eucharistic prayer. At smaller RCWP masses, like those at Therese, congregants are physically proximate to the Eucharist. When it comes time to receive Communion, everyone passes the paten and chalice to the person beside them. All worshippers, then, become Eucharistic ministers, offering one another the body of Christ and the blood of Christ."[48] As a different example, at the Church of the Beatitudes in Santa Barbara, California, which meets in the United Church of Christ's First Congregational Church, womenpriests Jeannette Love and Suzanne Dunn cannot change the fact that their host church has an elevated altar. During the Eucharistic prayer, however, when thirty-plus individuals circle the altar table, stand side by side, and join in the consecration, the equality of clergy and laity that RCWP strives toward can be more readily achieved.[49]

To be sure, womenpriests are not the first or only Catholic reform group to celebrate Eucharist in modified ways that invite the community to join the priest as Mass celebrants. RCWP's approaches derive from the practices of early Christian communities, contemporary theology, and the example of groups like Intentional Eucharistic Communities (IECs). IECs have celebrated the Eucharist in small, often laity-led communities since the late 1960s, in the wake of Vatican II. IECs sometimes have priests and sometimes do not: what matters is the communal commitment to break bread together in Jesus's name. Many RCWP worship communities are listed on the IEC website.[50] Bridget Mary Meehan has called the house church approach a "full circle" return "to basics," one that honors the likelihood that women participated actively in house church worship and Eucharistic meals in the early Christian centuries.[51] Meehan and others also credit theologians who have reframed Eucharistic understanding: Edward Schillebeeckx's *The Eucharist*, Bernard Cooke's *The Future of Eucharist*, and Paul Bernier's *Eucharist: Celebrating Its Rhythms in Our Lives*. Some womenpriests have studied different theologies of Eucharist in seminary and graduate programs, both Catholic and non-Catholic, and have woven these intellectual encounters into their liturgies.[52] RCWP's practice of Eucharist may not be pioneering, but it does represent continued intervention into the Roman Catholic Church's sacramental system. RCWP helps to make this intimate, female-facilitated Eucharist normative.

And what of the mystery of the Eucharist? For some of RCWP's women, it just happens—sometimes even through the decidedly modern medium of technology. A prime example of this is Canadian womanpriest Michele Birch-Conery's "conference-call Eucharists." When she lived on Vancouver Island in British Columbia, Birch-Conery found it difficult to establish a worship community because her hometown population was so mobile. Birch-Conery likened this challenge to missionary work: in order to effectively reach people, she had to be creative. Birch-Conery used the internet to address this problem. She devised a meetup ministry of conference-call liturgies. About once a month, she met remotely with people who wanted to celebrate Eucharist but could not easily travel. Birch-Conery and the congregants called in to a conference-call center. Birch-Conery prepared liturgical music (which she played on her stereo during the call) and emailed the order of liturgy in advance, so the people could follow along and participate. When the time came for the liturgy of the Eucharist, every individual participating—from their home, from a friend's home—extended their hands over the bread and wine that they had prepared or purchased for the Mass. Birch-Conery did the same in her office. She called the Spirit onto the gifts and made the sign of the cross. She did not ask the community to do this, she explained to me, lest they believe that they themselves were transubstantiating the gifts—which could make them uncomfortable. When the time came to receive Communion, the people either took it independently or passed it among themselves, depending on whether they were alone or with a small group. "They do not feel that it's not real," Birch-Conery said of this unconventional sacrament.[53]

For Birch-Conery, this approach beautifully fueled the "discipleship of equals" ideal: first, because people who would otherwise miss Mass were able to join in the celebration, and second, because participants had to be actively engaged for the liturgy to work. She did not think congregants' inability to see the priest or the other participants was a detriment; rather, she believed the distinctive setting eliminated distractions and increased attention to the language, music, and sacrament. Moreover, participants were called upon to make gestures and say words as the celebrant does. "It's pretty good sacramental mentoring, when you think of it," Birch-Conery explained. Though the community did not gather in the same physical space, they were together in cyberspace; though they did not sit in the room, they coexisted in the same conference-call room. "We are together in a technological age," Birch-Conery mused, "and we need to rethink" the realness of technological spaces. Conference-call Eucharists allow mystery to coexist with technology. When I asked Birch-Conery how transubstantiation happened even when she, the priest, was not physically present among the faithful, she exclaimed, "I just have to believe it happens!"[54] This is part of the mystery—upheld by Birch-Conery's faith. Sacramental mystery did not require assembling a congregation in the same location; mystery did, however, require the right words, the right gestures, and an ordained womanpriest's intentional spiritual mentoring.

Unlike Birch-Conery, some womenpriests are uncomfortable with transubstantiation. When I asked Bishop Andrea Johnson about RCWP's views on transubstantiation, she turned to church history. Transubstantiation is, she said, a "pseudoscientific" "medieval word" that reflects how Christians in the Middle Ages attempted to explain how Jesus entered into the bread and wine, fundamentally changing its substance. Rather than focus on discourse around transubstantiation, Johnson emphasized anamnesis, the memorial character of the Eucharist. In this approach to the Eucharist focused on remembrance, the people, as the community of faith, make present the body of Christ. Time collapses, and at liturgy, "we are past, present, and future." For Johnson, medieval language was not helpful for understanding the importance of sacraments in the twenty-first century.[55]

Birch-Conery and Johnson reveal two different iterations of "middle way" sacramental mystery. Using conference-call Eucharists, Birch-Conery retained traditional Roman Catholic ideas about transubstantiation while reforming it with both the authority of a womanpriest and the mediation of twentieth-century technology. Johnson, in contrast, was wary of medieval theological concepts uncritically transferred to the modern-day context. Instead, she envisioned womenpriests helping to usher in greater lay sacramental authority. Though she adhered to a more traditional-sounding discourse, Birch-Conery, too, was thinking about the laity, albeit differently than Johnson. Birch-Conery explained that womenpriests must meet the people where they are—and Catholics today equate sacraments with priesthood. To change things too quickly—for example, to eliminate the sacramental priesthood and usher in a pastoral priesthood—would be a failure of ordained service. Birch-Conery invoked the word *transitional* in describing what she felt RCWP needed to do and be.

Are womenpriests like Johnson rejecting sacramental mystery altogether? Or is theirs a postmodern move that acknowledges the construction of meaning through language and symbols, and therefore rejects a sacramental system that poses as science and demands lay adherence to a patriarchal system? Can mystery remain part of Catholic sacramental understanding even if centuries-old language around mystery shifts? RCWP raises but does not yet answer such questions.

"All Are Welcome": Sacramental Inclusivity

Etched into the altar table at the Therese of Divine Peace Inclusive Community are the words "All Are Welcome." Whether the chairs for that day's Mass are arranged in rows, arcs, or a circle, congregants orient themselves toward that welcoming message. When Elsie McGrath and Rose Hudson were ordained in November 2007, they included the well-known Catholic hymn "All Are Welcome," by Marty Haugen, in the liturgy. One verse chimes,

> Let us build a house
> Where love can dwell
> And all can safely live
> . . . .

> Built of hopes and dreams and visions,
> Rock of faith and vault of grace;
> Here the love of Christ shall end divisions
> ....
> All are welcome, all are welcome,
> All are welcome in this place.[56]

Therese of Divine Peace and all RCWP communities extend welcoming inclusivity to visitors. RCWP welcomes people whom the institutional church will not invite to the table. This helps bring about healing for those estranged from Rome.

RCWP wants its sacraments to enact inclusivity, whereas official Roman Catholic teaching sometimes uses sacraments to retain *ex*clusivity. For example, Protestant visitors to Catholic churches are not invited to receive Communion. The *Catechism* states that Christian groups "derived from the Reformation and separated from the Catholic Church" have not retained the fullness of Eucharistic mystery because they have not kept holy orders intact—specifically, apostolic succession and the sacramental priesthood. As such, "Eucharistic intercommunion with these communities is not possible."[57] RCWP eliminates this barrier. With an open table Communion service, anyone and everyone—Catholic, Protestant, or non-Christian—who wishes to partake of bread and wine, body and blood, can do so. When saying Mass, womenpriests make a point of extending a Communion invitation to everyone present, carefully distinguishing RCWP's position from the Roman Catholic Church's.

Some Roman Catholic priests use sacraments to publicly enact punitive measures, and excommunication is one form of boundary marking. Canon 915 bars excommunicated Catholics from receiving communion. Excommunicated womenpriests, then, have felt the sting of refusal when they visit their home parishes for Mass and are denied Communion. Before she was excommunicated *latae sententiae* in May 2008, Regina Nicolosi's archbishop asked her to stop receiving Communion—or else risk formal excommunication.[58] Eileen DiFranco was shocked when, in the wake of the 2008 declaration, her parish priest asked that she no longer take Communion "for the good of the parish." She described this parish as a liberal-minded "peace and justice church" that baptized the babies of gay couples and protested war and capital punishment. She had not imagined that her priest would bar her from receiving the Eucharist.[59]

RCWP's excommunicated womenpriests empathize with Catholics excluded from the sacraments. Exclusion happens frequently in the case of divorce, as many divorced or divorced-and-remarried Catholics believe that they are not welcome to receive Communion. Womenpriests acknowledge the pain many divorced Catholics feel and offer sacramental ministry to Catholics who feel excluded.[60] Many RCWP congregants are divorced, and this story ARCWP bishop Bridget Mary Meehan told about "Marie" is not uncommon: A divorced and remarried woman, Marie cried when she received Communion at Meehan's house church, for she had long felt unworthy to receive the Eucharist. As part of Meehan's house church, Marie came to feel that she had "come home at last" to the faith that had seemed to reject her. Later on, Marie invited Meehan into her home and asked for a special Mass for family and friends. Marie learned that, not only could she be welcomed to receive the sacraments, but she could participate as a "celebrant of the Eucharist."[61]

Likewise, a divorced community member in the Holy Spirit Catholic Community in Toledo, Ohio, acknowledged that having a womanpriest lead the sacraments had changed her understanding of sacraments. Her words alluded to past pain—perhaps stemming from her divorce—that had prevented her from taking Communion: "There are so many RULES in the Catholic Church and even though the male priests are sinners and breaking the rules themselves, most would not admit it. The women, on the other hand, admit their faults and try to do better. In our community, ALL [are] welcome to the table. Just like Jesus said Himself. Yet in my past experience, the very one keeping me from the table is also guilty of sin."[62] This cradle Catholic in her early fifties wanted an admission of imperfections from her priests, and she said she found this humility in RCWP's ordained women. In womenpriests' hands, the sacraments, which can be vehicles for punishment, which in turn can highlight feelings of sinfulness, become opportunities for healing and homecoming.

Weddings make up a large part of womenpriests' sacramental ministries, and this is particularly important for couples who cannot freely marry in the Roman Catholic Church. More than a civil union, Roman Catholic marriage is a sacramental commitment vowed before the community of God. Rome strictly forbids marriage for same-sex couples. Complications can arise when one or both members of a couple are divorced (without a formal church annulment), and in the case of cohabitation prior to marriage, and with ecumenical and interfaith marriages. The Roman church also requires that wedding ceremonies take place inside Catholic churches as a sign of the union's solemnity and commitment to the faith. RCWP's practice of marriage is different. A look at the RCWP regions' websites reveals myriad photographs of womenpriests presiding at weddings. Most ceremonies are outdoors: on the beach, on a grassy hill, in a park surrounded by trees. Womenpriests allow couples to modify the liturgy to meet their own vision; this may include using nonscriptural readings or extending the Eucharist to all persons present. RCWP gladly marries gay, lesbian, and trans couples, and the womenpriests appeal to a range of audiences, from the more traditionally Catholic to the more ritually experimental.[63] Womanpriest Victoria Rue and her partner Kathryn Poethig (who is not an RCWP womanpriest but does minister out of her Presbyterian background) together offered many sacraments and services through their Threshold Ministries and invited couples to personalize their ceremony.[64] Womenpriests like Mary Ann Schoettly have worked with interfaith couples. Schoettly described a wedding she celebrated where the bride was a cradle Catholic who wanted a woman to preside, and the groom wanted a religious ceremony. The couple had planned to use an Episcopal womanpriest until they found Schoettly, who offered them prenuptial preparation and the liturgical ceremony they envisioned.[65]

RCWP also aims to tend to Catholic bodies that have been unable to partake of the full sacramental menu. Instead of using wheat bread and alcoholic wine for Communion, as canon 924 stipulates, many RCWP communities offer gluten-free bread and grape juice. The bread is safe for those with gluten allergies, and the wine is safe for individuals who cannot consume alcohol. Gloria Carpeneto of Baltimore's Living Water community described this as an important gesture of inclusion, permitting people whose bodies are challenged in some way—with alcoholism, with gluten intolerance—to receive Eucharist fully, in the same way as their communicants.[66] Canadian womanpriest Monica Kilburn-Smith noted that baking gluten-free bread for liturgies is difficult work but an important step in making the Eucharist safe for all bodies.[67]

RCWP seeks to accommodate individuals' feelings of fragility and unworthiness by removing atonement language that depicts Christ as the sacrificial lamb. During the Agnus Dei, or "Lamb of God" supplication, the priest breaks the bread to symbolize Christ's suffering. While Roman Catholic communities (since the new translation of the Roman missal in 2010) say "Lord, I am not worthy that you should enter under my roof, but only say the word and my soul shall be healed," Eileen DiFranco's St. Mary Magdalene community says, "Lord, you make us worthy to receive you, and by your word, we have been healed."[68] Other communities remove blood atonement as well as the masculine title "Lord," instead substituting a more gender-neutral "God." These changes are not always easy for lifelong Catholics to make, and womenpriests can find themselves in a teaching mode with these modifications. When the Hildegard Community of the Living Spirit in Festus, Missouri, was only months old, womanpriest Rose

Marie Hudson had to be very deliberate in leading the worshippers to say, "*God, we are worthy* to receive you."[69] RCWP does not believe that language of unworthiness helps the faithful move closer to God.

RCWP's appeal to Catholics who feel spiritually "broken" speaks to the pull of sacramental grace and RCWP's ability to fill a void for some Catholics who are estranged from the Roman Catholic Church. This is why womanpriest Eleonora Marinaro has said that "reconciliation with the Roman Catholic Church after years of estrangement is a prime feature of our ministry."[70] The sacrament of reconciliation features prominently in womenpriests' sacramental ministries. Sometimes, reconciliation happens spontaneously: someone will be speaking to a womanpriest, learn she is ordained, and ask for absolution.[71] A number of established RCWP worship communities use penitential services and absolutions in lieu of individual confessions. But some people still want penance one on one. Eileen DiFranco recalled a woman from outside her worship community who sought her out for reconciliation because she "just felt the need to be absolved by a woman."[72] Mary Ann Schoettly was "delighted and very humbled" when a woman religious requested absolution.[73] Womanpriest Gabriella Velardi Ward and Canadian womanbishop Marie Bouclin specifically bring the sacrament of reconciliation into their work with victims of trauma and abuse, including those harmed by Catholic priests. Ward wrote about reconciliation requiring a change in selves and social systems: "Reconciliation with self, the world and God happens when survivors take steps toward empowerment, justice and the re-creation of self as they work against suffering [and] when they begin to break the conspiracy of silence and reclaim their truth."[74] The womenpriests try to offer sacraments that restore an individual's fractured relationship with the church and with God.

Paradoxically, these excommunicated womenpriests—not clerics in good standing with Rome—usher fallen-away Catholics back to the church. Just as the womenpriests themselves have broken the institutional church's rules as a way of ensuring their relationship with God and Jesus, RCWP invites others to reframe and restore their relationship with God by receiving sacramental ministries outside of formal Vatican authority. Those who are welcomed to the RCWP sacramental table trust the womenpriests' authority to perform sacraments and offer grace through the Holy Spirit. The womenpriests accept the responsibility gifted to them by their congregants and sacramental recipients. RCWP puts women into positions of sacramental power and presence: at the altar table consecrating the Eucharist, in a private setting hearing a confession, beside a couple exchanging their vows, or at a bedside anointing the sick. Here, a female body represents Roman Catholic religious and spiritual authority, and a woman gifts that power back to her lay congregants.

Conclusion: Navigating Tensions around RCWP's Sacramental Economy

As RCWP continues to develop a modified sacramental economy, questions arise. Where is the line between what is and is not "really" Roman Catholic? Do sacraments mean more, or less, or the same, when the boundaries around sacramental meaning are loosened or perforated? What makes a sacrament sacred? Wherein lies the mystery? And what, if anything, makes a bishop's power distinct from that of priests, deacons, and the laity? Two final examples illuminate the sacramental middle way that RCWP has created for creative and theological exploration.

First: catacomb priests. A small fraction of RCWP's ordained women (eleven, according to the group's website in the summer of 2019) have been ordained secretly, in what RCWP calls "catacomb ordinations," named for the underground crypts constructed by ancient Romans. These women do not feel safe becoming priests publicly, usually because they work for Catholic institutions or parishes or because they are women religious. Some secretly ordained women later "come out" as priests; others remain clandestine.

If these catacomb womenpriests cannot form a worship community, minister publicly, and celebrate sacraments with others, why do they become ordained? I put this question to an older woman, "Ruth," whom I met in the "no media" section of an ordination ceremony, where she sat to avoid being photographed and outed as an RCWP supporter. As a catacomb womanpriest, Ruth told me that she held hope that she would be able to live openly as a priest in her lifetime. I pressed further because her optimism took me aback: What could this woman, who was probably in her eighties, *do* as an ordained priest when she had to live secretly? Ruth explained that as a hospital chaplain, she could and did bless people. "Do your patients know you're a priest?" I asked. "No," she said, "but I know."[75]

What Ruth took to be important about her priesthood was not that others knew she was ordained but rather that she was able to gift a special blessing—something distinctly sacred—to her ailing patients. For Ruth, ordination was about an internal change that allowed her to bless the faithful—even if the faithful did not know a priest was blessing them. In Ruth's theology, priesthood was a special, secret bond between herself, some RCWP members, and God. Ruth's story expresses the Catholic sacramental imagination at its simplest and most elegant: even without the formalities of vestments, church buildings, holy oils, or formal rituals, priests can offer efficacious blessings. Ruth believed this. She believed it so fully that she risked her livelihood within her religious order to become a priest.

But at the same time, Ruth's understanding of herself as a secretly ordained priest removed the RCWP sacramental economy based in sharing authority between a priest and layperson. After all, someone receiving the sacraments cannot participate with the womanpriest if they do not know the individual ministering to them is ordained. In this way, as a catacomb priest, Ruth can deliver the sacraments, but she can't do as much to reform church sacraments as can publicly known womenpriests.

The second example is the ordination of Nancy Corran, who was ordained within and by an RCWP community (Mary Magdalene Apostle Catholic Community in San Diego, California) but *without* a bishop's laying on of hands. Corran's 2010 ordination offers an alternative understanding of holy orders, apostolic succession, and a lay community's power to call a person to priesthood. The MMACC community called Corran to priesthood and then ordained her themselves; Corran's apostolic succession came not through a bishop or RCWP but through the hands of nearly 150 MMACC community members.[76]

Though this approach differs from Rome's current practice of ordination, it holds historical validity, because ordination at a bishop's hands is not the only way that ordination has happened throughout history. Rome's practice today stems from the writings of church fathers like Ignatius of Antioch and Eusebius of Caeserea, who sought to assert authority and orthodoxy over diverse early Christian groups. A different model for ordination—but still within apostolic tradition—saw priesthood as connected to a teaching (and not a sacramental) authority that ensured the continuation of original faith traditions. In other words, Christian tradition has never held one singular definition of apostolic succession, and MMACC emulated an early-church model to ordain Corran.[77]

Corran was not ordained through or into RCWP but through and into MMACC specifically, and this caused debate within RCWP. Was it prudent to ordain women in this early-Christian mode when Rome still did not accept the validity of women's ordination through more routine, contemporary rituals?[78] Was a bishop necessary, and was the MMACC community's blessing sufficient? Complicating this issue at Corran's ordination was the presence of Dana Reynolds, an RCWP womanbishop who had resigned from RCWP earlier that year because of health issues and a new ministerial call. Reynolds explained later that she had attended Corran's ordination in solidarity, and like everyone gathered on that day, Reynolds laid hands on Corran. But speculations mounted. Was Reynolds in attendance as a "planted bishop," ensuring that Corran met Rome's definition of apostolic succession? Did someone ask Reynolds to attend in order to guarantee episcopal authenticity, should anyone question Corran's legitimacy?[79]

Difficult conversations came out of Corran's ordination, in terms of RCWP's structure, the role of bishops, and the autonomy of RCWP communities. In the end, RCWP formally supported MMACC's approach. Speaking to a local paper on RCWP's behalf, Bridget Mary Meehan explained, "There are many ways to be ordained. And we certainly consider [Corran's ordination] a valid ordination."[80] The controversy died down, and Corran went on to become pastor of MMACC. But the debates and rumors surrounding her ordination had revealed a point of contention within RCWP.

RCWP's actions highlight its desire to forge a path between reform and tradition. Conflicts within the movement show that RCWP must also navigate among conventional understandings of priesthood, progressive theologies, and historical knowledge. Sacramental transitions are taking place within RCWP and in womanpriest-led communities, but, as RCWP's ordained have told me time and again, they must meet the people where they are. In other words, if communities expect their womenpriests to emulate male priests, womenpriests cannot make radical departures from present practices. Corran's unorthodox ordination worked for MMACC, according to MMACC pastor Jane Via, because that "highly educated" community was spiritually prepared and theologically accepting of a community-driven ordination.[81] Not every RCWP community has similar demographics or a similar desire for sacramental experimentation. It stands to reason that differences among RCWP's communities might lead womenpriests to practice different ways of sharing sacramental authority. Without a centralized institution like the Vatican determining sacramental practice and meaning, RCWP's women get to be creative in serving their communities. At the same time, this complicates RCWP's goal of reform: What does sacramental reform look like? How much do geography and social class influence the womenpriests and their decisions?

Regardless of location, however, RCWP's actions and theological rhetoric suggest that RCWP tries simultaneously to preserve elements of mystery and empower the laity as the people of God. This raises questions about womenpriests' authority *as women*: Do womenpriests undermine their priesthood authority by sharing sacramental power with laity? Or, conversely, do they show confidence in their priesthood authority this way? In RCWP's sacramental equation, the laity play essential roles, participating in *contra legem* ordinations and the consecration of the Eucharist. Additionally, laity are empowered to choose, for example, womenpriests over legal male priests for baptisms and marriages. Both lay community members and ordained women become symbols in RCWP's sacramental economy: the womenpriests represent gender equality and a woman's sacramental power; the community represents RCWP's investment in lay sacramental authority and decision-making. For RCWP, sacraments are the location of grace, a way to strengthen faith, an indication of one's commitment to God, and a sacred, liminal space that provides creativity and healing.

CHAPTER 6

Ministries on the Margins

ORDINATION CREATES SACRAMENTAL POSSIBILITIES for womenpriests but does not provide an established parish to lead or offer a steady paycheck, housing, or medical care. When a male priest is ordained, the church (either a diocese or religious order) directs his next steps (e.g., to parish priesthood or chaplaincy, to teaching or campus ministry), all the while providing housing, food, transportation, health insurance, and stipends. Conversely, once womenpriests are ordained, they must look beyond these typical models of Roman Catholic ministerial priesthood and forge an ordained livelihood for themselves.

RCWP's womenpriests believe that what they do as ministerial priests will reveal their worth. Ministries to individuals and groups constitute the majority of the women's lives as womenpriests. They believe Jesus supports them, often noting his words from the Sermon on the Mount: "You will know them by their fruits. . . . Every good tree bears good fruit, but the bad tree bears bad fruit. A good tree cannot bear bad fruit, nor can a bad tree bear good fruit" (Matthew 7:16–20). Womenpriests also quote that moment in Acts of the Apostles when a respectable Pharisee named Gamaliel defends the apostles as they proselytize about Jesus. Gamaliel says to the apostles' opponents, "If this plan or this undertaking is of human origin, it will fail; but if it is of God, you will not be able to overthrow them—in that case you may even be found fighting against God!" (Acts 5:38–39). Here, womenpriests liken themselves to the apostles. Like the early Christians struggling to spread the faith, they believe God is on their side. Womenpriests view themselves as being like Christ in their aim of serving men and women "on the margins." As ARCWP bishop Bridget Mary Meehan explained, "Jesus stood on the margins and ministered to the marginalized, [and] so do women priests today!"[1] Framed in this way, ministries—and RCWP's rhetoric of ministry—transform RCWP's women from provocatively ordained rule breakers into committed social justice activists.

Womenpriests see themselves as marginalized and thus position themselves as uniquely suited to serve a marginalized audience. Womenpriests' ministries evolve out of the women's educational backgrounds, careers, and relationships. As "worker priests," many merge priesthood and career in order to earn a living and augment their priestly identities. Their work brings them into contact with the ministerial efforts of other ordained persons, including Protestants and non-Christians, making RCWP an unintentional ecumenical and interfaith endeavor within the margins of the Roman Catholic Church. And womenpriests' ministries put them squarely within contemporary debates about church reform that have suggested ministerial service does not require ordination in the first place.

In this chapter, I analyze womenpriests' descriptions and practices of ministry alongside their rhetoric of marginality. In complicating RCWP's idea of priesthood "on the margins," I argue that, perhaps surprisingly, Rome's rejection of women's ordination has given womenpriests a type of ministerial power that they would not have if they were legally ordained within the institution. When womenpriests describe themselves as "marginal," they position themselves outside the Roman Catholic Church. Part of this exclusion comes from the group's own *contra legem* actions, and part comes from Vatican statements regarding women's roles. In describing themselves as serving marginalized individuals while being marginalized themselves, RCWP aligns with other disempowered populations who are "outcasts" as a result of political, ecclesiastical, and institutional structures. But the language of marginalization can mask the opportunities RCWP has found on the margins. Elements of RCWP's ministerial priesthood—such as the validation of their vocational calls, professional careers that augment but do not depend on ordination, ecumenical partnerships, and practical and rhetorical support from non-Catholics as well as Catholic priests—emerge from an absence of institutional support and lead the womenpriests to draw on unexpected, creative resources and find support structures independent of the Roman Catholic Church. Put simply: the margins empower RCWP's women, rhetorically and ministerially.

Ministries, Margins, and an Argument for Women in Ministerial Priesthood

Language of marginalization binds RCWP to its "new model of priestly ministry."[2] In a 2006 YouTube video, Bridget Mary Meehan, who was then RCWP's public relations director, explained RCWP's vision of an ordained ministry to the margins. In this edited video, with photographs from RCWP ordinations, sacraments, and ministerial endeavors punctuating her words, Meehan defined marginality as it pertained to RCWP's ministries.

> In the Roman Catholic Womenpriests community, we reach out to those who have been alienated, hurt, or rejected by the institutional Catholic Church. There are many who feel like second-class citizens in their own church: divorced and remarried Catholics, gays and lesbians, and *all those on the margins* [emphasis mine] of church and society. We will minister everywhere we find a need for God's compassion and love. The world is our parish. Wherever we minister, Roman Catholic womenpriests offer a vision of an inclusive church where all are welcome at God's table of plenty, at the banquet of love. We offer a new model of priestly ministry in which all people and all ministries are equally valued. We work as partners and equals with others in our communities. We work in an interfaith context, respectful of other traditions. Inclusivity is our hallmark. It is not enough to ordain women into a patriarchal and hierarchical structure. The clerical structure needs to be transformed from a dominator model, with powers reserved to clergy, into an open, participatory model that honors the gifts of the Spirit in the people of God. The present gap between clergy and lay needs to be eliminated. We need to move from an unaccountable, top-down hierarchy to a people-empowered community of equals. We advocate a model of ministry based on partnership with the people we serve.[3]

In RCWP's ministerial philosophy, *marginality* refers to groups who face exclusion—from society, politics, and the church—on the basis of gender, sexual orientation, or marital status.

In Meehan's statement, a shared sense of marginalization allows the womenpriests to connect to Jesus—"Jesus ministered to people on the margins," Meehan pointed out in a survey response[4]—and to make sense of their call and commitment to Roman Catholicism. For womanpriest Diane Dougherty, Catholicism works best when serving marginalized people: "I remain Catholic because it . . . allows us to proclaim and live the gospel on the margins of society."[5] Another ordained woman expressed the following view: "My calling, and the way I see the calling of RCWP, is to live on the margins of the institutional church by being a prophetic voice."[6] By evoking a "prophetic" position, this womanpriest (like the movement itself) aligned herself with prophets in the Hebrew Bible who preached God's message but were ignored or ostracized by people in power. Indeed, many Christians who view themselves as marginalized have situated themselves discursively within a "prophetic tradition." Doing so places marginalized activists like RCWP's within the support and protection of God—a more powerful advocate than any institutional church.

Womenpriests' understandings of ministries are philosophical and deeply personal. It has often seemed to me that womenpriests become the priests they wish they had had. One example of this is womanpriest and social justice worker Judy Lee, who illustrates how womenpriests' personal experiences and lived theologies inform their ordained ministry to the margins. Like many of RCWP's womenpriests, Judy Lee infused ministries with sacraments, built pastoral service on professional and personal experiences, sought resources from local interfaith groups, and received vocational mentoring from non-Catholics and Catholics—including male priests. Lee and her life companion, a former Benedictine sister and womanpriest named Judy Beaumont, co-pastored Good Shepherd Ministries of Southwest Florida, with a mission to help the homeless through education, job skills, and mentorship.[7]

One of Lee's early ministerial undertakings was Church in the Park, a weekly Mass for homeless men and women in Fort Myers, Florida. This Mass took place in a city park filled with sounds of automobiles, squealing children, and rowdy pickup basketball games. Lee's interactive homily led the people gathered to share their reflections on the day's scripture reading. Homeless children and adults, some struggling with addiction, mental illness, and domestic abuse, could come together in the bustling urban space. Lee's Church in the Park ministry included a feeding program that served an average of one hundred people each week. Lee, who referred to herself as a "street preacher," wrote, "Every week we experience the miracle of the loaves and fishes, as the crowd swells and we still have just enough prepared by many loving hands. I am filled with thanksgiving."[8]

Lee's ministry did not begin with ordination: she worked with homeless populations for over twenty-five years before becoming a priest. Her call to ministry stemmed from her life experiences serving the poor and homeless. She grew up poor in Brooklyn and saw many family and friends struggle with mental illness and addiction. Lee's education focused on social work, counseling, and ministry, and she became a professor of social work at Yale Divinity School and the University of Connecticut School of Social Work.[9] She eventually tired of academia but struggled to accept what she understood as her vocational call to priesthood. Friends and colleagues—ordained and unordained, Catholic and non-Catholic—encouraged her to pursue priestly ordination. Once ordained through RCWP, Lee sought to emulate Jesus's passion for social justice and love of the poor. She explained her calling as a "sacramental ministry with the poor, the ill, the different, and the outcasts of society by virtue of color, caste, sexual orientation, mental or physical illnesses or challenges." She labeled herself a "border dweller" and "sometimes" an outcast, and so now, as a priest, she reaches out to people who exist "on the margins."[10] Womenpriests like Lee have the freedom to shape their pastoral work around their existing communities and personal passions.

Womenpriests' ministries are largely grounded in their worship communities, where they celebrate regular liturgies and pastor to their communities. Often, these communities emerge because of the women's priesthood. In the weeks before their ordination, Elsie McGrath and Rose Marie Hudson announced that they would begin offering weekly Mass at a downtown St. Louis community they had named Therese of Divine Peace Inclusive Catholic Community. The publicity that accompanied their 2007 ordination alerted local Catholics to this new group; plus, the women had a ready audience in nearby progressive, intentional Catholic communities like the local Catholic Worker house. Other times, newly ordained deacons and priests serve alongside other womenpriests in existing communities. For example, womanpriest Suzanne Dunn started Santa Barbara's Church of the Beatitudes in 2008, and Jeannette Love joined her as a co-pastor when she was ordained two years later. Stories like womanpriest Dena O'Callaghan's are not unusual: she attended one of Bridget Mary Meehan's home liturgies in 2009, and after hearing her story, Meehan encouraged O'Callaghan to discern ordination. O'Callaghan was ordained a priest the following year.[11] Some worship communities evolved out of other communities, as was the case for womanpriest Chava Redonnet, whose Oscar Romero community emerged from within the Rochester Catholic Worker house, and womanpriest Victoria Marie, whose Our Lady of Guadalupe Tonantzin Inclusive Catholic Community grew out of the Catholic Worker House Vancouver, where she lived.[12] Some communities gather weekly, others bimonthly, others monthly. Some communities see liturgies with only a handful of people in attendance, while other communities routinely get upward of one hundred participants. When I asked womenpriests how their sacraments and ministries had changed and evolved since their ordination, it was not uncommon to hear reports of adding Mass times or finding new spaces to rent for liturgy.

Not all womenpriests lead worship communities, however. After offering Masses in a nondenominational chapel at San Jose State University starting shortly after her 2005 ordination, womanpriest Victoria Rue found that her work changed. Even without her own formal community, her priesthood service continued: "My ministry is now my theatre making and retreat giving," she stated.[13] Certainly, "not every womanpriest is going to start a church," womanpriest Jeannette Love told me. "There are different ways of living out that call. It comes together in different ways for different people," and RCWP does not require womenpriests to start or serve a community.[14] Womanpriest Ruth Broeski had previously worked with Sophia Christi, a community in Eugene, Oregon, but was unaffiliated when I connected with her in summer 2014. She wrote, "When I was with Sophia Christi, I was more public and related to a greater number of people as one of their priests. Now I am clearly more freelance and respond in depth to the spiritual needs of whoever is in my life or is sent to me."[15] Womanpriest Elsie McGrath still leads Therese as of 2020 and also served RCWP for seven years in her role as program coordinator of the Great Waters Region. "More than half of my time is devoted to the women in the formation program and the women in the region," she explained.[16] Like McGrath, many womenpriests count service to the RCWP and ARCWP organizations among their ministries. In 2011 womanpriest Suzanne Thiel described her ministry as "primarily administrative," for in addition to her volunteer work with assisted living facilities, she served as a kind of executive director for RCWP-USA, managing the finances and organizational demands of this steadily growing nonprofit. Such diversity in ministry is "not a bad thing, because the Catholic public is very diverse," Thiel said.[17] In this way, RCWP envisions itself emulating the populations it serves.

The RCWP movement seems to believe that being on the margins automatically requires a rejection of hierarchicalism. But can womenpriests be ordained priests *and* marginalized, simultaneously? Progressive feminist theologians have challenged the notion that a true discipleship of equals can be attained in a religious system that ordains few while serving many. Mary Hunt has advocated ministry *without* ordination since the second Women's Ordination Conference meeting, in 1978. Defining "ministries" as "the infinite range of ways we serve our communities," Hunt argued in 2006 that feminist ministries can and must do justice work independent of hierarchical structures—and thus, she concluded, independent of an ordained priesthood. Criticizing groups like RCWP, Hunt stated, "While I understand and respect the moves toward various forms of ordination in which some Catholic women are engaged, I believe such efforts are fraught with problems that an emphasis on feminist ministries does not share." In Hunt's analysis, kyriarchical structures that distinguish clergy (made distinctly holy through a laying on of hands) from laity (who await the ministerial blessings of clerical authorities) will always lead problematically to ministries *to* as opposed to the ideal ministry *with*. All the more reason, says Hunt, to minister without clerical roles.[18]

Hunt's vision offered RCWP a cautionary message and raised questions: Does RCWP need ordination in order to achieve its ministerial goals? What, if anything, is ordination adding to these pastoral efforts? Without fully address- ing these questions, RCWP doubles down on service that is both ministerial and priestly. The movement's response to women's exclusion from priestly ministry is to put women into ministerial priesthood.

Ordaining women to illicit priesthood as a defiant act of social justice is one thing, but assisting women in finding and living out viable sacramental minis- tries is something else. This is one area where RCWP differs from ARCWP (which, recall, formed out of RCWP in 2010): rhetorically, at least, the Associ- ation of Roman Catholic Women Priests places greater emphasis on the min- istries that follow ordination, specifically as they pertain to peace and justice. ARCWP bishop Bridget Mary Meehan told me that ARCWP's women are "passionate about our community's witness for justice and peace issues . . . be- cause we see justice as constitutive to the Gospel and therefore all justice issues are interrelated."[19] With a somewhat different emphasis, RCWP's "primary goal is to prepare and ordain women. It's not social justice per se," explained Suzanne Thiel in 2011, speaking as "president of the board of the RCWP-USA" (a title she openly disliked because it sounded hierarchical). Thiel added that, of course, the group was committed to social justice and serving the marginalized—but one had to separate preparation and ordination from the ministerial service that followed.[20]

These differences indicate different visions of the relationship between priest- hood and ministry. RCWP-USA's vision is "a new model of ordained ministry in a renewed Roman Catholic Church," with a mission to "prepare, ordain, and support qualified women . . . who are called by the Holy Spirit and their com- munities to minister to the People of God."[21] ARCWP's original constitution, on the other hand, said, "We prepare and ordain women to serve the people of God in inclusive priestly ministry."[22] Both groups rely on marginalization language, but to somewhat different ends. In emphasizing formation, RCWP more rigorously prepares its women for discernment and sacramental action; in emphasizing ministry, ARCWP ordains women more quickly, forgoing depth of preparation in order to get women into ministry. Both branches share a con- certed effort to perform ministries *with* (and not *to*) marginalized people; the differences between them reveal the global RCWP movement's ongoing negoti- ations of *contra legem* priesthood alongside ministerial priesthood.

The Professionalization of Worker Priests

Womenpriests proudly refer to themselves as "worker priests." The women's ordination movement has championed the idea from its inception, and RCWP's
2004 constitution stated, "We perceive ourselves as worker womenpriests. This
means that we earn our money like other human beings in worldly endeavors."[23]
The idea of worker priests started in the mid-twentieth century in parts of Europe, primarily France, when (male) priests chose to work in factories in order
to be close to the people they serve. Recognizing the disillusionment many
working-class Catholics felt post–World War II, these priests shared in laypeople's economic struggles and working conditions.[24] I have not heard any womanpriest draw direct connections between RCWP and the European worker
priest practice, but I have frequently heard womenpriests suggest they are better
positioned to serve a wide range of people because they understand workers'
struggles.

In addition, womenpriests believe themselves better suited to combating
clericalism because they are not church dependent, as male priests are. Most
diocesan priests receive a monthly stipend, live in rectories (apartments or houses
located near their church), and use their salary to pay for clothing, groceries,
transportation, and other basic needs. Ordered priests receive food, housing,
transportation, and sometimes clothing. In exchange, male priests make vows
of obedience to a bishop (for diocesan priests) or a superior (for religious orders).
It behooves male priests, then, to stay within the bounds of Catholic polity,
because disobedient or disruptive priests can be disciplined or even lose their
career and economic stability. As Bishop Patricia Fresen wrote, "The financial
dependence of priests upon their bishop or their Order is a very strong aspect of
the power structure of the hierarchical church."[25] As a movement that aims to
avoid hierarchy and its abuses, RCWP casts its independence as a positive part
of its priestly model. A womanpriest cannot lose her livelihood because she has
disobeyed a bishop or branch of the movement.

Yet this freedom comes with a price, literally, because ordained women must
finance their priesthood themselves. Some women are retired and live on pen-
sions or savings. Some receive help from spouses' incomes. Many continue working jobs and holding careers. In this way, womenpriests are akin to male members
of Roman Catholicism's permanent diaconate, whose church work is volunteer
service. Because womenpriests must be financially independent worker priests,
the women often fuse their careers and their ministries.

Without institutional church directives, a womanpriest's ministerial service comes from her own initiative, personal connections, and what she regards as the guidance of the Holy Spirit. Some womenpriests frame this positively as freedom and flexibility, allowing them to take up liberal, progressive causes that diocesan priests do not support. Paradoxically, RCWP's professionalized priesthood reflects the group's "on the margins" status vis-à-vis Rome while revealing the privileges that come from an extra-ecclesiastical position.

Critics have pointed out, however, that the movement's emphasis on well-educated and professionally trained priests limits ordination to women who can afford it. RCWP's high bars for educational degrees might exclude the kinds of marginalized individuals RCWP purports to serve. At a March 2005 conference celebrating the thirtieth anniversary of the Women's Ordination Conference, Marian Ronan, a scholar of contemporary Catholicism, issued a warning to groups like RCWP when she said,

> Catholic faith communities that now ordain women should go out of their way to ordain women—and men—who do not have academic theological training, that is to say, who do not have seminary degrees or even college educations. In saying this, I am echoing the recommendation made by the African American Catholic scholar Sheila Briggs at the WOC conference in Milwaukee in the year 2000. By limiting ordination to those with advanced theological education, we exclude large numbers of God's people who lack the cultural and financial capital to avail themselves of such training. Some of these excluded Catholics will be people of color. In saying this I am not recommending that we stop ordaining people with seminary educations. But it is essential that the Eucharist sometimes be celebrated in Catholic communities by those whom Jesus came to call: the poor and the marginalized.[26]

Ronan's critique asked the women's ordination movement (including RCWP) to widen its vision of social justice concerns to include socioeconomic status, race, and ethnicity. For Ronan, RCWP's brand of social justice was simply too limited.[27] Ronan's warning had merit: RCWP's status on the margins makes the group unable to finance the educations of women who (1) do not already meet the requirements and (2) cannot afford schooling. Here, RCWP's outsider status might prevent the marginalized people RCWP wants to serve from becoming servant priests themselves.

For reasons like those Ronan raised, education and preparation have come to distinguish ARCWP from RCWP-USA. ARCWP tends to ordain women more quickly and without requiring a master's degree or equivalent. As Meehan described it, ARCWP is "flexible about our preparation program and allow[s] equivalences by providing custom design certificates to prepare candidates and provide ongoing education for our ordained members."[28] This suggests that ARCWP shifts the educational burden a bit, away from candidates and onto ARCWP. But not all RCWP members see this positively, and I have heard several women in RCWP-USA express concern that ARCWP is an "ordination factory." What is lost and what is gained in a rigorous preparation program? In a "flexible" program? How do differences between ARCWP and RCWP-USA appeal to different candidates, and how do these differences register with audiences and critics?

RCWP finds itself in a difficult place here. By necessity, it attends to perceptions of professionalism and legitimacy. In this way, RCWP behaves like the cautious career woman (or member of a racial or ethnic minority) who feels she must go above and beyond to prove her aptitude. And she must try even harder when she steps into male-dominated roles. As Roman Catholic priests who are women, RCWP's ordained must contend with gendered assumptions about women as well as traditionally held presumptions about what it means and what it looks like to be a priest. Amid these gender politics, the women's expertise is neither presumed nor honored. RCWP deploys womenpriests' educational merits, then, to demonstrate their competence.[29] But without RCWP-specific seminaries, RCWP cannot train every woman who feels called to ordination. The organization guarantees itself educated, professional pastors but (as yet) cannot open the door for women who cannot afford that credentialing on their own.

And credentialing is important to womenpriests, who wear their educational and career backgrounds as badges of honor that testify to their abilities and work ethic. RCWP thus flips the narrative and trajectory of Roman Catholic priesthood. Unlike young seminarians who discern the ministerial priesthood while working and living alongside like-minded men, the women who go on to be ordained through RCWP see priesthood as the logical next step in their life path.[30] As worker priests, these women find that RCWP priesthood becomes an extension of past ministerial and professional efforts, allowing them to draw deeply from their careers. Womenpriests' backgrounds support their case for priesthood.

Patterns emerge when looking at the women's career histories, which largely fall under education (teaching and administrative), health care / public health, counseling and mental health support, and chaplaincy.[31] My 2014 survey showed that of thirty-four RCWP respondents, seven were in education, elementary through higher education (three as college professors, four on staff or in administration), six worked in mental health fields like psychology or counseling, and two were in chaplaincy. Sixteen—nearly half—were retired or not working other jobs at the time. These patterns show tendencies toward service and healing professions and indicate that womenpriests gravitate toward interpersonal engagement.

In the survey, many womenpriests said their ministries and ministerial service had not changed much since their ordination. Monica Kilburn-Smith's response was fairly common: "Really, [my ministries have] stayed more or less the same. Just more of them."[32] In some ways, being ordained allows womenpriests to do more ministerially: in interviews, I heard about women who perform many more sacraments, who expanded their ministries to include LGBTQ issues, and who negotiate the challenges and shifting dynamics within their worship communities. Furthermore, a large number of women said they do their ministerial actions (such as hospital chaplaincy) without any outward sign of their identity, such as a Roman collar. It seems, then, that for many womenpriests, the point is not to be recognized as ordained; rather, priesthood ministries are often interpersonal and private. RCWP straddles, on the one hand, Mary Hunt's vision of ministry without ordination and, on the other, Rome's mode of ministerial priesthood. What they do ministerially as priests, they often do privately. Many women perform the same services with the same intentionality that they had for decades. Now, though, instead of being called "women religious" or "lay ministers," they are "worker priests."

Here again, time and money enter the equation: being a worker priest can be physically exhausting and economically precarious. Many women must blend their priesthood with a career or part-time job that keeps them financially secure. Here, being outside the church proves difficult. As Elsie McGrath said, "I see myself as a 'parish priest' without the privileges that term implied!"[33] In a similar vein, womanpriest Monica Kilburn-Smith critiqued the worker priest model, which does not provide financial support for ministry per se and is, as a result, "a great recipe for running ourselves into the ground."[34] Womanpriest Ann Penick likewise expressed pragmatic concerns about the worker priest ideal: "My responsibilities have increased, which has put a strain on me trying to juggle a demanding full-time job and also increasingly growing ministerial responsibilities."[35] Some womenpriests admitted having had to let go of some service work because the demands of ordained priesthood taxed their time and emotional resources. Womanpriest Gabriella Velardi Ward was looking forward to retiring from her career in architecture and devoting more time to her ministry, family, and creative projects. It is "hard" to be a worker priest, she pointed out, "living outside the priesthood as well as being responsible for everything else."[36]

How do RCWP's womenpriests compare with Protestant clergywomen, who are salaried? Books like Sarah Sentilles's *A Church of Her Own* remind us that the grass may not simply be greener on the Protestant side. Even in denominations that ordain women, female Protestant ministers face sexism, lower pay than male ministers, impediments to promotion and full-time work, and "sexual harassment, individual discrimination, and systemic discrimination."[37] The authors of another book, called *Clergy Women*, found that, throughout Christian ministry, all too often ordained women are held to a different standard of professional commitment, so that it becomes difficult "for clergy to find sufficient personal, family, or social time away from the demands of the church to enable them to be whole, healthy individuals."[38] Womenpriests share some of these problems that Protestant women have faced for decades.

But according to Sentilles's conclusions, there is good news for Roman Catholic womenpriests. Sentilles's research revealed that many Protestant women in denominations that ordain women internalize sexism as a result of their own personal failings; in contrast, Catholic women believe sexism is "institutional, not individual."[39] Sentilles speculated that Rome's outright rejection of women's ordination unites and inspires Catholic women; Protestant women, however, tend to disregard the systemic challenges and blame themselves. Once again, we see how womenpriests' marginalized position provides unexpected benefits. RCWP's struggles in work-life-ministry balance come not from Rome but are instead typical obstacles, exacerbated by an emerging movement's growing pains. Without having to fight systemic impediments to ordained ministry within a theology that proports to be gender-equal, as Protestant women do, RCWP's womenpriests have more autonomy to establish the terms and conditions by which they minister.

So why does ministry in combination with ordination remain attractive to RCWP's women? What does ordination do for women who already have extensive educations, professional careers, and backgrounds in service? First, the call to priesthood is again important. No longer doing social justice work as a substitute for the priestly role they desire, the women now minister as the priests they believe themselves called to be. Second, ordination legitimizes and professionalizes the ministerial lives they have long held. Now the women can serve others with an additional validating credential. Third, ordination allows the women to stand in a lineage of Roman Catholic servants who have dedicated themselves to living the gospel. For RCWP, all of this happens independent of the institutional church. Being on the margins means the women become priests, but not institutional representatives.

Ecumenism and Affirmation outside the Church

With no affirmation from Rome, womenpriests seek validation outside the church. Many interfaith and reform groups have supported RCWP over the years, including independent Catholics, Protestants, and non-Christians. From the margins, womenpriests can forge alliances with groups and individuals that Rome cannot. These relationships arise from necessity yet give RCWP ecumenical opportunities. Cooperative interfaith work is integral to RCWP's ministerial priesthood: RCWP's candidates rely on ordained and unordained people outside of Roman Catholicism to model, affirm, and encourage their journey toward ordination, and womenpriests weave ecumenical partnerships into their pastoral outreach and social activism. Seeing itself as marginalized by Rome, RCWP cultivates partnerships with other religious groups that Rome sees as outside the "one true Church."[40] RCWP publicizes its cooperation with interfaith groups and suggests that other Christian groups find value in ordaining female candidates, even though Rome does not. In doing so, RCWP uses non-Catholic support to argue for Catholic women's ordination.

The Roman Catholic Church has a mixed history with ecumenism. While publicly embracing the idea of "church unity," Rome insists that unity will be accomplished when all Christian churches unite (or *re*unite, in Vatican parlance) with Rome. The Roman Catholic Church was slow to participate in twentieth-century ecumenical activity and is conspicuously absent from the World Council of Churches, which comprises nearly 350 Christian groups worldwide. Vatican II and *Lumen Gentium* softened Rome's recalcitrance somewhat, and yet Rome's professed willingness to engage in ecumenical and interfaith dialogue has not led to structural or doctrinal changes. A 1995 book calling Rome to greater ecumenical efforts bemoaned the fact that, even thirty years after Vatican II, the Roman church remained "ecumenically aloof and immobile."[41] Women's ordination is a particular sticking point between Rome and other faiths, especially the Anglican Communion: as I mentioned in an earlier chapter, the Episcopal Church's decision to ordain women in the 1970s led to a heated exchange between Catholic and Episcopal leaders; more recently, the Vatican has invited Anglicans unhappy about women's ordination to transfer seamlessly to Roman Catholicism, in a structure called the "ordinariate" (or "Personal Ordinariate"). Although Rome likes to position itself as open to ecumenical exchanges, its self-appointed status as the single "true" church often precludes its full partnership.[42]

Protestant ways of envisioning and embodying ministry have influenced and inspired some of RCWP's women. Take, for example, Iris Müller, one of the Danube Seven and an RCWP founding mother. Born Protestant, Müller studied theology in Germany and qualified for ordination in her local Protestant church. Yet Roman Catholicism's sacraments and global community drew her in, and she converted. But once she became Catholic, Müller became, in her words, "a creature incapable of receiving Holy Orders." As she continued her theological studies at a Catholic university in Münster, she said, "the professors and most of the students expected me to simply accept the position of women in the Church without further question. But I decided to be faithful to my conviction, and to my call to ordination. So, as a former Protestant theologian, I [gave] witness that women were discriminated against in the Catholic Church and that their inferior status had to be reformed."[43] Müller joined forces with German academic Ida Raming, and the two became theological pioneers for the women's ordination movement.

Like Müller, several of RCWP's women were not born Catholic. Dana Reynolds, who was RCWP's first North American bishop, converted to Catholicism from Episcopalianism in 1999. Womanpriest Jane Via, ordained alongside Reynolds in Pittsburgh, Pennsylvania, in 2006, converted to Catholicism as a teenager. Womanpriest Alice Iaquinta was raised Evangelical Lutheran but became Catholic amid the hope and change of Vatican II. Discouraged at times, she "periodically gave up" on the Roman church. Yet while praying with the Quakers in 1994, she felt "the Spirit" nudging her: "It's time to go home," back to Catholicism. She was ordained a womanpriest thirteen years later.[44] Elsie McGrath converted to Catholicism at age seventeen when she married her Roman Catholic husband. Womanpriest Rose Marie Hudson long felt called to ministry in her Methodist tradition. She applied and was accepted into the formation program—but then her husband decided he wanted to become Catholic. Hudson then embarked on a prayer retreat where, like Iaquinta, she heard the Spirit: "You've been a Protestant for 38 years. Now you will become a Catholic and see what that faith community is like. Later you'll be a catalyst to help bring the whole church back together again."[45] Stories like these, conspicuous in the women's autobiographical statements, suggest a possible mutual transformation: just as the women themselves converted from Protestant to Catholic, they envision themselves as able to "convert" Roman Catholicism through their progressive stance on women's ordination. Because ordination was possible for these women before they were Catholic, they believe it should be possible for them now. Iron-ically, then, some of the Protestant groups that resulted from Martin Luther's breaking away from Rome five hundred years ago are now, in the twenty-first century, inspiring RCWP's women to break away from Catholic prohibitions of women's ordination.

Most womenpriests have stories of non-Catholics naming and affirming their calls to ministry, and they all say that these encounters intensified their commit-ment to Roman Catholicism. Instead of leaving the Roman church for a tradi-tion that would ordain them, RCWP's women take the Protestant affirmation they receive back to their Roman Catholic tradition. As womenpriests tell these stories, they argue that faithful, pastoral people affirm Catholic women's calls to ministry, even if Rome refuses to see it.

Womenpriests seem to relish the opportunity to talk about the ecumenical support they receive. Even though Rome is infinitely more powerful than the small RCWP movement, non-Catholic communities endorsing RCWP can undermine Rome's claims to superiority and uphold RCWP's argument that documents like *Inter Insigniores*, parts of canon law, and the 2008 decree of excommunication are merely man-made (read: Rome-made, patriarchy-made) laws lacking the fullness of religious truth. RCWP's ecumenical support even makes the Catholic patriarchy appear out of touch with fellow Christians. For womenpriests, when it comes to women's ordination, the higher law is not the Roman Catholic hierarchy but rather God's call, the Spirit's work, and the vi-sion of non-Catholics who honor a womanpriest's vocation. Ousted by Roman Catholicism, RCWP aligns with other traditions—not to adopt their religious beliefs, but to build partnerships. Wanting legitimacy, RCWP solicits and re-ceives help from other professional ministers and practicing Christians. Such support from outside the church—both a necessity and an opportunity—hap-pens because RCWP is "on the margins," and marginalization opens doors to extra-Catholic partnerships.

Covert or Controversial: Advocacy from Male Priests

Rome will not support RCWP, but some Roman Catholic male priests have come to womenpriests' aid. RCWP would not exist without the help of male prelates: because the group insists on being in the line of apostolic succession, male bishops had to ordain the Danube Seven in order to start the movement. Support from Catholic priests has continued in the forms of public arguments for women's ordination, sacramental training, and spiritual direction. This work is risky, for ordained men who support RCWP risk excommunication or laicization.

Several womenpriests are married to Roman Catholic priests who left the priesthood in order to marry. These men have little to lose from disobeying the Vatican.[46] When I inquired about influences from priest mentors, womanpriest Mary Theresa Streck mentioned her husband, Jay, "by far the most extraordinary mentor," whom she met when she was with the Sisters of St. Joseph and he was a priest in the Albany diocese. They married in 1984 and "continued a ministry to the impoverished in a housing project in Troy, New York."[47] Former Jesuit Don Cordero mentored his wife, Juanita, as well as Kathleen Kunster and Victoria Rue. Rue described Cordero as a "very progressive thinker about the priesthood," adding that by working together, "we taught each other about a reimagined priesthood."[48] Until he died from prostate cancer in 2007, Don and Juanita celebrated sacraments together, including a Mass in honor of their wedding anniversary.[49] Before their wives pursued illicit ordination, these men modeled a liminal priesthood state, wherein they were indelibly marked as priests yet were not functioning as priests.

Though not affiliated with the institutional church, the groups CORPUS and the Federation of Christian Ministries (FCM) champion the sacraments, pastoral care, and preaching, and they form alliances with women's ordination activists like those in RCWP. Started in 1974, CORPUS is a Catholic reform group "promoting an expanded and renewed priesthood of married and single men and women."[50] The FCM evolved out of the Society of Priests for a Free Ministry, which was the United States' first association of married priests and came from a post–Vatican II movement calling for clerical celibacy to be optional.[51] CORPUS and FCM members include married priests and their wives, as well as a smaller number of male priests involved in canonical service. In 2004 the wives of these married priests called on their husbands to "do something" to support women's ordination. Collaborations among the FCM, CORPUS, Women's Ordination Conference, and the emerging RCWP movement led to a sacramental mentorship program whereby RCWP candidates partner with a priest mentor. Some womenpriests, like Marie David and Jean Marchant, chose to work with their husbands.[52] A new, formal group took shape, called the National Catholic Ministries Alliance (NCMA), which sought to cultivate an "inclusive priesthood" (referring to gender and marital state) by "promoting the grassroots re-formation of ministries in the Roman Catholic Church."[53] As part of NCMA, mentors might offer spiritual direction, liturgical instruction, or sacramental modeling. Embodied practices of sacraments and liturgies cannot

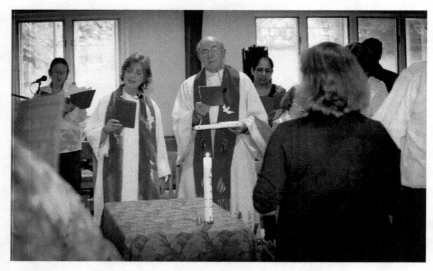

Womanpriest (now bishop, as of 2019) Jean Marchant and her husband, ordained Roman Catholic priest Ron Hindelang, concelebrate the Eucharist at Spirit of Life Community in Weston, Massachusetts, in May 2010. (Photograph by Judith Levitt.)

be easily learned from a book or assigned essay, and male priests' expert feedback has helped prepare RCWP's women for priesthood.

Womenpriests do work with practicing priests in good standing with the church, but they are understandably reluctant to give specifics about these mentoring relationships. I asked about priest mentors in the 2014 survey I conducted. Nearly all respondents talked about mentors but asked that I keep any identifying information in strict confidence. Womenpriests talked about help from male priests they had known for years and male priests they met only through RCWP. Some talked about guidance from religious brothers and women religious as well as male priests. Many talked about specific aid from their male priest mentors, such as teaching them to preside at sacraments, discussing liturgy, and identifying and meeting the community's needs. Some mentioned help from CORPUS. It was not uncommon that a womanpriest prepared a ceremony and "performed" it for a former priest, who could give "advice and pointers."[54]

RCWP uses these examples to demonstrate that Catholicism's problem is not individual men but rather a patriarchal system that privileges power over egalitarian decision-making. Womenpriests benefit from the men's support, in terms of liturgical and sacramental logistics, validation of call, and the ability to say that someone "within the system" is on their side. RCWP's women know male priests who encourage women's ordination but are afraid to act on their beliefs. Because priests are structurally dependent upon the institution, male priests have much to lose by supporting RCWP and the women's ordination movement. Speaking about a priest she knew personally, womanpriest Monica Kilburn-Smith described a man who "came out" in favor of women's ordination and was subsequently removed. He later recanted in order to get his career back. "The church has 'em by the balls," Kilburn-Smith said pointedly, "and if . . . the church squeezes, it hurts."[55]

Public punishments of male priests who endorse women's ordination are rare, but the examples of Ed Cachia and Roy Bourgeois show what consequences can befall priests who publicly support womenpriests. A parish priest in Ontario, Canada, Cachia said in 2005 that he hoped the upcoming St. Lawrence Seaway ordinations would mark "the beginning of a new and awesome change in the life of the church."[56] Cachia's bishop, Nicola De Angelis, required Cachia to retract his support of women's ordination. Until he did so, De Angelis said, Cachia would be removed from the rectory, suspended from public ministry, and given a reduced salary. Cachia did not recant and was dismissed from priesthood and excommunicated in 2006.[57]

According to Rome, Roy Bourgeois "excommunicated himself" in August 2008 when he attended, concelebrated, and delivered a homily at the ordination of Janice Sevre-Duszynska, his friend and fellow activist.[58] Bourgeois and Sevre-Duszynska had worked alongside each other for years as part of School of the Americas Watch, a grassroots organization Bourgeois started in 1990 to protest human rights abuses by the US government in Latin America.[59] But it was his activism supporting women's ordination that threatened his priesthood. Bourgeois's Maryknoll community stood by him as he continued to serve and minister as a priest in spite of the excommunication. Together with Dominican priest and canon lawyer Tom Doyle, who worked on his behalf, Bourgeois argued that he had a right to hold and voice opinions different from Rome's teachings. Nonetheless, Bourgeois was "canonically dismissed" from the Maryknoll Fathers and Brothers and laicized. The Congregation for the Doctrine of the Faith issued a press release about his dismissal on November 19, 2012, saying that Bourgeois refused to recant his position and reconcile with the church. Instead, "Mr. Bourgeois chose to campaign against the teachings of the Catholic Church in secular and non-Catholic venues. This was done without the permission of the local U.S. Catholic Bishops and while ignoring the sensitivities of the faithful across the country. Disobedience and preaching against the teaching of the Catholic Church about women's ordination led to his excommunication, dismissal and laicization."[60] This statement highlights the institutional church's problems with Bourgeois: disobedience, not securing bishops' permission before speaking, participating in public discourse about women's ordination, and talking about Roman teachings outside of Roman church venues. As a priest structurally within the Roman Catholic mainstream and not on the margins, he could not dissent publicly and keep his priesthood.

When Rome publicly punishes men like Bourgeois and Cachia, RCWP can spin the Vatican's reaction into a systemic critique of patriarchy, wherein a church that purports to follow Christ turns against its faithful servants. Additionally, priests who stand in favor of womenpriests, either publicly, as Bourgeois and Cachia did, or covertly, draw on the same language of "conscience" and "call" as RCWP's women, challenging Rome's ban on womenpriests using Rome's own words. Responding to his excommunication and explaining why he did not retract his support for ordaining women, Cachia wrote,

> Many have suggested to me "is it not worth a white lie for the sake of all the good work you will do[?"] As much as I would have liked to take the easy way out I could not. My statements that the Church should speak respectfully and should re-establish dialogue with women who are called to ordination are what I believe to be true. . . . The choice I was given was to lie to the people, or lose my position in the Church. . . . I lost everything my home, my job, my benefits, my pension, my security, but Jesus called us to stand by our convictions even to the point of suffering.[61]

Rhetorically suggesting a parallel between Jesus's willingness to suffer and Cachia's punishment for holding fast to his beliefs, Cachia cast the institutional church as dangerously shortsighted for silencing someone who is speaking his truth. To force him to recant would be to force him to lie, and Cachia positioned himself as a principled actor refusing to bow to such pressure. He would not and could not suggest that women who feel called to ordination are not called.

Bourgeois did something similar in a 2008 letter to the CDF regarding his excommunication, in which he used historical parallels to set himself against Rome. Like Cachia, he said he could not recant his support of women's ordination—because of his conscience. "Conscience is very sacred. Conscience gives us a sense of right and wrong and urges us to do the right thing. . . . Conscience is what compelled Rosa Parks to say she could no longer sit in the back of the bus. Conscience is what compels women in our Church to say they cannot be silent and deny their call from God to the priesthood. . . . And after much prayer, reflection and discernment, it is my conscience that compels me to do the right thing. I cannot recant my belief and public statements that support the ordination of women in our Church."[62] Bourgeois noted that he himself felt called to priesthood, and he could not tell a woman that his call was valid while hers was not. And as he understood it, to support these women was to honor his conscience, which was a more righteous demand than following the Roman church's rules, which he believed to be wrong.

With their performance of priestly dissent, these men drew a distinction between the Catholic Church and Catholic values, between obedience and conscience. Like RCWP, they talk about emulating Christ even at the expense of Roman Catholic laws. Because these priests had served the church for decades, they could not readily be dismissed as anti-Catholic radicals opposed to Rome's teachings, as the womenpriests were. With their actions, the men moved to the margins with the womenpriests, occupying a place they believed was faithfully Catholic and Christlike, in spite of Rome's determination otherwise.

Is RCWP unconsciously deferring to male priests' authority, thereby replicating the power dynamics they are trying to overturn? Or is RCWP's dependence on male priests a temporary, transitional necessity governed by the group's determination to have legitimacy and validity? RCWP's celebrated public relationships with some male priests, practicing and former, goads some observers who think the womenpriests rely too much on male priests to affirm their calls and strengthen their requests for gender-inclusive priesthood. It might seem the womenpriests are letting the men fight their battles. Consider: the movement depended on male bishops for its first ordinations in Europe, promoted and hosted Bourgeois's North American speaking engagements on the topic of women's ordination, and continues to draw on male priests' connections and expertise to prepare women for priesthood. RCWP's website features a short film called *Standing on the Shoulders* that is introduced with a paragraph that includes this statement of gratitude: "We are especially thankful for Fr Roy Bourgeois, Fr Bill Brennan, theologian Elizabeth Johnson and the many others who have risked so much to support the women's ordination movement."[63] Bourgeois's photograph has been featured on ARCWP's website with a reference to his "courageous" stance on women's ordination.[64] Invoking male priests' names and reputations can help capture an audience that would otherwise dismiss the women altogether. Having Bourgeois as an ally, for instance, is a boon for RCWP: a "genuine American Catholic hero," he is an incredibly well-known presence in Catholic social justice and is something of a present-day Daniel Berrigan.[65] If, as marginalized figures in the Roman Catholic Church, RCWP's women are powerless to have their voices heard or their calls validated, it makes sense to marshal all the support possible.

Yet by using men, womenpriests affirm priestly power, which is a distinctly male-gendered power. In spite of efforts to break down the lay-clergy divide and empower womenpriests, a reliance on male priests within the system belies the women's desire for self-sufficiency. Womenpriests may stand on the margins, but the importance they place on male priests raises the question: Are womenpriests standing beside powerful male prelates, making them their allies, or behind male prelates, making them their shields?

Conclusions: Freedom from Control, Opportunity to Change

Womenpriests' ministries include the women's relationships, worship communities, social justice activism, ecumenical connections, professional backgrounds, and credentialed service as priests. On the margins, womenpriests are unencumbered by Roman dictates. RCWP's priesthood thus becomes one of creativity and experimentation. Not relegated to silence or solitude, RCWP has found power on the margins. The margins have become a place of opportunity, community, and social justice. As a result of RCWP's ecumenical and interfaith work, the movement can rent or borrow locations—often in Protestant churches—for ordinations or weekly liturgies. The womenpriests can and do partner with progressive churches and DignityUSA (an organization for gay and lesbian Catholics) on issues like gay rights. In sum, womenpriests experience a freedom in their marginal state that surpasses the autonomy of male priests.

RCWP's women also fare better than many ordained Protestant women, who, in spite of denominational approval for their ministerial career, still face countless challenges. When womenpriests are placed alongside the Protestant clergywomen Sentilles researched, it becomes clear that RCWP's women paradoxically benefit from their outsider status. Whereas Protestant women must work with congregants who are not ready for a woman's authority, womenpriests attract individuals who are predisposed to accepting women as religious leaders and thereby avoid overt sexism and distrust from the people in their own worship communities and ministerial circles.[66]

The issue that has most riled RCWP's critics comes from RCWP's use of "margins" language that overlooks the nuances of race, class, and regionalism. Bourgeois and RCWP's members and supporters have compared RCWP's *contra legem* actions to the protests of civil rights activists like Rosa Parks.[67] Likewise, South African RCWP bishop Patricia Fresen has compared RCWP's strategy of breaking unjust laws to her and other activists' antiapartheid work in the 1970s.[68] Scholar Marian Ronan criticized RCWP for appropriating the civil rights language of black South Africans and African Americans and rejected the comparison of race-based suffering and "the exclusion from ordination of Roman Catholic women with graduate-level training in theology and pastoral studies."[69] She further called upon RCWP to consider the gap between Catholics in the Global North and in the Global South, thus questioning the need to bring "highly educated, Euroamerican women into the leadership class of the Roman Catholic Church."[70] In light of Ronan's concerns, RCWP's commitment to ordain educated, professionally polished, ministerially adept women could potentially drive a wedge between marginalized types: women marginalized by the church because of their gender, and individuals marginalized by society because of race, socioeconomics, or nationality.

Is RCWP's claim to marginality a rhetorical strategy aimed at bolstering support while deriding the Vatican's male decision-makers? Is it an oversight that reflects the womenpriests' second-wave-feminist focus on equal rights for women, with a secondary regard for mitigating racial, ethnic, and economic discrimination? Considering the RCWP movement's size and educational diversity—which is significant even given the womenpriests' demographic similarities—it is impossible to generalize here, as each individual has different backgrounds and understandings. The womenpriests are indeed committed to social justice ministries and reaching people on the margins; to date, many—though certainly not all—of those marginalized people look similar to the womenpriests in terms of skin color and economic privilege. It makes sense that an emerging movement like RCWP would start with familiar territory and spread out from there; just as womenpriests build on their past professional and ministerial experiences, they see most clearly the injustices they themselves have faced. Still, RCWP may want to soften or at least add nuance to this language, especially when the movement's public face is that of (seemingly) white, well-educated, professionally accomplished woman.

To be sure, gender identity is not a privilege women have ever enjoyed within the Roman Catholic Church. Throughout its history, the church has said that women were not made in God's image (Tertullian), that women need men to dominate them (Augustine), that women lack intellect and reason (Aquinas). As much as the modern Roman church seeks to argue for equality amid difference, in language reminiscent of *Plessy v. Ferguson*'s "separate but equal," women have been created by and within a religious system that says they cannot image Christ in sacramental, priestly performance. Regardless of the ways they seek to

reform the priesthood, they are always at risk of being viewed as either panto-
miming male priesthood or simply adding women to priesthood "and stirring."
But womenpriests believe—and the ordination movement depends on their
belief—that women minister differently, celebrate sacraments differently, and
image Christ differently. RCWP says that womenpriests can serve in ways male
priests cannot—not least because male priests live in male bodies, with all of
the privilege and power that come with the male gender. All the more reason,
then, that they view their female bodies as bringing something new, something
essential, something that has long been missing from the Roman Catholic ministerial priesthood.

CHAPTER 7

Womenpriests' Bodies *in Persona Christi*

CATHOLICISM PLACES BODIES AT the center of the worship experience, from Christ's battered body hanging on the crucifix to statues of Mary cradling an infant Jesus, from stained-glass images of saints and scripture to holy relics of bone encased in altar tables, from the smells of incense and candles to the sounds of organs and hymns. The Catholic tradition disciplines believers' bodies with sacramentals (like genuflecting or making the sign of the cross) and rituals (like receiving Communion, attending liturgy, or confessing sins). The Roman Catholic Church further disciplines bodies by limiting permissible sexual behavior (forbidden outside of heterosexual marriage), drawing firm boundaries around procreation (as the primary purpose of sexual intercourse, not to be impeded by birth control), and forbidding homosexuality (as "intrinsically disordered" and "contrary to the natural law"[1]). Roman Catholicism imprints itself on the bodies of the faithful.

Catholic women's bodies have their own symbolic significance, especially when paired with church teachings on essential women's roles. For much of the twentieth century, the "eternal woman" ideal told American Catholic women that they should aspire to be humble, tender, and pious. Ubiquitous in books and Catholic magazines, the "eternal woman" language said that it was "every woman's duty to sacrifice her body, her will, her work, even her personality, for the sake of her family and the kingdom of God."[2] She was a virtuous archetype of selflessness and surrender. By negating herself, she transcended time and place to benefit humankind. Symbolically, she represented not Christ's atoning sacrifice but rather the Virgin Mary's acceptance of God's will.

Womenpriests know well Catholicism's fixation on bodies. Canadian womanpriest Monica Kilburn-Smith told me during a phone interview that Catholic priesthood was "all about the penis"—that is, what men anatomically possess that women do not. For Kilburn-Smith, RCWP did the invaluable work of putting women into the roles, postures, and poses of the traditionally male-only

priesthood. Kilburn-Smith experienced apostolic succession and priestly vestments as theologically relevant parts of the Roman Catholic "visual vernacular."
"Women are the face of the divine, too," she explained passionately, and when
a woman sees a womanpriest at the altar, "it's not just you seeing me—it's you
seeing *you*."[3]

Baltimore-area womanpriest Gloria Carpeneto has also thought a lot about
bodies. Decades before being ordained, she worked as a certified massage thera-
pist and found that during massage, female clients would open up about deeply
personal and spiritual matters. Carpeneto speculated that physical touch put
the women emotionally in touch with their bodies and spiritual selves. In the
1990s, Carpeneto wrote a doctoral dissertation exploring women and embodied
spirituality in active and inactive Catholic women. Her research revealed that as
women aged, they shed feelings of shame and discomfort, often stemming from
church teachings, and instead embraced their physicality. This underscored for
Carpeneto how important it is for Catholic women to embrace the gift of embodiment. Once ordained, Carpeneto remained conscious of her body: when
standing before the congregation, she would hold her arms in a way that was
more circular than angular, so as to create a welcoming and inclusive pose. She
explained to me—in a twist on Marshall McLuhan's oft-cited phrase—"Your
body is the medium, and the medium is the message."[4]

These womenpriests' reflections highlight ways that Roman Catholicism
speaks not just through scripture and tradition but also, powerfully, through
indelible, visual, embodied symbols. These symbols allow Roman Catholicism
to constitute and discipline bodies—typically based on traditional gender roles.
And these symbolically enforced gender categories help the Vatican argue that
men are suitable "matter" for priestly ordination and women are not.[5]

The Roman Catholic Church has constituted a male priesthood through
centuries of repeat performances. With men's bodies the only "matter" deemed
appropriate for priesthood, women's bodies get cast as distinct, different, and
otherwise suited. Gendered priesthood is, thus, iterative—or an "action of gender [that] requires a performance that is repeated."[6] As men perform priesthood,
century after century, in one location after another, the very ideas of priests and
priesthood become discursively produced. Male bodies play the role of priest,
thus casting the male body as the only suitable matter for Catholic priesthood
and sacramental facilitation. Yet as the idea of iterability helps us see, new possibilities emerge in repeated performances. As symbols of social justice, agents
of active resistance against an all-male priesthood, and interventions into the
meaning of Jesus, womenpriests' bodies—including their gestures, actions, and

An RCWP deacon distributes Communion. Seeing ordained women wearing vestments, stoles, and wedding rings is a common occurrence at RCWP Masses. (Photograph by Judith Levitt.)

symbolic meanings—become theologically and materially important. Women-priests reinform Catholic stereotypes of bodies both female and ordained.

Pairing my ethnographic observations of womenpriests' bodies in action (e.g., what they wear, where they stand, how they relate physically to worshippers and sacraments) with womenpriests' self-disclosures about gender and embodied performances reveals how womenpriests create gendered, embodied priesthood. Womenpriests resist the construction of priests-as-male by offering their priesthood as female bodies in action: laying prostrate during the litany of saints in an ordination ceremony; becoming vested in familiar clerical garments; raising their arms, hands, and voices over the Eucharist; pouring water on children being baptized. Womenpriests provoke, prod, and push existing Catholic theological anthropology and teachings on gender complementarity. Women-priests have the ability to destabilize Catholic priesthood and newly inscribe the relationship between gender and ordained Catholic authority. Womenpriests' self-construction as Roman Catholic (women)priests commences with the matter of their bodies *doing*. In contrast to priesthood as a sacramentally made, sacred identity, a focus on bodies shows how priesthood is a construction, replayed time and again in performances of priesthood.

Dressing the Part:
Clerical Vestments and Roman Collars

Between hypersexualized media depictions of women, appearance-driven crit-icisms of female public figures, and fixation on a woman's age, when a woman steps into public view, her body and—all too often by extension—her very worth become vulnerable to critique and judgment. The identity and appearance of a priest carries assumptions as well. In traditional Catholic iconography, "priest" equals "male." The quintessential Roman Catholic priest—always a he—wears an alb, chasuble, and stole when saying Mass and a black shirt and Roman collar outside of Mass. He is authority. In sum, ideas of both women and Roman Catholic priests are fraught with social expectations and cultural baggage.

A womanpriest, combining the categories of female and priest, thus carries others' expectations in her body, gestures, and dress. She cannot escape interpre-tation and critique. She is symbol and signifying agent. As a woman, she is read-ily sexualized: she may be celibate or married, she may or may not have children and grandchildren, but either way, it matters. She defies the Roman Catholic institution by stepping into its most sacred, sacramental role. Sometimes she wears vestments and even a Roman collar, and thereby looks the part of "priest," and sometimes she rejects clothing that would signify her clerical status. What-ever she does, someone somewhere will say she is performing her gender or her priesthood—or both—incorrectly.

As a result, the way womenpriests dress presents opportunity and danger. RCWP explores and sometimes exploits this, both consciously and uncon-sciously troubling the singular association between "male" and "Roman Cath-olic clerical vestments." If the public will read women's bodies anyway, drawing meaning from the position and display of those bodies, and foist meaning upon female bodies, then RCWP has the ability to use clothing, vestments, and the Roman collar to recast the role of priest.

Womenpriests like Elsie McGrath know this all too well, which is why Mc-Grath wears a T-shirt that reads, "This is what a woman priest looks like!"[7] Her casual shirt allows her to playfully challenge the male-only priesthood in less-formal environments, like a grocery store or restaurant, and invites people reading her shirt (and thus her body) to rethink their image of a Roman Catholic priest. The womenpriests' bodies take part in a resignification process that chan-nels RCWP's desire for a reformed Roman Catholic priesthood into public dis-course, all the while suggesting that women can and do embody the priestly role.

Formal clerical dress lets womenpriests communicate their identities without words. But RCWP's women and their observers debate whether womenpriests should wear stereotypical priestly clothing, since clerical vestments and the Roman collar can symbolize patriarchy and kyriarchy. Womenpriests struggle to decide how and why to be recognized as Roman Catholic priests, lest their clothing signal the clericalism the movement seeks to avoid. Should transgressive womenpriests dress like traditional male priests in order to facilitate a symbol shift that begins inviting new mental pictures of the quintessential Catholic priest? Or do womenpriests dressed like familiar Catholic priests problematically replicate the kyriarchical structures they seek to overturn?

Especially in the early years, RCWP faced criticisms connected to vestments. Longtime women's ordination activist Mary Byrne expressed concern in a 2006 editorial for *Equal wRites* (a regional Women's Ordination Conference publication) responding to RCWP's Pittsburgh ordinations. Byrne affirmed the womenpriests' "resemblance to Jesus" but startled at the visual of priestly multitudes, especially around the Eucharist table. Byrne wrote that she and another ordination attendee exchanged "sad glances" and whispered, "It's still the same priestly caste." Byrne argued that women must not simply don the emperor's (that is, male priests') clothes.[8] Byrne's problem with the Pittsburgh ordination was that it included vestments, and her concern was exacerbated by sacramental gestures. Particularly jarring were the dozens of ordained women gathered around the altar table, in a festive spirit, with no unordained laity in sight. What RCWP likely intended as a celebratory moment with power in numbers was interpreted, by Byrne at least, as a triumphant show of kyriarchical power.

What, then, should a renewed Roman church and a renewed Roman priesthood look like? How can a woman be a priest in ways that are not merely iterative of men while adopting the clothing signifiers that signal her priesthood? For Byrne and others, seeing a group of women at the altar table, wearing vestments and saying the words of consecration, read as women replicating the clerical hierarchy. The issue of audience comes into play here. If RCWP's women are heralding their priesthood to church patriarchs who deny their calling and their priesthood, showing scores of women in albs and stoles and chasubles communicates a provocative message. If, however, RCWP is nodding to feminist theologians who have long called for the end of the lay-clergy divide, such staged photo opportunities seem in poor taste.

RCWP launches these critiques upon itself from time to time, leading womenpriests to thoughtful and diverse approaches to questions of clerical dress.

For instance, when saying liturgy, the women nearly always wear a stole—but sometimes they pair the stole with an alb, and sometimes also with a cincture. Some womenpriests dress more formally on holidays like Christmas or Easter, and some wear more vestments for Masses in churches than Masses in homes. Bridget Mary Meehan, a bishop, wears a stole when presiding at liturgy but wears vestments when she is ordaining.[9] Some women wear an alb and stole for liturgy and a stole alone for anointings or the sacrament of reconciliation. In a statement revealing that womenpriests try to be aware of the situation and the needs and expectations of the people they serve, womanpriest Debra Meyers said, "It depends. Sometimes I wear an alb, chasuble and stole. Other times I wear just a stole. It depends on what the group or individual needs."[10] Similarly, Meehan wrote that she had allowed the community with which she celebrates to determine whether or not she wears liturgical vestments, thereby sharing decision-making authority with the laity in her worship community.[11] Other womenpriests provide simple vestments for their community members to wear. Womanpriest Mary Theresa Streck explained, "I wear a stole and I have a bucket of stoles that I pass out to anyone who wants to wear one."[12] Womanpriest Victoria Rue mentioned a similar practice: for liturgy, she wears "a stole, but then everyone else wears a stole, too."[13]

These practices reveal that womenpriests try to avoid the pitfalls of "adding women and stirring." While the movement has not arrived at a uniform solution, the women have felt empowered to personalize their clothing practices. Streck and Rue try to eliminate the lay-clergy divide by providing stoles for everyone at liturgy. All worshippers' bodies, then, and not just the ordained's, wear the stole, which is a visible symbol of holy orders. In this way, the stole does not distinguish the ordained but becomes a marker of shared authority. Meehan's decision to let her community determine her level of dress reveals deference to unordained worshippers. In these ways, womenpriests attempt to use liturgical dress to mark ordained and unordained bodies as equal before God.

RCWP's ordained women also debate what to wear *outside* of liturgies, and most contention centers on the Roman collar. Many womenpriests oppose the collar, reading it as the height of the kind of clericalism that Catholic feminists condemn. In lieu of the collar, womenpriests find other ways to signal their priesthood. Many wear small RCWP pins or the ARCWP logo pendant. Womanpriest Monica Kilburn-Smith will often wear "cross necklaces of various kinds—as do other Catholics and Christians," suggesting her concern with being like the people.[14] Womanpriest Debra Meyers explained, "Since we generally frown upon wearing collars I find that wearing a large (6″) cross lets people know they can approach me concerning spiritual matters."[15] Meyers wanted to be sure she could be recognized so she could serve pastorally, but the Roman collar—which would definitely signal her ordination—was unacceptable to her, given its history.

Yet some womenpriests have worn and do wear the collar. Former RCWP bishop Dana Reynolds reported that people perceived and treated her differently when she wore the collar, even when she was driving in her car. She conceded that there could be value in the collar—primarily in being identifiable as a minister—but overall, Reynolds found the collar to be "a wall" dividing priest and layperson.[16] When we talked, womanpriest Mary Ann Schoettly had worn the collar only twice. One instance made her very uncomfortable, because she felt it was too "showy" and not about ordination at all. The second instance—during a demonstration for women's ordination—felt "very appropriate [and] made a statement that could not have been made otherwise."[17] Some womenpriests reject the collar outright while others use it selectively. In the 2014 survey I conducted, which came nearly a decade into RCWP's presence in North America, all but one woman who wore the collar said, with something of a disclaimer, that they only did so on certain occasions for very specific reasons. Womanpriest Wanda Russell said she wore a collar "ONLY when a special event is happening,"[18] and womanpriest Beverly Bingle explained that she would wear the collar in "very few instances," only "when I'm officially participating in some activity where it is useful to communicate a Roman Catholic presence," such as a demonstration against war or the death penalty or when there will be television coverage.[19] These womenpriests know that the Roman collar can communicate powerful messages, and they have learned through their priesthood to control the messages their clothing can send.

Questions of audience are again important here. Responding to my question about how, if at all, she signals her priestly identity, Elsie McGrath offered the following: "I have no need to signal I am ordained unless I am taking public part in a peaceful demonstration or ecumenical service of some kind that involves clergy of all denominations, in which case I wear either a Roman collar or a stole."[20] An unnamed womanpriest shared something similar, saying that she did not dress to stand out as a priest "unless the event(s) I'm attending need me to be singled out as a clergy, like the gay pride parade. I will then [wear] a black shirt and white tabbed [Roman] collar."[21] Other women echoed this need to dress like a priest when contending with social justice concerns. Ann Penick wore the clerical collar for "special occasions, such as the Unity Walk in Washington, DC, to commemorate 9/11." She went even further, though, and

sometimes would wear it to Masses when there were many children in attendance, because "that's what these children identify as priest. It's about meeting
them where they are."[22] As priests, the women seemed ready to reflect on the
relationship among their bodies, their dress, and their movement's reform goals.
As women in a culture that patrols women's bodies, womenpriests are sensitive
to what their bodies and clothing communicate—about themselves, their movement, and their Catholic faith.

When womenpriests wear the Roman collar or stoles and albs at public functions, they give Roman Catholicism a particular interfaith or social justice presence—and often support causes that go against the Roman church's messaging.
For example, myriad womenpriests participate in gay pride events and affiliate
with local Dignity chapters (a reform group supporting gay and lesbian Catholics) or Metropolitan Community Churches (or MCC, an open-Communion
worship community providing sanctuary and welcome for LGBTQ persons).[23]
When womenpriests appear in public, dressed to be recognized as priests, they are
deliberately performing a liberative, feminist theological approach to certain social
issues. Their embodied presence offers Roman Catholic support—not with formal
institutional decrees, but with priestly participation. When womanpriest Janice
Sevre-Duszynska marched and protested as part of the School of the Americas
Watch—sometimes in her alb and cincture, sometimes in a simple priestly stole—
she brought a feminine priestly persona to the demonstration. Marching alongside
male priests as well as laity, she displayed commitment to her own understanding
of Catholic values.[24] Her marching delivered a twofold meaning: she called Catholics' attention to abuses surrounding the School of the Americas, and she physically
declared, "Ordained women are here." Her dress communicated both priesthood
and Catholic social activism, with an important tension: she pushed against certain Roman Catholic teachings (that women cannot be ordained) while upholding fundamental teachings about social justice. Likewise, when she donned an
alb and cincture and witnessed for women's ordination at national bishops' meetings, her small frame and simple attire offered a striking contrast to the ordained
men's more ornate and authoritative ways of being clergy. Because of the contrast
between her body and theirs, Sevre-Duszynska's priestly presence stood out. She
invited audiences to read her body as simultaneously asking, "What would Jesus
do?" and answering, "He would be standing here, with me."

Womanpriest Marie David was quick to explain that she did not believe
vestments *made* her a priest, but that, importantly, they helped her to be *seen*
as a priest. Clothing and dress are part of the liturgical "dance" in which

womenpriests take part, and David vested for liturgy and wore the Roman collar in ecumenical circles where she felt it important that she be recognized as a priest.[25] Womanpriest Monica Kilburn-Smith told me that she would be content to avoid vestments altogether, but she realized that clothing offered a visual that helped connect the people to God. Putting a female head over familiar vestments became, she said, a "visual prophecy" for the church and its members.[26] And so, some womenpriests embrace vestments' potential to break down gender distinctions that say only men can be priests. This lets the women embody both Christ and the quintessential Roman Catholic priest that grips the imagination of Catholics and non-Catholics.

As I have mentioned, as a social movement strategy, RCWP's women welcome traditional dress (liturgical and extraliturgical) at times when they can make a statement, either supporting a social justice cause (especially one that runs counter to Rome's official position), standing alongside ordained men and women from other Christian and non-Christian traditions, or placing themselves and the movement in the spotlight. But what about at other times? For example, I saw some womenpriests wearing the Roman collar at the 2015 Women's Ordination Worldwide (WOW) conference in Philadelphia. Walking from session to session, surrounded almost entirely by people who support women's ordination, some womenpriests made the choice to dress as a traditional priest. Why? Perhaps these womenpriests knew cameras were following conference events and dressed for publicity. Or perhaps the "quintessential male priest" image appeals to these womenpriests, in that when they think of being a priest, the Roman collar is what they envision. Perhaps these women felt that it was important to display a more traditional form of Roman Catholic priesthood, in response to the antipriesthood reformers at the conference who argued for removing priesthood and tradition from WOW's vision altogether.

Womenpriests' clothing choices reflect the RCWP movement's ongoing struggle to reconcile tradition with transgression: to be the priests they aspire to be means, to some degree, being immediately recognizable as priests—even if doing so sometimes means exacerbating the lay-clergy divide that RCWP aims to assuage. And yet, if all womenpriests eschewed traditional dress altogether, RCWP would miss an opportunity to benefit from the authority that comes from costuming, since womenpriests' transgressive actions are underscored when a woman puts on the clothing that signals authority long reserved for men alone. In this way, clothing can be both an opportunity and a trap for women seeking a reformed Catholic Church.

Complementarity and Queering

RCWP participates in traditional normalizing practices and transgressive queering practices—often simultaneously. At times, the group subscribes to gender complementarity to argue the importance of having both men and women in priestly leadership. At other times, the group offers rationales, imagery, and practices that overturn notions of male-female difference, thus queering Catholic priesthood.

Doing so, womenpriests capitalize on a tension endemic to Roman Catholicism. Even Vatican leadership has seemed uncertain about the disconnect between a celebration of Mary, motherhood, and maternal qualities on the one hand and an all-male, paternalistic priesthood on the other. John Paul II offered a negotiation of this tension in his 1988 letter to priests for Holy Thursday, in which he heralded Mary as a role model for male priests who display maternal qualities. Speaking to priests about their role in "the Church's motherhood," he wrote, "If each of us [ordained men] lives the equivalent of this spiritual motherhood in a manly way, namely as a 'spiritual fatherhood,' then Mary, as a 'figure' of the Church, has a part to play in this experience of ours." Here, John Paul II suggested that male priests could break through the gender binary and take on maternal traits, thanks to Mary and "mystery." Priests could thus be maternal under the right circumstances and with sufficient intent. The pope did not suggest, however, that mystery might go both ways—that is, he didn't propose letting essentially maternal women take on fatherly traits for the purpose of pastoral priesthood.[27]

RCWP finds itself within this doctrinal tension: a Catholic culture with gender differences so strictly bifurcated that one must create arguments to show how some genders might, with God's help, emulate the finest characteristics of the other gender. Perhaps it is to be expected, then, that RCWP replicates Rome's own discursive challenges around gender and sexuality, and criticisms cut both ways. When the pope extols "feminine genius" but affirms a male-only priesthood, he seems to deny the Catholic faithful the distinct benefits of male *and* female priesthoods.[28] Likewise, it seems disingenuous for RCWP to lean into the ideas (and even benefits) of gender complementarity while fighting the implications of separate gender roles.

In the rest of this chapter, I will unpack RCWP's various positions, both normalizing and queering, around gender complementarity. Women's ordination activists—including womenpriests—argue that Paul's famous passage in

Galatians 3:28 ("There is no longer Jew or Greek, there is no longer slave or free, there is no longer male or female; for all of you are one in Jesus Christ") is evidence that gender differences should not block paths to Christ—or to ordination. Yet RCWP is not ready to elide "male" and "female." Rather, the movement sometimes keeps gender boundaries for the purpose of argument. How the movement navigates sacred and secular teachings about gender, and how the movement performs a female priesthood, reveal the challenges and opportunities rife in debates over women's ordination and sacred authority.

Gender Complementarity: Wives, Mothers, Essentially Female

At the St. Lawrence Seaway ordination in July 2005, Jim David introduced his wife, Marie David, as a candidate for ordination. With love and pride in his voice, he praised her suitability for priesthood and described Marie's mothering as a form of ministering to their children.[29] By drawing attention to Marie's mothering body, Jim expanded the idea of the Catholic priestly body, collapsing Rome's boundary between priest and woman. Placing maternal gestures alongside ordained ministry, as Jim David did, creates an alignment between them. With this juxtaposition, he invited the audience to consider the similarities between motherly tasks like tending during illness, consoling during sorrow, teaching life lessons, and making sacrifices, and priestly, pastoral work such as visiting the sick, comforting the aggrieved, offering blessings, giving homilies, and leading worship communities. RCWP's priests do not have to strive for the "spiritual motherhood" John Paul II championed: within the logic of Catholic theological anthropology, womenpriests instinctively have this pastoral ability.

Christine Mayr-Lumetzberger, RCWP bishop and member of the Danube Seven, and her husband, Michael Mayr, used a marriage analogy to make their case for women's unique, innate abilities to be priests. Mayr-Lumetzberger argued that ordained women will "open the second eye of the male church." She explained that womenpriests offer a way for the church to move toward the future and said that, just as in a marriage where the wife prepares meals and tends to the relationship, so too would womenpriests care for and guide the Roman church and its patriarchs. "[The male clergy] will not find it alone," she said. "We [womenpriests] are the pathfinders, and we give them ideas."[30] Michael Mayr agreed. He said that he wanted to see in the Roman Catholic Church the "motherly role" that male priests cannot fill. His marriage to Mayr-Lumetzberger had taught him that one spouse is only one half of human life: two are needed to make a whole. He wanted the same wholeness for the Roman Catholic priest-hood, and that required ordaining women.[31]

Rome, too, uses a nuptial analogy, but in defense of the all-male priest-hood. In 1976, *Inter Insigniores* emphasized the scriptural precedents of the bride-bridegroom analogy, which stems from an interpretation of Song of Songs wherein God (the bridegroom) declares faithfulness to Israel (the bride) in spite of Israel's infidelities. Early Christians would later adopt this analogy, seeing it as Christ (the bridegroom) expressing devotion to the church (the bride). In this formation, the church is gendered female—hence references to the church as "she" or "her" in papal documents. When the priest stands *in persona Christi*, therefore, he is the Christ-groom to the church's bride. Male priests uphold Christ's maleness as well as the bride-bridegroom symbolism when they stand in Christ's place as sacramental leaders of the Roman Catholic Church.[32]

Womenpriests have shown that they are not afraid to use Rome's own teach-ings to reach very different conclusions. Jim David elevated the unique status of motherhood in ways reminiscent of John Paul II's writings while countering Rome's assertion that only men are suitable for priesthood. Mayr-Lumetzberger and Mayr used the Roman church's emphasis on marriage to argue for the ne-cessity of allowing women into priesthood. These examples show that RCWP does not seek to dismantle Rome's ideas about gender, motherhood, or marriage. Instead, it shares premises with Rome but ultimately concludes that women are suitable for priesthood, and indeed essential for the church. Womanpriest Kath-leen Kunster performed a similar intellectual move as a seventh grader who be-lieved she had a vocation to priesthood. When her parish priest told her that a woman could not be a priest because she could not be a "father to the people," Kunster thought to herself, "I can be a mother to the people."[33] Womenpriests frequently and strategically draw on Catholic women's distinct experiences *as* women, particularly around marriage, motherhood, and female sexuality. They deploy Rome's logic of gender to argue that the priesthood is incomplete without the unique female body.

In this way, womenpriests obey papal teachings to some extent. John Paul II's 1995 "Letter to Women," for example, called on women to fill specific, God-given roles, as modeled by Jesus's mother, Mary: "There is great signifi-cance to that 'womanhood' which was lived in such a sublime way by Mary . . . a powerfully evocative symbolism, a highly significant 'iconic character,' which finds its full realization in Mary and which also aptly expresses the very essence of the Church as a community consecrated with the integrity of a '*virgin*' heart to become the '*bride*' of Christ and '*mother*' of believers" (emphases in original).[34] John Paul II equated womanhood with being a mother, wife, and virgin. Although these roles cannot be held simultaneously by any woman (the Virgin Mary excepted, per Catholic doctrine), this triad is the Roman Catholic superlative to which women must strive.

Are womenpriests who argue from motherhood, marriage roles, and innate female characteristics replicating Rome's prescribed gender roles in an ostensibly provocative form? In some ways, yes. The majority of womenpriests are (or were) married and have children (and often grandchildren and even great-grandchildren), and therefore they have, in a very real sense, attained the Roman Catholic ideal for women. It makes sense that womenpriests, many in their fifties, sixties, and seventies, would have imbibed sacred and secular messages on female identities; they "do" Catholic femininity with a feminist flair. Womenpriests trade on their ability to be wives, mothers, *and* priests. Their online biographies suggest that they (1) have largely followed institutional church dictates for women by becoming wives and mothers, and (2) enhance the existing all-male priesthood community by bringing maternal experiences to their ministries. Kunster's biography, for instance, first listed her myriad professional and pastoral accomplishments and then said that she "delights in her daughter and son-in-law, four grandchildren, and two great-grandchildren."[35] Most biographies indicate the women's personal histories, thus indicating indirectly something about their sexual histories. The women's public personas become those of priests with sexual bodies—bodies that, surprisingly, coincide with church mandates about women's sexual and maternal roles.[36]

Where the majority of womenpriests deviate from Roman Catholic teaching, then, is in breaking canon 1024 and becoming ordained *contra legem*. Radically upending traditional gender roles is not on every womanpriest's agenda. In second-wave feminist form, many womenpriests seek equality first and foremost: the ability to have equal opportunities within the Roman church while living out roles as wives and mothers. For these womenpriests, gender complementarity does not harm but rather helps their case for women's ordination: by acquiescing to the Vatican's stated differences between men and women, some activists can better argue that womenpriests are a logical necessity for a functioning, ministerially adept priesthood. RCWP often repeats a quote about embodiment by Sister Joan Chittister, who said that without women's presence in Church leadership, "We look at questions with one-half of the human brain, we make decisions with one-half of the human brain, we see with one eye and we stand on one leg, and our decisions show it."[37] This line of argument says that—because of gender complementarity—women's bodies, sexual identities, and gendered experiences are essential for bringing priesthood to its fullest expression.

Some of RCWP's arguments for ordaining women, then, track with both the Roman Catholic gender binary and the idea that womenpriests are needed to bring women's distinct voices and experiences in Catholic pastoral care. RCWP is rhetorically dependent on clear differences between gendered bodies. Both consciously and unconsciously, RCWP attempts to call Rome's bluff by arguing that if women are as uniquely important as Rome avows, women's priestly presence is essential to a functioning church. The womenpriests' discursive efforts echo literary critic Gayatri Spivak's "strategic essentialism," whereby disempowered groups play into the essentialism put forth by dominant forces in order to better achieve their goals through unity.[38] RCWP's approach here further exposes the potential described in feminist theorist and philosopher Luce Irigary's take on strategic essentialism (which she labeled "mimesis") wherein women play into stereotypes in order to expose and subvert the illogic of stereotypes.[39] RCWP argues that women must step into male-only roles *as women* in order to subvert gender norms around priesthood. Yet RCWP does not subvert gender essentialism entirely, because it remains reliant on traditional Catholic womanhood.

Deconstructing the Gender Dichotomy

Bringing women into priesthood makes for a jarring modification of the priestly prototype. In spite of RCWP's selective deference to Roman Catholicism's gender complementarity, the movement offers new interpretations and performances of sacred and sexual(ized) ordained bodies. Among RCWP's membership are female-gendered individuals, noncelibate bodies, and self-identified lesbian and bisexual women. The way RCWP merges women's bodies and sexual identities with the archetype of a Roman Catholic priest is a form of queering whereby RCWP occupies liminal spaces that complicate traditional presuppositions about celibate male priesthood. RCWP's approach is both/and: womenpriests are challenging and queering boundaries of sex, gender, and sexuality through female priesthood while simultaneously using gender complementarity to argue for their distinct, feminine suitability for priesthood. Both approaches are potentially transgressive, albeit for vastly different reasons.

For decades, women's ordination advocates have argued that women and girls must be able to see themselves in the priest and, by extension, in Jesus Christ.

Womenpriests are one symbolic way of dismantling the rigid association between priests and cisgender men, between holiness and the male gender. By including openly gay women in sacramental priesthood, RCWP troubles Rome's unidirectional association of male to priest to Christ to God the Father, and invites nonconforming Catholics (like lesbians or bisexuals) to image Christ. RCWP's own gender transgression (i.e., making priests of women) extends to others who defy the Catholic gender binary and sexual ethics.

Per her online biography, womanpriest Cheryl Bristol is "lesbian by birth, Catholic by choice."[40] She credited motherhood (she has a son) with shaping her ministry, and she believed people found it easier to talk to her about LGBT issues because she was openly lesbian. Bristol is a mother but not a wife; she chose Catholicism though it did not choose her (the Roman Catholic Church prohibits lesbians from acting on same-sex attraction and has excommunicated her for illicit priesthood); she credited her otherness with making her a better priest. She remained Catholic while calling out the Catholic Church as discriminatory: she argued that LGBT people need their church to be "a place to find inspiration to grow spiritually and a springboard from which to live out their faith."[41] With its lesbian priests—some partnered, some single; some with children, some without—RCWP affirms the ministerial holiness of individuals who do not fit Catholic standards of gender and sexuality. By putting sacraments into the hands of openly gay womenpriests, RCWP collapses the Roman Catholic disjuncture between sacred and (homo)sexual.

Ordination allows RCWP's lesbian women to bring an ordained commitment to their self-identity and past activism. Of the thirty-four RCWP members who responded to my 2014 survey, seven identified as gay/lesbian or bisexual. One of these was Toni Tortorilla.[42] Tortorilla wrote her RWCP website biography to describe a politically motivated path to ordination, which began when antigay legislation came to a vote in her home state of Oregon, pushing her to join with a "sympathetic priest" in starting "an outreach ministry to the gay and lesbian community."[43] This event became part of her calling and ministry. Like straight womenpriests who talk about spouses, children, and grandchildren, womenpriests in same-sex relationships use their biographies to draw attention to their sexual identities. Womanpriest Victoria Rue's biography mentioned her decades-long relationship with partner Kathryn Poethig as well as her pastoral work with Dignity NYC and LGBT people. Womanpriest Jennifer O'Malley's biography mentioned her ministry to the gay and lesbian community and said that she lived with Liz Carlin, her partner "of 20+ years."[44] These ordained women defy the church through both *contra legem* ordination and their same-sex partnerships. They destabilize normative priesthood (by being female, lesbian and noncelibate) while also destabilizing stereotypes of lesbians (by being committed Roman Catholics).[45]

This destabilization continues with RCWP's ministerial activism, as many womenpriests work with gay and lesbian communities. By advocating for LGBT civil rights—as priests, no less—RCWP defies Rome's formal teachings on homosexuality.[46] A number of womenpriests publicize their support for gay and lesbian issues in their RCWP biographies. As mentioned earlier, some womenpriests work with Dignity and champion the idea that LGBT Catholics can and should be able to "express their sexuality in a manner that is consonant with Christ's teaching"—and not be confined to lives of celibacy.[47]

RCWP's public priesthood further dismantles the maleness and heterosexuality of Jesus Christ. RCWP's frank discussion of womenpriests' sexual lives has the potential to bring an embodied materiality and unapologetic sexuality to Jesus via womenpriests' physical embodiment of Jesus (as priests in a sacramental mode). In "Touching the Taboo: On the Sexuality of Jesus," theologian Kwok Pui-Lan called the silence surrounding Jesus's sexuality "the greatest taboo in Christianity."[48] Kwok argued, "That Jesus must be seen as asexual, unmarried, and celibate is a direct result of an erotophobic church maintained for a long time by a celibate, male, and dominating clerical hierarchy. They have projected onto Jesus their values and ideals as a means to control behavior and maintain their sacred status. . . . The asexual Jesus functions to perpetuate the social values of these elite males."[49] Kwok's article intervenes in a particular discourse around Jesus's sexuality—one set forth and championed, typically, by white male scholars. She calls for theologies that take Jesus's sexual body as a starting point for an increased awareness of the material conditions that impact lives, bodies, and sexual selves: "The body of Jesus—as the incarnate flesh of God—brings into sharp relief the demarcations between the sacred and the profane."[50] Womenpriests stand *in persona Christi* as women, and sometimes as sexually active women, thereby drawing attention to the body's materiality and sexuality in a way that has long been overlooked or underrepresented in Roman Catholic iconography. Because women are often cast as "body" (and "emotion" or "feeling," in contrast to men as "mind" and "intellect"[51]), now the sexual and maternal stereotypes so often attached to women's bodies become a source of empowerment, heightening the provocative image of womenpriests *in persona Christi* and deepening the association between Christ incarnate and historically marginalized populations—in this case, Catholic women. If women are viewed as more embodied, more material, more profane than males, then womenpriests' bodies standing *in persona Christi* can invite more robust considerations of Christ's humanity—including his body and his sexuality. Like Christ as Word made flesh, as God incarnate, the womenpriests are both fully human (as women) and wholly sacred (as priests signifying Jesus).

Womenpriests also have the potential to disrupt traditionally male language for God. Male priests standing in for Christ indirectly stand in for God. Traditional metaphors for God are already heavily masculine: "Father," "Lord," "King," and "Good Shepherd" point to male roles, as does imagery of God as judge, warrior, and "rock" (Deuteronomy 32:15). This language further inscribes the notion that God is male while obstructing feminine biblical personifications of God, specifically motherhood metaphors around birthing, nurturing, and caring for bodies.[52] Literally female, literally standing *in persona Christi*, womenpriests can upend male metaphors for God while inviting female metaphors for God to emerge.

Of course, RCWP's women do not all view sex and gender the same way. Just as Kwok worked to destabilize normative assumptions about Jesus's sexual desires, womenpriests like self-described "biotheologian" Roberta Meehan have called into question not just the implications of Jesus's maleness but the literal maleness and male body of Jesus. Whereas RCWP's women disdain canon 1024 for excluding women ("Only a baptized man can validly receive sacred ordination"; some translations say "male"), Meehan argued that canon 1024's real problem is a lack of specificity: What is a "man" and what is a "male," Meehan asked, and what makes "maleness" essential for ordination? She criticized the Vatican for using the term *male* in a way that implied common knowledge but was actually rooted in a sexist historical time. Meehan asked, How can Rome preclude women from ordination when Rome has never defined "male" biologically and seems unaware of recent biological findings complicating a straightforward male-female dyad? Rejecting the gender binary, Meehan wrote that some people are "sexual mosaics" and that it can be difficult to (1) determine sex based on external genitalia alone and (2) argue convincingly that male and female are mutually exclusive categories.[53] She posed provocative questions to underscore her point: Would or could the Roman church "validly ordain" someone who was externally male but had a female internal gonadal structure? What about individuals with female external but male internal structures? Meehan demanded that Roman leaders explain the criterion for defining "male" in canon 1024. This goes beyond justice for admitting men *and* women into priesthood, Meehan warned: should Rome ignore emerging science, it "could easily repeat the problems caused by the Galileo incident."[54]

Merging Meehan's research with Kwok's observations, we might ask, *What type of male was Jesus?*[55] What were the internal gonadal structures of the twelve apostles? Have there been leaders in Christianity's two thousand years who were actually "female" in terms of genetic makeup? How many individuals could not seek ordination because of female external genitalia when in fact they were genetically male? By challenging the very premises of culturally held views of sex and gender, Meehan aimed to destabilize the gender binary that has upheld a male-only ordination for centuries. Her critique cut beyond a dismantling of gender essentialism: she called out the institutional church for not understanding—biologically, scientifically—what it means when speaking about sex and gender. She accused the church of using loaded terms like *male, female, man,* and *woman* uncritically and unreflectively. If material bodies are the reason women cannot be ordained—because of Jesus's (presumably) male body, the (presumably) male bodies of the apostles, or the fact that (apparent) women's bodies have different genitalia than men's—Meehan summoned the church to contend with *biological* materiality.[56]

In fairness to Rome, most womenpriests are not prepared to contend with biological materiality either. Most womenpriests argue for women's ordination—again evoking Spivak's strategic essentialism—by reframing the ways women have been traditionally defined and othered in Catholic discourse as a source of power. This approach, while not radical, *is* confrontational, as it brings women into the priesthood as wives and mothers, thereby affirming some Catholic teachings (around gender complementarity) while aggressively flouting others (specifically related to a male-only priesthood and canon 1024). Performing priesthood in these ways, RCWP invites feminine virtues to penetrate Catholic patriarchy. Ethicist Christine Gudorf pointed out that, as women have been ordained in Protestant traditions, "it has become commonplace . . . to hear references to traditional feminine traits (sympathy, support, empathy, sensitivity, patience) that are required of ministers in addition to more intellectual or authoritative qualities useful in preaching that used to be considered masculine but that are becoming more neutral."[57] It seems reasonable to presume, then, that an influx of Roman Catholic ordained women into Catholic priesthood could reorient the faithful toward new expectations and ideals for their priests. Publicity and exposure can chip away at familiar priestly forms, allowing paternal *and* maternal qualities to inform a new ideal of quintessential priesthood.

RCWP's other possible path is the more radical, the more transgressive, and the more potentially transformative. When womenpriests disassemble gender boundaries altogether, however unintentionally, they unveil a "shift from di-morphism to polymorphism" and posit not just new ways of being priests but new ways of seeing Christ and understanding the incarnation.[58] This sweeping change may also be the most strategically viable in the long run: as noted in the last chapter, studies of ordained Protestant women reveal continued sexism in the forms of lower pay; comments about women's bodies, clothing, and appear-ance; and different expectations of female clergy.[59] At this relatively early stage of RCWP's emergence, RCWP has a unique opportunity to dismantle the gen-der binary in priesthood altogether. By focusing on the sacramental authority that stems from Catholic priesthood, womenpriests could argue for what they already perform: a woman's ability to facilitate sacraments and minister sacra-mentally, independent of gender. Because RCWP's women stand in the role of Christ, they can bring a wider swath of human characteristics to Catholics' understanding of Jesus. Instead of casting Jesus in a strict gender role, as the Roman Catholic Church does, RCWP might best attract and serve Catholics in North America and Western Europe by blurring lines between male and female. This might eventually (if even inadvertently) open up space to trouble other presuppositions about Jesus—specifically, as Kwok ultimately envisioned, Jesus's racial and ethnic makeup.

I suggest we read RCWP both ways. What womenpriests do rhetorically and what they do performatively, while often in tension, are not mutually exclusive: both constitute RCWP's distinct form of Roman Catholic priesthood. Wom-enpriests are, to repeat Monica Kilburn-Smith's words, upending the "visual ver-nacular." Where RCWP goes in the future with their rhetoric and practices of priesthood will indicate much about the types of reforms they desire for Roman Catholicism; furthermore, their success or missteps in drawing people to their movement—as worshippers and as priests—will indicate much about the mag-nitude of reform twenty-first-century Catholics are willing to tolerate.

Of course, RCWP's future might continue to be both/and. RCWP's individ-ual members follow their ministerial callings in personalized directions. Some women seek priesthood as wives in heterosexual marriages; some womenpriests are committed to celibacy; some womenpriests are openly lesbian or bisexual. This range of options—for individuals who are sexual or celibate, who are part-nered or single, who are cisgender or trans—can offer ever-expanding ideas of Jesus as an embodied, incarnate savior: a savior for all Catholics, not just het-erosexual men.

Conclusions: Familiarity and Flexibility
in the Womanpriest's Body

Womenpriests' bodies communicate messages—often disparate ones. A range of ideas, ministries, and experiences motivate womenpriests' priesthoods and influence how they dress as priests, discuss their personal lives, and understand themselves as illegally ordained women. The women also hold different primary audiences in mind with their provocative practices of priesthood: some wish to challenge canon 1024, some want to stand for social justice, some want to model leadership for Catholic women, and some seek to expand ideas of Jesus Christ. All womenpriests use their bodies as the medium—but the messages are not singular.

Nor are womenpriests' embodied priesthoods uniformly interpreted. Some critics see RCWP's *contra legem* actions as the epitome of schism and disrespect; others cringe at a woman making traditionally male gestures and replicating patriarchy. Still others see something different altogether, and survey respondents told me that womenpriests helped them reimagine sacraments, priesthood, and Jesus. "It is nice to see a person that looks like me in a leadership position in my church," said a woman from Resurrection Community in Ohio.[60] Another Resurrection Community member saw her womanpriest as a "peer image . . . rather than an elite separate role."[61] Womenpriests make the liturgy more "about shepherding and . . . collaborative, affirming, and inclusive of the laypeople, empowering people in their own call from God."[62] The experience of liturgy is "softer, gentler."[63] Another wrote that, because of womenpriests, "I'm thinking even more of feminine images of Jesus. Just being in service with womenpriests and women deacons and people supporting them gives me a deeper sense of Scriptures and Parent and child and the love between them being the Spirit. I experience Jesus as sister as well as brother and mother."[64] One respondent mused, "I'm not sure whether it's because our pastor is a woman, but I now experience the priesthood as more oriented to service and collaboration."[65]

These interpretations are resoundingly gendered. Perhaps it is no surprise that womenpriests are read, first and foremost, as *women*priests. RCWP reiterates these points, thereby allowing its priesthood to rest largely on conventional analyses of women's bodies. This may serve the group in these early years, when arguments for justice and gender equality have more weight with RCWP's likely Catholic audience than would a dramatic reversal of traditional gender roles.

Still, questions abound. Do womenpriests appeal to their audiences because they are women and are thus naturally and instinctively a certain kind of priest? Or do they appeal to audiences because, *as women*, they are barred from ordained priesthood? Does RCWP play to a type of priesthood that is familiarly female? Do womenpriests replicate male priests' gestures because this is what they know from decades of faithful Catholic worship? Or do they strike some abstract, personal balance between the feminine and masculine in order to create for themselves an individualistic priesthood within a community of Catholic womenpriests?

One thing seems certain: RCWP's new image of a priestly body has arrived on the contemporary Catholic scene at an opportune time. In the wake of the Catholic sex-abuse crisis, when celibate male priest are viewed as having potentially predatory and dangerous sexual habits, women's priestly bodies offer the church—and the idea of "Roman Catholic priest"—new opportunities. Marie Bouclin suggested that her ordained ministry received so much attention because of the abuse scandal: "Perhaps because the pedophilia scandal has hit this diocese particularly hard, many Catholics here support me. They believe it is time women and married men were ordained, that the Church needs priests who understand the 'realities of ordinary life.' They know that I'm married, have raised three children and I have a grandchild. They also seem to know that my only motive is to serve and help heal the wounds of abuse in the church I love."[66] Audiences read Bouclin as a positive priestly figure: not only is she not male, but she is a wife, mother, and grandmother, and her actions read as healing and service oriented. She is right to link support of RCWP with the sex-abuse scandal: one survey respondent told me that having a womanpriest changed her idea of priesthood because "I do not have fear [of my womanpriest] wielding power over me in any way, #1, because she includes us in decision making for our community, #2, I don't have to fear her abusing me. . . . Unfortunately, I was one of those women abused by a male priest when I was a teenager."[67] If male priests' bodies inspire fear and distrust, womenpriests' bodies represent new potential.

As womenpriests walk the line between tradition and transgression, between reiteration and transformation, their bodies are read and reread, cast and recast, as markers of gendered, sexual, and Catholic identities. RCWP offers the potential for destabilizing gender and priestly identity but does not fully commit to a complete overhaul of complementarity and theological anthropology. Perhaps the destabilization of gender is not an ideal aim while the Roman Catholic

Church still needs dramatic healing from the horrible sex-abuse crisis. Additionally, while white male bodies are associated with hegemonic systems of racism, colonialism, and elitism, perhaps the jarringly different "read" of a woman's body can provide the alternative Christ symbol that a struggling church needs. To be sure, amid the mystery of the sacraments stands the materiality of the body and women's bodies' creative potential.

Conclusion

THE DECISION ON WHEN to end formal research on an evolving topic was always going to be an arbitrary one. I undoubtedly could have continued exploring RCWP for years, but an end date of 2015 afforded me a solid decade of material on RCWP in North America. Still, some things have changed since 2015, for RCWP as a movement, for the Roman Catholic Church, and for academic studies on women's ordination and leadership, and these items are worth noting.

In 2018, political scientists Benjamin R. Knoll and Cammie Jo Bolin published *She Preached the Word: Women's Ordination in Modern America*, based on results of their extensive 2015 and 2016 Gender and Religious Representation Survey. By focusing on a wide range of religious traditions—including Roman Catholicism, Protestant Christianity, Mormonism, Islam, and Judaism—they were able to offer an extensive yet focused analysis of American attitudes about women in positions of religious authority. Many of Knoll and Bolin's conclusions echo what I found researching RCWP. For instance, Americans are more likely to support ordained women if they have had experience with clergywomen or women in positions of leadership. Perhaps not surprisingly, individuals who support and individuals who oppose ordained women rely on similar stereotypes for women and men to argue their point. If congregants belong to a highly institutionalized faith, such as Roman Catholicism or Mormonism, they become more amenable to accepting women as priests *if* the (male) leadership makes that move first, with scriptural and/or theological justification. For instance, if patriarchs from the Church of Jesus Christ of Latter-day Saints (Mormon) were to receive a revelation from God calling for women in the priesthood, or if Vatican leaders were to use scripture and Catholic tradition to reverse course on an all-male priesthood, church members are increasingly likely to accept women's ordained leadership.[1] *She Preached the Word* aims to explain why women's advances toward equality stalled in the 1990s and to rekindle these discussions with empirical evidence, specifically around women in religious leadership.[2] It should prove to be a helpful conversation partner for studies on movements like

RCWP and, particularly, for research on RCWP congregants, which I only briefly tackled in *Womanpriest*.

In August 2016, Pope Francis started a commission to investigate women in the permanent diaconate. The mandate of the Study Commission on the Women's Diaconate was to examine both history and theology—two Roman Catholic elements that RCWP actively contends with—to see if the possibility exists of ordaining women to the diaconate. Some commission members had publicly argued previously for women deacons, citing church history, while others had said women deacons should be impossible because women priests are forbidden. In May 2019, Francis told reporters that the commission had completed its work and was unable to come to an agreement. Francis's conclusion? This question needs further study.[3]

No matter what the Francis papacy decides to do (or not do) on this issue, the Vatican is taking absolutely no steps toward women's ordination to priesthood. In recent years, Rome has reaffirmed the male-only priesthood and *Ordinatio Sacerdotalis*'s "definitive character."[4] Speaking as prefect of the Congregation for the Doctrine of the Faith (CDF), Archbishop Luis Ladaria wrote in 2018, "The church has always recognized herself bound by this decision of the Lord, which excludes that the ministerial priesthood can be validly conferred on women."[5] Activist groups including Women's Ordination Conference (WOC) and RCWP were quick to criticize Ladaria's remarks, but their increased efforts to include women in the church's decision-making structures has meant nothing in terms of legal priestly ordination.

Another recent change is the A Church for Our Daughters movement, which arose in response to declining church attendance among US women. A 2016 Pew Research Center survey found that, while American women continue to attend weekly church services at higher rates than men, women's rates of attendance are declining more rapidly than men's. Between 1972 and 1974, women averaged 36 percent and men 26 percent weekly attendance. By the early twenty-first century, those numbers were 28 percent and 22 percent, respectively, meaning that women's churchgoing behavior had declined by twice as much (8 percent versus 4 percent) as men's.[6] In part as a response to this data, as well as declining rates of Mass attendance among millennial Catholic women specifically, a number of Catholic reform organizations formed A Church for Our Daughters, which believes Rome's teachings on gender and sexuality are a primary cause of the decline. A Church for Our Daughters seeks dialogue with church leaders about this issue. RCWP-USA and ARCWP joined in forming this reform community, along with groups like Call to Action; CORPUS; Women's Alliance for Theology, Ethics, and Ritual (WATER); and WOC.[7]

The Roman church and, by extension, the priesthood continue to be under siege and scrutiny. Revelations of priests' sexual abuse of children, women, and women religious continue to emerge in a relentless litany. In August 2018, a grand jury report named three hundred priests in abuse impacting one thousand children in Pennsylvania.[8] These problems are not limited to the North American church: painful scandals have unfolded in Australia, Chile, the Philippines, and Ireland (where, a 2009 report found, the abuse of children in Catholic orphanages and schools was "endemic").[9] This, combined with his loss of hope in the "otherwise revolutionary" Pope Francis, motivated former priest James Carroll to write a piece for *The Atlantic* in May 2019 titled "Abolish the Priesthood." His reasons for losing faith in Roman Catholic priesthood and institutions resonated also in RCWP's reasons: rigid clerical structures, mandatory celibacy, systemic disempowerment of the laity, the refusal to ordain women. Carroll called on the faithful to become faithful exiles from the church. Keep "the pillars of Catholicism," he argued, and maybe someday the Vatican will "catch up."[10] Indeed, RCWP has been saying and doing the same thing since 2002—but by keeping the priesthood with women in it.

Of course, RCWP's women have not been formally recognized by the Roman Catholic Church as valid and licit priests. Although their Episcopal role models, the Philadelphia Eleven, saw the legalization of women's ordination two years after their irregular ordination, RCWP's women have had no comparable outcome, nor can they see signs of Vatican acceptance in the near future. Women-priests today also receive less media attention, probably because their controversial ordinations seem more routine now. Parish priests and local dioceses still issue condemnatory statements about womanpriest ordinations, but large-scale disagreements—shaped often by the media as battles between powerful prelates and Catholic grandmas—are less frequent.

RCWP, for its part, continues attracting more candidates for ordination, and womenpriests continue to grow their ministries. RCWP has also become more activist, it seems, in the Trump era. RCWP-USA and ARCWP are active on social media, especially Facebook, and both have Twitter accounts. RCWP-USA frequently posts articles about women's ordination, championing activists and progressive theologies while criticizing what it sees as Rome's obtuseness. ARCWP is similarly involved and additionally comments on a range of issues, including the Trump administration's policies on separating migrant families, Catholicism's lack of full acceptance of LGBTQ Catholics, police violence against black Americans, and the January 2017 Women's March on Washington. More and more, RCWP ministries include this social media component.

To think about RCWP in all its creativity, complexity, and contradictions, we must think of its past, present, and possible future. In this conclusion, I lay out the implications and inferences for RCWP going forward, for scholars, contemporary Catholics, and others following progressive feminist movements like RCWP. I offer my concluding thoughts, pose my remaining questions, and suggest avenues for future research.

Beyond Catholicism:
RCWP and Non-Catholic Women's Movements

Other groups seeking women's equality in religious leadership have come to see RCWP as a valuable conversation partner. The way that womenpriests blend tradition and transgression resonates in other resistance movements, making RCWP a beacon and leader for non-Catholic reformers. At the Women's Ordination Worldwide conference in September 2015, Kate Kelly, who founded the Mormon Ordain Women movement in 2013, appeared on a panel titled "Equal in Faith" alongside RCWP bishop Patricia Fresen, as well as the Anglican Church's Christina Rees, Reconstructionist Jewish rabbi Rebecca Alpert, and Muslim activist Asra Nomani. The panelists shared stories of their religious tradition's distinct histories and rationales for dividing male and female roles, and they brainstormed ways to work constructively across religious boundaries.[11] Through these interfaith discussions that combine strategy and solidarity, RCWP sees how its own questions and challenges converge with feminist-aligned religious others.

Much like the Roman Catholic Church, the Church of Jesus Christ of Latter-day Saints teaches that a male-only priesthood connects to God-given gender roles and—with a focus not unlike Catholicism's emphasis on the nuptial analogy—the importance of set roles within the family.[12] All worthy Mormon men hold the priesthood, whereas no women do or can. Unlike the estimated (depending on the survey) 60 to 75 percent of American Catholics who support the ordination of women priests, only about 10 percent of Mormons believe worthy women should hold the priesthood. Significantly, however, the LDS numbers skyrocket to about 77 percent when respondents are given a hypothetical scenario in which church patriarchs receive a divine revelation permitting women to be priesthood holders.[13] In other words, Mormon women who want priesthood will not likely get far within their own church if they rely on public opinion, as RCWP frequently attempts to do by generating media coverage and telling their stories of being called by God. In better news for Mormon women, their religion's trust in ongoing revelation means that women's fortunes could change literally in an instant, should God speak to Mormon leadership. Whereas Mormonism emphasizes an open canon and divine revelation, RCWP must (and does, rhetorically) contend with a church tradition that's two thousand years old, nearly ten times older than Mormonism. So while RCWP and Ordain Women share many aims, feminist theologies, and embodied actions, their paths to ordination wind through very different institutional mazes.

In some ways, Orthodox Jewish women stand closer to the Roman Catholic struggle, with notable changes happening since 2015. Although other branches of Judaism (Reform, Reconstructionist, and Conservative) have ordained women to the rabbinate, Orthodox Judaism has not. Orthodox Jewish arguments lean heavily on law and tradition.[14] Like Roman Catholic women, Orthodox Jewish women have agitated for entry to the rabbinate. In October 2015, the Rabbinical Council of America (consisting of over one thousand Orthodox rabbis) voted to formally prohibit women's ordination to the rabbinate; this vote came six years after the founding of Yeshivat Maharat, a religious school for women in New York City that had ordained nearly a dozen women to the rabbinate, though with the honorific title *maharat* ("female leader") rather than *rabbi*.[15] The approach to ordination taken by the women of Yeshivat Maharat—to just "do it" in spite of male opposition—resonates with RCWP's own tactics. Like RCWP's womenpriests, Jewish maharats appeal to certain elements of tradition and to an overlooked history of female religious authorities. Also like RCWP's womenpriests, some of these ordained women refer to themselves as rabbis, even if the men in power would disagree.[16]

Orthodox Jewish disagreements about women's ordination extend well beyond the American context: much debate is symbolically enacted at the Western Wall, a remnant of the Second Temple of Jerusalem, now considered Judaism's holiest prayer site. Since the group Women of the Wall began in 1988 attempting public prayer at the wall, wearing *tallitot* (prayer shawls) and reading the Torah, they have faced angry and violent opposition. One Israeli rabbi said, "A woman at the Wall is like a pig at the Wall," and men have attacked the women with words, spittle, chairs, and feces.[17] But change is happening, if slowly: in February 2016, Israel announced a decision to allow space at the Western Wall where men and women can pray together, instead of being segregated by sex, as before.[18] Women of the Wall have been credited with (or blamed for) helping to instigate this change, showing that embodied protests wrapped in faithful if disobedient action can inspire change.[19]

Comparisons between Catholics, Mormons, and Orthodox Jews are instructive and offer future scholars a rich place to begin. While activists can (and do) support one another and share ideas, the juxtaposition of these groups reveals not only theological differences among the religions but also core challenges with which their women must contend. Centralized, institutional power blocks progressive, feminist aims, as does the reach of global religions with millions of members worldwide who do not support women's leadership as akin to men's. All three of these groups have used some strategic essentialism to argue that, yes, women are inherently different from men, which is why their elevated leadership is vital to the religion's health. Orthodox Judaism and Catholicism, especially, must grapple with traditions dating back nearly two thousand years and navigate ways to remain relevant in the modern world. And each of these groups has tried to present itself as protesting reverently, respectful of the faith and committed to God's expectations of humankind.

In light of these comparisons, RCWP's ordained women come into sharper relief. They stand out in the landscape of contemporary feminist agitators by creating a dexterous form of contemporary Roman Catholicism that allows them to fit in, to participate, to lead, to embody ministerial holiness—as women. They have had to make strategic decisions, rooted in theology, sacred texts, and institutional histories, that Mormon and Orthodox Jewish women have not; to be certain, those groups have their own challenges to face, their own obstacles to surmount. Most significantly, because sacraments are central to the Roman Catholic (and not the Mormon or Jewish) experience, sacraments are of utmost importance for RCWP, and womenpriests have come to believe themselves to be conduits of the Roman Catholic sacramental tradition. Given their backgrounds, life experiences, and encounters with Catholic feminism, they could accept only a church that allowed them involvement as priests. When the institutional church repeatedly failed to allow that, they created it themselves.

Finally, partnerships among Catholic women, Mormon women, Jewish women, and more, should offer valuable comparisons in the coming years.

Where Is Roman Catholicism?

In its early years, RCWP showed itself to be a movement with a fraught relationship to the institutional church, to say the very least. In attempting to change institutional Rome for the better, RCWP has removed itself from the institution, per *latae sententiae* excommunication, and taken Roman Catholicism elsewhere—away from Rome. Rome's Catholicism still exists, of course; like a large flame, burning for centuries, it is difficult to douse. But RCWP has taken some of that fire and carried it to *contra legem* communities.

RCWP's brand of Roman Catholicism is *not* located institutionally, in brick-and-mortar buildings or Rome's archives or the office of the papacy or the authority of bishops. So, then, where *is* its Catholicism? Rome's loss of hierarchical control becomes a gain for RCWP's women: they have at their disposal the resources of the faith, and now they will make of it what they will. Having removed the locus of authority from the institutional church, RCWP makes "church" happen anywhere and everywhere, in spaces and places that could not "be Catholic" previously (like Protestant chapels or Jewish synagogues), at the hands of people (read: women) who could not "make Catholicism happen" before. RCWP captures a Roman Catholic essence while moving away from physical, tangible, rule-bound matter. What RCWP deems important is not in the institution but in the Catholic idioms people wish to share. Instead of the institutional church determining what it means to be a good Catholic, churchgoers themselves get to determine their own religious destiny and make their own rules—while keeping certain tradition-based rituals and sacraments to guide them.

I often think of RCWP through the analogy of English Puritans in the New World: unlike the Separatists who settled in Plymouth and wanted to separate entirely from the Church of England, the Puritans wanted to be a "city on a hill," modeling "purified" reform. RCWP's ordained are not Separatists, indifferent to the church they left behind. Rather, RCWP seeks to build a city on a hill with womenpriests, sacramentally empowered laity, and new Christological emphases. Womenpriests do not want to join the Roman church as it is: they want the Roman church to join them. RCWP wants to "purify" Rome out of its current existence and into an entirely new entity that embraces women's leadership, reaches out to marginalized populations, and curtails its own clerical authority for the good of the laity. Womenpriests are not asking to enter the hallowed halls of Vatican authority; instead, they want the patriarchy to see, understand, appreciate, and emulate them. As womanpriest Diane Dougherty explained, "Hopefully we [womenpriests] are reconfiguring the Roman [from] a dominating organizational structure to an egalitarian collaborative engine."[20] Even after decades of what RCWP views as sexism and ostracism, RCWP aims for Rome's approval, which—RCWP believes—would result in positive progressive and feminist changes in the future church.

I think also of RCWP as a proto-restorationist movement. Like nineteenth-century American restorationist groups such as the Latter-day Saints, women-priests argue that they—and not Rome—create the kind of church community Jesus actually envisioned; that they—and not Rome—are capturing the ethos of first-century Christian gender progressivism; that they—and not Rome—are the ones who can offer what people need in a spiritual marketplace with a dizzying array of options. In doing so, RCWP is raising the kinds of questions that Puritans, Mormons, and the Stone-Campbell Movement did before. How can a group—and how much can a group—surgically extricate a faith tradition from its long-standing host institution? When and for how long does a new movement need the host to survive? And what new theological ideas might arise as the scalpel cuts?

RCWP wants to move a mountain; Rome swats at RCWP as at a pesky fly. As small as the group seems, and as impractical as its goals may appear to skeptics, its Puritan/"purifying" and restorationist antecedents suggest it has the potential to make an impact. What is not clear is whether it can impact *Rome*. Even outside of the mother church, but with what it holds as the faith's central tenets and theologies, it is in solid yet uncertain historical company.

Thinking about RCWP: Spiritual, but Religious

RCWP holds implications for scholars and students thinking through the rise of "spirituality" in late-twentieth-century and early-twenty-first-century Western religions. But instead of declaring themselves "spiritual but not religious"—a now-ubiquitous catchphrase that I have never heard a single womanpriest use—RCWP crafts a religious space in which Catholics (and non-Catholics) can be spiritual *as well as* religious. "Spiritual" and "religious" are not mutually exclusive categories in RCWP communities; instead, the womenpriests and their supporters are, to evoke the title of scholar Laurel Zwissler's 2007 article "Spiritual, but Religious." Like Zwissler's subjects, RCWP's women "refuse to relinquish 'religion' to conservatism. They also assert the right to continue to draw on their religions as resources in their social justice work [and] they do not want to force their 'religious' interpretations onto the 'spiritual' experiences of others."[21] In the contemporary Catholic world, where some identities are excluded from certain church roles and rituals, RCWP brings "religion" to bear on spiritual searching only insofar as it promotes a sense of self-worth and a more intimate relationship with God. For RCWP, Roman Catholicism has many of the right resources and proper tools—Catholics just need guidance applying those tools in spiritually healthy ways.

In interviews and surveys, womenpriests' language is often peppered with references to "spirituality" and "the individual," both hallmark concepts for SBNRs (i.e., people who identify as "spiritual, but not religious"). Additionally, womenpriests believe they have the right—based on Rome's own emphasis on conscience—to use Catholicism's resources to create their own religious meanings and relationships with God. What makes RCWP significant for SBNRs is that it loops back around to religion, accepting it instead of rejecting it.[22] And, as Zwissler notes, problems can arise for religious activists committed to social justice; these individuals, like womenpriests, exist "in a liminal position between more conservative members of their religious traditions and those in their activist communities who dislike religion."[23] In so many ways, this describes RCWP perfectly: they rile conservatives with their activism (transgression), and they unsettle activists with their religious behavior (tradition). Unlike those who (either self-reflectively or uncritically) label themselves SBNR today, RCWP proudly replicates parts of the Roman Catholic tradition, keeping religion intact by using Catholic idioms and actions, and keeping spirituality intact via individuality and autonomy.

RCWP helps forge this bridge between religion and spirituality in the form of a Roman Catholic priesthood practiced and performed by illegally ordained womenpriests. While of course their *contra legem* actions invalidate them in many Catholics' eyes, the women's *priesthood*, however illegal, validates them for others—the same others who prioritize Catholicism's spiritual, experiential, and nondoctrinal elements. Priesthood holds undeniable meaning for followers of a faith tradition rooted for millennia in ordained authority through apostolic lineage, wherein priests deliver sacramental sustenance enveloped in grace and mystery. For RCWP's women, being priests—and being able to call themselves priests—is central to the group's mission and vision: being priests lends authority; being priests provides the ultimate provocation; being priests allows women into priesthood; and being priests allows the movement's members to see themselves as remaining connected to Catholicism. In this way, RCWP's form of spirituality remains tethered to Roman Catholicism's formal religiosity, just as RCWP's religious replication makes space for more individualistic theologies.

And so, RCWP invites observers of contemporary Western religion to consider how feminist faith commitments can blur the boundaries between religious formality and spiritual fluidity. In using the RCWP movement to enact their own relationship to Roman Catholicism, womenpriests use priesthood to tether themselves more tightly to tradition, all the while making more precarious their standing within institutional Catholicism. Then, as leaders within this transgressive form of *contra legem* Catholicism, they share their "spiritual but religious" faith with their congregants.

What Does the Future Hold for RCWP?

Womenpriests argue that female priests are necessary for *this* time and place. This transitional language has been a motif since the movement's founding. RCWP has often written that it is "a renewal movement within the Roman Catholic Church and that [it] will dissolve when canon 1024 is changed to open ordination to women."[24] RCWP bishop Patricia Fresen echoed the transitional message in 2005: "We are in a transitional time," between the need to ordain clergy and, perhaps, a future day when leadership will come from a community, with no need for ordination.[25] In 2014, womanpriest Irene Senn wrote, "Our movement has the potential to be the transition[al] step between the institutional church and its hierarchy and the evolving (but still not prevalent) church in which all are equal (ordained not set apart from lay)."[26] Womenpriests see themselves as being for the present moment, where the problems exist and the people stand ready to address them. If they succeed in their aims of changing (or, in my framing, purifying) the Roman church, women will be ordained, the lay-clergy divide will be weakened, and RCWP will, having achieved its aims, be needed no longer.

But that aspirational future is far away, and as we look beyond the present incarnation of RCWP toward its possible future, observers of contemporary Catholicism must note the temporal issues that RCWP raises. The fact that the movement sees itself as offering guidance and spiritual support during a transitional moment shows that some of Roman Catholicism's most invested (if not most deferential) members are experiencing and expecting a paradigm shift in Roman Catholicism.[27] As many womenpriests I have talked to understand it, something new is on the horizon. It has been five hundred years since the Protestant Reformation, and they say that the time is ripe for another. Here, finally, the Protestant analogy so often used to deride womenpriests may one day prove apt: like RCWP's women, Augustinian priest Martin Luther had no intention of leaving behind the Catholic Church or his Catholic identity when he posted his Ninety-Five Theses and agitated for reforms. He was a Catholic who held fidelity and dissent in tension as he became a key figure in the Protestant

Reformation. Womenpriests talk of reforming the church, yet they stand poised to do something different, if the Spirit moves them.

RCWP says that it is building something for now and not for all time. At present, RCWP holds in tension a number of conflicting forces: rejecting power, knowing and honoring its audience, and wanting to change the Roman Catholic patriarchy when hundreds of millions of the world's Catholics have little investment in the kinds of reforms RCWP envisions. It would perhaps be easier to build a successful protest movement if RCWP were more willing to bend on some of these items. But to be a *reform* movement, RCWP must retain trust in the long-standing hold of Roman Catholic faith, theology, and traditions. Flawed as these are in the progressive Catholic imagination, RCWP wants to usher worshippers and the church into a new paradigm with female priests, lay authority, and a dismantled kyriarchy.

RCWP is an unfolding case study of the very transition to which they aspire. The movement straddles the line between institutional (hence the adjective "Roman" in their name) and experiential (in terms of spiritual seeking). RCWP offers both, practices both, and experiments with both, simultaneously. Womenpriests are remaking Catholicism as we know it. The group's focus on women is the beginning—not the end—of imagined Catholic reform. Including women is, for RCWP, required to set in motion twenty-first-century Roman church renewal. RCWP does not desire an all-women-led church but a Roman Catholic Church that includes women at all levels of leadership so that the vital future renewal will be just, egalitarian, and viable for all Roman Catholics. They believe the inclusion of women will kick-start the necessary reforms, but it will not *ensure* the necessary reforms. Rather, eschewing power and aspiring to a "discipleship of equals" are still required. And for RCWP, as revealed in their rhetoric and practices, women are the invaluable starting point for change, in part because they are *women*, with particular gifts and tendencies, and in part because they are marginalized, with a particular perspective.

We must acknowledge, however, that RCWP's idealized and specialized brand of Catholicism likely holds little appeal for most Catholics worldwide. So far, RCWP consists of well-educated, mostly white women living in the Global North. A small—though certainly growing—number of women have been ordained outside of North America and Europe, but by and large, living as excommunicated, *contra legem* womenpriests is a somewhat privileged (if also socially perilous) state, available to women who can survive and thrive in their culture even after disobeying the Roman Catholic Church and challenging gender binaries. This is not true for all Catholic women around the globe. RCWP's actions can obscure the realities of lived Catholicism for the vast majority of Catholics in other parts of the world. Womenpriests' version of gender-equal priesthood will not appeal to all people, nor would it work in all historical times and places. RCWP's Catholicism is thus not universal but distinctly contemporary and Western.

With these global trends in view, Rome will not be rushing to ordain women any time soon. As historian Philip Jenkins noted in his book *The Next Christendom*, "The conservatism of [the Catholic Church], so often denounced and derided, must partly be seen as a response to the changing demographics of world religion."[28] Those Western Catholics accusing Rome of failing to appreciate the nuances around questions of women's ordination, for example, are possibly overlooking the dominance of Catholic cultures in the Global South, which would consider such a departure from tradition to be anathema. Per Jenkins, "The hierarchy knows that many liberal issues dear to American or West European Catholics are unpalatable to many socially traditional societies of the South."[29] In addition, while RCWP, WOC, and other groups constantly point to priest shortages as an imperative for women's ordination, Europe and North America already fare far better in priest-to-believers ratios.[30]

At present, the issue of womenpriests is of grave importance only to certain subsets of Western Catholicism and not at all important to the growing numbers of Catholics in Latin America, Africa, and Asia. If this is so, the women's ordination issue might well be the fulcrum on which hinge future changes in the church: northern Christians will not accept Catholicism without it, while southern Christians cannot envision a Catholicism with it. The question "What is Catholicism?" casts a wide net, and while Western Catholic voices resonate more loudly in the American and European media, the majority of global Catholics (as well as Christians) simply do not share these concerns. Try as RCWP might to impact Rome and reverse a historical mandate against ordained women, womenpriests truly have more in common with progressive elements of Protestant denominations, Mormonism, and Judaism than with their own—more conservative and gender-traditional—Catholic brothers and sisters. As strongly as RCWP is holding onto sacramental and traditional elements of Catholicism, their cultural location in the West indicates the rifts between Catholic cultures worldwide.

In the coming years, we may discover that RCWP has heralded an emerging trend, far too important to overlook, that marks an irreparable departure among Catholics worldwide. While the Global South values traditional male authority and the doctrines and decrees that accompany it, Catholics in the Global North find themselves caught between rejecting religious structures outright or creatively maneuvering to merge the religious with the individual, the doctrinally bound with the spiritually evolving. RCWP represents this latter development in seeking to keep Roman Catholicism viable. Often, educated women with feminist leanings reject religious systems altogether, dismissing them as unfailingly sexist. Womenpriests, in contrast, have doubled down on Roman Catholicism's intrinsic and soteriological value. RCWP is—maybe inadvertently—helping to restore Roman Catholicism's reputation by pointing to its spiritual and sacramental viability, even while, paradoxically, Roman Catholic leadership rejects the womenpriests themselves. Quite simply, womenpriests want ordination because they want Roman Catholicism—the history, the traditions, the culture, the sacraments.

What, then, will the future hold for RCWP? Part of this question will be answered in the future dynamics among the different groups. Conflict certainly arises among and within the RCWP regions, on matters ranging from theology to bureaucracy to retreat logistics. This is to be expected from impassioned, dedicated women, and respectful disagreement can help focus the movement's mission and future goals. RCWP tends to avoid discussing publicly its internal conflicts, as a matter of strategy. At the September 2015 Women's Ordination Worldwide conference, I attended a workshop titled "Inclusive and Empowered: The Women Priests Movement, Renewing the Church Now," featuring women from both RCWP-USA and ARCWP. Toward the end of the session, as the contributors' formal comments ended, the audience began asking—with increasing intensity—what *actually* distinguished RCWP-USA and ARCWP; evidently, conference-goers were not convinced that the groups had any substantive differences. I watched as the contributors struggled to address this question with any specificity. One womanpriest, in attendance but not on the panel, said, finally, that they had to be careful not to appear "schismatic," lest "the boys" in Rome point to the movement and say, "There's a cat fight."[31] Conflict within the movement will continue to arise in the future as it has in the past, and RCWP is sensitive to appearances of infighting and the likely gendering of conflicts. How the women will handle their differences amid the similarities that bond them together, all while in the fraught environment of *contra legem* priesthood, will steer the movement's future.

I have heard some womenpriests wonder aloud whether RCWP might best be viewed as a kind of religious order, that is, a group of devoted individuals committed to specific ways of living one's faith and beliefs in the world. If they are unable to transition the church to Western feminist progressivism, perhaps

RCWP will go this route. As a religious order—or a consortium of several similar but distinct religious orders (RCWP-USA, ARCWP, RCWP-Canada, etc.)—the group might find strength amid regional differences. As Victoria Rue said, it has been difficult for the womenpriests "to embrace and...balance [their] differences," in part because they "have never articulated a charism that [they] all share," across all RCWP groups.[32] A charism—that is, a distinct spiritual orientation or mission shared by all members—could help unite the movement. Determining a charism would require decision-making, because, unlike many religious orders (think Jesuits or Franciscans), RCWP was not founded by a charismatic leader who implanted a charism into the movement from the outset.

A shared charism or a deliberate categorization as something other than a transitional protest group might, in the years ahead, help RCWP attract younger generations and more diverse Catholic populations. At present, RCWP speaks most clearly to Catholic women raised with Vatican II's progressive promises—like the vast majority of womenpriests themselves. How, then, will RCWP draw women from among younger generations? What changes to message and practice would the group have to make to do so? Additionally, RCWP currently draws very (politically and religiously) liberal women. Might the movement at some point appeal to more conservative women who also feel a call to priesthood and cherish Catholicism's traditions and sacraments? In other words, RCWP's blend of tradition and transgression might someday appear more conservative *of church traditions*, traditions that are diminishing in an increasingly secular Western context.

I wonder also how RCWP will continue to reject kyriarchical forms in the hopes of creating a more democratic "discipleship of equals." As I have suggested before, surely this will depend largely on the individual womanpriest's congregation, which is itself a kind of democratic response to "meeting the people where they are." But RCWP's sharpest critiques from Catholic feminist theologians have warned about replicating hierarchy, and this is something around which RCWP proceeds cautiously, even defensively. As I have described, RCWP has developed formal organizational, administrative, and regional structures since the 2002 Danube ordination. Although some womenpriests view the emerging governance structures as helpful and necessary, others recoil at what looks to be a path toward the power differentials RCWP seeks to reform. Again, RCWP is a case study for difficult questions: Is it possible for a movement to grow and strengthen without falling into an inevitable trap of hierarchical thinking? Or, how can leadership and organizational structure avoid becoming hierarchical? Or, more finely put, is there a way for reform movements based in and seeking to reform an institutional model to truly practice a "discipleship of equals"? Will womenpriests find a way to simultaneously be leaders in their communities and organized on a national and international level without linking this leadership and organization to power and authority—specifically the types of power that corrupt and the types of authority that infantilize laypeople? Can womenpriests who reject what they view as Rome's repressive power structures create a governance model that is true to their values? Considering that these are the types of questions that have already led RCWP to splinter into different organizational and governance modes, these matters are imperative for RCWP's future. It will behoove us to watch for the different models of leadership and partnership that arise within the RCWP communities. We should also make note of possible differences among groups, like RCWP-USA, ARCWP, and the Canadian and European branches.

In this book, I have left unturned some topics that would provide valuable material for future scholars. *Womanpriest* has not deeply explored RCWP liturgies—specifically, how does RCWP design and practice liturgies in comparison to, for instance, Women-Church groups, or Ecumenical Catholic Communion churches, or other groups that position themselves as independent of Rome? It would be illuminating to examine how liturgical styles and choices either signal or influence theology and practice among priests and worshippers. In addition, most womenpriests have edited parts of the lectionary and sacramentary to include more gender-inclusive terms (e.g., referencing "Mother and Father God") and to downplay patriarchal language (such as "Lord" and "Master"). Other womenpriests have worked with congregants to write their own parts of the Mass, like the Gloria and Lamb of God, which a liturgist may find rich for analysis.

Similarly instructive would be research on the womenpriests who bring contemporary Catholic mysticism into their prayer lives and priesthoods. Some womenpriests draw on the mystical traditions of medieval women, and the creative theologies this inspires reveal the decision-making inspiring Catholics today. Also meriting scholarly attention is an ethnographic study of RCWP congregants specifically. Who are these RCWP-curious and loyal congregants who worship with womenpriests week after week? It may be telling to compare these individuals and their theologies with the Catholics who remain dedicated to Catholicism's institutional forms. Additionally, in the past few years, a number of women have been ordained through RCWP outside of North America and Western Europe. Learning more about these women—who hail from South Africa, the Philippines, Taiwan, Venezuela, and Columbia—could shed light on different worldwide "Catholicisms" and the gender politics different Catholics confront. If, as I have argued throughout *Womanpriest*, RCWP is a reform movement that holds a magnifying glass to what its womenpriests really believe to be important and invaluable within the Roman Catholic tradition, a study of non-Western womenpriests could reveal the crucial areas of difference and intersection in global Catholicism.

In what is likely a provocative question, considering how *Womanpriest* has emphasized the deliberate "Roman" labeling in RCWP's rhetoric, I wonder how long "Roman" will remain part of Roman Catholic Womenpriests' group identity. Might RCWP someday purposefully jettison its "Roman" descriptor and, by extension, its mission of overturning canon 1024? This question of RCWP's "Roman-ness" is one area where I noted incremental changes in my years studying the movement. Whereas the movement's founding mothers in Europe and North America saw themselves retaining "Roman" as a matter of principle and protest, crucial to RCWP's vision, there are today ordained womenpriests who sound more like Independent Catholics, disinterested in Rome's rules or reactions. When I queried women about their Roman-ness in 2014, for example, ARCWP's Maureen McGill responded, "It depends on what you mean by Roman," and womanpriest Debra Meyers wrote, "Most of us don't really care what the 'Romans' have to say about our ministry or our ordinations anymore." Wanda Russell, also with ARCWP, was more definitive about keeping "Roman": "Yes. We cling to the best of the Roman Church."[33] Most believe the "Roman" label to be invaluable, but a handful of women I interviewed are already calling for the movement to drop the word "Roman." Perhaps the decade of Vatican immobility on women's ordination is nudging womenpriests to look elsewhere for their movement's mission. If changing canon law is an insurmountable challenge, there may be other ways for womenpriests to make Catholicism meaningful.

All this is to say, just as *Womanpriest* has shown RCWP to be an invaluable case study for contemporary Catholicism, feminist religious action, and questions of religious authority and reform, RCWP can continue to be so into the future, in a multitude of possible iterations. Scholars would do well to keep an eye on RCWP and the ways it changes. Whether it grows or shrinks, splinters or consolidates, develops more formalized, institution-like organization or further decentralizes, the group will continue to communicate to us about the ever-evolving relationships between individual and institution, gender and authority, tradition and transgression.

Where Is Everyone? (And Why Not RCWP?)

One of my largest lingering questions about RCWP is this: "Where is everyone?" If RCWP is providing Catholics what they claim to want—particularly progressive Catholics who are suspicious of the institution and want more modernizing reforms—why are RCWP services not standing-room only? The more I researched and discovered how closely RCWP's women try to stay aligned with many Roman Catholic elements, the more it seemed likely that other Catholics would fill RCWP's pews—or, in many cases, womenpriests' living rooms and folding chairs. The more I heard womenpriests speak directly—and sacramentally, and liturgically—to problems confronting the contemporary church, the more I expected to find those Catholics—who want married priests, womenpriests, acceptance for LGBTQ Catholics, clergy who are not "out of touch" and hierarchical—cramming RCWP Masses.

But this is not what I found. The typical RCWP Mass draws ten to twenty congregants, not hundreds. RCWP ordination ceremonies often draw very large numbers, but many who attend do so in solidarity or curiosity and do not intend to stay on as congregants. So what kinds of conclusions might we draw about individuals absent from RCWP Masses? What of the people who could worship with RCWP's women but do not? Why *not* RCWP? Here I am thinking not of the millions of Catholics and former Catholics who have not yet heard about the RCWP movement but rather of those who could come to RCWP communities but do not. My thoughts here stem from those informal conversations I had with people about my project over the years: strangers I encountered while traveling, non-Catholics I talked with at academic conferences, friends who made offhand comments in social contexts, students who tried to reconcile what they thought they knew of Catholicism with what they were learning—all of this proved illuminating in informal ways. I offer four tentative conclusions.

First, dissension from the institutional church takes work. It takes emotional, spiritual, and intellectual energy. Dissenting means taking a position, explaining oneself, severing some ties while building others. And thoughtful dissent requires theological dexterity. This is not work every Catholic is prepared to do. Many people I have talked with have the passion to simultaneously love and critique the church, but they do not have the tools to do so in a way that provides resolution. Many Catholics know they need something more than what the current Roman Catholic Church is offering them, but they do not know how to cultivate an alternative: contemporary, progressive theologies only infrequently make their way from the Catholic pulpit to the pews. What many Catholics know of their religion comes from childhood catechism, required religious instruction (surrounding, for example, first Communion, confirmation, and marriage), and homilies. They have no reason outside of self-motivation to read the scholarship, theology, and critiques of kyriarchy that have motivated RCWP's women—and that many church leaders view as threatening to the faith. Even most ordained priests today are unfamiliar with the theologies that inspire conscientious disobedience, and so, unsurprisingly, the laity are largely unprepared for "valid but illicit" female priests.

Second, many Roman Catholic parishes, particularly in North America, offer large communities that enrich members' lives socially as well as spiritually. Parents with children in Catholic grade schools, congregants who love singing in large choirs, and parishioners who engage in large-scale volunteer efforts cannot as yet find such opportunities within RCWP communities.[34] The rationale here is not so much theological as social and cultural. To choose an RCWP community over a large diocesan parish could mean missing out on large-parish events, like Lenten fish fries or fundraising trivia nights; or forgoing your children's chance to attend Catholic schools and make the sacraments of reconciliation, Communion, and confirmation with other Catholic students; or participating in standing-room-only Masses on Christmas and Easter. Some people, then, bypass RCWP communities because what they most value about being Catholic is not priestly leadership or traditional theology but family traditions, holiday celebrations, and Catholic cultural markers. This is also why a sizable number of RCWP worshippers remain connected to their old parishes. RCWP, as yet, cannot compete with large parishes.

Third, myriad Catholics who are frustrated with Catholicism have left the church behind altogether. They are burned out. Their relationship with Catholicism—and often with religion in toto—cannot be salvaged at this time. These individuals are not "seekers," are not struggling to rectify and return. I think of these as the people who, when I tell them about RCWP, respond in one of two ways: "Good for them! Glad someone is doing it!" or "What's the point? It won't change anything." Embedded in these remarks is an unstated resignation: "I myself wouldn't bother." Many of RCWP's potential audience are not choosing between RCWP and the institutional church: they are choosing between RCWP and no church. In other words, many of RCWP's possible congregants are unreachable. What RCWP offers them is too little, too late. These individuals may applaud RCWP's efforts, but only from a comfortable distance.

Finally, I suspect the act of disobedience and the threat of excommunication scare some away from RCWP. RCWP's women have adopted a posture of defiance in the face of excommunication, but few Catholics are as willing to risk their relationship with their religion. Two things are simultaneously true here. One, most people I have talked to about Catholicism think it silly to believe a priest or bishop or even pope had any say in their individual relationship with God and their soul's eternal destination. And yet, two, I have to acknowledge—for this has been reverberating throughout *Womanpriest*, after all—that the teaching that the Roman Catholic Church is heaven's gatekeeper is deeply hardwired within the faithful. Many have a hard time articulating their discomfort with womenpriests once they learn the women are all excommunicated. Talking with contemporary Catholics, it can be easy to see the cognitive dissonance between what believers intellectually think and what their souls fear. And often with this fear comes fatigue.

If I am correct on this final point, the lack of committed congregants is not about RCWP and its limitations: it is about fear and fatigue among current and former Catholics. Their lack of appearance at RCWP services might not be about RCWP but about Roman Catholicism. So many times, I have found myself listening to progressive Catholics—usually baby boomers or Generation Xers—who are railing against the institutional church. The sources of their derision run the gamut, from local diocesan politics ("Bishop Smith is so conservative and not at all pastoral") to theological teachings ("The theology is so confusing! It does not make sense that there are no married priests or women priests in this day and age") to horror ("I can't believe those priests abused all those children"). But what have these individuals done with their frustration? Many have continued to go to Mass, remaining Catholic as they had always been Catholic. Their discomfort with the church was palpable, but their behavior had not changed.

Why not? Perhaps because even within a troubled and troubling church, there is a sense of soteriological certainty. Paradoxically, the Roman Catholic elements that RCWP holds tight—the traditions and rituals, the sacraments and prayers, the words and influences of Jesus, the embodied discipline—might be precisely what keeps even unenthusiastic and yet dutiful Catholics within non-RCWP Catholicism. These Catholics value the "smells and bells" of Catholicism because they signal something familiar and safe. Being "within" the Roman church (and not worshipping with excommunicated womenpriests) offers trust that one is saved, that one is checking the right boxes to get to heaven. It is easier to do nothing different than something dramatic like RCWP—especially if one's soul might, *might*, be at stake.

RCWP often catches people who are drawing their last breaths of Roman Catholic air. These are the people pained, often deeply, by decades of sexism, the sex-abuse crisis, and dwindling trust in the value of a strict Catholic religiosity. Womenpriests offer hope to these individuals, but it may not be enough. Some worshippers, surely, believe that ordained women will be a panacea to fix problems in the Roman Catholic Church. But of course, womenpriests cannot fix everything, nor do they aspire to change everything. This group of nearly 250 individuals does, however, aim to transform a two-thousand-year-old institutional church that has over a billion members worldwide—and that goal is certainly daunting enough. Whether they can provide Catholic sustenance to struggling Roman Catholics looking for reasons to stay is a question that only time can answer.

Postscript: A Return to Therese of Divine Peace

As a researcher using methods of critical ethnography, I sought to remain intentional and careful throughout my research, remembering the potential impact of my academic perspective in interpreting womenpriests' stories. In remaining attuned to my own reactions to RCWP, I came to realize that I had embarked on a Roman Catholic journey of my own. My personal responses to womanpriest-led liturgies revealed much to me, personally and intellectually, about Catholicism's ability to implant itself in bodies and souls. Early in my research, sometimes attending RCWP Masses left me feeling sad—because it wasn't quite the same, and I wanted renegade womenpriests to be able to capture what I understood to be "the correct" Catholicism.

For example, sometimes I wished for a kneeler. Because womanpriest-led Masses cannot be held in Catholic churches, I never knelt during them—and this absence showed me that my Catholic-disciplined body craved kneelers. I also felt the absence of Catholic "smells and bells": the candles or incense, the statues and stained glass, the crucifix looming over the altar. Certain things come to mark one's experience of Catholicism, and these were staples of mine—though I did not realize that until such hallmarks were gone.

Other times I wished for the anonymity that a large parish church affords, where I can sneak into a pew, sit quietly, and be alone yet present within a community. Yet most RCWP services are so small that one cannot hide. New visitors stand out and draw many questions. With this small size comes intimacy and friendship—and hugging—among the gathered. Enthusiastic affection is not a trademark of Catholic Masses in most diocesan communities, and the friendly greetings before and after RCWP Masses reminded me more of evangelical Protestant services than Catholic ones.

But in time, I adjusted to the differences of RCWP Masses. The physical, experiential, and even spiritual differences I experienced throughout my ethnographic study helped me consider RCWP's significance in and beyond Catholicism. I discovered that I liked engaging more deeply: shared homilies, concelebration of the Eucharist, conversations with other worshippers before and after Mass. I noticed anew the parts of the Mass when they felt not perfunctory but participatory. With a womanpriest at the altar, feminine imagery and feminist theological ideas sprang to life in my mind. And then, when the new English translation of the Roman missal arrived in 2010, with some jarring (to me) new language, I took comfort in RCWP liturgies because the womenpriests had rejected these changes. For example, while English-speaking Roman Catholics everywhere now responded to the priest's "The Lord be with you" with the unfamiliar "And with your spirit," RCWP Masses kept the decades-old utterance "And also with you." In other words, RCWP liturgies came to feel more familiar than legal diocesan Masses.

On a more intellectual level, the more I researched the Catholic Church's long history of viewing women as less holy than men, the less I was able to sit through a "valid and licit" Mass without nagging discomfort. I struggled to find room within formal Catholicism for my evolving, ever-unfolding sense of self and my place in the world. RCWP's liturgies increasingly made sense to me as an illegal but invigorating alternative to the form of Catholicism I had known for decades.

For my part, I realized through my research that what RCWP communities could not provide in terms of the Catholic familiarity of my youth, they made up for in spirit, community, and intellectual rigor. In my experience, RCWP offers both womenpriests and worshippers a salve for the religious and existential struggles that mar the contemporary Catholic faithful. I found gratitude in an environment that welcomed me, no matter where I was on my constantly shifting Roman Catholic journey.

And this journey continues, with RCWP in view. Once I was no longer conducting interviews or seeking new data, I attended RCWP Masses not because I needed to but because I wanted to. Those few times each year when I return to St. Louis, my hometown, I attend Mass at Therese of Divine Peace. It seems fitting that my present and future relationship with RCWP connects with my past, that is, with the people and in the place where my research began in 2007.

When I attend church at Therese of Divine Peace, I am surrounded by adults—most several decades older than myself—who delight in each other's company. I have watched the many ways womanpriest Elsie McGrath has gifted her ordained authority to the lay people at Therese, as everyone is involved in making Mass possible. Those who participate in the music ministry do so joyfully, sharing their gifts with their community. Elsie and another original member of Therese, a musician named Rodger Kalbfleisch, wrote words and music for parts of the Mass. I have now attended Therese just enough to recognize this music and sing along. I listen to Elsie's thought-provoking and impassioned homilies, which always touch upon current events and call the community to conscientious action and prayer. I reflect on comments from other Mass-goers when Elsie invites discussion during the homily. I hug everyone around me during the sign of peace. I participate in the concelebration of the Eucharist. It all feels normal now.

It has become my practice to attend Christmas Eve Mass at Therese. Like the "midnight" Masses of my childhood, Therese's Christmas Eve vigil starts not at midnight but a few hours earlier. Every Christmas Eve, I park my car in a near-empty lot and walk about fifty yards to the Hope Chapel of the Unitarian Universalist church. The golden-orange glow from the worship space's floor-to-ceiling windows pierces the darkness of the December night. I hear piano, strumming guitar, and sounds of a small choir preparing for a celebration. I walk in. Almost immediately, I find Elsie and we greet one another with a warm hug. Therese parishioners surround me, welcoming me. Many remember me, year after year, and reintroduce themselves, and ask how the book is coming along. Like the Roman Catholic liturgy, like the Catholic liturgical calendar, my annual visits to Therese are becoming ritualized. I find comfort in this familiarity.

I take a seat, and my eyes search for Therese's simple nativity scene, which I have come to love. Every year it moves to a new location, because every year the worship space is set up differently. Every year, I cherish the first sight of the statue once I find it. It is a singular wooden statue of the Holy Family, without a manger or barnyard animals or magi. Joseph's body wraps around Mary's; her nesting arms await Jesus's arrival. The small Christ child figure will be placed in his mother's embrace once the liturgy begins.

After the Christmas Eve Masses, Therese's members exchange gifts. Some come with seasonal gift bags to distribute; some share cookies and pastries. Elsie passes around a homemade calendar containing important dates for the Therese community. They share stories with one another.

Whether they give much thought to the Roman Catholic legality of their worship, I do not know. I suspect that, by now, this question has become uninteresting to them. Their midnight Mass at Therese is, in their eyes, holy, sacred, sacramental. I even suspect that many of the questions I have taken up in this book—about the international RCWP initiative, RCWP's history and changing tensions and challenges—only concern them slightly. My questions are not their questions; what I care about as a researcher is not why they attend Therese. They come because they are surrounded by friends and a chosen family. They are able to see a woman in the role of priest, something many of them have wanted for decades and some of them did not really consider before Elsie.

The Christmas Eve vigil is simple and intimate—certainly simpler and more intimate than the elaborate, formal Mass with thousands of attendees taking place less than a mile away at the Cathedral Basilica of St. Louis. Unobtrusively, in a Mass facilitated by a *contra legem* womanpriest, the Therese community embodies their chosen Roman Catholic faith and the mystery of Jesus's incarnation. Like the small carved wooden infant Jesus, nestled in his mother's arms in Therese's nativity set, this mystery—of sacrament, of grace, of Christ's life and death—has rested simply and quietly at the core of the Therese Mass. And like the Jesus of the nativity, Therese of Divine Peace rests in a woman's arms. Above all, this is what the RCWP movement creates: an expression of Roman Catholicism wherein one trusts and believes that God works sacramentally, bestows grace, and rewards the faithful—through the hands of a womanpriest.

APPENDIX A

Interview Subjects and Primary Sources

RCWP ordinations and liturgies, along with interviews, created the experiential foundations for my ethnographic methods. I started my ethnographic research in earnest in 2009, after receiving IRB approval through the University of North Carolina at Chapel Hill.

Ordination services attended

Minneapolis, Minnesota (August 16, 2009)
Rochester, New York (May 1, 2010)
Baltimore, Maryland (June 4, 2011)
Falls Church, Virginia (June 22, 2013)

Liturgies attended

Therese of Divine Peace (several liturgies, including a baptism), St. Louis, Missouri
Hildegard Community of the Living Spirit, Festus, Missouri
St. Praxedis Catholic Community, New York, New York
Spiritus Christi (RCWP-led Mass), Rochester, New York
Living Water Community, Baltimore, Maryland
Church of the Beatitudes, Santa Barbara, California
Mary Magdalene Apostle Catholic Community, San Diego, California

I started my ethnographic work before ARCWP branched off from RCWP-USA. As a result, the majority of Masses I attended were RCWP (or RCWP-USA), and not ARCWP, with the exception of the Falls Church, Virginia, ordination in 2013.

I conducted all of my research while living in North Carolina, and for most of that time, I was a graduate student. Not until 2013 did the Tar Heel State see its first womanpriest—who even then lived two hours away from my home in Durham. Logistical and financial challenges precluded me from weeks-or months-long immersions into a particular RCWP community or communities. Thankfully, other scholars were starting to do academic, ethnographic work at the local level, and two theses—one a master's thesis focused on the Sophia Inclusive Catholic Community in Sussex County, New Jersey, and the other an undergraduate thesis examining Therese of Divine Peace in

St. Louis—provided me with narrative data on several worshippers within these two RCWP communities, and thus proved a valuable supplement to my own interviews.[1]

In conducting interviews, I went out of my way to make the experience as convenient as possible for my subjects. Many preferred to write their responses to my questions, saying this gave them time to reflect and complete the interview over several days. In the following list, I indicate whether the interview subjects were ordained with RCWP at the time I spoke with them. I do not distinguish RCWP-USA from ARCWP affiliation here.

Interviews

Rose Marie Hudson, RCWP, July 9, 2009 (in person)
Elsie Hainz McGrath, RCWP, July 9, 2009 (in person)
Marybeth McBryan, RCWP, July 17, 2009, and February 19, 2014 (telephone)
Patricia Hughes Baumer, August 17, 2009 (in person)
Mary Kay Kusner, RCWP, September, 17, 2009 (email and telephone)
Gabriella Velardi Ward, RCWP, January 9, 2010 (telephone)
Dorothy Irvin (archaeologist), March 17, 2010 (in person)
Laura Singer, (then president of Women's Ordination Conference), November 17, 2010 (telephone)
Jane Via, RCWP, November 22, 2010 (telephone)
Dana Reynolds, RCWP, December 14, 2010 (telephone)
Eileen DiFranco, RCWP, January 4, 13, and 18, 2011 (email and telephone)
Chava Redonnet, RCWP, January 6, 2011 (telephone)
Joan Houk, RCWP, January 8, 2011 (telephone)
Mary Ann Schoettly, RCWP, January 8 and 9, 2011 (email and telephone)
Ida Raming, RCWP, January 9, 2011 (email)
Theresa Novak Chabot, RCWP, January 20, 2011 (telephone)
Janice Sevre-Duszynska, RCWP, January 23, 2011 (telephone)
Marie David, RCWP, February 11, 2011 (telephone)
Gloria Carpeneto, RCWP, February 16, 2011 (telephone)
Mary Frances Smith, RCWP, March 4, 2011 (email)
Monique Venne, RCWP, March 27, 2011 (email)
Roberta Meehan, RCWP, April 10 and 14, 2011 (telephone)
Michele Birch-Conery, RCWP, April 19, 2011 (telephone)
Monica Kilburn-Smith, RCWP, April 20, 2011 (telephone)
Marie Bouclin, RCWP, April 26 and 27, 2011 (email)
Rachel Wood, May 10, 2011 (telephone)
Andrea Johnson, RCWP, May 11, 2011 (telephone)
Morag Liebert, RCWP, May 20, 2011 (email)
Suzanne Thiel, RCWP, May 25, 2011 (telephone)
Alta Jacko, RCWP, May 28, 2011 (email)

Cheryl Bristol, RCWP, June 1, 2011 (email)
Olivia Doku, RCWP, June 14, 2013 (in person)
Suzanne Dunn, RCWP, June 15, 2013 (in person)
Jeannette Love, RCWP, June 15, 2013 (in person)

I met womenpriests and other women's ordination activists in other contexts as well and enjoyed important discussions with them, but I do not include these as formal interviews. As examples, I am grateful for the chance to talk informally with Marian Ronan (Catholicism scholar and RCWP critic) at a conference, and I took a workshop on "Theater as Pedagogy" led by womanpriest Victoria Rue at the 2011 American Academy of Religion conference in San Francisco. I also presented on a panel with womanpriest Eileen DiFranco at the 2017 Berkshire Conference and enjoyed conversation with her afterward.

Pink Smoke over the Vatican

Filmmaker Jules Hart started work on the documentary *Pink Smoke over the Vatican* in 2005, just as RCWP appeared in North America. She interviewed more than thirty-five individuals, including RCWP bishops, priests, and deacons; spouses and partners of ordained women; authors and activists committed to church reform; participants at RCWP Masses; and ordained men critical of RCWP. She filmed ordination ceremonies at Gananoque in 2005 (the first North American ordination), Pittsburgh in 2006 (the first US ordination), and Santa Barbara in 2007. She filmed liturgies at Rochester's Spiritus Christi church, the 2005 WOW conference in Ottawa, and various others in Northern California. She conducted formal interviews and shot informal footage in people's homes. I marvel with awe and gratitude at Hart's generosity in sharing this nonarchived footage with me.

Her interviews proved invaluable: not only did she begin her research years before I had even heard of the RCWP movement, but she was able to get interviews with European womenpriests who rarely travel to the US and only reluctantly grant interviews (in part because of language barriers). She also talked to ordained men critical of RCWP, whereas I—conducting interviews five or more years later—had no luck getting clergy to talk frankly about the movement.

Pink Smoke over the Vatican is unapologetically a work of advocacy that champions RCWP's actions and reviles the Catholic hierarchy for centuries of misogyny. Hart never intended otherwise. It is worth stating, then, that her interview questions are not *my* interview questions. What Hart wanted and needed from her subjects is not identical to what I would have pursued through ethnography and fieldwork. As a result, I have used the *Pink Smoke* footage with awareness of how the documentary genre could alter the subject's storytelling.

Interviews from Pink Smoke over the Vatican

2005

Angela Benavoglia
Patricia Fresen, RCWP
Jeanne Gallo
Rea Howarth
Dorothy Irvin
Joanna Manning
Christine Mayr-Lumetzberger, RCWP
Michael Mayr
Charles Nicolosi
Regina Nicolosi, RCWP
Mary Rammerman
Dana Reynolds, RCWP
Christine Schenk
Janice Sevre-Duszynska, RCWP
Jane Via, RCWP

2006

Dagmar Braun Celeste, RCWP
Don A. Cordeo
Juanita Cordero, RCWP
Patricia Fresen, RCWP
Anna Kolhede, San Jose State University student
Kathleen Strack Kunster, RCWP
Fr. Ron Lengwin, spokesperson for Catholic Diocese of Pittsburgh
Jean Marchant, RCWP
Scarlette McKenzie, San Jose State University student
Kathryn Poethig
Dana Reynolds, RCWP
Father Jose Rubio, San Jose State University campus ministry chaplain
Victoria Rue, RCWP
Janice Sevre-Duszynska, RCWP

2007

Patricia Fresen, RCWP
Kathleen Strack Kunster, RCWP

2009

Roy Bourgeois

Events in Pink Smoke over the Vatican

2005

Spiritus Christi Mass (July 21, 2005)
Women's Ordination Worldwide worship service
Preordination events, St. Lawrence Seaway (July 25, 2005)
Ordination, St. Lawrence Seaway (July 25, 2005)
Mass, Victoria Rue's house church (September 25, 2005)
Mentor meeting (April 10, 2005)

2006

Pittsburgh ordination press conference (July 30, 2006)
Ordination, Pittsburgh (July 31, 2006)
Mass, San Jose State University (April 23, 2006)
Mass, San Jose State University (May 7, 2006)
Mass, San Jose State University (May 21, 2006)
Mass, Don and Juanita Cordero's house church (August 11, 2006)
Dinner after Cordero house church Mass (August 11, 2006)

2007

Ordination, Santa Barbara (July 21, 2007)
Blessing oils (August 2, 2007)

2014 Electronic Surveys

In the summer of 2014, I created two online surveys through Survey Monkey, one for womenpriests and one for RCWP's community members. For the womenpriests survey, I received responses from thirty-five ordained RCWP members, including thirty-four women and one man. The respondents primarily lived in the United States, but some were in Canada and one in English-speaking Europe. For the RCWP communities survey, I received thirty responses. The online surveys aimed to capture the voices of womenpriests whom I would not have the opportunity to meet as well as to allow me to hear again from women I had previously interviewed in order to see what, if anything, had changed in their priesthoods. Talking to congregants had always been secondary to my research—behind talking with the womenpriests themselves—but grew increasingly significant as I sought to understand womenpriests' ministries and theological significance within their worship communities.

2014 Survey Respondents

Beverly Bingle
Mary Bergan Blanchard
Ruth Broeski
Mary Grace Crowley-Koch
Diane Dougherty
Christine Fahrenbach
Ann Harrington
Jim Lauder
Morag Liebert
Rita Lucey
Rosa Manriquez
Victoria Marie
Maureen McGill
Elsie McGrath
Bridget Mary Meehan
Debra Meyers
Ann Penick
Josie Petermeier
Victoria Rue
Wanda Russell
Irene Senn
Dorothy Shugrue
Rosemary Smead
Monica Kilburn Smith
Mary Theresa Streck
Toni Tortorilla
Gabriella Velardi Ward

Seven respondents answered some or all of the questions but did not include their names. One respondent is a catacomb priest, and I will not use her name.

Websites

Several websites helped shape my understanding of the many reform movements and ministries in contemporary Catholicism. While not all sites were/are meticulously maintained and updated, all offer a glimpse into the wider world of Catholic reform today—a world of which RCWP is a part.

Association of Roman Catholic Women Priests (www.arcwp.org)
Call to Action (www.cta-usa.org)
Catholic Network for Women's Equality (www.cnwe.org/)
A Church for our Daughters (http://achurchforourdaughters.org/)

CORPUS (www.corpus.org)

DignityUSA (www.dignityusa.org/)

Ecumenical Catholic Communion (www.ecumenical-catholic-communion.org/index
   .html)

Federation of Christian Ministries (www.federationofchristianministries.org)

Future Church (www.futurechurch.org)

Global Ministries University (www.globalministriesuniversity.org)

Intentional Eucharistic Communities (www.intentionaleucharisticcommunities.org)

Mary Magdalene Apostle Catholic Community (www.mmacc.org)

Roman Catholic Womenpriests (www.romancatholicwomenpriests.org)

Römisch-katholischen Priesterinnen (www.priesterinnen.net)

Southeastern Pennsylvania Women's Ordination Conference (www.sepawoc.org)

Spiritus Christi (www.spirituschristi.org)

United States Conference of Catholic Bishops (usccb.org)

Voice of the Faithful (www.votf.org)

We Are Church (www.we-are-church.org)

Women Priests for the Catholic Church (www.womenpriests.org)

Women's Alliance for Theology, Ethics, and Ritual (www.his.com/~mhunt)

Women's Ordination Conference (http://womensordination.org)

Women's Ordination Worldwide (www.womensordinationworldwide.org)

Interview Questions for Womenpriests

This is an exhaustive list of the questions I used for interviews and surveys, which reflect my growing understanding of the movement and the womenpriests themselves. In other words, these questions evolved and expanded between 2009, when I received IRB approval to begin ethnographic research, and 2014, when I created a survey using SurveyMonkey. In what you will see below, for instance, question 16 asks women why they decided to seek a *contra legem* ordination, and the multiple-choice options emerged years into my research, once I had enough data to identify patterns in the women's descriptions of their vocational callings. Questions about differences between RCWP and ARCWP came after the split between these entities. Questions asking about the respondent's relationship with "God/Godde/Higher Power" reflect the ways I had heard womenpriests talk about the divine.

During in-person and over-the-phone interviews, I would often begin with questions like these and find that our conversation focused almost exclusively on, for instance, sacraments or ministry. The survey I conducted in the summer of 2014 included all of these questions, and as with my in-person interviews, most survey respondents gravitated toward questions that most spoke to them.

The online survey gave me a chance to compare responses from RCWP-USA and ARCWP women, as well as compare the handful of responses from Canada and Europe to those from America.

All womenpriests were offered anonymity; very few wanted it. A greater number were willing to be quoted only if I cleared their quotations with them before publishing.

In quoting the respondents (for this survey and email interviews), I retain their choices in capitalization.

Basic Demographic Questions

1. What year were you born?
2. What is your gender?
3. Where do you live (city, state, country)?
4. What educational degrees have you received (and in what years)?
5. Which of these best describes you? (cradle Catholic, convert to Catholicism, other)
6. Given the church's position on women's ordination, why have you chosen to remain Catholic?

7. What do you consider the most important issues confronting the Roman Catholic Church?
8. What is your current relationship status?
9. Which of the following best describes you? (heterosexual/straight, gay/lesbian, bisexual, other)
10. How many children do you have (including biological, adopted, and from blended families)?
11. How many grandchildren do you have (including biological, adopted, and from blended families)?
12. Do you have a job, jobs, or a career in addition to your service as an ordained person?
13. When (month and year) and where were you ordained to the diaconate? To the priesthood? To the episcopate?
14. At what age were you first ordained?

Discernment Process

15. At what age did you first experience a call to priesthood? Feel free to comment on this call.
16. What is the reason you decided to seek a *contra legem* ordination?

> (You may select more than one option.)
> To honor a call to priesthood
> To work for justice in the Roman Catholic Church
> To protest the all-male priesthood
> To be a role model for women and girls in the church
> To stand within the lineage of activist Christian women
> Other (please specify)

17. What does being ordained allow you to do that you could not do before?
18. Before you were ordained through RCWP, were you an ordained or consecrated member of any other religious order or organizations?
19. Did you work with a priest mentor as part of your discernment and prepara19. tion process?
20. With which group or region do you affiliate? (USA-West, USA-East, USA-Midwest, USA-Great Waters, USA-Southern, Canada-West, Canada-East, Europe-West, Weiheämter für Frauen, ARCWP)

Role within RCWP/ARCWP and within Leadership and Ministry

21. Do you hold an office or position with RCWP/ARCWP?
22. What do you call yourself? (Multiple answers possible: womanpriest/womandeacon/womanbishop; woman priest/woman deacon/woman bishop; priest/deacon/bishop; other (please specify))

23. What do the people you serve call you? (Multiple answers possible: Reverend; Mother; Your first name; other (please specify))
24. What do you wear to signal you are ordained when celebrating sacraments?
25. What do you wear outside of liturgy and sacraments, if anything, to signal you are ordained?
26. Do you think RCWP and ARCWP are "Roman," as the groups' names suggest? Why or why not?
27. What do you see as the important differences between your movement's different regions and organization (e.g., RCWP vs. ARCWP, USA vs. Europe, Canada-West vs. Canada-East, etc.)?
28. Do you regularly lead a faith community?
29. What is the name of your faith community?
30. How did you choose this name?
31. How often do you meet for liturgy?
32. How many people regularly attend worship?
33. How would you describe your community demographically?
35. Do you lead this community with other members of RCWP? Or with members of other faith traditions?
35. Do you partner with other religious communities in your area? If so, what groups and what kinds of interfaith/ecumenical work do you do?

Sacraments

36. What sacraments have you performed? (Multiple answers possible: Eucharist; baptism; reconciliation; marriage; holy orders; confirmation; anointing of the sick)
37. Can you describe, in just a few words, what it's like to administer sacraments as an ordained person?
38. Do you use an organization (like the Federation of Christian Ministries) to "legitimate" your sacraments?
39. In working with liturgical forms, what have you kept from the traditional Roman Catholic rite and what have you modified? Have you made changes to your liturgy in the wake of the new Roman missal in 2011?

Interfaith and Ecumenical Work

40. What kinds of ecumenical and/or interfaith work have you done as a member of RCWP/ARCWP?
41. Have members of other religious traditions (Christian and non-Christian) helped you discern your call to ordination? If so, how?

Changes and Transitions, Personally and in the Movement

42. Since you have been ordained, how have you seen RCWP change?
43. Since you have been ordained, how has your worship community (if applicable) changed and evolved?
44. Since you have been ordained, how have your ministries changed and evolved?
45. How has your personal theology changed, if at all, since becoming ordained?
46. How has your relationship with [God/Godde/your Higher Power/etc.] changed, if at all, since becoming ordained?
47. What do you see as the future for RCWP? (acceptance and integration into the institutional Roman Catholic Church; separation from Rome as a distinct sect; integration into an existing group or denomination; other (please specify))
48. What would you like to see happen to or for RCWP?
49. If you could convince your fellow RCWP members of one thing, what would it be?

Various

50. What are your thoughts about Pope Francis?
51. If Pope Francis called you tomorrow and said, "We have reconsidered. Your ordination is valid. Come join us!" what would you say and do?
52. The research for this book focuses on topics like ordination ceremonies, sacraments, ministries, families, bodies, and sexuality. If you have any examples or stories about these or other topics that you are willing to share, please do so here.
53. What should I be asking you? What have I missed?

Data and Interview Questions for RCWP Communities

Although womenpriests are the central focus of this book, RCWP's ordained women do not exist in isolation. The following offers some basic information about the people who regularly attend Mass and are active in RCWP-led communities. Most of the following information comes from three studies: a 2014 electronic survey I conducted through the RCWP and ARCWP listservs; a 2011 MA thesis for Drew University's Theological School ("Waiting for Wisdom: Sophia's Response to the Roman Catholic Church's Position on Priesthood"), written by Allison Delcalzo; and an undergraduate thesis in women and gender studies from Washington University in St. Louis ("All Are Welcome: The Roman Catholic Women's Ordination Movement and the Motivations of Participants"), written by Caitlyn Gaskell.[1] I have also developed a strong sense of RCWP congregants through news stories, documentary interviews, and participant observation. Data combined with ethnographic research revealed distinctive patterns within North American RCWP communities (no parishioners outside of the US and Canada opted to take my survey), especially when compared to recent trends in American Catholic demographics (as reported primarily by the Pew Research Center).

Demographics of RCWP Congregants

RCWP congregants (or community members, i.e., people who regularly attend RCWP liturgies) are as diverse as the womenpriests themselves yet are united—also like the womenpriests—by shared beliefs about the need for Roman Catholic Church reform, spiritual growth, and the role modeling of Jesus. I have culled some preliminary data about RCWP parishioners in order to place womenpriests in a wider though still immediate context.

First and foremost, RCWP's worshippers are women, by a strong majority: Delcalzo's respondents were 85 percent women, Gaskell's were 67 percent women, and women in my survey were 82 percent.[2] While women are indeed better represented in the general American Catholic population, Pew's findings of 54 percent average women membership (to men's 46 percent) shows that RCWP's appeal to women is dramatic.[3] One can reasonably assume that many women join RCWP because of the powerful allure of a womanpriest, something for which countless Catholic women have long waited. This is even more the case for women of older generations, who grew up during Vatican II and its aftermath, seeing the rise of Catholic feminism and being part of a transforming Catholicism. And indeed, RCWP's worshippers are older: 100 percent of the parishioners Delcalzo surveyed were over the age of fifty. All but two people I surveyed were over the age of fifty, and twenty-five of my twenty-eight respondents were born before the start of Vatican II. The two oldest members from my survey were born in 1934 (and thus turned eighty the year they took the survey in 2014), and the youngest, born in 1983, was the only one of the twenty-eight born after 1966. When Gaskill interviewed Therese members in 2008 and 2009, she found a much younger average population (ranging in age from twenty-two to "late sixties") than I have seen in my recent visits to Therese, where members appear to be in their fifties, sixties, and older.[4] To be sure, the American Catholic population is an older group as a whole, with an average age of forty-nine (in 2015), which is higher than the American average of forty-six and significantly higher than the average age of not-religiously-affiliated Americans, thirty-six.[5] In spite of this trend, nearly 50 percent of American Catholics fall between the ages of eighteen and forty-nine.[6] Clearly, RCWP skews much older.

Openness to the idea of womenpriests may also stem from RCWP community members' significant educational achievements. Whereas 46 percent of American Catholics are likely to have a high school degree or less, 27 percent are likely to have some college, 16 percent have a bachelor's degree, and 10 percent have a postgraduate degree, RCWP's parishioners have devoted remarkably more time to education and degree seeking. Of Delcalzo's respondents, 30 percent had bachelor degrees alone, 50 percent had a master's degree, and 19 percent had multiple master's degrees. All of Gaskell's respondents had college degrees, and 53 percent had graduate degrees. Of my respondents, 64 percent had one or more graduate degrees.

Race is another factor that significantly distinguishes RCWP communities from American Catholics at large: all of Delcalzo's respondents in New Jersey and 93 percent of Gaskell's in St. Louis identified as white.[7] Compare this to the 2014 Pew Research Center Religious Landscape Study, which found that 59 percent of American Catholics are likely to be white, with 34 percent Hispanic, 3 percent black, 3 percent Asian, and 2 percent "other." And yet, although the RCWP data tips wildly toward white, the regional demographics where Delcalzo's and Gaskell's communities were located should not be ignored: nearly-all-white parishes in Sussex County, New Jersey, and St. Louis, Missouri, are not unusual. More telling would be RCWP communities in California or the American Southwest reporting 90 percent–plus white parishioners. As yet, that data is unavailable. Moreover, there are very few womenpriests in the Louisiana, Texas, New Mexico, and Arizona corridor, where huge swaths of the Hispanic Catholic population reside.[8] More significant, I believe, is a fact I mentioned earlier in the book: the majority of RCWP's community members tend to resemble the womenpriests themselves—older, well educated, and white. Womenpriests seem to attract communities that demographically resemble them.

My survey found 50 percent of parishioners were married, 33 percent were single, and 18 percent were divorced, which is fairly consistent with the American Catholic averages of 52 percent married, 8 percent living with a partner, 12 percent divorced, 7 percent widowed, and 21 percent never married.[9] Delcalzo's study found more divorced and divorced-and-remarried members. Fifteen percent of Delcalzo's respondents identified as homosexual, compared with 20 percent in Gaskell's study and 14 percent (identified lesbian, gay, or bisexual) in my survey; unfortunately, there is no Pew data on practicing gay and lesbian Catholics for comparison. Because of the church's rigidity about same-sex relationships and divorce, one might presume RCWP communities would have more individuals longing for Catholicism in a judgment-free environment. Then again, many such individuals may have given up altogether on finding nurture within Catholic spirituality.

2014 Survey

In the summer of 2014, I conducted an electronic survey of members of RCWP communities. With the help of administrators, I sent the survey through the RCWP and ARCWP listservs, and willing womenpriests could forward the link onto their congregants. The main purpose of the survey was to get a greater sense of how RCWP parishioners understand and interpret the womenpriests' presence as a Catholic community leader.

In quoting the respondents, I retain their choices in capitalization.

Basic Demographic Questions

1. What year were you born?
2. Where do you live (city, state, country)?
3. What educational degrees have you received (and in what years)?
4. What is your occupation?
5. Which of the best describes you? (cradle Catholic, convert, other)
6. What do you think are the most pressing issues confronting the Roman Catholic Church today?
7. Which of the following best describes your current relationship status?
8. Which best describes you? (heterosexual, gay/lesbian, bisexual, other)
9. How many children do you have (including biological, adopted, and from blended families)?
10. How many grandchildren do you have (including biological, adopted, and from blended families)?

Experience within the Worship Community

11. In which womanpriest community do you attend Mass?
12. Who is/are your womanpriest(s) and/or deacon(s)?
13. How many years have you been a part of this community?
14. How did you first learn about RCWP and this worship community?
15. Was this your first experience with a female priest? If so, can you describe what that was like, initially?
16. In addition to this community, do you participate in any other religious communities?

Experience with Ordained Catholic Women

17. Does having a womanpriest change your experience of the priesthood? If so, explain.
18. Does having a womanpriest change your experience or understanding of Roman Catholicism? If so, explain.
19. Does having a womanpriest change your experience of the sacraments? If so, explain.
20. Does having a womanpriest change your experience or understanding of Jesus? If so, explain.

Lay Involvement

21. In what ways have you been involved in your worship community?
22. In what ways would you like to be involved in your worship community?

Envisioning the Future

23. What do you envision as the future of the RCWP movement?
24. What do you envision as the future of the Roman Catholic Church?

Various

25. My research focuses on topics like ordination ceremonies, sacraments, ministries, families, bodies, and sexuality. If you have any examples or stories about these or other topics that you are willing to share, please do so here.
26. What should I be asking you? What have I missed?

ACKNOWLEDGMENTS

As soon as I could read, I wanted to write. From a young age, I often proclaimed assuredly, "No matter what I do, I know I want to be an author!" Of course, my younger self could not appreciate how challenging academic authorship would be.

All the more profoundly deep, then, are my thanks. The people I acknowledge here have helped guide and support me through a number of transitions, many of them confounding. The most influential of you have helped me see how indispensable kindness and generosity are—in writing and in academia.

I owe thanks to people who helped me during my graduate program at the University of North Carolina at Chapel Hill. My committee—Julie Byrne, Todd Ochoa, Tony Perucci, Randall Styers, Tom Tweed, and my wonderful adviser, Laurie Maffly-Kipp—posed invaluable questions throughout the process and modeled how academic conversations happen and why they are important. I am also grateful for scholarly mentoring from Bart Ehrman and Grant Wacker, two dedicated teachers and role models, and from Della Pollock, who introduced me to the best practices of oral history. My mentors at the UNC Writing Center, where I tutored, allowed me to discover and then cherish a mastery of the writing process. Just as important, the Writing Center's Dissertation Boot Camp provided a fun, supportive writing structure I did not even know I needed, but which certainly contributed to my dissertation's completion. UNC libraries offered vital help, and special thanks goes to the UNC Media Resource Center, where I spent over one hundred hours watching and transferring documentary film footage. I am grateful for travel grants from UNC, specifically from the Perry family and the Graduate and Professional Student Federation. And I am thankful to many graduate school friends who helped over the years by reading chapters or participating in writing and accountability groups, especially Anne Blankenship, Brandi Denison, John-Charles Duffy, Carrie Duncan, Dan Guberman, Shannon Harvey, Cyn Hogan, Marc Howlett, Shenandoah Nieuwsma, and Claire Novotny.

I was incredibly fortunate to participate in two formative seminars. Harvard Divinity School's Debates on Religion and Sexuality, in 2011, led by the brilliant and kind Mark Jordan, provided me a community of junior scholars, all of us trying to create compassionate, impactful work. I am grateful for their comments on my project. Most of all I thank Kelsy Burke, who as a writing-exchange colleague pushed me to greater clarity while providing constant encouragement.

I also participated in the 2015–2016 Teaching and Learning Workshop for Pre-tenure Religion Faculty at Colleges and Universities through the Wabash Center for Teaching and Learning in Theology and Religion. If there is a pure gift for academics in religious studies, this is it, as the program helps participants forge genuine and supportive academic relationships. The Wabash Center and my amazing cohort transformed my heart and my soul; my cup runneth over. I must especially thank Patricia O'Connell Killen, our seminar director, for helping me hone my book's thesis—and for teaching me much about academic introductions in the process. I thank also Eugene Gallagher, for always being an email away and never ceasing to lend his wisdom to any question I pose.

I am thankful to friends and colleagues at Guilford College who rooted me on as I prepared this manuscript amid the rigors of a first academic job. I am thankful for the research support I received from Guilford's faculty development committee. I cherish the opportunities I have had on campus to share my work with students and faculty. Special thanks go to friends in the Religious Studies Department and the WGSS (women's, gender, and sexuality studies) program. I am particularly grateful for Sarah Thussen's friendship, and huge thanks goes to Diya Abdo for unending love and support. Thanks go also, of course, to my wonderful students, whose enthusiasm about RCWP surprised me and propelled me forward. At Guilford, the great students are not simply great—they are astonishing, and I am so lucky to work with them. They help me think about how I think, and they motivate me to speak and write with clarity. Special thanks to Katharine Fullerton and Laura Sippel, who served as research assistants working through the tedium of footnote details.

Thank you to Fred Nachbaur at Fordham University Press for his patience and guidance. Thank you to series editor John Seitz for believing in this project; you have been a gracious source of support, and I remain grateful for the ways you have helped me think more deeply about RCWP, through your own research and your comments at the 2014 American Catholic Historical Association meeting. Huge thanks go to the copyeditor for your conscientious attention to details. Thank you also to the anonymous peer reviewers for helpful questions and comments.

I cannot say enough about the incredible Catholic feminists and activists I spoke to throughout this process. My most heartfelt thanks goes to each and every womanpriest who took time to speak to me, email me, fill out surveys, or even just offer a quick hug at the end of a Mass. These women inspire with their actions, theologies, and deep faith. No two conversations with womenpriests were the same, and my understanding of RCWP and contemporary Catholicism is all the better for it. I reflect with awe on the many women I got to know throughout this project. Some women were contemplatives and mystics who constantly sought God's voice in their lives; some were organizational masters who used their leadership talents to grow a budding young movement; some were pastoral spirits who aimed to meet people "where they are," on scales small and large; some were natural teachers with much to show and share with others. Most women were a combination of these. All the women exhibited astonishing faith in God, in Roman Catholicism, and in themselves. It was this last trait I did not expect to find, nor find so striking. The Roman Catholic Church can and does produce remarkably strong women.

My greatest thanks goes to Elsie McGrath, my St. Louis hometown womanpriest, who has created a Catholic worship community where I truly feel peace. I want to thank also Suzanne Thiel, for frequent help with data and statistics; Suzanne Dunn and Jeannette Love (and Perrier), for being incredible hosts when I traveled to Santa Barbara; Olivia Doku, for a delightful and candid lunch conversation in Pismo Beach, California; and Eileen DiFranco, for lively discussion when we presented on a panel together at the Berkshire conference in June 2017.

To all the womenpriests, I sincerely hope you recognize yourselves in these pages, even if you disagree with some of my conclusions and analyses. And to all the womenpriests I did not get to interview, particularly those ordained since I concluded my ethnographic research, I hope you too will see yourselves in the RCWP movement described here. I do know that your movement is growing and evolving rapidly, and there are details important to you that I may have missed or downplayed.

Womanpriest would not be here, now, without the help of two women. Katie Rose Guest Pryal took a manuscript in which I had defensively hidden my voice and instructed me to "write with more arrogance." Her instruction has transformed the way I think about (and teach) writing. Julie Byrne has helped steer this project from its inception, generously giving her time and expertise to shape me from grad student to scholar. She has always known the right questions to ask and the best tone to strike. I am so glad there are brilliant women offering guidance to young academics like myself, and I am so thankful to have crossed paths with these inspiring, capable minds. May I someday give to others what they have given to me.

Still other women have offered their expertise and kindness to make this book possible. Mary Henold's first book on Catholic feminism served as an early inspiration for me, and I have since benefited from her wise counsel as I edited my own work. Mary Hunt's brilliance comes from her willingness to ask the hard questions, and my project benefited from this. Kathryn Burns has been unfaltering in giving her time and expertise, and she has been on the receiving end of more than one panicked email—and, happily, more than one joyful phone call. She has been a true cheerleader.

Two talented artists also added to this project. Jules Hart's documentary film footage for her project, *Pink Smoke over the Vatican*, was an invaluable gift that nearly doubled my access to interviews. I still marvel at her trust in sending the raw footage to my doorstep. I met Judith Levitt at the May 2010 Rochester ordination, and I was thrilled about her photojournalism project on RCWP. I could not be more honored to include some of her photographs here, and I thank her for her generosity.

The contemporary Catholic world is one of rich and intersecting networks, and I am grateful to the people who helped me connect with interview subjects, groups, and worship communities, and who have helped me think through the on-the-ground implications of my work. Here I thank the ministerial Joseph Laramie, the intrepid Anne Perkins, the openhearted Jane Redmont, and Janet and Leo Dressel, the best godmother and uncle a person could have.

I thank family, friends, and acquaintances who knew about the book and asked curious and supportive questions over the years—your interest was encouragement. To my wonderful Woodcroft neighbors, field hockey teammates, workout buddies at the gym, trivia teams, and the staff at Bean Traders in Durham, North Carolina—you have helped keep me strong, sustained, and smiling in more ways than you know.

I thank friends for constant support, enriching conversation, laughter, and levity. Throughout this project, I have been lucky to call many people friends, some of whom I have already mentioned, plus Liz DeGaynor, Diane Faires, Anna Kelly, Sarah Malino, Mandy McMichael, Mary Ryan, and Ben Saypol. Above all, I owe tremendous thanks to Sarah O'Donnell Hays, not only for loyal friendship, but for being that incisive, "real" Catholic critic who read countless drafts, paragraphs, and sentences. Her skills as a librarian paired with her sharp mind have made this a better book, for academics and nonacademics alike.

Thank you to my families for their love and support. While the world of academia is foreign to them, I always know that my family, Al, Dana, Terri, Keith, Liz, and Vera (and Gus!) are cheering for me. Thanks go to my second family as well, Dan, Stephanie, Caroline, and Julie Wechsler, who have done so much for me and truly made graduate school bearable. I give love and gratitude to my furriest family, Albert, Marshall, Hamilton, and Phineas, each of whom is "my best."

I have dedicated *Womanpriest* to Catholics. Though I was not seeking it out, this project has shown me the incredible ache so many Catholics carry with them today, as well as the indefatigable creativity and hope that enliven the faith of those who will not give up. Few agree 100 percent on the best path forward, but so many believe the traditions are worth keeping—even if (and perhaps mostly when) the best solutions seem transgressive. For the pain, the persistence, the patience and impatience—this book is for Roman Catholics who hold fast to life-sustaining mysteries, even when answers are slow to unfold.

Introduction

1 Therese of Divine Peace, Mass and baptism, St. Louis, MO, field notes, December 27, 2009.

2 Therese Mass, St. Louis, MO, field notes, July 13, 2008.

3 I interviewed Marybeth McBryan again about four years after Chloe's baptism. When I asked her about Chloe's receiving Communion, she did not remember anything out of the ordinary. I relayed to her my memory of events, which she confirmed: "We had made it a policy that anyone who was at that Mass, child or Catholic or not, we welcome anyone to the table." She even remarked that Chloe had probably received Communion at Therese before. (Marybeth McBryan, telephone interview with author, February 19, 2014.) I want to emphasize that Therese's policy on giving Communion to children is not official RCWP policy but rather represents the community's freedom to make decisions that make sense for them. Later in the book I will talk about another community, Church of the Holy Spirit in Manchester, New Hampshire, where womanpriest Theresa Novak Chabot upheld Rome's typical ages for first Communion.

4 On May 29, 2008, the Congregation for the Doctrine of the Faith issued a general decree titled "Regarding the Crime of Attempting Sacred Ordination of a Woman." The decree reads, "Both he who has attempted to confer holy orders on a woman, and the woman who has attempted to receive the said sacrament, incur in *latae sententiae* excommunication, reserved to the Apostolic See." The decree is highlighted in the preface of RCWP's 2008 book *Women Find a Way: The Movement and Stories of Roman Catholic Womenpriests*, edited by Elsie Hainz McGrath, Bridget Mary Meehan, and Ida Raming (College Station, TX: Virtualbookworm.com Publishing Inc., 2008), 1–2.

5 Raymond L. Burke and Henry J. Breier, "Declaration of Excommunication of Patricia Fresen, Rose Hudson, and Elsie McGrath," *St. Louis Review*, March 14, 2008, 10.

6 Congregation for the Doctrine of the Faith, "Warning Regarding the Attempted Priestly Ordination of Some Catholic Women," July 10, 2002, reprinted in *The Papal "No": A Comprehensive Guide to the Vatican's Rejection of Women's Ordination,* by Deborah Halter (New York: Crossroad Publishing, 2004), 235.

7 "Embracing and Shaping Our Future," Intentional Eucharistic Communities, accessed December 10, 2019, https://intentionaleucharistic.org/; "About Us" and "FAQ," Ecumenical Catholic Communion, accessed August 12, 2010, http://www.

ecumenical-catholic-communion.org/index.html; Julie Byrne, *The Other Catholics: Remaking America's Largest Religion* (New York: Columbia University Press, 2016); John P. Plummer and John R. Mabry, *Who Are the Independent Catholics?* (Berkeley, CA: Apocryphile Press, 2006).

IECs are "small faith communities, rooted in the Catholic tradition, which gather to celebrate Eucharist on a regular basis." They use shared governance and describe themselves in post-Vatican II era "church of the people" language. Some IECs remain closely tied to the institutional church, and some are independent. Worship communities that are part of the Ecumenical Catholic Communion retain Western Christian tradition with respect to Jesus's life and ministry, the sacraments, and apostolic succession but do not consider themselves "Roman" or bound by papal authority.

8 Halter, *The Papal "No,"* 144–145. Ramerman's ordination was performed by Bishop Peter Hickman, who himself was ordained in the Diocese of Ecumenical and Old Catholic Communities and who was a leader in the Ecumenical Catholic Communion. Significantly, Ramerman was ordained by Hickman, the Spiritus Christi community, and international interfaith clergy—it was not only Hickman who had power to call and ordain. See also "The Apostolic Succession of Peter E. Hickman," Ecumenical Catholic Communion, accessed December 18, 2018, www.ecumenical-catholic-communion.org/eccpdf/apostolic_succession.pdf.

9 The two bishops involved in the Danube ordination—Romulo Braschi and Rafael Regelsberger—had questionable credentials, which I'll examine later in this book. Other bishops who were in good standing participated in ordaining RCWP's first generation of deacons and priests, but RCWP is protecting these men from reprisal and will not reveal their identities while they are living. Many womenpriests have told me that the bishops' names are contained in notarized documents being kept in a European safe-deposit box, to be revealed when the bishops die.

10 *The Code of Canon Law* (Washington, DC: Canon Law Society of America, 1999), 1024.

11 The RCWP website was updated in summer 2019. The website shows 19 bishops (13 active, 6 retired), 191 priests (1 retired, 9 catacomb), and 20 deacons. It lists 13 support members (1 retired) and 15 total deceased. This brings a total of 229 ordained persons (active and retired) in the worldwide RCWP movement; this number grows to 242 if we count unordained support members; this gives a total of 257 including deceased persons.

The vast majority of ordained are in the United States. Canada has 16; Colombia has 9; South Africa, Germany, and Austria each have 4; and Norway, Scotland, France, Spain, Venezuela, and Taiwan each have 1.

Roman Catholic Womenpriests, "Meet the Ordained," Roman Catholic Womenpriests, accessed December 19, 2019, https://www.romancatholicwomenpriests.org/meet-the-ordained/.

12 At a keynote speech at the Southeast Women's Ordination Conference in 2005, Bishop Patricia Fresen said of the growing RCWP movement, "We believe we need to reform the church structures from within. By staying outside of official church structures,

we will achieve nothing. We are already excluded and this would mean accepting our exclusion." Patricia Fresen, 2005, accessed November 10, 2010, http://www.womensor-dination.org/content/view/65/117/. "A new model of ordained ministry in a renewed Roman Catholic church" was an oft-repeated expression in the movement early years, in formal documents and informal interviews. "Homepage: Mission," Roman Catholic Womenpriests, accessed May 14, 2015, http://romancatholicwomenpriests.org/. Now, the phrase features on the title banner of the RCWP website. "Welcome to RCWP," Roman Catholic Womenpriests, https://www.romancatholicwomenpriests.org/.

13 "Excerpts from Pope Francis's Interview with Reuters," Reuters, June 20, 2018, https://uk.reuters.com/article/uk-pope-interview-excerpts/excerpts-from-pope-francis-interview-with-reuters-idUKKBN1JG2UN; John Bacon, "Pope: Women Will Be Banned from Priesthood Forever," *USA Today*, November 1, 2016, https://www.usatoday.com/story/news/nation/2016/11/01/pope-women-banned-priesthood-forever/93118528/.

14 For a helpful chart tracing the number of priests from 1965 to 2013, see "Frequently Requested Church Statistics," Center for Applied Research in the Apostolate, accessed May 11, 2019, http://cara.georgetown.edu/frequently-requested-church-statistics/.

15 Verónica Giménez Béliveau, "Why the Catholic Church Is 'Hemorrhaging' Priests," The Conversation, May 25, 2018, https://theconversation.com/why-the-catholic-church-is-hemorrhaging-priests-97198. The issue of whether Roman Catholicism is facing a vocational crisis is a murky one. First, the numbers do not tell a clear story: Should observers pay attention to the number of priests or to the ratio of priests to parishioners? Second, there is disagreement about what story the numbers tell. Progressive groups (including RCWP, CORPUS, and the Women's Ordination Conference) look at declining numbers of priests and argue that the ordination of women and married men would address the problem. More conservative Catholics look at the decline and blame the negative impact of liberal policies and secular cultures. (See, for example, Marco Tosatti, "Return of the Vocations Crisis," *First Things*, August 10, 2017, https://www.firstthings.com/web-exclusives/2017/08/return-of-the-vocations-crisis.) Finally, and further complicating the question, in 2013, some news sources began reporting that more men were entering seminaries, suggesting a possible increase in vocations: Cathy Lynn Grossman, "After Years of Decline, Catholics See Rise in Number of Future Priests," Religion News Service, September 24, 2013, http://www.religionnews.com/2013/09/24/years-decline-catholics-see-rise-number-future-priests/.

16 Ruth A. Wallace, *They Call Her Pastor: A New Role for Catholic Women* (Albany, NY: SUNY Press, 1992); Jerry Filteau, "Panelists Urge Laity to Take the Lead," *National Catholic Reporter*, January 7, 2011, 12; Zoe Ryan, "Demographic Opportunity Knocking for Schools," *National Catholic Reporter*, March 4, 2011, 1a.

17 Pew Research Center, "Chapter 4: Expectations of the Church," *U.S. Catholics Open to Nontraditional Families*, September 2, 2015, https://www.pewforum.org/2015/09/02/chapter-4-expectations-of-the-church/. In this Pew study, the category "Catholic" describes people who claim Catholicism as their primary religious affiliation. "Cultural Catholics" identify with a faith other than Catholicism (Protestantism or "none") but

also say they consider themselves "Catholic or partially Catholic." "Ex-Catholics" no longer identify as Catholic at all. That explanation is here: Pew Research Center, "Chapter 1: Exploring Catholic Identity," *U.S. Catholics Open to Nontraditional Families*, September 2, 2015, https://www.pewforum.org/2015/09/02/chapter-1-exploring-catholic-identity/.

18 Benjamin R. Knoll and Cammie Jo Bolin, *She Preached the Word: Women's Ordination in Modern America* (New York: Oxford University Press, 2018), 40. Knoll and Bolin created the Gender and Religious Representation Survey for *She Preached the Word*, drawing on "a combined series of four nationally representative telephone and internet public opinion polls" (31).

19 David Agren, "Univision Poll Shows Strong Support for Church Teaching in Asia, Africa," Catholic News Service, February 11, 2014, https://www.catholicnews.com/services/englishnews/2014/univision-poll-shows-strong-support-for-church-teaching-in-asia-africa.cfm.

20 Congregation for the Doctrine of the Faith, *Inter Insigniores* ("Declaration on the Question of the Admission of Women to the Ministerial Priesthood"), October 15, 1976, Vatican Archive (web), http://www.vatican.va/roman_curia/congregations/cfaith/documents/rc_con_cfaith_doc_19761015_inter-insigniores_en.html

21 Pope John Paul II, *Ordinatio Sacerdotalis* ("On Reserving Priestly Ordination to Men Alone"), May 22, 1994, Vatican Archive (web), http://w2.vatican.va/content/john-paul-ii/en/apost_letters/1994/documents/hf_jp-ii_apl_19940522_ordinatio-sacerdotalis.html. A helpful and readable overview of the church's position comes from Sara Butler, a theology professor and Missionary Servants of the Most Blessed Trinity sister who once believed women should be ordained in Roman Catholicism but later found church arguments convincing. Sara Butler, "Women's Ordination: Is it Still an Issue?," Archdiocese of New York, March 7, 2007, http://www.laici.va/content/dam/laici/documenti/donna/teologia/english/womens-ordination-still-an-issue.pdf.

22 In "Women's Ordination: Is it Still an Issue?," Sara Butler talks about a late-fourth-century bishop, Epiphanius of Salamis, who viewed women's ordination as a heresy. Also, in 2018, German cardinal Walter Brandmüller said that anyone supporting women's ordination has "left the foundation of the Catholic faith" and "fulfils the elements of heresy which has, as its consequence, the exclusion from the Church—excommunication." See Nick Hallett, "Cardinal Brandmüller: Those Who Call for Women Priests Are 'Heretics' and 'Excommunicated,'" *Catholic Herald*, May 22, 2018, https://catholicherald.co.uk/news/2018/05/22/cardinal-brandmuller-those-who-call-for-women-priests-are-heretics-and-excommunicated/. Additionally, in the original documents warning and then excommunicating the Danube Seven, Roman officials invoked the term *schismatic* to describe Romulo Braschi and his community. Congregation for the Doctrine of the Faith, "Warning Regarding the Attempted Priestly Ordination of Some Catholic Women"; Congregation for the Doctrine of the Faith, "Decree of Excommunication Regarding the Attempted Priestly Ordination of Some Catholic Women," August 5, 2002, in Halter, *The Papal "No,"* 236. When St. Louis archbishop Raymond Burke excommunicated Patricia Fresen, Rose Hudson, and Elsie

McGrath in March 2008, he frequently used the word *schism*. He said that Fresen had acted "in the manner of the leader of a schism" and that all three women "by the commission of the most grave delict of schism [had] lost membership in, good standing in, and full communion with the Roman Catholic Church." Raymond L. Burke and Henry J. Breier, "Declaration of Excommunication of Patricia Fresen, Rose Hudson, and Elsie McGrath," *St. Louis Review*, March 14, 2008, 10. Finally, in a much decried juxtaposition in 2010, the church published revisions to Vatican law that said, in the same breath, that the sexual abuse of minors *and* the attempt to ordain women were crimes, or "grave delicts." See Richard McBrien, "Linking Sexual Abuse and the Ordination of Women," *National Catholic Reporter*, September 13, 2010, https://www.ncronline.org/blogs/essays-theology/linking-sexual-abuse-and-ordination-women.

23 A group called the Federation of Christian Ministries (FCM) legally certifies the sacraments for American womenpriests, since the Roman Catholic Church will not. FCM will be taken up later in the book.

24 Pope Paul VI, *Lumen Gentium* ("Dogmatic Constitution on the Church"), November 21, 1964, Documents of the Second Vatican Council, Vatican Archive (web), http://www.vatican.va/archive/hist_councils/ii_vatican_council/documents/vat-ii_const_19641121_lumen-gentium_en.html.

25 Gary Wills, *Why Priests? A Failed Tradition* (New York: Viking, 2013). Wills's book traces the history of priesthood—how it arose in early Christianity and evolved over the centuries—to pose the question of whether Catholic Christians need priests today.

26 Reading American Catholic women in dualistic and dialectical terms—as I do here with RCWP—has a long history in Catholic historical scholarship. In his study of women's devotions to St. Jude, Robert A. Orsi places St. Jude's devoted women "in an oscillating dialectic between 'fantasy and reality,' self and other, objective and subjective, past and present, submission and resistance." Julie Byrne characterizes the Immaculata Mighty Macs—a little-known powerhouse Catholic women's basketball team—as "hidden in plain view, affirming and subverting Catholicism." Mary J. Henold shows how women can be simultaneously "Catholic and feminist" by carving out positions of "sustained ambivalence" within their church. Henold notes that this language of "both/and" characterizes other studies: Mary Jo Weaver viewed women religious as "inside outsiders," Sheila Pew Albert described 1990s Catholic feminists as "revolutionary loyalists," and Miriam Therese Winter talked about Catholic women as "defecting in place."

See Robert A. Orsi, *Thank You, St. Jude: Women's Devotion to the Patron Saint of Hopeless Causes* (New Haven, CT: Yale University Press, 1996), 210; Julie Byrne, *O God of Players: The Story of the Immaculata Mighty Macs* (New York: Columbia University Press, 2003), 208; Mary J. Henold, *Catholic and Feminist: The Surprising History of the American Catholic Feminist Movement* (Chapel Hill: University of North Carolina Press, 2008), 199–200. Here, Henold is building on Mary Farrell Bednarowski's *Religious Imagination of American Women*, in which Bednarowski talks about "ambivalence" and "contradictions" in women's experiences within religious communities. Mary

Farrell Bednarowski, *Religious Imagination of American Women* (Bloomington: Indiana University Press, 1999).

27 As my project blurs the line between women's religious history and feminist theology, I acknowledge Rita Gross's call for scholars to more carefully distinguish religious studies from theology, specifically when studying women and feminism. To be sure, this project resembles that of other Catholic studies scholars who honor their subjects' theological motivations without drawing theological conclusions. Here I am thinking of Sarah McFarland Taylor and John Seitz. Rita M. Gross, "Where Have We Been? Where Do We Need to Go? Women's Studies and Gender in Religion and Feminist Theology," in *Gender, Religion, and Diversity: Cross Cultural Perspectives*, ed. Ursula King and Tina Beattie (New York: Continuum, 2004), 17–27; Sarah McFarland Taylor, *Green Sisters: A Spiritual Ecology* (Cambridge, MA: Harvard University Press, 2007); John Seitz, *No Closure: Catholic Practice and Boston's Parish Shutdowns* (Cambridge, MA: Harvard University Press, 2011).

28 Inspired heavily by D. Soyini Madison's instructive techniques, I held to Madison's advice that researchers must "be accountable for the consequences of our representations and the implications of our message—because they matter." D. Soyini Madison, *Critical Ethnography: Method, Ethics, and Performance* (Thousand Oaks, CA: Sage, 2012), 5.

29 See, similarly, Taylor, *Green Sisters*, xviii.

30 In fall 2007, the CDF had not yet issued a standing decree that any woman attempting ordination, or anyone attempting to ordain a woman, would be excommunicated *latae sententiae*. Burke's threats of excommunication, then, stand out as an approach for addressing RCWP's actions before the May 2008 general decree automatically excommunicating all of RCWP's women.

31 I should say, though, that I have had some conservative Catholic friends express concern for me because of my proximity to RCWP. One could argue that by attending ordination ceremonies and Masses led by womenpriests, concelebrating the Eucharist with womenpriests, and praying with womenpriest-led communities, I put my soul—or at the very least my relationship to Catholicism—in peril.

32 In other words, as an ethnographer, I kept in view how struggles around justice and power shaped the womenpriests' lives. One challenge I faced was reminding myself to treat my subjects with as much thoughtful care as I would give to subjects who appear inherently more vulnerable—like the subjects Madison studies in Sub-Saharan Africa who face challenges around human rights, economic viability, and access to natural resources. D. Soyini Madison, *Critical Ethnography: Method, Ethics, and Performance*, 2nd ed. (Thousand Oaks, CA: Sage, 2012), 5.

33 "Roman Catholic Womenpriests Program of Preparation for Ordination," emailed to me by womanpriest May Kay Kusner on September 22, 2009. These are specifically the units Kusner used for her discernment process toward ordination, as each region uses a somewhat modified program.

34 RCWP-USA redesigned its website in the summer of 2019, leading to the removal

or relocation of many documents. Throughout this book, I cite the newest versions of RCWP's and ARCWP's websites unless content has changed or been deleted.

35 Because of my difficulty finding conservative Catholic critics to speak about RCWP and women's ordination, I am all the more grateful for Jules Hart's documentary, as she did interview a handful of dissenters. Yet I understand that she, too, had difficulty getting dissenters to speak on camera.

36 Elsie McGrath, email to author, January 5, 2011.

37 I do not use the term *womanpriest* to make claims about the authenticity or inauthenticity of the women's ordained status as Catholic priests, nor do I use *womanpriest* to essentialize the women as gendered beings or to argue for a simple definition of what makes someone a "woman."

38 Some of these men were ordained through the movement, and some were ordained through the Roman Catholic Church and have since left the institutional church. This points to one of the challenges posed by the very name "Roman Catholic *Women*priests." RCWP's website simply calls these men "deacons" and "priests."

39 When I first started studying RCWP, the group promoted itself as an alternative path to ordination for men who were disabled or otherwise barred from Roman Catholic priesthood. They use this argument less nowadays. The question of whether men who are "disabled" (or differently abled) can become priests is a murky one with no uniform practices. Canon 1029 states, "Only those are to be promoted to orders who, in the prudent judgment of their own bishop or of the competent major superior, all things considered, have integral faith, are moved by the right intention, have the requisite knowledge, possess a good reputation, and are endowed with integral morals and proven virtues *and the other physical and psychic qualities* in keeping with the order to be received" (emphasis mine). This canon, combined with informal conversations I have had with ordained men, suggests that orders and dioceses can make a determination on a case-by-case basis.

40 Peter Rowe, "Sing a New Song Unto the Lord: The Transgender, Nonbinary Rev. Kori Pacyniak," *The San Diego Union-Tribune*, February 16, 2020, https://www.sandiegouniontribune.com/news/religion/story/2020-02-16/first-transgender-nonbinary-priest-ordained. Intriguingly, also in February 2020, an RCWP member told me about a second transgender womanpriest, one ordained earlier than Pacyniak but who is closeted.

41 A WOW (Women's Ordination Worldwide) 2015 conference panel titled "Inclusive and Empowered: The Women Priests Movement, Renewing the Church Now" included both RCWP and ARCWP priests speaking about their ministries and renewal efforts. I found it difficult to discern a difference between the two branches of the movement in terms of the womenpriests' motivations for ordination, ministerial actions, and experiences of priesthood. WOW 2015, Philadelphia, PA, field notes, September 19, 2015.

42 Julie Byrne, *The Other Catholics: Remaking America's Largest Religion* (New York: Columbia University Press, 2016).

43 Pamela Schaeffer, "WOC Gathers to Promote Women's Ordination amid Conflicting Visions, Goals," *National Catholic Reporter*, December 1, 1995. Theologian Elisabeth Schüssler Fiorenza said "ordination is subordination" at this WOC event. I take up Schüssler Fiorenza's criticisms of women's ordination in Chapter 4.

Chapter 1. Called

1 Kathryn Poethig, interview, April 19, 2006, unused documentary footage from *Pink Smoke over the Vatican*, directed by Jules Hart (2011; Eye Goddess Films, 2013), DVD.

2 Juanita Cordero, "Doors Closed and Doors Open," in *Women Find a Way: The Movement and Stories of Roman Catholic Womenpriests*, eds. Elsie Hainz McGrath, Bridget Mary Meehan, and Ida Raming (College Station, TX: Virtualbookworm.com Publishing Inc., 2008), 140–143; Gabriella Velardi Ward, "Draw Me, We Shall Run," in *Women Find a Way*, 68–75; Gabriella Velardi Ward, telephone interview with author, January 9, 2010; "Meet the Ordained: Mary Grace Crowley-Koch," Roman Catholic Womenpriests, December 17, 2019, https://www.romancatholicwomenpriests.org/meet-the-ordained/; Kathleen Strack Kunster, "Biography of a Priest," in *Women Find a Way*, 152–154; Janice Sevre-Duszynska, interview, July 19, 2005, unused documentary footage from *Pink Smoke*, dir. Jules Hart.

3 Victoria Rue, interview, April 19, 2006, unused documentary footage from *Pink Smoke*, dir. Jules Hart; Congregation for the Doctrine of the Faith, "Letter to the Bishops of the Catholic Church on the Pastoral Care of Homosexual Persons," October 1, 1986, Vatican Archive (web), http://www.vatican.va/roman_curia/congregations/cfaith/documents/rc_con_cfaith_doc_19861001_homosexual-persons_en.html.

4 Victoria Rue, response to "Womenpriests" survey created by the author, SurveyMonkey (web), May 29, 2014.

5 Victoria Rue, interview, April 19, 2006, unused documentary footage from *Pink Smoke*, dir. Jules Hart. Don Cordero passed away in 2007.

6 Congregation for the Doctrine of the Faith, "6. The Ministerial Priesthood Illustrated by the Mystery of the Church," *Inter Insigniores* ("Declaration on the Question of the Admission of Women to the Ministerial Priesthood"), October 15, 1976, Vatican Archive (web), http://www.vatican.va/roman_curia/congregations/cfaith/documents/rc_con_cfaith_doc_19761015_inter-insigniores_en.html.

7 Janice Sevre-Duszynska, interview, July 19, 2005, unused documentary footage from *Pink Smoke*, dir. Jules Hart.

8 Janice Sevre-Duszynska, telephone interview with author, January 23, 2011.

9 Marie Evans Bouclin, *Seeking Wholeness: Women Dealing with Abuse of Power in the Catholic Church* (Collegeville, MN: Liturgical Press, 2006).

10 Marie Bouclin, "Call to Ministry: Binding the Wounds of Clergy Abuse," in *Women Find a Way*, 48–54: 52.

11 Bouclin, "Call to Ministry," 51. Bouclin in no way underplays the severity of child

sex abuse when she draws attention to the lesser-studied problems of adult clerical abuse. She concedes that adult female victims often manifest codependency, lack self-esteem, do not maintain healthy personal boundaries, and are people pleasers. While she acknowledges that only a small minority of priests take advantage of women like this, she aims to show how patriarchal dominance is especially damaging for these vulnerable women, who are more likely to believe they need a male mediating force in their lives.

12 See John Jay College of Criminal Justice, *The Nature and Scope of Sexual Abuse of Minors by Catholic Priests and Deacons in the United States 1950–2000* (Washington, DC: United States Conference of Bishops, February 2004), http://www.usccb.org/issues-and-action/child-and-youth-protection/upload/The-Nature-and-Scope-of-Sexual-Abuse-of-Minors-by-Catholic-Priests-and-Deacons-in-the-United-States-1950-2002.pdf; BishopAccountability.org, accessed January 10, 2016, http://www.bishop-accountability.org/.

13 Russell Heimlich, "Clergy Sexual Abuse and the Catholic Church," Fact Tank, Pew Research Center, March 29, 2010, https://www.pewresearch.org/fact-tank/2010/03/29/clergy-sexual-abuse-and-the-catholic-church/.

14 See John C. Seitz, *No Closure: Catholic Practice and Boston's Parish Shutdowns* (Cambridge, MA: Harvard University Press, 2011).

15 Although women and women religious in Catholic dioceses and archdioceses have also been accused of victimizing children, this happens in far smaller numbers—and with much less publicity. Still, we know that women do sexually abuse children, and this is as yet an understudied topic. In a 2006 book, *Women Who Sexually Abuse Children*, author Hannah Ford says it is very difficult to know how many perpetrators of sexual violence against children are women; some studies say less than 1 percent; others say 1–4 percent. Of those convicted of sexual assault of children, some studies say, roughly 1.5–2 percent are women. Ford points out that these low numbers could reflect cultural disbelief about women as perpetrators more than actual rates of abuse. Hannah Ford, *Women Who Sexually Abuse Children* (West Sussex, England: John Wiley & Sons, 2006).

16 Bouclin, "Chapter 3: Power and the Priesthood," in *Seeking Wholeness*, 22–40.

17 Bouclin cites the Protestant example as instructive: not until Protestant churches began ordaining women did accusations of clergy sex abuse receive more serious attention and support. She credits Dr. Marie Fortune of the FaithTrust Institute for providing this information. Bouclin, "Call to Ministry," 50.

18 Bouclin, "Call to Ministry," 52.

19 Marie Bouclin, email interview with author, April 26 and 27, 2011.

20 Bouclin, "Call to Ministry," 51–52.

21 On this point, Bouclin critiqued the Roman church's "subtle ploy" to "[overvalue] symbolic womanhood (in the form of Mary) and at the same time [refuse] to grant women full human status." Bouclin, *Seeking Wholeness*, 47.

22 Bouclin, interview. Bouclin is not alone in her work with abuse victims or in discovering that her female ministerial priesthood is helping fallen-away Catholics reconnect with their faith. Like Bouclin, Gabriella Velardi Ward has long worked with

trauma and abuse victims, including those harmed by priests. When discerning a call to ordination, Ward envisioned leading a reconciliation service for survivors of trauma and thus playing a role in the mediation of God's grace that happens through sacraments. The sacrament of reconciliation takes on additional meaning for survivors. Ward wrote, "Reconciliation with self, the world and God happens when survivors take steps toward empowerment, justice and the re-creation of self as they work against suffering. Reconciliation happens when survivors can begin to feel authentically, truthfully, the feelings that may include anger and the pain of becoming visible. Reconciliation happens when they begin to break the conspiracy of silence and reclaim their truth." Now a womanpriest, Ward built on her history as a spiritual director for survivors of child abuse, and the reconciliation she does now has sacramental elements. Ward, "Draw Me, We Shall Run," 73.

23 Eleonora Marinaro, "Coming Home," in *Women Find a Way*, 86–88: 87.

24 Monica Kilburn-Smith, "Womenpriests" survey, May 29, 2014.

25 No name given, "Womenpriests," survey created by author, *Survey Monkey*, SurveyMonkey Inc., (Palo Alto, CA, 2014), Web, July 17, 2014; Gabriella Velardi Ward, "Womenpriests," survey created by author, *Survey Monkey*, SurveyMonkey Inc., (Palo Alto, CA, 2014), Web, July 9, 2014.

26 The poem "Hound of Heaven" was written in 1893 by Francis Thompson, a Roman Catholic English poet.

27 Rue, "Womenpriests" survey, May 29, 2014.; No name given, "Womenpriests" survey, July 2, 2014; Monica Kilburn-Smith, "Womenpriests" survey, May 29, 2014; Christine Fahrenbach, "Womenpriests" survey, July 2, 2014.

28 Cordero, "Doors Closed and Doors Open," 140–143.

29 Lauren [pseudonym created by author], interview with author, July 17, 2009.

30 In September 2009, womanpriest Mary Kay Kusner sent me the program of preparation for ordination that she used. Her process is representative of but not identical to that of the other ordained women. In her program, unit one emphasized personal autobiography and reflection. Unit two focused on baptism. Unit three explored anointing with oils. Unit four analyzed the Holy Spirit and the fire of Pentecost. Unit five centered upon the Eucharist, while unit six looked at penance. Unit seven unpacked human sexuality in light of RCWP's rejection of mandatory celibacy. Unit eight looked at ministry broadly. Unit nine required the candidate to examine, personally and rigorously, her call to ordination. Unit ten had the candidate receive practical training for preaching and celebrating the sacraments.

31 Kathleen Kautzer refers to RCWP as a "feminist seminary," noting that the movement sponsors "a formation program that prepared women and men for ordination as deacons and priests." Insofar as a seminary is a centralized location for both shared study and community formation, I disagree with this characterization. Kautzer is correct that RCWP and ARCWP help prepare Catholic women for ordination, but this formation program is too diverse to merit the term "feminist seminary," which implies unity and similarity. Womenpriests do not study together in one geographical location and thus

do not have a seminary experience in any way akin to that of Catholic male seminarians or even Catholic or Protestant divinity school students. Kathleen Kautzer, *The Underground Church: Nonviolent Resistance to the Vatican Empire* (Boston: Brill, 2012), 261.

32 A handful of my interviews included discussion of the formation program and the lack of uniformity in its requirements. Because this was (and, in some regions, remains) a delicate issue, I will not cite these interview subjects by name.

33 This pattern of well-educated womenpriests started with the Danube Seven—Gisela Forster, Iris Müller, and Ida Raming, three of the seven, held doctorates—and continued into the early wave of North American ordinands; Gloria Carpeneto, Michele Birch-Conery, Suzanne Dunn, Kathleen Kunster, Judy Lee, Roberta Meehan, and Jane Via all have PhDs. Many women have master of divinity degrees from Catholic schools—a credential shared by male priests—including Joan Houk, Alice Iaquinta, Kathleen Kunster, Toni Tortorilla, and Kathy Vandenberg. Other women have advanced degrees in fields (ostensibly) unrelated to ministry, such as Judith McClosky's master of library science and Monique Venne's master of science in meteorology. A number of women with graduate degrees directed their thesis or dissertation work toward questions surrounding Catholic women and feminist theology, including Gloria Carpeneto, Michele Birch-Conery, Mary Ann Schoettly, Mary Frances Smith, and, of course, Ida Raming, whose dissertation "The Exclusion of Women from Priesthood: Divine Law or Gender Discrimination?" has inspired much women's ordination activism since the 1970s.

Each of the thirty-four ordained individuals connected to RCWP (thirty-three women, one man) who responded to my 2014 survey had a college degree. Three women had BAs alone, three women were working toward additional graduate degrees, and eight women had doctorates. The survey revealed fifty-one completed advanced degrees (master's, doctor, and juris doctor) among the thirty-four respondents. The names and statistics I offer here are a mere snapshot of RCWP's cumulative educational background.

34 Michele Birch-Conery and Juanita Cordero were with the Sisters of the Holy Names; Patricia Fresen was a Dominican sister for decades until her ordination required her departure; Jeannette Love was a religious sister for nineteen years. Marie Bouclin and Olivia Doko are former sisters who later married. Suzanne Dunn and Bridget Mary Meehan still identify as Sisters of Christian Charity (a consecrated order committed to the spirit of Vatican II) in their RCWP biographies. Kathy Redig and Christine Myer-Lumetzberger entered convents as teenagers but later left and married. In addition to these consecrated women, scores of womenpriests worked within the church. Elsie McGrath worked for the St. Louis archdiocese, and she and her husband ran marriage preparation courses; Pat Sandall served the Los Angeles archdiocese for over twenty-five years as a catechist, pastoral associate, and religious education director. Mary Meyer-Gad worked for archdiocesan offices in Chicago and Detroit.

Chapter 2. Rome's Mixed Messages

1 Rev. Michael G. Murtha, "Diocesan Official Responds to Our Leaflets: 'Dissenting Catholics' Are Not Truly Catholic," *Equal wRites* (Ivyland, PA), June–August 2004, 4.

2 Mary Frances Smith, email interview with author, March 4, 2011.

3 Monique Venne, email interview with author, March 27, 2011.

4 Eileen DiFranco, email interview with author, January 13, 2011.

5 Several such stories have made it to print: Kaya Oakes's memoir, *Radical Reinvention: An Unlikely Return to the Catholic Church,* traced the author's return to Roman Catholicism after a foray into atheism; she discovered that she could not abandon the faith that keeps pulling her back, and she found Catholic kinship with other progressives. In *Sister Trouble: The Vatican, Bishops, and Nuns,* Marian Ronan not only investigated the faith-filled activism of the American church's beleaguered sisters but candidly disclosed her own spiritual location as a critically engaged Catholic scholar inexorably located within the church. The expression "defecting in place" comes from a 1994 study of the same name, which looked at both Catholic and Protestant women and concluded, "Many feminists of faith, however alienated or angry, are not pulling out of the churches, but instead are 'defecting in place.'" Kaya Oakes, *Radical Reinvention: An Unlikely Return to the Catholic Church* (Berkeley, CA: Counterpoint, 2012); Marian Ronan, *Sister Trouble: The Vatican, Bishops, and Nuns* (North Charleston, SC: Create Space Independent Publishing Platform, 2013); Miriam Therese Winter, Adair T. Lummis, and Allison Stokes, eds., *Defecting in Place: Women Claiming Responsibility for Their Own Spiritual Lives* (New York: Crossroad, 1994), 196.

6 Two books that provide rich histories of the Catholic women's ordination movement and church statements about women and ordination are Deborah Halter, *The Papal "No": A Comprehensive Guide to the Vatican's Rejection of Women's Ordination* (New York: Crossroad Publishing, 2004), and Mary Jeremy Daigler, *Incompatible with God's Design: A History of the Women's Ordination Movement in the U.S. Roman Catholic Church* (Lanham, MD: The Scarecrow Press, 2012).

7 Michael J. Bayly, "'We Are All the Rock': An Interview with Roman Catholic Womanpriest Judith McKloskey," Progressive Catholic Voice, August 2008, accessed December 31, 2019, http://thewildreed.blogspot.com/2008/08/we-are-all-rock.html.

8 Pope Paul VI wrote, "Through the common sharing of gifts and through the common effort to attain fullness in unity, the whole and each of the parts receive increase. Not only, then, is the people of God made up of different peoples but in its inner structure also it is composed of various ranks. This diversity among its members arises either by reason of their duties, as is the case with those who exercise the sacred ministry for the good of their brethren, or by reason of their condition and state of life, as is the case with those many who enter the religious state and, tending toward holiness by a narrower path, stimulate their brethren by their example. ... Between all the parts of the Church there remains a bond of close communion whereby they share spiritual riches, apostolic workers and temporal resources. For the members of the people of God are called to share these goods in common." Pope Paul VI, *Lumen Gentium* (Dogmatic Constitution

on the Church), November 21, 1964, Documents of the Second Vatican Council, Vatican Archive (web), http://www.vatican.va/archive/hist_councils/ii_vatican_council/documents/vat-ii_const_19641121_lumen-gentium_en.html; Angelo Maffeis, *Ecumenical Dialogue*, trans. Lorelei F. Fuchs (Collegeville, MN: Liturgical Press, 2005); Halter, *The Papal "No,"* 69–73; John Wilkins, "Ordinariate Gets Up and Running," *National Catholic Reporter*, May 27, 2011, 1, 6–7.

9 It is important—and historically correct—to note that progressive Catholics are not the first to use the "people of God" theme to argue against decisions and doctrines with which they disagree. See, for example, Leslie Woodcock Tentler's research on racial initiatives in the Detroit archdiocese in the 1960s: Leslie Woodcock Tentler, "The American Reception and the Legacy of the Second Vatican Council," in *The Long Shadow of Vatican II: Living Faith and Negotiating Authority since the Second Vatican Council*, ed. Lucas Van Rompay, Sam Miglarese, and David Morgan (Chapel Hill: University of North Carolina Press, 2015), 37–57.

10 "Roman Catholic Womenpriests Responds to Pope Francis's Interview" (press release), Roman Catholic Womenpriests, accessed December 31, 2019, http://maryofmagdala-mke.org/subpage3.shtml.

11 "About Us," Association of Roman Catholic Womenpriests, accessed December 31, 2019, https://arcwp.org/about-us/.

12 By emphasizing feminist activism after Vatican II, I am in no way attempting to dismiss decades of women's social action before Vatican II. Many groups then were explicitly Catholic and socially concerned; these groups did not self-identify as "feminist." Kathleen Sprows Cummings shows that socially active Catholic women during the Progressive Era found solidarity in their Catholic identity and not their female identity. They opposed women's suffrage and affirmed the ideal role for women was in private, domestic spheres. In contrast, St. Joan's International Alliance (founded in London in 1911 as the Catholic Women's Suffrage Society) began amid the women's suffrage movement and worked against traditional teachings on gender roles. Other examples of groups that merged Catholicism with women's social concerns include the Sister Formation Conference, which argued for greater education and professionalization for women religious; the Grail Movement, wherein women became, rather than consecrated sisters or nuns, "lay apostles" serving the church; and the Christian Family Movement, which served the family, emphasized social justice, and saw women as its primary leaders. Kathleen Sprows Cummings, *New Women of the Old Faith: Gender and American Catholicism in the Progressive Era* (Chapel Hill: University of North Carolina Press, 2009); Mary J. Henold, *Catholic and Feminist: The Surprising History of the American Catholic Feminist Movement* (Chapel Hill: University of North Carolina Press, 2008); Anne Marie Pelzer, "St. Joan's International Alliance, a Short History 1911–1977," Wijngaards Institute for Catholic Research, accessed November 11, 2011, Womenpriests.org, www.womenpriests.org/interact/pelzer.asp.

13 Henold, *Catholic and Feminist*, 21. Mary Fainsod Katzenstein echoes Henold's arguments about the importance of Vatican II on Catholic women's activism and self-understanding. Katzenstein, *Faithful and Fearless*, 158.

14 *Pacem in Terris* was a 1963 encyclical written by Pope John XXIII and was not one of the sixteen conciliar documents of Vatican II. Still, it gets swept up in discussions of the spirit of Vatican II and further elevates John XXIII's status in the minds of progressive Catholics. Both *Gaudium et Spes* and *Pacem in Terris* spoke of "conscience," suggesting that God had imbued humankind with the ability to distinguish right from wrong. In *Pacem in Terris*, Pope John XXIII wrote, "The world's Creator has stamped man's innermost being with an order revealed to man by his conscience; and his conscience insists on his preserving it. Men 'show the work of the law written in their hearts. Their conscience bears witness to them.' And how could it be otherwise? All created being reflects the infinite wisdom of God." Today, RCWP cites Joseph Ratzinger (the future Pope Benedict XVI)—who as cardinal and pope never gave any indication that he would entertain discussion of women's ordination—because of a particular statement he made on conscience in 1967: "Over the Pope as expression of the binding claim of ecclesiastical authority, there stands one's own conscience which must be obeyed before all else, even if necessary against the requirement of ecclesiastical authority." Not surprisingly, Catholic feminists from the 1970s onward cite the importance of following their conscience. See Pope John XXIII, *Pacem in Terris* ("Encyclical of Pope John XXIII on Establishing Universal Peace in Truth, Justice, Charity, and Liberty"), April 11, 1963, Vatican Archive (web), http://www.vatican.va/holy_father/ john_xxiii/encyclicals/documents/hf_j-xxiii_enc_11041963_pacem_en.html; "Roman Catholic Womenpriests' Response to Vatican Decrees of Excommunication" (press release), June 1, 2008, Roman Catholic Womenpriests, accessed April 23, 2014, http:// romancatholicwomenpriests.org/archivepressreleases.htm. RCWP's website no longer contains this press release, but it can be found here: http://www.bishop-accountability. org/news2008/05_06/2008_06_01_VoiceFromTheDesert_RomanCatholic.htm. Some sources citing Ratzinger indicate that he was writing in the *Commentary on the Documents of Vatican II*, but do not give specific publication information.

15 Raming and Müller's petition was published in a 1964 book titled *We Shall Keep Quiet No More! Women Speak to the Second Vatican Council*, compiled by Gertrud Heinzelmann. Heinzelmann self-published this book because, it has been said, publishers were uneasy about such a controversial topic. The book is incredibly difficult to locate, and my knowledge of it comes from secondary sources, which give this citation: *Wir schweigen nicht langer! Frauen aussern sich zum II Vatikanischen Konzil,* ed. Gertrud Heinzelmann (Zürich: Interfeminas-Verlag, 1964).

16 To be very clear, Vatican II did not structurally include or empower women. Very few women were even allowed to attend council sessions. Countless women clamored for a participatory voice yet felt overlooked on the eve of monumental reforms. For more on the history of women and Vatican II, see Angela Bonavoglia, *Good Catholic Girls: How Women Are Leading the Fight to Change the Church* (New York: Harper Collins, 2005); Kenneth A. Briggs, *Double Crossed: Uncovering the Catholic Church's Betrayal of American Nuns* (New York: Doubleday, 2006); Henold, *Catholic and Feminist*; Carmel McEnroy, *Guests in Their Own House: The Women of Vatican II* (New York: Crossroad,

1996); and Ruth A. Wallace, *They Call Her Pastor: A New Role for Catholic Women* (Albany, NY: SUNY Press, 1992).

17 Peter Steinfels, *A People Adrift: The Crisis of the Roman Catholic Church in America* (New York: Simon & Schuster, 2003), 257.

18 Pope Paul VI, *Humanae Vitae* (Of Human Life), July 25, 1968, Vatican Archive (web), http://www.vatican.va/holy_father/paul_vi/encyclicals/documents/hf_p-vi_ enc_25071968_humanae-vitae_en.html, 16; Robert McClory, *Turning Point: The Inside Story of the Papal Birth Control Commission* (New York: Crossroad, 1995); Robert Blair Kaiser, *The Politics of Sex and Religion* (Kansas City, KS: Leaven Press, 1985); Leslie Woodstock Tentler, *Catholics and Contraception: An American History* (Ithaca, NY: Cornell University Press, 2004), 4.

19 Ann Harrington, response to "Womenpriests" survey created by the author, SurveyMonkey (web), May 24, 2014; Rosa Manriquez, "Womenpriests" survey, May 23, 2014; Anonymous, "Womenpriests" survey, May 29, 2014.

20 "Meet the Ordained: Alice Marie Iaquinta," Roman Catholic Womenpriests, accessed July 4, 2015, https://www.romancatholicwomenpriests.org/meet-the-ordained/.

21 Mark Chaves, *Ordaining Women: Culture and Conflict in Religious Organizations* (Cambridge, MA: Harvard University Press, 1997), 84–129; Congregation for the Doctrine of the Faith, Inter Insigniores ("Declaration on the Question of the Admission of Women to the Ministerial Priesthood"), October 15, 1976, Vatican Archive (web), http://www.vatican.va/roman_curia/congregations/cfaith/documents/rc_con_cfaith_ doc_19761015_inter-insigniores_en.html. To clarify arguments made in the controversial *Inter Insigniores*, the CDF later released "A Commentary on the Declaration": Congregation for the Doctrine of the Faith, "A Commentary on the Declaration," January 27, 1977, reprinted in Halter, *The Papal "No,"* 196–210. Admittedly, we cannot know with certainty that Jesus's body was male; we do know that tradition attributes social and biological maleness to Jesus.

22 Congregation for the Doctrine of the Faith, *Inter Insigniores*.

23 Pope John Paul II, *Ordinatio Sacerdotalis* ("On Reserving Priestly Ordination to Men Alone"), May 22, 1994, Vatican Archive (web), http://w2.vatican.va/content/john-paul-ii/en/apost_letters/1994/documents/hf_jp-ii_apl_19940522_ordinatio-sacerdotalis.html. Scholars have debated whether this was the pope's way of claiming infallibility without speaking *ex cathedra*, which had been in the past the formal way of conveying infallible doctrine. Certainly, Archbishop Raymond Burke viewed *Ordinatio Sacerdotalis* as infallible and said as much when he formally excommunicated Patricia Fresen, Rose Hudson, and Elsie McGrath: "Noting that the three women have publicly affirmed, by word and deed, the validity of the ordination of women to the priesthood, in contradiction to the perennial, constant and infallible teaching of the Catholic Church..." Raymond L. Burke and Henry J. Breier, "Declaration of Excommunication of Patricia Fresen, Rose Hudson, and Elsie McGrath," *St. Louis Review*, March 14, 2008, 10.

24 Questions surrounding the infallibility of the Vatican's position have been raised in the *National Catholic Reporter*: John L. Allen, "Infallibility Debate Intensifies:

Australia Case Latest in Tensions That Have Swirled since Vatican I," *National Catholic Reporter*, May 27, 2011, 10, 12; Jerry Filteau, "Complex Questions of Infallibility," *National Catholic Reporter*, May 27, 2011, 1, 10; "Ordination Ban Not Infallibly Taught," *National Catholic Reporter*, May 27, 2011, 35. For a discussion of *Ordinatio Sacerdotalis*, as well as a summary of scholarly discussion about the document's potentially infallible nature, see Halter, *The Papal "No,"* 94–107.

25 Pope John Paul II, "Letter of Pope John Paul II to Women" June 29, 1995, Vatican Archive (web), http://www.vatican.va/content/john-paul-ii/en/letters/1995/documents/hf_jp-ii_let_29061995_women.html.

26 Halter, *The Papal "No,"* 79, footnote 315. Certainly, the Catholic Church's current emphasis on gender complementarity is a notable departure from centuries of church-endorsed subordinationism, which says that because women were created after men (in the second creation story, Genesis 2:4ff), women are subordinate and inferior to men. This way of distinguishing men and women has a long history in the church and in Western thought, owing to philosophers like Aristotle and theologians like Augustine and Thomas Aquinas. Some examples: St. Irenaeus argued that nature and the law make women subordinate to men; Tertullian intimated that only men—and *not* women—are made in the image of God, and he cast women as dangerous sources of lust and sexual temptation; Augustine wrote that the order of nature dictates that men rule over women; Thomas Aquinas suggested that women lack intellect and reason; and Bonaventure argued that women cannot be ordained because they do not bear the image of God (*"imago Dei"*). These arguments are often cited in Catholic feminist literature as evidence of the kinds of harmful female subordinationism that has characterized some patriarchs' thinking throughout Roman Catholic history. A wealth of resources about the discussion of women in early and medieval church texts can be found at www.womenpriests.org/index/, under "Fathers of the Church."

27 Pope John Paul II, *Mulieris Dignitatem* ("On the Dignity and Vocation of Women"), August 15, 1988, Vatican Archive (web), http://www.vatican.va/content/john-paul-ii/en/apost_letters/1988/documents/hf_jp-ii_apl_19880815_mulieris-dignitatem.html; Pope John Paul II, *Christifideles Laici* ("Apostolic Exhortation on the Vocation and the Mission of the Lay Faithful in the Church and in the World"), December 30, 1988, Vatican Archive (web), http://www.vatican.va/holy_father/john_paul_ii/apost_exhortations/documents/hf_jp-ii_exh_30121988_christifideles-laici_en.html; Pope John Paul II, "Letter to Women."

28 Congregation for the Doctrine of the Faith, *Inter Insigniores*.

29 Congregation for the Doctrine of the Faith, *Inter Insigniores*.

30 Henold, *Catholic and Feminist*, 15–25; Readers interested in educated and progressive nuns will appreciate also Amy L. Koehlinger, *The New Nuns: Racial Justice and Religious Reform in the 1960s* (Cambridge, MA: Harvard University Press, 2007).

31 Henold, *Catholic and Feminist*, 123–124; Ida Raming, *The Exclusion of Women from the Priesthood: Divine Law or Sex Discrimination?* trans. Norman R. Adams (Metuchen, NJ: Scarecrow Press, 1976); Mary Jo Weaver, "Chapter 5: Enlarging the

Discipline: Roman Catholic Feminist Theologians," in *New Catholic Women: A Contemporary Challenge to Traditional Religious Authority* (San Francisco: Harper and Row, 1985), 145–179.

32 Henold, *Catholic and Feminist*, 66, 104–115, 117–136; Ann Marie Gardiner, ed., *Women and Catholic Priesthood: An Expanded Vision: Proceedings of the Detroit Ordination Conference* (New York: Paulist Press, 1976).

33 Statement of Archbishop Bernardin, news statement, October 3, 1975, quoted in Gardiner, *Women and Catholic Priesthood*, 193–197. The NCCB is now called the United States Conference of Catholic Bishops (USCCB).

Bernardin's letter touched on themes of theology, discussion, and progress—all of which tie into women's ordination. Bernardin called the question of women's ordination "a serious theological issue," albeit one that had generated lively discussion and could "contribute to a better understanding of ministry, priesthood, and the role of women in the Church." Saying that "candor and a sense of responsibility" impelled him to address this women's ordination question, Bernardin stated, "Honesty and concern for the Catholic community, including those of its members who advocate the ordination of women, also require that Church leaders not seem to encourage unreasonable hopes and expectations, even by their silence." Bernardin went on to say that the church "must make sure that people are truly convinced of women's dignity and equality," and acknowledged, "The Church will suffer, indeed it will be betrayed, if women are given only a secondary place in its life and mission." He concluded with a call for "charity and mutual respect" between the two sides of this debate, "in order to be as certain as is humanly possible that we are indeed at all times seeking to know and do the will of Jesus Christ." See Gardiner, *Women and Catholic Priesthood*, 195, 197.

34 Patricia Hughes Baumer, interview with author, August 17, 2009.

35 Baumer, interview.

36 Of course the *Humane Vitae* birth control issue shows that American bishops can strongly voice one view and still be overruled by Rome. A connection between WOC and the NCCB prior to *Inter Insigniores* would not have guaranteed a different outcome.

37 Hughes came to see *Inter Insigniores* as perhaps a positive indication that WOC was pushing the right patriarchal buttons. She recalled a January morning in 1977, just after the release of the *Inter Insigniores* English translation, when one of her seminary professors greeted her with a big hug. "Congratulations," he said. "You got the bear to growl." Hughes interpreted the professor's remarks to mean that WOC had caught Rome's attention. Now that the CDF had laid out theological reasons barring women's ordination, feminist theologians could dismantle those arguments and offer alternatives.

38 Information about Judmilla Javorova comes from Miriam Therese Winter, *Out of the Depths: The Story of Ludmilla Javorova, Ordained Roman Catholic Priest* (New York: Crossroad, 2001), as well as Halter, *The Papal "No,"* 9–11. Javorova says that seven other women were ordained in Czechoslovakia and Slovakia, by Davidek and other bishops, but these women priests left the church because of the pressure and difficulties of remaining secret. Ludmilla is unique because she remained a priest.

39 Clandestine Catholicism didn't originate in mid-twentieth-century Czechoslovakia: the church had implemented similar survival tactics, with Pope Pius XI's approval,
in Mexico (1920s) and Moscow (1926). Rome then saw a need for similar actions in
late-1940s Romania.

40 Winter, *Out of the Depths.*

41 Winter, *Out of the Depths.*

42 "Frequently Asked Questions," Roman Catholic Womenpriests, accessed November 18, 2019, https://www.romancatholicwomenpriests.org/faqs/. The Women's Ordination Conference also tells Javorova's story on their website and brought her to the
United States in 1997 to talk about her experiences.

Womenpriests.org includes a translation of an interview with Javorova from the
Austrian publication *Kirche intern*: Werner Ertel and Georg Motylewicz, "Yes, I Am
a Catholic Woman Priest!," *Kirche intern* 9, no. 11 (1995): 18–19, trans. Mary Dittrich,
Wijngaards Institute for Catholic Research, accessed November 14, 2010, http://www.
womenpriests.org/called/javo_rep.asp.

43 See Leonard Swidler and Arlene Swidler, eds., *Women Priests: A Catholic Commentary on the Vatican Declaration* (New York: Paulist Press, 1977), 338–346; Wijngaards Institute for Catholic Research at womenpriests.org has reproduced parts of the
Swidlers' book, and the PBC report, which was printed as an appendix in the book, can
be viewed on the website: http://www.womenpriests.org/classic/append2.asp (accessed
April 12, 2014).

44 Pope Leo XIII established the Pontifical Biblical Commission in 1902. The
group's intended purpose was to facilitate and regulate Catholic studies of the Bible.
While it was originally an independent group within the Vatican's structures, in 1971
Pope Paul VI amended the group's rules, and one result was that the PBC became a
subgroup of the Congregation for the Doctrine of the Faith. The PBC no longer made
its own declarations; rather, its conclusions were issued through the CDF. This may
explain why the CDF did not publicize the PBC's findings on women's ordination. See
Leonard Swidler and Arlene Swidler, eds., *Women Priests: A Catholic Commentary on
the Vatican Declaration* (New York: Paulist Press, 1977); John R. Donahue, "A Tale of
Two Documents," in Swidler and Swidler, eds., *Women Priests*, 25–34; Halter, *The Papal
"No,"* 37–41.

45 In American religious parlance, Episcopalians are often grouped with Protestants,
yet here, as I emphasize the unique connections between Catholicism and the Anglican
Communion, a distinction is valuable: the Episcopal Church is a direct descendant of
the Church of England, also known as the Anglican Church. When the US earned its
independence from Great Britain, what had been the Anglican Church in the British colonies became known as the Episcopal Church. Anglicans—and, thus, Episcopalians—are born of both Catholicism and Protestant Reform traditions. They have
described themselves as "Protestant, yet Catholic."

46 Chaves, *Ordaining Women*, 170.

47 Carter Heyward, *A Priest Forever: One Woman's Controversial Ordination in the*

Episcopal Church (Cleveland, OH: Pilgrim Press, 1999), 3. For more on Episcopal women's push toward ordination, see Norene Carter, "The Episcopalian Story," in *Women of Spirit: Female Leadership in the Jewish and Christian Traditions*, ed. Rosemary Radford Ruether and Eleanor McLaughlin (New York: Simon and Schuster, 1979), 356–372.

48 Other women were ordained irregularly between the Philadelphia Eleven's ordination in 1974 and the 1976 change. Although Episcopal women can now be ordained deacons, priests, and bishops, there is still a struggle for equality in the Episcopal Church and its Anglican counterpart. Three US dioceses refuse to ordain women, and the issues of women bishops and openly gay clergy divide the Anglican Communion today.

49 Pope John Paul II, "The Vatican and Canterbury Exchange of Letters," *Origins* 16, no. 8 (July 17, 1986): 153–155, cited in Halter, *The Papal "No,"* 70.

50 Archbishop Robert Runcie's letter to Cardinal Jan Willebrands, reprinted in "The Vatican and Canterbury Exchange of Letters," *Origins* 16, no. 8 (July 17, 1986): 156–158, and cited in Halter, *The Papal "No,"* 71.

51 Peter Hebblethwaite, *The Next Pope* (New York: HarperSanFrancisco, 1995), 164.

Chapter 3. Conflict and Creativity

1 Peter Steinfels, *A People Adrift* (New York: Simon & Schuster, 2003), 10.

2 Ann Penick, response to "Womenpriests" survey created by the author, SurveyMonkey (web), May 29, 2014; Catacomb priest, "Womenpriests" survey, June 3, 2014; No name given, "Womenpriests" survey, May 25, 2014.

3 Elsie McGrath, "Womenpriests" survey, May 25, 2014.

4 Tom Roberts, "The 'Had It' Catholics," *National Catholic Reporter*, October 11, 2010, http://ncronline.org/news/faith-parish/had-it-catholics. Roberts writes, "The adult population of the United States was 228.1 million in 2008. So if one in 10 U.S. adults were former Catholics, that 22.8 million would make ex-Catholics, if one considered them a denomination, the second largest in the country behind Catholics, who list 68.1 million members, according to the National Council of Churches' 2010 Yearbook of American and Canadian Churches. The ex-Catholics would far outnumber the next largest denomination, Southern Baptists, who claim 16.2 million adherents." Note that as of 2019, surveys of American religiosity showed that the number of "nones"—people citing "no religious affiliation"—was basically equivalent to the number of Catholics and evangelicals (the latter being a group that cuts across denominational boundaries). Jack Jenkins, "'Nones' Now as Big as Catholics, Evangelicals in the U.S.," *Religion News Service*, March 21, 2019, https://religionnews.com/2019/03/21/nones-now-as-big-as-evangelicals-catholics-in-the-us/.

5 Peter Steinfels, *A People Adrift* (New York: Simon & Schuster, 2003), 10.

6 "Map: The Roman Catholic Diaspora," *National Geographic*, accessed January 3, 2015, http://news.nationalgeographic.com/

news/2013/03/130311-roman-catholic-diaspora-map/; "The Global Catholic Population," Pew Research Center, February 13, 2013, http://www.pewforum.org/2013/02/13/
the-global-catholic-population/.

7 "America's Changing Religious Landscape," Pew Research Center, May 12, 2015,
https://www.pewforum.org/2015/05/12/americas-changing-religious-landscape/.

8 Of course, not everyone believes that a smaller Roman Catholic Church would
be a weaker church. Pope Benedict XVI is often claimed to have said that he wanted
"a smaller but purer church." Many have debated what Benedict meant by this: Was
he calling for a more exclusive church, intolerant of dissent, or was he underscoring
the need for Catholicism to make some unpopular moves in order to hold and model
Christian values? I have heard RCWP's women cite Benedict and assume the former to
prove the importance of *contra legem* ordinations to keep the church open and inclusive.
See Joseph A. Komonchak, "'A Smaller but Purer Church'?," *Commonweal*, October 21,
2010, https://www.commonwealmagazine.org/smaller-purer-church.

9 Stephanie Yeagle, "Survey Shows a Divided Global Church," *National Catholic
Reporter,* February 28–March 13, 2014, 17. While not directly related to the question
of women's ordination, abortion is always a valuable touchpoint for Catholic surveys:
the Univision study Yeagle cites found that 60 percent of Catholics in the US, Europe,
and Latin America believed abortion should be allowed in some cases, while 60 percent
of Catholics in Africa and the Philippines believed abortion should never be allowed.

10 There are, of course, millions of Catholics who remain uncritical of these problems. I have spoken informally with American Catholics who are either surprised or
angered to hear of my research on womenpriests. They do not see gender inequality as a
problem in their church. Neither do many Catholics believe the sex-abuse crisis is reason
to question the church's foundations. I acknowledge that these perspectives exist, and
in abundance.

11 Kaya Oakes, "Why the Church Is Struggling to Hold onto Millennial Catholics,"
Religion Dispatches, July 20, 2015, http://religiondispatches.org/why-the-church-is-
struggling-to-hold-onto-millennial-catholics/. Oakes's article stems from her research
for her book *The Nones Are Alright: A New Generation of Seekers, Believers, and Those
in Between* (Maryknoll, NY: Orbis Books, 2015). The survey about millennials that
Oakes cites is described here: Michael Lipka, "Millennials Increasingly Are Driving
Growth of 'Nones,'" Pew Research Center, May 12, 2015, http://www.pewresearch.org/
fact-tank/2015/05/12/millennials-increasingly-are-driving-growth-of-nones/.

12 Kathleen Kautzer, *The Underground Church: Nonviolent Resistance to the Vatican
Empire* (Boston: Brill, 2012), 29–30.

13 Kautzer, *The Underground Church,* 1.

14 "RAPPORT," Women's Ordination Conference, accessed January 3, 2015, http://
www.womensordination.org/programs/rapport/. The only American among the Danube Seven, Dagmar Celeste, was a former WOC board member. RCWP bishop Andrea
Johnson served as WOC's executive director from 1996 to 2000; she was also a member
of RAPPORT. Kathy Vandenberg attended the 1978 national WOC meeting; Bishop

Olivia Doko joined WOC in the 1980s; Janice Sevre-Duszynska worked as a leader for WOC's Ministry of Irritation (another name for what WOC calls a "ministry of witnessing and prayerful protest" that seeks to keep women's ordination on the minds of the people in the pews—and the prelates at the altar). Other women learned about RCWP movement through WOC: Eileen DiFranco learned of RCWP and met Patricia Fresen at a local WOC chapter meeting; Mary Ellen Robertson also heard about RCWP through her membership in WOC. Judith McClosky was long involved in WOC. Such connections work internationally as well. RCWP Canada bishop Marie Bouclin served as a coordinator for WOW from 2002 to 2006. Morag Liebert, a Scottish womanpriest, worked for fifteen years with a UK group committed to women's ordination.

15 "Home," "Distinctives," and "FAQ," Ecumenical Catholic Communion, accessed August 12, 2010, http://www.ecumenical-catholic-communion.org/index.html.

16 "One Spirit One Church: The Catholic Dioceses of One Spirit," Catholic Dioceses of One Spirit, accessed December 2009, www.onespiritcatholic.org.

17 Kautzer, *The Underground Church*. Kautzer sees RCWP and independent Catholic groups as having "severed their connections to the Roman Catholic Church and emphasiz[ing] their divergence from the institutional church in their literature and religious education programs" (226). Importantly, however, RCWP does not want to sever its connections nor diverge from the Roman church; RCWP believes it can best reform the church by remaining connected in important historical, traditional, sacramental ways. Byrne, for her part, knows and acknowledges some womenpriests' discontent with being categorized as independent Catholics. Julie Byrne, *The Other Catholics: Remaking America's Largest Religion* (New York: Columbia University Press, 2016), 35.

18 Email to author, July 5, 2016. I do not have permission to connect this email's author with its content, so this womanpriest will remain anonymous.

19 See appendix C for demographic data on womanpriest communities.

20 RCWP communities do include Protestant worshippers, often from the churches renting or gifting liturgical space to the womenpriests, but RCWP appeals to Roman Catholics first and foremost.

21 "Many Americans Mix Multiple Faiths," Pew Research Center, December 9, 2009, http://www.pewforum.org/2009/12/09/many-americans-mix-multiple-faiths/.

22 No name given, response to "RCWP Communities" survey created by the author, SurveyMonkey (web), May 27, 2014.

23 Caitlin N. Gaskell, "All Are Welcome: The Roman Catholic Women's Ordination Movement and the Motivations of Participants" (undergraduate honors thesis, Washington University, March 2009), 67. Gaskell created pseudonyms for her interview subjects.

24 "Jan," a vowed woman religious in her late sixties, long felt like "a nervous wreck" at her parish Mass; for example, she struggled to adjust her own vocal proclamations of the church's formal creeds to match what she personally believed. At Therese, though, she could "live the faith I profess without being judged, without being weird or standing out." Gaskell, "All Are Welcome," 89.

34   *Notes*

25 Gaskell, "All Are Welcome," 91.

26 Allison Delcalzo, "Waiting for Wisdom: Sophia's Response to the Roman Catholic Church's Position of Priesthood" (master's thesis, Drew Theological School, May 2011), 58.

27 Dorothy Shugrue, "Womenpriests" survey, June 6, 2014.

28 Patricia Le Bar Plogmann, "RCWP Communities" survey, May 23, 2014.

29 Kathleen Gibbons Schuck, "RCWP Communities" survey, May 23, 2014.

30 Linda Nie, "RCWP Communities" survey, May 24, 2014.

31 Joanna Truelson, "RCWP Communities" survey, May 23, 2014.

32 Joan Moorhem, "RCWP Communities" survey, July 3, 2014.

33 Anonymous, "RCWP Communities" survey, July 4, 2014.

34 Nie, "RCWP Communities" survey, May 24, 2014.

35 Laurie Snyder, "RCWP Communities," survey, May 29, 2014.

36 Delcalzo, "Waiting for Wisdom," 60–61.

37 Anonymous, "RCWP Communities" survey, May 24, 2014.

38 Of course, sometimes womenpriests inspire their parishioners to seek ordination. This happens not infrequently. Two of my twenty-eight survey respondents—Kathleen Gibbons Schuck and Joanna Truelson—discerned a call to ordination after being RCWP parishioners. Womenpriests embody possibilities few have considered, and RCWP offers paths to ordination few have considered. Seeing womenpriests in action plants a seed, extends an invitation, and allows Catholic women to hear what they believe to be a vocational call from God, for perhaps the first time in their lives.

39 Theologian Elisabeth Schüssler Fiorenza is credited with coining the term "discipleship of equals" in her 1983 book, *In Memory of Her*, and expounding upon it in future works. Her idea is one in which there is no hierarchy (or patriarchy or—in Schüssler Fiorenza's most familiar parlance—kyriarchy) within Christian communities, but rather, all persons are equal. This equality comes not from any social standing (or lack thereof) but from following Jesus as faithful disciples.

Elisabeth Schüssler Fiorenza, *Discipleship of Equals: A Critical Feminist Ekklesia-logy of Liberation* (New York: Crossroad, 1993); Elisabeth Schüssler Fiorenza, *In Memory of Her: A Feminist Theological Construction of Christian Origins* (New York: Crossroad, 1983).

40 Carolyn Osiek and Margaret Y. MacDonald, *A Woman's Place: House Churches in Earliest Christianity* (Minneapolis, MN: Fortress Press, 2006).

41 This characterization of the early Christian church(es) and hierarchical development is within the (current) scholarly mainstream and can be found in the majority of textbooks covering New Testament history and early Christendom. Some scholars have taken this information and drawn more political conclusions about women's roles in the early church and Jesus's desires for a reformed Judaism. For two examples of feminist arguments, see Schüssler Fiorenza, *In Memory of Her*, now a classic in this area, as well as Karen Jo Torjesen, *When Women Were Priests: Women's Leadership in the Early Church and the Scandal of Their Subordination in Early Christianity* (San Francisco: Harper,

1993). See also Gary Wills, *Why Priests? A Failed Tradition* (New York: Viking, 2013); Wills's approach is not feminist, but he does argue against the necessity of hierarchical priesthood, considering his own understanding of its early Christian origins. On the other hand, some scholars are starting to challenge this historical narrative: for example, Benjamin L. White, "The Traditional and Ecclesial Paul of 1 Corinthians," *Catholic Biblical Quarterly* 79, no. 4 (October 2017): 651–669.

42 "Constitution," Roman Catholic Womenpriests-USA, April 2, 2012, http://romancatholicwomenpriests.org/pdf/RCWP_Constitution_2012.pdf; "RCWP Documents," Roman Catholic Womenpriests, accessed February 7, 2016, http://roman-catholicwomenpriests.org/documents.htm. At the time of writing, RCWP-Canada did not have any operating documents posted online.

43 "Constitution," Association of Roman Catholic Womenpriests, accessed February 7, 2016, http://arcwp.org/constitution/.

44 Diane Dougherty, "Womenpriests" survey, July 6, 2014; Dorothy Shugrue, "Womenpriests," survey, July 6, 2014; Mary Theresa Streck, "Womenpriests," survey, May 28, 2014.

45 Dougherty, "Womenpriests" survey, July 6, 2014; Ruth Broeski, "Womenpriests" survey, May 23, 2014; Anonymous, "Womenpriests" survey, July 1, 2014; Bridget Mary Meehan, "Womenpriests" survey, July 6, 2014; No name given, "Womenpriests" survey, May 23, 2014; Ann Harrington, "Womenpriests" survey, May 24, 2014.

46 Gabriella Velardi Ward, "Womenpriests" survey, July 9, 2014; Victoria Marie, "Womenpriests" survey, May 25, 2014.

47 Comments section of Bridget Mary Meehan, "Roman Catholic Women Priests Ordain Four Women in Chicago," YouTube video, 1:07, November 16, 2008, accessed May 16, 2009, http://www.youtube.com/watch?v=0ifFLNIA4WM; Comments section of OrdainWomen, "Breaking the Silence on Women's Ordination on the 15th Annual World Day of Prayer," YouTube video, 7:24, March 26, 2009, accessed May 16, 2009, http://www.youtube.com/watch?v=BvRC98iq-Cc. I retained all spelling, grammar, and punctuation of the original comments.

48 Angela Bonavoglia, interview, July 23, 2005, unused documentary footage from *Pink Smoke over the Vatican*, directed by Jules Hart (2011; Eye Goddess Films, 2013), DVD.

49 Mary Grace Crowley-Koch, "Womenpriests" survey, July 1, 2014.

50 "Meet the Ordained: Mary Kay Kusner," Roman Catholic Womenpriests, accessed July 4, 2015, https://www.romancatholicwomenpriests.org/meet-the-ordained/.

51 Mary Kay Kusner, telephone interview with author, September 17, 2009.

52 Mary Kay Kusner, email to author, September 17, 2009.

53 Beverly Bingle, "Womenpriests" survey, May 23, 2014.

54 Dagmar Celeste, "Soli Deo Amor: Story of a Vagabond Troubadour," in *Women Find a Way: The Movement and Stories of Roman Catholic Womenpriests*, eds. Elsie Hainz McGrath, Bridget Mary Meehan, and Ida Raming (College Station, TX: Virtualbookworm.com Publishing Inc., 2008), 6.

55 Kathy Sullivan Vandenberg, "Prophetic Obedience," in *Women Find a Way*, 123.

56 Dougherty, "Womenpriests" survey, July 6, 2014.

57 No name given, "Womenpriests" survey, July 2, 2014.

58 Penick, "Womenpriests" survey, May 29, 2014.

59 Mary J. Henold, *Catholic and Feminist: The Surprising History of the American Catholic Feminist Movement* (Chapel Hill: UNC Press, 2008), 6.

60 These words come from Coon's personal website, www.normajeancoon.com, now unavailable. Citations from her website can be found in articles such as Zoe Ryan, "Woman Deacon Recants, Seeks Reunion with Church," *National Catholic Reporter*, March 14, 2011, 1, 8.

61 Ryan, "Woman Deacon Recants."

Chapter 4. Ordination

1 Mary Fainsod Katzenstein, *Faithful and Fearless: Moving Feminist Protest inside the Church and Military* (Princeton, NJ: Princeton University Press, 1998). Katzenstein writes of feminists agitating for change within patriarchal organizations: "Sometimes by their mere presence, but more often by claiming specific rights, and by demanding in certain facets the transformation of the institutions of which they are a part, feminists have reinvented the protests of the 1960s inside the institutional mainstream of the 1990s" (7).

2 Katzenstein, *Faithful and Fearless*, 7.

3 The ceremony was filmed for *Pink Smoke over the Vatican*, directed by Jules Hart (2011; Eye Goddess Films, 2013), DVD. While this was the first public RCWP ordination in North America, a private diaconate ordination had taken place in Cape Cod, Massachusetts, earlier the same year.

Much information in the following section comes from the following sources: Juanita Cordero and Suzanne Avison Thiel, *Here I Am, I Am Ready: A New Model of Ordained Ministry* (n.p.: Roman Catholic Womenpriests-USA, Inc., 2014); Domenic D. Nicassio, "Canadian Archbishop Says Women's Ordination Ritual Will Not Be Valid," Catholic News Service, June 8, 2005, http://www.catholicnews.com/data/stories/cns/0503401.htm; Doug Struck, "Nine Defy Vatican's Ban on Ordination of Women," Washington Post Foreign Service, July 26, 2005, http://www.washingtonpost.com/wp-dyn/content/article/2005/07/25/AR2005072501586.html; "Movie of the (St. Lawrence) Ordination," Roman Catholic Womenpriests, accessed November 1, 2010, http://www.romancatholicwomenpriests.org/photo_gallery.htm.

4 St. Lawrence Seaway Ordination, ceremony filming, July 25, 2005, unused documentary footage from *Pink Smoke over the Vatican*, dir. Jules Hart.

5 Mayr-Lumetzberger celebrated this liturgy with Spiritus Christi's Jim Callahan, Mary Ramerman, and Denise Donato. In 1999, when it was still a Roman Catholic church called Corpus Christi Church, the congregation elected to leave the Rochester diocese over conflicts on gay and lesbian weddings, an open table Eucharist, and

women's ordination. "Herstory," Women's Ordination Worldwide, accessed January 8, 2020, http://womensordinationcampaign.org/herstory; Janice Sevre-Duszynska, "Witness Wagon Follows the Vision," Women's Ordination Conference, accessed May 20, 2015, http://www.womensordination.org/archive/pages/art_pages/art_WitWag.htm; "History," Spiritus Christi, accessed May 20, 2015, http://www.spirituschristi.org/#/welcome/history.

6 St. Lawrence Seaway Ordination, ceremony filming, July 25, 2005, unused documentary footage from *Pink Smoke over the Vatican,* dir. Jules Hart.

7 The Danube River boat both offered symbolism and met practical needs. As with the St. Lawrence ceremony three years later, the boat evoked images of Jesus, who fished with his apostles and calmed stormy waters. The boat also suggested motion, smooth progress forward, gliding through waters teeming with life. Pragmatically, the boat provided a worship space for the ceremony, for the ordinands held no hope for an ordination in a Roman Catholic church. By sailing in the Danube's international waters between Austria and Germany, the women did not break canon law in any particular Catholic diocese and thus could avoid messy jurisdictional issues. The boat also allowed organizers to control attendance and ensure that protesters did not disrupt the ceremony. The Congregation for the Doctrine of the Faith had already threatened anyone who attended the ordination—even journalists—with excommunication. Ordinand Gisela Forster claimed that Rome sought unsuccessfully to stop the ceremony by suing to rent out the *Passau* pleasure boat on which the ordination was to take place. But the ceremony would not be stopped. The ordination took place as planned, and on the feast day of apostles Peter and Paul—a day historically known for ordinations of men—the cadre later known as the Danube Seven became priests.

Technically this was not RCWP's first ordination. In order to be ordained priests at the very public Danube ceremony, the women had to already be deacons. Three months prior, on Palm Sunday, March 24, 2002, in a private residence, six women had been ordained to the diaconate: Gisela Forster, Iris Müller, Ida Raming, and Viktora Sperrer of Germany and Christine Mayr-Lumetzberger and Adelinde Roitlinger of Austria. Sperrer did not go on to priesthood ordination; apparently her local bishop put great pressure on her, and she decided to withdraw. Then at the Danube ceremony, just before the priesthood ordinations, two women were ordained deacons: Pia Bruner of Germany and Angela White (a pseudonym for Austrian-born Dagmar Celeste) of the United States. The women made certain to follow the correct order toward ordination, starting with the office of deacon and moving to priest; to skip over any step would have been, in the organizers' view, to proceed incorrectly.

Gisela Forster, "The Start: The Danube Seven and the Bishop Heroes," in *Women Find a Way: The Movement and Stories of Roman Catholic Womenpriests,* eds. Elsie Hainz McGrath, Bridget Mary Meehan, and Ida Raming (College Station, TX: Virtualbookworm.com Publishing Inc., 2008), 9–13; Dorothea McEwan, "Valid but Illegal (6 July 2002)," Wijngaards Institute for Catholic Research, July 6, 2002, http://www.womenpriests.org/called/mcewan.asp. For more general information on the Danube

Seven, see: John L. Allen Jr., "Ordinations Ignite Debate over Tactics: Women Face
Excommunication for Actions," *National Catholic Reporter*, July 19, 2002; John L. Allen
Jr., "Seven Women 'Ordained' Priests June 29," *National Catholic Reporter*, July 1, 2002;
Christine Mayr-Lumetzberger, "Reflections on My Way: God's Call to Me," in *Women
Find a Way*, 14–18; Iris Müller, "My Story, Condensed," in *Women Find a Way*, 19–20;
Ida Raming, "Situation of Women in the Roman Catholic Church: Canonical Back-
ground and Perspective," in *Women Find a Way*, 21–26; Dagmar Braun Celeste, "Soli
Deo Amor: Story of a Vagabond Troubadour," in *Women Find a Way*, 4–8.

See also Rea Howarth, "Witness to Her Story: German & Austrian Women Ordained Priests," Wijngaards Institute for Catholic Research, July 2, 2002, http://
www.womenpriests.org/called/howarth.asp; Cordero and Avison Thiel, *Here I Am,
I Am Ready*.

8 Ida Raming and Iris Müller, "Statement Regarding the Ordination of Women in
Austria (29 June 2002)," June 21, 2002, Wijngaards Institute for Catholic Research,
http://www.womenpriests.org/called/ramista2.asp.

9 Mayr-Lumetzberger, "Reflections on My Way: God's Call to Me," in *Women Find
a Way*, 14.

10 The Danube Ordination Movement began as a small grassroots group in Austria
and Germany called Kirche Von Unten. Emerging in the late 1990s, Kirche Von Unten
divided into smaller groups in the Austrian cities of Linz, Innsbruck, and Vienna. Each
subgroup began preparing for ordination. Gisela Forster explained that the program
drew about thirty women all desiring ordination: teachers, nurses, women religious, and
theologians. Gisela Forster, "The Start: The Danube Seven and the Bishop Heroes," in
Women Find a Way, 9–13.

11 Raming and Müller, "Statement Regarding the Ordination of Women."

12 Raming and Müller, "Statement Regarding the Ordination of Women."

13 Raming and Müller detail their joining with Christine Mayr-Lumetzberger and
Gisela Forester in Ida Raming and Iris Müller, *"Contra Legem"—A Matter of Conscience*
(Berlin: Lit Verlag, 2010), 66–69, 75–81.

14 Ida Raming, email interview with author, January 9, 2011. I believe this bishop
is the one named in Raming and Müller's book: "We also took part in this search [for
a Roman Catholic bishop willing to violate existing church law by ordaining women],
which led us to ask the so-called 'women's bishop' Auxiliary Bishop Ernst Gutting of the
Diocese of Speyer, who both orally and in writing had advocated ending patriarchy in
the church, whether he would be willing to ordain women, at least to the diaconate. To
this modest request, he replied: 'You are aware that I have always felt free in certain cases
to think otherwise than the Vatican; however, to act in such a way would cause such a
scandal that it would only make the situation of women in the Church worse.' This was
a disappointing rejection of our request." Raming and Müller, *"Contra Legem,"* 75–76.

15 The website for Braschi's church is at http://jesustheking.20fr.com/ (accessed November 19, 2010). It seems Braschi was made a bishop not once but twice: in 1998 by
Roberto Padin from the Catholic-Apostolic Church of Brasil, and in 1999 by Jeronimo

Podesta, who'd been a bishop in Argentina until his social and reform activism put him on the outs with the hierarchical church. It is unclear why Braschi felt the need to be ordained twice, though the practice is not uncommon: *sub conditione* ("subject to condition") ordinations are the church's way of ensuring that, if the first ordination didn't "work," the second would amend the error. For information on Braschi and the Danube ordinations, see Allen, "Seven Women 'Ordained,'"; and Allen, "Ordinations Ignite Debate." For a letter Forster wrote to the press in the days surrounding the Danube ordination, in which she specifically addresses Braschi's qualifications, see Gisela Forster, "Statement on the Bishop's Ordination and Ordination of Women Priests," trans. John Wijngaards, Wijngaards Institute for Catholic Research, accessed November 19, 2010, http://www.womenpriests.org/called/forster3.asp.

16 Of course the church would not publicly agree with this hairsplitting: as the *National Catholic Reporter*'s John Allen explained of the 2002 Danube ordination, "In reality, Braschi's episcopal status makes no theological difference, since official Catholic doctrine holds that it is impossible to ordain a woman no matter who performs the ritual. Politically, however, the challenge to that doctrine would be more dramatic if it came from a legitimate bishop." Allen, "Seven Women 'Ordained'"; Allen, "Ordinations Ignite Debate over Tactics."

17 RCWP's female bishops have expressed different views on Braschi's legitimacy. Prior to the ordination, Forster released a letter quoting Braschi's explanations and defending his qualifications and ministerial sensibilities. She further explained that he had rigorously vetted the candidates to ensure their suitability for priesthood. When I asked Ida Raming about Braschi, she was also quick to defend him. She pointed out that he had parted ways with the Roman church because, unlike most other hierarchs in Argentina at the time, he'd gone underground to support the people over the government. She asserted that his "ordination as bishop is in the line of apostolic succession although he was no longer under the jurisdiction of the [Roman Catholic Church] when he ordained us in 2002."

Bishop Patricia Fresen felt differently about Braschi. When the opportunity arose for her to be ordained a bishop in 2005, she fervidly wanted a bishop whose history would not raise questions, as Braschi's did. Though she acknowledged Braschi was a Roman Catholic bishop, the fact that he was outside the church—Fresen referred to him as "excommunicated"—meant, to her, that he should not perform sacraments. Fresen desired to stay "in the church"—her willingness to be ordained depended on it—and so she agreed to become a bishop only after speaking with Bishop X, an unnamed male bishop allegedly in "good standing" with the Vatican, who had participated in earlier ordinations. Fresen did not refer to this man as "Bishop X" in her interviews; the RCWP-published book *Here I Am, I Am Ready* identifies Fresen's consecrating bishop as Bishop X.

Gisela Forster, "Statement"; Raming, email interview; Patricia Fresen, interview, August 1, 2006, unused documentary footage from *Pink Smoke over the Vatican*, dir. Jules Hart.

18 Bishop X's identity may not be such a well-kept secret. Though RCWP will not confirm or deny the claim, several sources have identified Bishop X as Dusan Spiner. Like Ludmilla Javarova, Spiner was secretly ordained a bishop by Felix Davidek in Communist-era Czechoslovakia, and the Vatican ruled his ordination valid. If Spiner is Bishop X, his apostolic lineage would raise far fewer questions than Braschi's and Regelsberger's. *National Catholic Reporter*'s John Allen is a well-respected, neutral source who alleged that Dusan Spiner was Bishop X in his article, "Ordinations Ignite Debate over Tactics." I emailed Allen asking for confirmation, as I noticed that a number of sources naming Spiner got their information from Allen's reporting (e.g., Halter, *The Papal "No,"* 147). Allen was not able to consult his specific notes from the story identifying Spiner but said, "In general, I can tell you that I'm not in the habit of printing something if I'm not sure." John Allen, email to author, March 24, 2011.

19 Cordero and Thiel, *Here I Am, I Am Ready*. This book identifies the man as Bishop X and includes a photograph, taken mostly from behind, of him presenting the Gospels to the newly ordained deacons.

20 Allen, "Ordinations Ignite Debate"; Forster, "The Start"; Raming, email interview; McEwan, "Valid but Illegal"; Brigitte Enzer Probst, "A 'Messy Church'—A Church That Dares to Dirty Its Hands," Wijngaards Institute for Catholic Research, accessed January 15, 2015, http://www.womenpriests.org/called/forster3.asp.

21 Halter, *The Papal "No,"* 147; Allen, "Ordinations Ignite Debate." The quote from Braschi comes from Halter's book, and she in turn cites Allen as her source. Allen does say Braschi "acknowledged that he has no authority to perform an ordination for the Roman Catholic Church," but it is unclear where the exact words Halter uses come from.

22 Allen, "Seven Women 'Ordained.'" It's worth noting that in *Here I Am, I Am Ready*, the authors indicated Braschi said *"Brüder,"* German for "brothers," and not *hermanos*, as Allen reported.

23 McEwan, "Valid but Illegal." The eyewitness accounts I refer to come from "The Ordination of Catholic Women in Austria on the 29th of June 2002," Womenpriests. org, accessed November 17, 2010, http://www.womenpriests.org/called/29june02.asp, under "Detailed eyewitness reports." I also rely on John Allen's two *National Catholic Reporter* articles and the Danube Seven's stories from *Women Find a Way*.

24 To again emphasize this point: the church saw the Danube ordinations as "invalid" regardless. The ordinands, for their part, believed it possible for women to be validly ordained. Thus, what could *in*validate their ordinations would be the questionable validity and standing of the ordaining bishop(s). Hence, a *sub conditione* ordination was a way to protect the validity of the Danube Seven's ordinations, given the Seven's understanding of the possible validity of their ordinations.

25 I asked Ida Raming about the *sub conditione* ordination, but she declined to comment. In an interview with Jules Hart in *Pink Smoke over the Vatican*, however, Patricia Fresen revealed that some of the Seven—though she did not know how many—did go through an "extended ordination ceremony with some validly ordained bishops in full communion with Rome," to be quite certain of their ordained status should Braschi's

ordination be deemed invalid. This extra ceremony was done privately, in what RCWP calls a "catacomb ordination." Allen, "Ordinations Ignite Debate," *National Catholic Reporter*, July 19, 2002; Raming, email interview; Patricia Fresen, interview, August 1, 2006, Jules Hart, *Pink Smoke*, Documentary Footage.

According to *Here I Am, I Am Ready*, the first ordained womenbishops—Christine Mayr-Lumetzberger and Gisela Forster—were made bishops by Bishop M (yet another unnamed male bishop) on October 20, 2002, in a private ceremony. But "since there had been questions regarding the previous ordinations, both Christine and Gisela were ordained bishops *sub conditione* during an episcopal ordination on 19 May 2003 in Europe, at which Bishop X presided." Cordero and Avison Thiel, *Here I Am, I Am Ready*.

26 As mentioned previously in these notes, the 2014 publication *Here I Am, I Am Ready* named two secret bishops, X and M, and Patricia Fresen described a small group of bishops in Europe who support women's ordination. Thus there were at least two male bishop advocates, possibly more.

27 Cordero and Avison Thiel, *Here I Am, I Am Ready*; Patricia Fresen, interview, August 1, 2006, unused documentary footage from *Pink Smoke over the Vatican*, dir. Jules Hart; Rose Marie Berger, "Rocking the Boat," *Sojourners*, March 2007, http://sojo.net/magazine/2007/03/rocking-boat. Priests who publicly support women's ordination *have* been excommunicated as a result, specifically Fathers Ed Cachia (of Canada, in 2006) and Roy Bourgeois (of the United States, after an extended back-and-forth with Rome and the Maryknoll fathers, in 2012).

28 Patricia Fresen, interview, August 1, 2006, unused documentary footage from *Pink Smoke over the Vatican*, dir. Jules Hart.

29 Patricia Fresen, interview, July 20, 2005, unused documentary footage from *Pink Smoke over the Vatican*, dir. Jules Hart. Fresen did not refer to this man as "Bishop X" in her interviews, but the RCWP-published book *Here I Am, I Am Ready* identifies Fresen's consecrating bishop as Bishop X.

30 Christine Mayr-Lumetzberger, interview, July 25, 2005, unused documentary footage from *Pink Smoke over the Vatican*, dir. Jules Hart.

31 Patricia Fresen, "A New Understanding of Priestly Ministry: Looking at a Church in Crisis," in *Women Find a Way*, 29.

32 For example, see Helena Moon, "Womenpriests: Radical Change or More of the Same?," *Journal of Feminist Studies in Religion* 24, no. 2 (Fall 2008): 115–134.

33 I focus here on the 1995 WOC meeting because of its proximity to the first Danube ordination and because this is where Schüssler Fiorenza's "ordination is subordination" phrase gained a wide audience. To be sure, the WOC membership had never been in total agreement about tactics and goals, and Mary J. Henold documents some of the tensions at the second WOC meeting in 1978 in her book *Catholic and Feminist: The Surprising History of the American Catholic Feminist Movement* (Chapel Hill: University of North Carolina Press, 2008), 197–232.

34 Quoted in Pamela Schaeffer, "WOC Gathers to Promote Women's Ordination amid Conflicting Visions, Goals," *National Catholic Reporter*, December 1, 1995. In

late 2014, I could no longer access Schaeffer's article on ncronline.org but did find it here: http://www.thefreelibrary.com/WOC+gathers+to+promote+women%27s+or-dination+amid+conflicting+visions,...-a017839236.

For an expanded history of Schüssler Fiorenza's and Radford Ruether's critiques of the desirability of women's ordination, starting in the 1970s, see Rosemary Radford Ruether, "Should Women Want Women Priests or Women-Church?," *Feminist Theology* 20, no. 1 (2011): 63–72.

35 Schaeffer, "WOC Gathers."

36 Schaeffer, "WOC Gathers."

37 Mary Hunt's keynote speech, "Different Voices / Different Choices," addressed the actions of the growing RCWP movement most directly. Hunt was a primary mover behind Women-Church (now Women-Church Convergence), a movement that started in 1983 and combined Catholic theology and secular feminism, creating a community for worship, discussion, and social action. In her keynote, Hunt began by listing four ways that the thinking on women's ordination had changed and why this thinking had to continue to evolve. Hunt's driving concerns were that womenpriests would be co-opted by institutional power and that kyriarchy would be reinscribed on ordained women. Hunt summoned women to participate ministerially as laity, in keeping with the call of Vatican II. She offered a different vision: women's ministries must be "feminist, global, interreligiously connected, and justice-seeking." Only then would any Catholic feminist movement be adhering to its own values and to twenty-first-century challenges. Mary E. Hunt, "Different Voices / Different Choices: Feminist Perspectives on Ministry—A Contribution from the United States" (keynote speech, Women's Ordination Worldwide conference, Ottawa, Ontario, July 23, 2005), transcript, Wijngaards Institute for Catholic Research, www.womenpriests.org/wow/hunt.asp.

38 Ruether, speaking on "The Church as Liberation Community from Patriarchy," called for the dismantling of clericalism. She lamented how the early, egalitarian Christian movement became institutionalized through a linking of clergy and power. The sacrament of Eucharist, she said, had become a "clerical power tool," separating the laity from the clergy and thus from the church. Rosemary Radford Ruether, "The Church as Liberation Community from Patriarchy: The Praxis of Ministry as Discipleship of Equals" (keynote speech, Women's Ordination Worldwide conference, Ottawa, Ontario, July 23, 2005), transcript, Wijngaards Institute for Catholic Research, http://www.womenpriests.org/wow/ruether.asp. This website says Ruether's keynote was in 2006; this is an error.

39 Elizabeth Schüssler Fiorenza, "We Are Church—A Kindom of Priests" (keynote speech, Women's Ordination Worldwide conference, Ottawa, Ontario, July 23, 2005), transcript, Wijngaards Institute for Catholic Research, http://www.womenpriests.org/wow/fiorenza.asp. "Women's Ordination Movement" is capitalized in the online reprinting of Schüssler Fiorenza's speech, for reasons that are unclear.

40 I found *Equal wRites* (a periodical from a local WOC chapter in southeastern

Pennsylvania) to be an invaluable resource for seeing these debates unfold: http://sepa-
woc.org/NewsLetter.htm.

41 Erin Hanley, "WOC Support Ordinations—Sign of Renewal for the Church,"
Wijngaards Institute for Catholic Research, July 11, 2002, http://www.womenpriests.
org/called/woc_usa.asp.

42 Laura Singer, telephone interview with author, November 17, 2010. Singer explained to me that WOC had decided to exist in a state of "ambiguity" with RCWP,
supporting the group while continuing to push for church reforms and other models of
women in ordained ministry. WOC made a conscious decision to move away from the
heady academic and theological focuses spelled out by WOW's 2005 keynote speakers
and focus instead on the "people in the pews." The group expends considerable energy
trying to discern the best ways to reach Catholics who love their faith tradition, who love
the sacraments, and who may advocate women's ordination—but who are not necessarily well versed in feminist theological writing. WOC is, in Singer's words, the "big tent"
where conversations about church reform and visions for the future can take place—
even if not everyone agrees on the best next steps.

43 Ruether, "Should Women Want Women Priests or Women-Church?," 71.

44 Mary Hunt, "Catholic Women's Ordination: Forty Years of Success and Challenges to Come" (keynote speech, Women's Ordination Worldwide conference, Philadelphia, Pennsylvania, September 18, 2015), transcript, http://static1.squarespace.com/
static/50c6050ae4b0cd7ca3db88a1/t/56cecd01044262547c44846b/1456394219689/
WOC+GGGJ+2015.

45 The theologians and academics have, more or less, agreed to disagree—and to
keep RCWP in check. As of 2019, Schüssler Fiorenza, Radford Ruether, and Hunt all
sit on the WOC national advisory board, alongside RCWP bishop Andrea Johnson,
and womanpriest Jennifer O'Malley is on WOC's national board of directors. RCWP
still receives critiques from WOC's more progressive, academic side, as well as from
other feminist scholars who question RCWP's methods and ministries. "Board of Directors and Staff," Women's Ordination Conference, accessed March 27, 2015, http://
www.womensordination.org/about-us/board-of-directors-and-staff/; Moon, "Womenpriests: Radical Change or More of the Same?"; Marian Ronan, "Living It Out: Ethical
Challenges Confronting the Roman Catholic Women's Ordination Movement in the
21st Century," *Journal of Feminist Studies in Religion* 23, no. 2 (Fall 2007): 149–169.

46 Tom Feran, "Catholic Women Priests Ordain Six in Emotional Ceremony Despite Church's Stance," Cleveland.com, May 15, 2014, http://www.cleveland.com/
metro/index.ssf/2014/05/catholic_women_priests_ordain.html; Sadhbh Walshe, "For
Women Priests, a Moment of Justice—and Excommunication," *Aljazeera America*,
May 23, 2014, http://america.aljazeera.com/articles/2014/5/23/catholic-women-priests.
html; Lila Percy, "Female Priests Defy Catholic Church at the Altar," *All Things Considered*, National Public Radio, June 12, 2011, http://www.npr.org/2011/06/12/137102746/
women-priests-defy-the-church-at-the-altar; Tamara Evans, "Kentucky Woman Goes
against Roman Catholic Law; Ordained as Priest," WDRB.com (Louisville, KY),

April 27, 2013, http://www.wdrb.com/story/22097974/kentucky-woman-goes-against-roman-catholic-law-ordained-as-priest; Lindsey Smith, "Catholic Church Advises Parishioners in Kalamazoo to Avoid Ordination of Female Priest," Michigan Radio, May 28, 2014, http://michiganradio.org/post/catholic-church-advises-parishioners-kalamazoo-avoid-ordination-female-priest; Patrick Yeagle, "Women Priest Defies Catholic Diocese," *Illinois Times*, July 17, 2014, http://illinoistimes.com/article-14204-woman-priest-defies-catholic-diocese.html.

47 Doug McAdam, "The Framing Function of Movement Tactics," in *Comparative Perspectives on Social Movements*, eds. Doug McAdam, John D. McCarthy, and Mayer N. Zald (New York: Cambridge University Press, 1996): 339.

48 Bridget Mary Meehan, email to author, December 10, 2007.

49 Many of RCWP's tactical decisions around its ordinations echo those of civil rights activists in the 1960s. See Doug McAdam, *Freedom Summer* (New York: Oxford University Press, 1988), 150–154; McAdam, "The Framing Function of Movement Tactics," 338–355.

50 Rose Marie Hudson, interview with author, July 17, 2009.

51 "Roman Catholic Womenpriests to Be Ordained in St. Louis" (press release), Roman Catholic Womenpriests, October 15, 2007, http://www.romancatholicwomenpriests.org/.

52 "Roman Catholic Womenpriests to Be Ordained in St. Louis."

53 Michele Munz, "Cheering Crowd Attends Disputed Ordination of Two Women as Priests," *St. Louis Post-Dispatch*, November 12, 2007; James Rygelski, "Archbishop Says Women Seeking Ordination Risk Excommunication," Catholic News Service, November 8, 2007, http://www.catholicnews.com/data/stories/cns/0706386.htm; "St. Louis Archbishop Warns of Excommunication over Women's Ordination," Associated Press, November 7, 2007, http://www.iht.com/articles/ap/2007/11/07/america/NA-REL-US-Women-Priests.php; "St. Louis Archdiocese Angered by Synagogue's Hosting of Women Priests Ceremony," Fox News, November 10, 2007, http://www.foxnews.com/story/0,2933,310360,00.html.

54 Rygelski, "Archbishop Says"; Raymond L. Burke, "Attempted Ordinations to the Priesthood," in *St. Louis Review*, November 9, 2007.

55 During the 2004 presidential election, for instance, Burke announced that any Catholic politician who publicly supported legalizing abortion must be denied Communion—and he named Democratic presidential candidate John Kerry specifically. Burke further decreed that any Catholic voter supporting a pro-choice candidate because of his or her pro-choice stance should be refused Communion. The archbishop also demanded that a local Catholic hospital, Cardinal Glennon Children's Hospital, withdraw an invitation to singer Sheryl Crow to perform at a benefit concert because she supported embryonic stem cell research; when the hospital refused, he resigned from its board of directors. He also got entangled in a public and prolonged dispute with St. Stanislaus Kostka, a Polish Catholic parish in St. Louis, over whether the archdiocese or the St. Stanislaus board controlled church property and assets. When the conflict could not be resolved,

Burke excommunicated the St. Stanislaus priest and lay board members, accusing them of schism. See "Backers Join Ousted Priest in 'Illicit' Mass," Associated Press, December 26, 2005, https://www.nytimes.com/2005/12/26/us/backers-join-ousted-priest-in-illicit-Mass.html; Christopher Leonard, "Archbishop Blasts Sheryl Crow Appearance," Associated Press, April 25, 2007, https://www.washingtonpost.com/wp-dyn/content/article/2007/04/25/AR2007042502745_pf.html; John Thavis, "Archbishop Burke Says He'll Continue Politics-Abortion Campaign," Catholic News Service, November 29, 2004, https://archive.is/20130102070613/http://www.catholicnews.com/data/stories/cns/0406521.htm.

56 Rygelski, "Archbishop Says"; Pamela Schaeffer, "Woman Rabbi Takes the Heat for Woman Ordinations," *National Catholic Reporter*, November 9, 2007, http://www.natcath.org/NCR_Online/archives2/2007d/110907/110907h.htm; Raymond L. Burke, "Attempted Ordinations to the Priesthood," in *St. Louis Review*, November 9, 2007.

57 Elsie McGrath, interview with author, July 17, 2009.

58 Hudson, interview with author, July 17, 2009.

59 Schaeffer, "Woman Rabbi Takes the Heat; Pamela Schaeffer, "Though Church Bans Women Priests More and More Women Are Saying 'Why Wait?'," *National Catholic Reporter*, December 7, 2007, http://natcath.org/NCR_Online/archives2/2007d/120707/120707a.htm; Pamela Schaeffer, "Profiles of Five Women Priests," *National Catholic Reporter*, December 7, 2007, http://natcath.org/NCR_Online/archives2/2007d/120707/120707p.htm; "Finished Playing by the Rules," editorial, *National Catholic Reporter*, December 7, 2007, http://natcath.org/NCR_Online/archives2/2007d/120707/120707v.htm.

60 McGrath, interview; Hudson, interview.

61 Meehan, email to author.

62 Raymond L. Burke and Henry J. Breier, "Declaration of Excommunication of Patricia Fresen, Rose Hudson, and Elsie McGrath," *St. Louis Review*, March 14, 2008, 10.

63 McAdam, "The Framing Function of Movement Tactics."

64 Greg Archer, "Roman Catholic Female Priests Growing in Numbers: An Insider's Perspective," Huffington Post, June 12, 2009, https://www.huffpost.com/entry/roman-catholic-female-pri_b_214625.

65 Mark Chaves, *Ordaining Women: Culture and Conflict in Religious Organizations* (Cambridge, MA: Harvard University Press, 1997), 90–91.

66 Field notes, Rochester ordination, Rochester, NY, May 1, 2010.

67 Rosemary Radford Ruether, *Sexism and God-Talk: Toward a Feminist Theology* (Boston: Beacon Press, 1983), 137.

68 Daphne Hampson, "Feminism and Christology," in *Feminism and Theology*, eds. Janet Martin Soskice and Diana Lipton (New York: Oxford University Press, 2003), 287.

69 Schaeffer, "WOC Gathers." Schaeffer does note that Schüssler Fiorenza deliberately located her arguments in and alongside the biblical Jesus, which seemed to herald a forthcoming strategy for ordination activists like RCWP.

70 The Wijngaard Institute for Catholic Research website (headlined "Women Can

Be Priests") at womenpriests.org has a list of Catholic scholars who do and do not favor the ordination of women. The list is a valuable starting place but does not include the nuances of different authors' visions for the future of women's ordination. "Catholic Scholars," Wijngaard Institute for Catholic Research, accessed May 25, 2015, http://www.womenpriests.org/scholars.asp.

71 Gary Macy, *The Hidden History of Women's Ordination: Female Clergy in the Medieval West* (New York: Oxford University Press, 2008), 5–6.

72 Macy, *The Hidden History of Women's Ordination*, 5. Macy's scholarship built upon a foundation that most scholars agree on: in the eleventh and twelfth centuries, Western Christianity's ideas about ordination and what it meant to be ordained shifted. Leading up to the eleventh century, a person holding an ordained office was not viewed as having special powers to perform sacred, sacramental acts. Rather, someone who was ordained was special because a particular community had called this individual to service. Furthermore, before the eleventh century, ordination was not a way of moving up a hierarchical ladder. Instead, a deacon could be ordained a bishop without ever having been a priest; a priest need not have been a deacon. In fact, a number of popes were never ordained priests (Macy 25).

But times were changing. The church consolidated papal—and thus patriarchal—authority as Catholicism's influence extended into secular realms. What is more, the church had to distinguish itself from groups it deemed heretical, and altering the church's ordination and sacramental foundations allowed leaders to distinguish "legitimate" authority from its more "heretical" brand. Canonical records show that between the twelfth and thirteenth centuries, theologians began to differentiate between "nonsacramental consecration" for women and "sacramental ordination" for men. With this change came a newfound emphasis on a priest's Eucharistic role: now, only a properly "ordained" priest could make Christ present in the Eucharist. As such, ordination became a way of separating clergy from laity (Macy 41–42). Using the Fourth Lateran Council in 1215 as a point of demarcation, Macy argued that, once this change took place, the offices women held—such as deaconess, abbess, presbyter (the ancient term for "elder" and the precursor to modern notions of "priest"), and bishop—ceased to be considered ordained offices. A distinction emerged among the terms *ordinare*, *consecrare*, and *benedicere*, when before there had been none. Now, an "ordained" priest possessed a sacramental authority that a "consecrated" woman religious did not. The ceremony for ordination also changed during this time, and the laying on of hands became a requirement for an authentic conferring of holy orders. Being called to ordination was no longer about ministering to a particular community but about celebrating the sacraments.

73 Macy, *The Hidden History of Women's Ordination*, 86.

74 Macy, *The Hidden History of Women's Ordination*, 86.

75 Macy himself remained agnostic on whether his findings on ancient and medieval women's ordination should impact the question of ordained women in the twenty-first century.

76 "Resources," Roman Catholic Womenpriests, https://www.romancatholicwomenpriests.org/resources/. RCWP calls Macy's book a "must read" and says of the book,

"One of the most comprehensive and scholarly surveys of the history of women's ordinations in the Roman Catholic Church—a very thorough study with over 130 pages of notes and cited bibliography."

77 Bridget Mary Meehan, "There Have Always Been Women Priests," *Bridget Mary's Blog*, January 24, 2008, http://bridgetmarys.blogspot.com/2008/01/there-have-always-been-women-priests-by.html.

78 Dorothy Irvin, interview, July 23, 2005, unused documentary footage from *Pink Smoke over the Vatican*, dir. Jules Hart.

79 Dorothy Irvin, interview. In her conversations with me, Irvin credited Joan Morris's book *The Lady Was a Bishop: The Hidden History of Women with Clerical Ordination and the Jurisdiction of Bishops* (New York: Macmillan, 1973) for turning her on to this material. Irvin noticed that Morris's book referenced frescoes and mosaics but contained no photographs. Morris told Irvin that the publisher had found the photographs too expensive to print. Irvin thus made it her mission to circulate images of these women. Dorothy Irvin, interview with author, March 17, 2010.

80 RCWP's efforts to equate their ordinations with reclaiming a lost history came some years after the original 2002 Danube ordination. In the Danube Seven's preordination arguments, they did not allude to Phoebe or Junia, nor did they invoke the latest scholarship (academic or historical) on women in early Christianity. As the movement has grown, it has found new ways to argue its legitimacy.

81 "Order of Worship," worship aid, Roman Catholic Womenpriests, Sixth Midwest Region Ordination, August 16, 2009.

82 Rosemary Radford Ruether, "Women Priests Offer Differing Approaches to Valid Ordination," *National Catholic Reporter*, August 10, 2010, https://www.ncronline.org/news/global-sisters-report/women-priests-offer-differing-approaches-valid-ordination.

Chapter 5. Sacraments

1 Chava Redonnet, telephone interview with author, January 6, 2011.

2 *Catechism of the Catholic Church*, 2nd ed. (New York: Doubleday, 1995), 1131.

3 *Catechism of the Catholic Church*, 2nd ed. (New York: Doubleday, 1995), 1131.

4 Catechism of the Catholic Church, 1129. Rome has softened this rhetoric since Vatican II yet still asserts that salvation comes through the Roman church alone. As an example of Rome's continuing insistence on Catholicism as the one church that Christ instituted and its continuing reluctance to see Protestant churches as equivalent to Catholic churches, see Congregation for the Doctrine of the Faith, "Responses to Some Questions Regarding Certain Aspects of the Doctrine on the Church," June 29, 2007, Vatican Archive (web), http://www.vatican.va/roman_curia/congregations/cfaith/documents/rc_con_cfaith_doc_20070629_responsa-quaestiones_en.html.

5 These are paraphrases of different Catholic definitions of *sacrament*. Liam Kelly, *Sacraments Revisited: What Do They Mean Today?* (New York: Paulist Press, 1998), 1–3.

Even in antiquity, the words *sacrament* and *mystery* were closely connected, for both implied rites of initiation. Church father Tertullian seems to have been, in the early third century, the first to use the word *sacrament* (or *sacramentum*, in Latin) to describe rites of initiation into the Christian faith and to distinguish Christian practices from pagan ones (known as *mysterion* after the Greek word). It was Augustine of Hippo who connected sacraments to efficacy, ushering in the idea of sacraments as "an outward sign of inward grace." A simple, readable document explaining Catholic sacraments can be found on the website for the Diocese of Westminster (UK), http://rcdow.org.uk/att/files/faith/catechesis/baptism/sacraments.pdf.

6 *Catechism of the Catholic Church*, 1076.

7 Congregation for the Doctrine of the Faith, "Permanent Value of the Attitude of Jesus and the Apostles," *Inter Insigniores* ("Declaration on the Question of the Admission of Women to the Ministerial Priesthood"), October 15, 1976, The Holy See, http://www.vatican.va/roman_curia/congregations/cfaith/documents/rc_con_cfaith_doc_19761015_inter-insigniores_en.html.

8 Congregation for the Doctrine of the Faith, "The Ministerial Priesthood in Light of the Mystery of Christ," *Inter Insigniores*.

9 Congregation for the Doctrine of the Faith, "The Ministerial Priesthood in Light of the Mystery of Christ," *Inter Insigniores*.

10 *Catechism of the Catholic Church*, 1257.

11 *Catechism of the Catholic Church*, 1256.

12 Congregation for the Doctrine of the Faith, "Warning Regarding the Attempted Priestly Ordination of Some Catholic Women," reprinted in Deborah Halter, *The Papal "No": A Comprehensive Guide to the Vatican's Rejection of Women's Ordination* (New York: Crossroad Publishing, 2004), 235.

13 Theresa Novak Chabot, telephone interview with author, January 20, 2011; Bishop of Manchester John McCormack to Theresa Novak Chabot, 30 September 2010, in the author's possession.

14 Rachel Wood, telephone interview with author, May 10, 2011.

15 Wood, interview. For another take on this story, see: Sarah M. Earle, "Don't Deny Me Your Prayers," *Concord Monitor* (Manchester, NH), March 20, 2011.

16 Wood, interview.

17 The FCM will be taken up more in chapter 6. "Federation of Christian Ministries' History," Federation of Christian Ministries, accessed June 9, 2015, http://www.federationofchristianministries.org/index.php/fcm-history); Mary Ann Schoettly, email interview with author, January 8, 2011; Mary Ann Schoettly, telephone interview with author, January 9, 2011.

18 This quote comes from the "Statement from the Rev. Robert Gorski, Moderator of the Curia on the Organization 'Roman Catholic Womenpriests,'" which the Diocese of Manchester (NH) placed in church bulletins in 2010. I received a copy of this statement from Theresa Novak Chabot.

19 Dorothy Irvin, "But They Have No Community!," in *The Rebound 2003, 2004,*

2005, 2006, 2007: The Archaeology of Women's Traditional Ministries in the Church, 28–29 (unnumbered pages). "The Rebound" is a collection of images, maps, documents, letters, speeches, and essays, all connected to issues of women's ordination from ancient times to the present, which Dorothy Irvin assembled, printed, spiral bound, and sold. In addition to Irvin's article on this practice of local parishes recording the names of RCWP-baptized children, I have had several womenpriests tell me that they have had male priests do the same for them. Each of these women, however, asked to remain anonymous around this issue, lest the male priests be identified and punished.

20 Peter Stanford, "Christine Mayr-Lumetzberger: 'Defying the Pope? It's Not Like Paying a Parking Fine,'" *The Independent*, April 24, 2011, http://www.independent. co.uk/news/people/profiles/christine-mayrlumetzberger-defying-the-pope-its-like-not-paying-a-parking-fine-2274074.html.

21 Bridget Mary Meehan, "Bishop Christine Mayr-Lumetzberger Has Presided at Funerals and Weddings with Roman Catholic Male Priests in Austria—A Step Forward!," *Bridget Mary's Blog*, April 26, 2010, http://bridgetmarys.blogspot.com/2010/04/bishop-christine-mayr-lumetzberger-has.html.

22 *Catechism of the Catholic Church*, 1223.

23 Congregation for the Doctrine of the Faith, "Responses to Question Proposed on the Validity of Baptism Conferred with the Formulas," February 1, 2008, Vatican Archive (web), http://www.vatican.va/roman_curia/congregations/cfaith/documents/rc_con_cfaith_doc_20080201_validity-baptism_en.html. The issue is also taken up here: "CDF Rules Feminist-Inspired Baptisms Invalid," Catholic News Agency, February 29, 2008, http://www.catholicnewsagency.com/news/cdf_rules_feministinspired_baptisms_invalid/.

24 Therese of Divine Peace, Mass and baptism, St. Louis, MO, field notes, December 27, 2009.

25 Marie David, telephone interview with author, February 11, 2011.

26 Gloria Carpeneto, telephone interview with author, February 16, 2011.

27 "Order of Worship," worship aid, Roman Catholic Womenpriests, Sixth Midwest Region Ordination, August 15, 2009.

28 Redonnet, interview. Redonnet is correct that Spiritus Christi is not currently getting the kind of attention RCWP is drawing from church officials, but Spiritus Christi—when it was still known as Corpus Christi—had its share of diocesan trouble in the late 1990s. In 1998, Rochester bishop Matthew Clark removed Father Jim Callan from leadership; Clark was likely feeling Vatican pressure because Rome frowned upon the parish's willingness to allow women on the altar, bless gay unions, and invite non-Catholics to Communion. Many members of the Corpus Christi parish broke away and formed Spiritus Christi. In February 1999, the Rochester diocese declared that the new parish's members had excommunicated themselves. This *latae sententiae* excommunication is the same that applies to RCWP's women. I found a brief history of Spiritus Christi, told by Spiritus Christi, at "About Us: Our History: History of Spiritus Christi Church," Spiritus Christi, accessed February 11, 2011, http://spirituschristi.org.

29 Victoria Rue, interview, April 19, 2006, unused documentary footage from *Pink Smoke over the Vatican*, directed by Jules Hart (2011; Eye Goddess Films, 2013), DVD.

30 *Catechism of the Catholic Church*, 1582, 1597; "Priests in the Early Church and in Vatican II," Vatican Archive (web), http://www.vatican.va/roman_curia/congregations/cclergy/documents/rc_con_cclergy_doc_23111998_pvatican_en.html.

31 "Priests in the Early Church and in Vatican II."

32 Redonnet, interview.

33 Rose Marie Hudson, "I Think I See a Priest," in *Women Find a Way: The Movement and Stories of Roman Catholic Womenpriests*, eds. Elsie Hainz McGrath, Bridget Mary Meehan, and Ida Raming (College Station, TX: Virtualbookworm.com Publishing Inc., 2008), 105.

34 Kathy Sullivan Vandenberg, "Prophetic Obedience," in *Women Find a Way*, 125.

35 Mary Frances Smith, email interview with author, March 4, 2011.

36 Eileen DiFranco, "A *Contra Legem* Life," in *Women Find a Way*, 59.

37 Kathleen Strack Kunster, "Biography of a Priest," in *Women Find a Way*, 154.

38 Monique Venne, email interview with author, March 27, 2011.

39 Monica Kilburn-Smith, telephone interview with author, April 20, 2011.

40 Roberta Meehan, telephone interview with author, April 10 and 14, 2011.

41 *The Code of Canon Law* (Washington, DC: Canon Law Society of America, 1999), 897.

42 *Catechism of the Catholic Church*, 1357; *The Code of Canon Law*, 900.

43 For a full description of the official parts of the Roman Catholic Mass, see United States Conference of Catholic Bishops, "Chapter 2: The Structure of the Mass, Its Elements, and Its Parts," *General Instruction of the Roman Missal* (Washington, DC: United States Conference of Catholic Bishops, 2011), accessed June 14, 2015, http://www.usccb.org/prayer-and-worship/the-Mass/general-instruction-of-the-roman-missal/girm-chapter-2.cfm.

44 *Catechism of the Catholic Church*, 1353.

45 Eileen DiFranco, email interview with author, January 4, 13, and 18, 2011; DiFranco, "A *Contra Legem* Life," 56–62.

46 Bridget Mary Meehan, "Holy People, Holy Music, Holy House Church: A Roman Catholic Womanpriest's Story," in *Women Find a Way*, 89–94: 93, 90.

47 St. Praxedis Catholic Community, Mass, New York, NY, field notes, February 14, 2010.

48 Therese of Divine Peace Inclusive Community, Mass, St. Louis, MO, field notes, July 5, 2009; Therese of Divine Peace Inclusive Community, Mass and baptism, St. Louis, MO, field notes, December 27, 2009.

49 Church of the Beatitudes, Mass, Santa Barbara, CA, field notes, June 15, 2013.

50 "Home," Intentional Eucharistic Communities, accessed July 21, 2015, http://intentionaleucharistic.org/. A helpful introductory article to IECs is Tom Roberts, "Excellent Parishes, Small Communities Work Out Future," *National Catholic Reporter*, September 7, 2001, http://www.natcath.org/NCR_Online/archives2/2001c/090701/090701m.

htm. When I checked the publicly searchable directory of IEC communities in July 2015, a dozen of the communities listed—just about 10 percent—were RCWP communities.

51 Bridget Mary Meehan, "House Churches: Back to Basics: Christ-Centered, Spirit-Empowered Communities," in *Women Find a Way*, 44–46. For scholarship on house churches, see: Cynthia M. Baker, *Rebuilding the House of Israel: Architectures of Gender in Jewish Antiquity* (Stanford, CA: Stanford University Press, 2002); Carolyn Osiek and Margaret Y. MacDonald, with Janet H. Tulloch, *A Woman's Place: House Churches in Earliest Christianity* (Minneapolis, MN: Fortress Press, 2006).

52 Womanpriest Mary Ellen Robertson explained that she encountered Bernier's book during a course called "The Sacrament of Eucharist," and his ideas helped her think about incorporating the entire community into a liturgical celebration. Mary Ellen Robertson, "My Story," in *Women Find a Way*, 119.

53 Michele Birch-Conery, telephone interview with the author, April 11, 2011.

54 Birch-Conery, interview.

55 Andrea Johnson, telephone interview with the author, May 11, 2011.

56 I originally found this ordination video on Google Videos in the fall of 2007. It has since been moved to YouTube. "Roman Catholic Womenpriests: St. Louis," Google Videos, November 15, 2007, http://www.video.google.com/. Bridget Mary Meehan, "Roman Catholic Womenpriests: St. Louis," YouTube video, 9:59, May 18, 2013, https://www.youtube.com/watch?v=Dqnr3SSnt-0.

57 *Catechism of the Catholic Church*, 1399–1400.

58 Mary Frances Smith, "An Interview with Regina Nicolosi," in *Women Find a Way*, 137.

59 DiFranco, email interview. DiFranco went on to tell me about her return visit to her parish for a funeral, two years after her priest asked her not to receive Communion. Enacting what she believed to be her assigned role as an unwanted guest, she sat in the back of the church and did not come forward to take Communion. But some parishioners acted on her behalf: some sat with DiFranco in the back pews, using their presence and physical proximity to signal acceptance of her, and some brought her Communion, thereby including her in the community celebration of Christ's saving action. Significantly, DiFranco's parishioners felt empowered to follow their conscience and their own understanding of Christ, rather than adhere strictly to church-made rules.

60 Marybeth McBryan, interview with author, July 17, 2009; Redonnet, interview; Schoettly, email interview; Schoettly, telephone interview; Dagmar Braun Celeste, *We Can Do Together: Impressions of a Recovering Feminist First Lady* (Kent, OH: Kent State University Press, 2002).

61 Bridget Mary Meehan, "House Churches," in *Women Find a Way*, 44; Bridget Mary Meehan, "Holy People, Holy Music, Holy House Church," in *Women Find a Way*, 92.

62 No name given, response to "RCWP Communities" survey created by author, SurveyMonkey (web), May 27, 2014.

63 In the official Catholic understanding of marriage, it is not the officiant who

does the marrying; rather, the couple marries each other. The priest presides and facilitates, and of course makes celebrating the Eucharist possible in weddings that include a full Mass.

64 Victoria Rue, "Threshold Ceremonies," Threshold Ceremonies website, accessed January 8, 2011, http://home.earthlink.net/~humanint/site/index.html. This Threshold Ceremonies website is no longer active, though mention of Threshold Ceremonies still appears on Rue's personal website: Victoria Rue, "Roman Catholic Women Priest," Victoria Rue website, accessed January 5, 2020, http://www.victoriarue.com/html/woman_priest.html.

65 Schoettly, email interview.

66 Carpeneto, telephone interview.

67 Kilburn-Smith, telephone interview.

68 DiFranco, email interview.

69 Hildegard Community of the Living Spirit, Mass, Festus, MO, field notes, December 26, 2010.

70 Eleonora Marinaro, "Coming Home," in *Women Find a Way*, 86–88: 87.

71 Marie Bouclin, email interview with author, April 26 and 27, 2011. Other women-priests report similar incidents.

72 DiFranco, interview.

73 Schoettly, email interview.

74 Gabriella Velardi Ward, "Draw Me, We Shall Run," in *Women Find a Way*, 68–75: 73.

75 Rochester ordination, Rochester, NY, field notes, May 1, 2010.

76 "Pastoral Team," Mary Magdalene Apostle Catholic Community, accessed June 19, 2015, http://www.mmacc.org/#/about-us/pastoral-team. Corran was a Presbyterian woman in her midthirties with an extensive background in ministry and theology who took a profession of faith into the Catholic Church "as embodied by MMACC" at Easter 2010. MMACC copastors at the time were Jane Via, a Roman Catholic womanpriest since 2006, and Rod Stephens, an openly gay Roman Catholic priest who no longer served the institutional church and who had become affiliated with RCWP through Via.

77 Rosemary Radford Ruether, "Women Priests Offer Differing Approaches to Valid Ordination," *National Catholic Reporter*, August 10, 2010, http://ncronline.org/news/women/women-priests-offer-differing-approaches-valid-ordination. In her article, Ruether cites Gary Macy, The Hidden History of Women's Ordination (New York: Oxford University Press, 2008); Kurt Aland, A History of Christianity, vol. 1 (Philadelphia, PA: Fortress Press, 1985), 120; and Walter Bauer, Orthodoxy and Heresy in Early Christianity (Philadelphia, PA: Fortress press, 1971). See also: Rosemary Radford Ruether, *Women-Church: Theology and Practice of Feminist Liturgical Communities* (San Francisco: Harper and Row, 1985), 5, 284; Christopher Cadelago, "Congregation Ordains Catholic Female Pastor," *Sign On San Diego*, August 1, 2010, http://www.signonsandiego.com/news/2010/aug/01/congregation-ordains-catholic-female-pastor/. In this article, Bridget Mary Meehan, an RCWP bishop, says Corran's ordination is valid and "quite historic."

78 Years before Corran's ordination, RCWP had posed the possibility of ordaining women through a new mode of apostolic succession. Bishop Patricia Fresen wrote in 2008 that RCWP might in the future use another apostolic tradition to ordain Catholic priests:

> It is possible that, once women's right to be ordained equally with men, and in the same way, is more firmly established, there may be some new developments. . . . I suggest that our whole understanding of apostolic succession could be considerably broadened. Apostolic succession rightly means that the tradition of laying-on of hands for community ministry comes down to us through the centuries from the time of the early Church, and in fact goes back even beyond that. When we trace what we call apostolic succession, it usually goes back, in its written form, to some time during the Middle Ages. This is a hierarchical form of apostolic succession, passed down from one bishop to the next. It could still be accepted as apostolic succession, I propose, if the community—not the bishop—were to lay on hands. That would fit the communitarian model.

MMACC ordained Corran in this way: with lay hands, not a bishop's. Patricia Fresen, "A New Understanding of Priestly Ministry: Looking at a Church in Crisis," in *Women Find a Way*, 29.

79 The women I talked to did not feel comfortable speaking about the MMACC ordination without anonymity. Reynolds did not speak about the controversy, but she did mention having attended Corran's ordination. She felt it was one of the most "exquisite, powerful experiences" she had ever had, and she championed the idea of a *community* calling someone to ordination—as was the case in Jesus's time, she said. Dana Reynolds, telephone interview with author, December 14, 2010.

80 Cadelago, "Congregation Ordains Catholic Female Priest."

81 Jane Via, telephone interview with author, November 22, 2010.

Chapter 6. Ministries on the Margins

1 Bridget Mary Meehan, response to "Womenpriests" survey created by author, SurveyMonkey (web), July 6, 2014.

2 This language of "a new model of priestly ministry" occurs in Bridget Mary Meehan's 2006 video, which I analyze shortly. The phrase "a new model of ordained ministry in a renewed Roman Catholic Church" is the banner subtitle on RCWP-USA's website as of the summer of 2019. ARCWP's banner as of late 2019 now reads "a renewed priestly ministry in a community of equals."

3 godtalk, "A New Model of Priestly Ministry: Roman Catholic Womenpriests," YouTube video, 3:44, October 28, 2006, https://www.youtube.com/watch?v=LMYrQOpK58M.

4 Meehan, "Womenpriests" survey.

5 Diane Dougherty, "Womenpriests" survey, July 6, 2014.

6 No name given (USA-West), "Womenpriests" survey, July 17, 2014.

7 Good Shepherd Ministries of Southwest Florida was a nonprofit [501(c)3] started in 2003 and related to the Good Shepherd Inclusive Catholic Community, started in 2008 when Lee was ordained. Beaumont was ordained a priest in 2012. Under Lee and Beaumont's leadership, these entities worked in conjunction with the Lamb of God Lutheran-Episcopal Congregation, the progressive Catholic organization Call to Action, local Roman Catholic parishes, and other "interfaith friends," as Lee called them. In January 2020, there was no information online about Good Shepherd Ministries of Southwest Florida or the Good Shepherd Inclusive Catholic Community, possibly because Beaumont died in 2018.

8 Judy Lee, "A Priest of the Poor," in *Women Find a Way: The Movement and Stories of Roman Catholic Womenpriests*, eds. Elsie Hainz McGrath, Bridget Mary Meehan, and Ida Raming (College Station, TX: Virtualbookworm.com Publishing Inc., 2008), 77–85.

9 Lee holds a doctor of social work degree from Yeshiva University, a master's degree from Columbia University School of Social Work, and a doctor of ministry degree from Global Ministries University.

10 Judy Lee, "A Priest of the Poor," in *Women Find a Way*, 77–85: 77–78.

11 Dena O'Callaghan, response to "RCWP Communities" survey created by author, SurveyMonkey (web), May 28, 2014.

12 Victoria Marie, "Womenpriests" survey, May 25, 2014.

13 Victoria Rue, "Womenpriests" survey, May 29, 2014.

14 Jeannette Love, interview with author, June 15, 2013.

15 Ruth Broeski, "Womenpriests" survey, July 16, 2014.

16 Elsie McGrath, "Womenpriests" survey, May 25, 2014.

17 Suzanne Thiel, telephone interview with author, May 25, 2011.

18 Mary E. Hunt, "Catholic Feminist Ministries in a Discipleship of Equals" (speech, Call to Action conference, Milwaukee, Wisconsin, November 3–4, 2006). One context for this 2006 speech was the problems Hunt saw illustrated in the United States Conference of Catholic Bishops 2006 document "Ministry to Persons with a Homosexual Inclination: Guidelines for Pastoral Care," which she criticized as "top-down with no consultation with LGBTQ people." For more on Hunt's vision of the future of feminist ministries, see Mary E. Hunt, "Roman Catholic Ministry: Patriarchal Past, Feminist Future," *Proceedings of the Second Conference on the Ordination of Roman Catholic Women*, November 1978, http://www.womenpriests.org/classic2/hunt.asp; Mary E. Hunt, "Different Voices / Different Choices: Feminist Perspectives on Ministry—A Contribution from the United States" (keynote speech, Women's Ordination Worldwide conference, Ottawa, Ontario, July 23, 2005), transcript, Wijngaards Institute for Catholic Research, http://www.womenpriests.org/wow/hunt.asp.

19 Meehan, "Womenpriests" survey, July 6, 2014.

20 Suzanne Thiel, telephone interview with author, May 25, 2011.

21 "International Vision Statement," Roman Catholic Women Priests, accessed December 11, 2019, http://rcwpmidwest.org/IVS2014.pdf.

22 "Constitution/Constitución," Association of Roman Catholic Women Priests, accessed June 27, 2015, http://www.arcwp.org/constitution.html. I suspect that much of this language of serving people on the margins came from Meehan, who articulated it in the YouTube video and who is now a bishop with ARCWP. ARCWP's constitution has since been rewritten and is now more closely aligned with RCWP-USA's: "The Association of Roman Catholic women priests, therefore, responds to this call from the Holy Spirit, in our time, by preparing, ordaining and supporting qualified women and men, from all states of life, who are committed to a model of Church grounded in Jesus' vision of an open table, where all are welcome." See "Constitution," Association of Roman Catholic Women Priests, accessed January 8, 2020, https://arcwp.org/constitution/.

23 "History: Original Draft Constitution," Roman Catholic Womenpriests, accessed August 8, 2011, http://romancatholicwomenpriests.org/NEWhistory.htm.

24 Not surprisingly, worker priests in twentieth-century Europe drew concerns from Rome because of their proximity to the labor cause and unions, which were connected to Marxist ideas, which in turn exacerbated Vatican fears about Communist threats. Andreas Freund, "The Worker-Priest Movement in France Has Received New Papal Encouragement," *New York Times*, May 27, 1979, https://www.nytimes.com/1979/05/27/archives/some-clerics-also-wear-a-blue-collar.html.

25 Patricia Fresen, "A New Understanding of Priestly Ministry," in *Women Find a Way*, 32.

26 Marian Ronan, "Celebrating Our Triumphs, Committing Ourselves to Change" (speech, Southeast Pennsylvania Women's Ordination Conference, Philadelphia, Pennsylvania, March 12, 2005), transcript, accessed June 29, 2015, http://www.womensordination.org/archive/pages/art_pages/art_Ronan3-05.htm.

27 Significantly, Ronan was one of two keynote speakers at this anniversary event; the other was RCWP womanbishop Patricia Fresen. RCWP would have its first North American ordination four months later on the St. Lawrence Seaway, and Fresen was then in the early stages of articulating the young group's vision for American audiences. Contrary to Fresen's summons to stand up for justice in honor of "prophetic obedience," Ronan's speech issued cautionary advice, asking her audience to consider the people who might be excluded from this nascent brand of ordained ministry.

28 Meehan, "Womenpriests" survey, July 6, 2014.

29 Two articles that tackle questions of gender and professionalism specifically in higher education are Jo-Anne Dillabough, "Gender Politics and Conceptions of the Modern Teacher: Women, Identity and Professionalism," *British Journal of Sociology of Education* 20, no. 3 (1999): 373–394; and Theodore Glasser, "Professionalism and the Derision of Diversity: The Case of the Education of Journalists," *Journal of Communication* 42, no. 2 (June 1992): 131–140.

30 Of course, no singular type of man (in terms of age, ethnicity, or background) is drawn to the Catholic priesthood. A book that explores the United States' largest seminary for second-career priests, Sacred Heart, outside of Milwaukee, is Jonathan Englert's *The Collar: A Year inside a Catholic Seminary* (New York: Houghton Mifflin,

2006). For an accessible overview of priesthood formation since the Reformation, see Charles M. Murphy, *Models of Priestly Formation: Past, Present, and Future* (New York: Crossroad, 2006).

31 Some examples: Victoria Rue taught women's studies and comparative religion at San Jose State University; Debra Meyers and Rosemary Smead are university professors; Jane Via taught college courses in early Christianity before going to law school and becoming a prosecutor for San Diego County; Roberta Meehan taught biology for many years; Janice Sevre-Duszynska worked with ESL students as a high school teacher; Alice Iaquinta taught college for over thirty-five years and wrote, simply, "I am a teacher." Some women have training in health care, and some have backgrounds in body care. Mary Frances Smith, Mary Ellen Robertson, Morag Liebert, and Eileen DiFranco had long careers in nursing. Marie David, Gloria Carpeneto, and Monica Kilburn-Smith were trained as Reiki masters. Kathy Vandenberg, Kathleen Kunster, Suzanne Dunn, Toni Tortorilla, Christine Fahrenbach, and Mary Bergan Blanchard all have extensive backgrounds in counseling; Marie Bouclin and Gabriella Velardi Ward have counseled abuse victims, including those abused by priests. The wider category of pastoral ministry characterizes other women's work: Rose Marie Hudson worked in prison ministry, and Regina Nicolosi served as a chaplain in long-term care and worked with young men in a corrections facility.

32 Monica Kilburn-Smith, "Womenpriests" survey, May 29, 2014.

33 McGrath, "Womenpriests" survey, May 25, 2014.

34 Kilburn-Smith, "Womenpriests" survey, May 29, 2014.

35 Ann Penick, "Womenpriests" survey, May 29, 2014.

36 Gabriella Velardi Ward, "Womenpriests" survey, July 9, 2014.

37 Sarah Sentilles, *A Church of Her Own: What Happens When a Woman Takes the Pulpit* (Orlando, FL: Harcourt, Inc., 2008), 17.

38 Barbara Brown Zikmund, Adair T. Lummis, and Patricia Mei Yin Chang, *Clergy Women: An Uphill Calling* (Louisville, KY: Westminster, 1998), 23.

39 Sentilles, *A Church of Her Own*, 4. In fact, Sentilles credited Catholic women for helping her realize "how devastating Protestant sexism is." She discussed this further in chapter 11, which is dedicated to "Catholic Womenpriests" (249–267).

40 Typically, the adjective *ecumenical* characterizes exchanges between Christian churches, while *interfaith* extends to non-Christian groups. Throughout this section, I use *ecumenical* to refer specifically to intra-Christian work, and I use *interfaith* to describe efforts that may include Christianity but extend beyond it.

41 Jon Nilson, *Nothing Beyond the Necessary: Roman Catholicism and the Ecumenical Future* (New York: Paulist Press, 1995), 9.

42 Pope Paul VI, *Lumen Gentium* ("Dogmatic Constitution on the Church"), November 21, 1964, Documents of the Second Vatican Council, Vatican Archive (web), http://www.vatican.va/archive/hist_councils/ii_vatican_council/documents/vat-ii_const_19641121_lumen-gentium_en.html; Angelo Maffeis, *Ecumenical Dialogue*, trans. Lorelei F. Fuchs (Collegeville, MN: Liturgical Press, 2005); Deborah Halter, *The Papal*

"No": A Comprehensive Guide to the Vatican's Rejection of Women's Ordination (New York: Crossroad Publishing, 2004), 69–73; John Wilkins, "Ordinariate Gets Up and Running," *National Catholic Reporter*, May 27, 2011, 1, 6–7.

43 Iris Müller, "My Story, Condensed," in *Women Find a Way*, 19–20. Müller offers an extended autobiography in *"Contra Legem"—A Matter of Conscience*, which she coauthored with Ida Raming and which expands on Müller's arguments for Catholic women's ordination based on her experiences in and knowledge of the Lutheran example. Ida Raming and Iris Müller, *"Contra Legem"—A Matter of Conscience* (Berlin: Lit Verlag, 2010), 7–45.

44 Alice Iaquinta, "Coming Full Circle: The Journey Back to the Beginning," in *Women Find a Way*, 127.

45 Rose Marie Dunn Hudson, "I Think I See a Priest," in *Women Find a Way*, 104.

46 Mary Grace Crowley-Koch, Juanita Cordero, Marie David, Gisela Forster, Jean Marchant, Dena O'Callaghan, and Mary Theresa Streck are some examples of ordained women who are or were married to Catholic priests.

47 Mary Theresa Streck, "Womenpriests" survey, May 28, 2014.

48 Rue, "Womenpriests" survey, May 29, 2014.

49 Juanita Cordero, "Doors Closed and Doors Open," in *Women Find a Way*, 140–143.

50 "About CORPUS USA," CORPUS.org, http://corpus.org/index.php/about-corpus.

51 "Federation of Christian Ministries' History," Federation of Christian Ministries, https://www.federationofchristianministries.org/about-fcm/fcm-history.html.

52 William J. Manseau, "Roman Catholic Womanpriest Sacramental Mentorship, an Emerging Ecclesial Presbyterial Collegiality in Process," in *The Rebound 2003, 2004, 2005, 2006, 2007: The Archaeology of Women's Traditional Ministries in the Church*, ed. Dorothy Irvin, 61–62.

53 William J. Manseau, "National Catholic Ministries Alliance," Women's Ordination Conference, accessed July 6, 2015, http://www.womensordination.org/national-catholic-ministries-alliance/.

54 Various respondents, "Womenpriests" survey.

55 Monica Kilburn-Smith, telephone interview with author, April 20, 2011.

56 "Father Ed Cachia and the Reign of Terror (from the *Catholic New Times*, with permission)," in *The Rebound*, 45–46.

57 Edward Cachia, "Fr. Cachia's Response to Excommunication," Women's Ordination Conference, accessed July 6, 2015, http://www.womensordination.org/archive/pages/art_pages/art_FrCachiaApr06.htm. Note that, in the wake of his excommunication, Cachia and others set up a small faith community called Christ the Servant Catholic Community. Cachia said he felt called to "minister to those who are disillusioned with the current dysfunctionality of the Roman Catholic Church," a goal that resonates with those of RCWP. Unfortunately, this document is no longer available at this link, and I could not find it elsewhere.

58 Bourgeois's participation in Sevre-Duszynska's ordination seemingly would not automatically render him excommunicated *latae sententiae* because the CDF's May 2008 decree specifies excommunication for the women who attempt ordination and anyone who attempts to confer ordination upon them. Bourgeois can be said to have been excommunicated *ferendae sententiae*, however, because he received formal notice from the CDF after Sevre-Duszynska's ordination that he had incurred this penalty. Joshua J. McElwee, "Maryknoll: Vatican Has Dismissed Roy Bourgeois from Order," *National Catholic Reporter*, November 19, 2012, http://ncronline.org/news/people/maryknoll-vatican-has-dismissed-roy-bourgeois-order.

59 "About," School of the Americas Watch, accessed May 10, 2019, http://www.soaw.org/about/.

60 Reprinted in McElwee, "Maryknoll: Vatican Has Dismissed Roy Bourgeois."

61 Cachia, "Fr. Cachia's Response to Excommunication."

62 Roy Bourgeois, "My Journey from Silence to Solidarity," Wijngaards Institute for Catholic Research, accessed July 6, 2015, http://www.womenpriests.org/my-journey-from-silence-to-solidarity/. Note also Bourgeois's letter to the *New York Times* on the issue of women's ordination: Roy Bourgeois, "My Prayer: Let Women Be Priests," *New York Times*, March 30, 2013, http://www.nytimes.com/2013/03/21/opinion/my-prayer-let-women-be-priests.html.

63 "Resources," Roman Catholic Womenpriests, accessed January 6, 2020, https://www.romancatholicwomenpriests.org/resources/.

64 "Our Ministries," Association of Roman Catholic Women Priests, accessed July 7, 2015, http://www.arcwp.org/ministry.html. The ARCWP website has since changed but Bourgeois is still featured, appearing in three photographs. See "Ministries," Association of Roman Catholic Woman Priests, accessed January 6, 2020, https://arcwp.org/ministries/.

65 Marian Ronan, "Giving Thanks for Father Roy," *An American Catholic on the Margins* (blog), November 22, 2012, https://marianronan.wordpress.com/2012/11/22/giving-thanks-for-father-roy-2/.

66 Sentilles, *A Church of Her Own*.

67 In 2003, a sister from the National Coalition of American Nuns (NCAN) compared Fresen to Rosa Parks. Thanking Fresen for following God's call and risking excommunication, this NCAN sister wrote, "Like Rosa Parks, your action speaks loudly to our Church and the world. Like Rosa Parks, you will nudge our Church in changing an unjust law that restrains women and ignores their full personhood. With ordination, we as women can claim the same position as men in the Church's social structure much like Rosa Parks did in the civil society in the United States." See Sister Beth Rindler, SFP, to Patricia Fresen, *Equal wRites* (Ivyland, PA), June–August 2004, 11.

68 Patricia Fresen, "Prophetic Obedience: The Experience and Vision of Roman Catholic Womenpriests" (speech, Southeast Pennsylvania Women's Ordination Conference, Philadelphia, Pennsylvania, March 2005), transcript, accessed July 8, 2015, http://www.womensordination.org/archive/pages/art_pages/art_Fresen2005.htm.

69 Marian Ronan, "Living It Out: Ethical Challenges Confronting the Roman Catholic Women's Ordination Movement in the 21st Century," *Journal of Feminist Studies in Religion* 23, no. 2 (Fall 2007): 149–169, 166.

70 Ronan, "Living It Out," 164.

Chapter 7. Womenpriests' Bodies *in Persona Christi*

1 *Catechism of the Catholic Church*, 2nd ed. (New York: Doubleday, 1995), 2357–2359.

2 Mary J. Henold, *Catholic and Feminist: The Surprising History of the American Catholic Feminist Movement* (Chapel Hill: University of North Carolina Press, 2008), 26.

3 Monica Kilburn-Smith, telephone interview with author, April 20, 2011. Kilburn-Smith's critique struck out at the legacy of medieval theology. Invoking Thomas Aquinas's description of sacraments as a balance of matter and form—the matter being the tangible vehicle for the sacrament, such as water for baptism or bread and wine for Eucharist, and the form being the invocative words—Kilburn-Smith criticized the church for being fixated on matter, and specifically the gendered body as matter.

4 Gloria Carpeneto, telephone interview with author, February 16, 2011.

5 In 1988's apostolic letter *Mulieris Dignitatem* ("On the Dignity and Vocation of Women"), Pope John Paul II described motherhood and virginity as "two particular dimensions of the fulfillment of the female personality" and therefore intimately tied to a woman's vocation. Later that same year, in the Apostolic Exhortion *Christifideles Laici*, the pontiff again emphasized women's "specific vocation" and the way "the anthropological foundation for masculinity and femininity" clarifies "women's personal identity in relation to man [as] a diversity yet mutual complementarity, not only as it concerns roles to be held and functions to be performed, but also, and more deeply, as it concerns her make-up and meaning as a person." Pope John Paul II, *Mulieris Dignitatem* ("On the Dignity and Vocation of Women"), August 15, 1988, Vatican Archive (web), http://w2.vatican.va/content/john-paul-ii/en/apost_letters/1988/documents/hf_jp-ii_apl_19880815_mulieris-dignitatem.html; Pope John Paul II, *Christifideles Laici* ("Apostolic Exhortation on the Vocation and the Mission of the Lay Faithful in the Church and in the World"), December 30, 1988, Vatican Archive (web), http://w2.vatican.va/content/john-paul-ii/en/apost_exhortations/documents/hf_jp-ii_exh_30121988_christifideles-laici.html. For a fuller discussion of these papal documents in the context of women's ordination, see Deborah Halter, *The Papal "No": A Comprehensive Guide to the Vatican's Rejection of Women's Ordination* (New York: Crossroad Publishing, 2004), 76–85.

6 Judith Butler, *Gender Trouble: Feminism and the Subversion of Identity* (New York: Routledge, 1990), 140.

7 McGrath's shirt was a play on the well-known expression, often found on shirts, "This is what a feminist looks like."

8 Mary Byrne, "To Ordain or Not to Ordain...," *Equal wRites* (Ivyland, PA), September–November 2006: 9–10.

9 Bridget Mary Meehan, response to "Womenpriests" survey created by author, SurveyMonkey (web), July 6, 2014.

10 Debra Meyers, "Womenpriests" survey, May 23, 2014.

11 Bridget Mary Meehan, "Holy People, Holy Music, Holy House Church," in *Women Find a Way: The Movement and Stories of Roman Catholic Womenpriests*, eds. Elsie Hainz McGrath, Bridget Mary Meehan, and Ida Raming (College Station, TX: Virtualbookworm.com Publishing Inc., 2008), 92.

12 Mary Theresa Streck, "Womenpriests" survey, May 28, 2014.

13 Victoria Rue, "Womenpriests" survey, May 29, 2014.

14 Monica Kilburn-Smith, "Womenpriests" survey, May 29, 2014.

15 Meyers, "Womenpriests" survey, May 23, 2014.

16 Dana Reynolds, telephone interview with author, December 14, 2010.

17 Mary Ann Schoettly, email interview with author, January 8, 2011.

18 Wanda Russell, "Womenpriests" survey, May 23, 2014.

19 Beverly Bingle, "Womenpriests" survey, May 23, 2014.

20 Elsie McGrath, "Womenpriests" survey, May 25, 2014.

21 No name given, "Womenpriests" survey, May 23, 2014.

22 Ann Penick, "Womenpriests" survey, July 17, 2014.

23 It is certainly true that many legally ordained Catholic male priests support gay and lesbian rights. The official Roman church position, however, remains staunchly opposed to homosexuality and same-sex marriage.

24 Janice Sevre-Duszynska, interview, July 19, 2005, unused documentary footage from, *Pink Smoke Over the Vatican*, dir. Jules Hart.

25 Marie David, telephone interview with author, February 11, 2011.

26 Kilburn-Smith, telephone interview.

27 Pope John Paul II, "Letter of the Holy Father John Paul II to Priests for Holy Thursday 1988," March 25, 1988, Vatican Archive (web), http://www.vatican.va/content/john-paul-ii/en/letters/1988/documents/hf_jp-ii_let_19880325_priests.html. See also Deborah Halter, "Motherhood in a Manly Way," in *The Papal "No,"* 74–75.

28 Pope John Paul II, "Letter of Pope John Paul II to Women," June 29, 1995, Vatican Archive (web), http://www.vatican.va/content/john-paul-ii/en/letters/1995/documents/hf_jp-ii_let_29061995_women.html.

29 St. Lawrence Seaway Ordination, ceremony, July 25, 2005, unused documentary footage from *Pink Smoke over the Vatican*, dir. Jules Hart.

30 Christine Mayr-Lumetzberger, interview, July 25, 2005, unused documentary footage from *Pink Smoke over the Vatican*, dir. Jules Hart. Mayr-Lumetzberger was speaking not in her native German tongue but in English, and perhaps struggled to express her ideas fully.

31 Michael Mayr, interview, July 25, 2005, unused documentary footage from *Pink Smoke over the Vatican*, dir. Jules Hart.

32 Congregation for the Doctrine of the Faith, *Inter Insigniores* ("Declaration on the

Question of the Admission of Women to the Ministerial Priesthood"), October 15, 1976, Vatican Archive (web), http://www.vatican.va/roman_curia/congregations/cfaith/documents/rc_con_cfaith_doc_19761015_inter-insigniores_en.html; Halter, *The Papal "No,"* 42–62; Sara Butler, "Women's Ordination: Is it Still an Issue?," Archdiocese of New York, March 7, 2007, http://www.laici.va/content/dam/laici/documenti/donna/teologia/english/womens-ordination-still-an-issue.pdf.

33 Kathleen Kunster, "Biography of a Priest," in *Women Find a Way*, 152–154.

34 Pope John Paul II, "Letter of Pope John Paul II to Women."

35 "Meet the Ordained: Kathleen Kunster," Roman Catholic Womenpriests, accessed January 6, 2020, https://www.romancatholicwomenpriests.org/meet-the-ordained/.

36 I have noticed this pattern in RCWP's biographies—online, in interviews, and in publications like *Women Find a Way*—since I began studying the movement in 2007, and thus this tendency is neither a recent development nor a choice being phased out over time. The womenpriests' practice reminds me of similar patterns in professional and academic biographies, where women are more likely to talk about families (husbands, children, grandchildren, and even pets), whereas men are more focused on professional accomplishments.

37 In RCWP's "Response to Cardinal Rigali's Statement on the Ordination of Women in Philadelphia," RCWP wrote, "In refusing to recognize the priestly vocations of women, Sister Joan Chittister said quite accurately that the Roman Catholic Church forces itself to see with one eye, hear with one ear, and walk with one leg." See "Response to Cardinal Rigali's Statement on the Ordination of Women in Philadelphia," Roman Catholic Womenpriests, April 26, 2009, accessed December 11, 2015, http://romancatholicwomenpriests.org/responseo1.htm. RCWP's response to Rigali is no longer on the RCWP website but can be found on Bridget Mary Meehan's blog: Bridget Mary Meehan, "Response to Cardinal Rigali's Statement on the Ordination of Women in Philadelphia," *Bridget Mary's Blog*, April 26, 2009, accessed January 6, 2020, http://bridgetmarys.blogspot.com/2010/04/bishop-christine-mayr-lumetzberger-has.html.

38 Gayatri Chakravorty Spivak, *Outside in the Teaching Machine* (New York: Routledge, 1993).

39 Luce Irigary, *This Sex Which Is Not One*, trans. Catherine Porter with Carolyn Burke (Ithaca, NY: Cornell University Press, 1985).

40 "Biographies," Association of Roman Catholic Womenpriests, accessed December 13, 2015, http://arcwp.org/biographies/. In January 2020, Cheryl Bristol no longer appeared as a member of RCWP or ARCWP.

41 Cheryl Bristol, email interview with author, June 1, 2011.

42 Toni Tortorilla, "Womenpriests" survey, July 2, 2014.

43 "Meet the Ordained: Toni Tortorilla," Roman Catholic Womenpriests, accessed January 7, 2020, https://www.romancatholicwomenpriests.org/meet-the-ordained/.

44 "Ordained," Roman Catholic Womenpriests, accessed December 13, 2015, http://romancatholicwomenpriests.org/ordained.htm. For this note, I am citing the older version of the RCWP website, since in the newest version, Rue and O'Malley have modified their biographies, though still mention "spouse of twenty eight years…Kathryn Poethig"

and "wife, Elizabeth Carlin," respectively. I take it as significant that in these new iterations of their biographies, both womenpriests emphasize that, since the legalization of same-sex marriage, their partners are now *spouses*.

45 Janine Denomme was ordained to priesthood in May 2010, just about a month before she passed away, and the RCWP website honors her "in memoriam" as, among other qualities and accomplishments, the "cherished partner of Hon. Nancy Katz." Judy Lee and Judy Beaumont were RCWP's first ordained lesbian pair, as Lee was ordained (a deacon and priest) in 2008 and Beaumont was ordained to the diaconate in 2011 and the priesthood in 2012. The women are partners "in ministry and life since 1989." "Ordained," Roman Catholic Womenpriests.

46 Roman Catholicism's position on homosexuality has long been paraphrased as "love the sinner, hate the sin." Some argue that this is a more benign position than that of some Protestant denominations, for the Catholic Church says gay and lesbian people are welcome to be full participants in Catholic life—they just cannot act on their sexual desires (as sex must only happen within marriage, and the Roman Catholic Church bars same-sex marriages). Others contend that this position is not loving. One book tackling the "love the sinner, hate the sin" rhetoric so prevalent in Roman Catholicism (though not focused exclusively on Roman Catholicism) is Janet R. Jakobsen and Ann Pellegrini, *Love the Sin: Sexual Regulation and the Limits of Religious Tolerance* (New York: New York University Press, 2003).

47 "Statement of Position and Purpose," DignityUSA, https://www.dignityusa.org/ purpose. Womanpriest Eileen DiFranco's biography announces her heterosexuality— specifically, by saying that she and her husband Larry have four children and two grandchildren—and tells readers that she was "the first woman priest to preside at Dignity, Philadelphia." Similarly, Bishop Regina Nicolosi's biography referenced her husband, Charles, the "love of [her] life," and says that she "celebrates Eucharist with Dignity and other small faith communities." Both straight women allied with gay communities. Canadian womanpriest Linda Spear does not mention a spouse or partner, and an article about her on the RCWP Canada website says that she once served as "President of Dignity, Montréal." "Stories: A Roman Catholic Priest at Sutton," RCWP Canada, accessed December 13, 2015, http://rcwpcanada.x10.mx/docs/Herstory.html; "Meet the Ordained," Roman Catholic Womenpriests, accessed January 7, 2020, https://www. romancatholicwomenpriests.org/meet-the-ordained/.

48 Kwok Pui-Lan, "Touching the Taboo: On the Sexuality of Jesus," in *Sexuality and the Sacred*, ed. Marvin M. Ellison and Kelly Brown Douglas, 2nd ed. (Louisville, KY: Westminster John Knox, 2010), 119–134: 121.

49 Kwok, "Touching the Taboo," 122.

50 Kwok, "Touching the Taboo," 124.

51 These male-female binaries are often discussed in feminist theology, including in Anne M. Clifford, *Introducing Feminist Theology* (New York: Orbis Books, 2001), 19.

52 Clifford, "Chapter 3: Feminist Perspectives on God," in *Introducing Feminist Theology* (New York: Orbis Books, 2001), 102–104. See also Athalya Brenner, "The Hebrew

God and His Female Complements," in *Feminism and Theology*, eds. Janet Martin Soskice and Diana Lipton (New York: Oxford University Press, 2003).

53 Meehan developed what she calls the "polydimensional-continuum theory." Historically, an individual's sexual identity was determined based on "gross observation of the external genitalia." Instead, Meehan contends that the physical expression of sex is just one part of the polydimensional continuum and is not enough to determine whether one is "male" or "female." What must also be taken into consideration are internal gonadal structure, chromosomal identity, genetic expression, nervous system response, and hormonal response. Meehan explained that sometimes, a person appears male based on external genitalia but has a female internal gonadal structure; the converse also occurs. Roberta Meehan, telephone interview with author, April 10 and 14, 2011; Roberta Meehan, "Biology for Theologians: A Scientific Look at Male-Only Ordination," Wijngaards Institute for Catholic Research, accessed November 20, 2011, http://www.womenpriests.org/body/meehan2.asp. It strikes me that, with her arguments, Meehan anticipates much of the discourse around trans identities that have characterized discussions of gender in the 2010s, though she does not remark upon trans (or intersex) identities specifically.

54 Meehan, telephone interview; Meehan, "Biology for Theologians."

55 Mark Jordan asks similar provocative questions about Jesus's body from a theological perspective: Mark D. Jordan, "Chapter 5: Telling God's Body: The Flesh of Incarnation," in *Telling Truths in Church: Scandal, Flesh, and Christian Speech* (Boston: Beacon Press, 2003), 79–98.

56 Meehan is not the only scholar challenging gender essentialism and its implications for Christianity. Ethicist Christine E. Gudorf analyzed the challenges that arise for religion as sexual dimorphism erodes: Christine E. Gudorf, "The Erosion of Sexual Dimorphism," in *Sexuality and the Sacred*, 141–164. Abrahamic religions distinguish men from women "in terms of social function, worth, and relation to each other and to God" (144). Twentieth-century studies of sex and sexuality, however, undercut dimorphism, and biology has found chromosomal patterns that go beyond the simple XX and XY forms. "Polymorphous sexuality" is a more apt description of sexual realities—and Gudorf recommends that religions transition from dimorphous to polymorphous sexualities in order to make sense of these new, complex ways of understanding sex and gender. Meehan would agree and would add that one way religions like Catholicism must adjust to changing biological understandings of sex and gender is to "welcome *everyone* to discern a vocation to the priesthood." Meehan, telephone interview.

57 Gudorf, "The Erosion of Sexual Dimorphism," 157.

58 Gudorf, "The Erosion of Sexual Dimorphism."

59 Sarah Sentilles, *A Church of Her Own: What Happens When a Woman Takes the Pulpit* (Orlando, FL: Harcourt, Inc., 2008).

60 Rebecca Johnson, response to "RCWP Communities" survey created by author, SurveyMonkey (web), May 23, 2014.

61 Patricia Le Bar Plogmann, "RCWP Communities" survey, May 23, 2014.

62 No name given, "RCWP Communities" survey, July 2, 2014.

63 Sharon DeGreeff, "RCWP Communities" survey, July 19, 2014.

64 Linda Nie, "RCWP Communities" survey, May 24, 2014.

65 Joan Moorhem, "RCWP Communities" survey, July 3, 2014.

66 Marie Evans Bouclin, "Life as a Roman Catholic Woman Priest," *New States-man*, March 31, 2008, http://newstatesman.com/blogs/the-faith-column/2008/03/catholic-woman-priest-women.

67 Sharon DeGreeff, "RCWP Communities" survey, July 19, 2014.

Conclusion

1 Benjamin R. Knoll and Cammie Jo Bolin, *She Preached the Word: Women's Ordination in Modern America* (New York: Oxford University Press, 2018): 47–62.

2 Knoll and Bolin, *She Preached the Word*, 13–14.

3 Gerard O'Connell, "Pope Francis Says Commission on Women Deacons Did Not Reach Agreement," *America*, May 7, 2019, https://www.americamagazine.org/faith/2019/05/07/pope-francis-says-commission-women-deacons-did-not-reach-agreement.

4 Pope John Paul II, *Ordinatio Sacerdotalis* ("On Reserving Priestly Ordination to Men Alone"), May 22, 1994, Vatican Archive (web), http://w2.vatican.va/content/john-paul-ii/en/apost_letters/1994/documents/hf_jp-ii_apl_19940522_ordinatio-sacerdotalis.html.

5 Quoted in Joshua J. McElwee, "Vatican's Doctrinal Prefect Reaffirms Ban on Women Priests, Calls Teaching 'Definitive,'" *National Catholic Reporter*, May 29, 2018, https://www.ncronline.org/news/vatican/vaticans-doctrinal-prefect-reaffirms-ban-women-priests-calls-teaching-definitive.

6 David McClendon, "Gender Gap in Religious Service Attendance Has Narrowed in U.S.," FactTank, Pew Research Center, May 13, 2016, http://www.pewresearch.org/fact-tank/2016/05/13/gender-gap-in-religious-service-attendance-has-narrowed-in-u-s/.

7 Jamie Manson, "Reform Groups Challenge U.S. Bishops to Create 'A Church for Our Daughters,'" *National Catholic Reporter*, June 8, 2016, https://www.ncronline.org/blogs/grace-margins/reform-groups-challenge-us-bishops-create-church-our-daughters; "Declaration for Our Daughters," A Church for Our Daughters, accessed July 2, 2018, http://achurchforourdaughters.org/declaration.

8 Report I of the 40th Statewide Investigating Grand Jury (Office of the Attorney General, Commonwealth of Pennsylvania, August 2018), http://media-downloads.pacourts.us/InterimRedactedReportandResponses.pdf?cb=32148.

9 Report by Commission of Investigation into Catholic Archdiocese of Dublin (Department of Justice and Equality, November 29, 2009), http://www.justice.ie/en/JELR/Pages/PB09000504; Henry McDonald, "'Endemic' Rape and Abuse of Irish Children in Catholic Care, Inquiry Finds," *The Guardian*, May 20, 2009, https://www.theguardian.com/world/2009/may/20/irish-catholic-schools-child-abuse-claims.

10 James Carroll, "Abolish the Priesthood," *The Atlantic*, June 2019, https://www
.theatlantic.com/magazine/archive/2019/06/to-save-the-church-dismantle-the
-priesthood/588073/.

11 Women's Ordination Worldwide, Philadelphia, PA, field notes, September 15, 2015.

12 I want to acknowledge that in August 2018, Russell M. Nelson, president of the
Church of Jesus Christ of Latter-day Saints, made a statement requesting that the terms
Mormon and *LDS Church* no longer be used to refer to the church. Church members
are working to comply with this; it is as yet unclear what Nelson's request will mean for
academics in the field of Mormon studies.

13 Jana Reiss, "Mormon Women and Priesthood: 5 Depressing New Survey Findings," Religion News Service, December 15, 2015, http://religionnews.com/2015/12/15/
mormon-women-and-priesthood-5-depressing-new-survey-findings/; Pew Research
Center, "Chapter 4: Expectations of the Church," *U.S. Catholics Open to Nontraditional Families*, September 2, 2015, http://www.pewforum.org/2015/09/02/
chapter-4-expectations-of-the-church/.

14 Sally Priesand, the first American woman rabbi, was ordained in 1972 by Hebrew
Union College and her Reform congregation. In 1974, Sandy Eisenberg Sasso was or-
dained by the Reconstructionist Rabbinical College. The first woman ordained within
Conservative Judaism was Amy Eilberg, in 1985. Of the three women, Eilberg's ordina-
tion was the hardest won, as Conservative women had begun talking about ordination
in the early 1970s but faced barriers not unlike those Christian women faced. See Malka
Drucker, *Women and Judaism* (Westport, CT: Praeger, 2009); Pamela Susan Nadell,
Women Who Would be Rabbis: A History of Women's Ordination, 1889–1985 (Boston:
Beacon Press, 1998); Riv-Ellen Prell, *Women Remaking American Judaism* (Detroit, MI:
Wayne State University Press, 2007).

15 Kimberly Winston, "Modern Orthodox Judaism Says 'No' to Women Rabbis,"
Religion News Service, November 2, 2015, http://www.religionnews.com/2015/11/02/
modern-orthodox-judaism-says-no-women-rabbis/.

16 Elana Sztokman, "The New Critical Mass of Orthodox Women Rabbis," *The
Sisterhood* (blog), Forward, June 18, 2015, http://forward.com/sisterhood/310280/the
-current-wave-of-orthodox-women-rabbi/#ixzz403l41Nf2; JTA, "First Woman Orthodox
'Rabbi' Is Hired by Synagogue," *The Sisterhood* (blog), Forward, January 3, 2016,
http://forward.com/sisterhood/328427/first-woman-orthodox-rabbi-is-hired-by
-synagogue/#ixzz403nMcwcP.

17 Kelly Hartog, "Jewish 'Women of the Wall' Defy Law to Pray," Religion
Dispatches, September 21, 2009, http://religiondispatches.org/jewish-women-of-the
-wall-defy-law-to-pray/.

18 Emily Harris, "New Western Wall Rules Break Down Barriers for Jewish
Women," *Weekend Edition Saturday*, National Public Radio, February 6, 2016,
http://www.npr.org/sections/parallels/2016/02/06/465805423/new-western-wall
-rules-break-down-barriers-for-jewish-women.

19 Shayna Weiss, telephone interview with author, June 25, 2017. I extend very special

thanks to Shayna for her willingness to speak to me, academically and personally, about women seeking the rabbinate in Orthodox Judaism.

20 Diane Dougherty, response to "Womenpriests" survey created by author, Survey-Monkey (web), July 6, 2014.

21 Laurel Zwissler, "Spiritual, but Religious," *Culture and Religion* 8, no. 1 (March 2007): 66.

22 I am thinking here of this quote: "The 'spirituality' model focuses on the autonomous subject, who can construct paths of meaning that connect to the transcendent, even if on the edge of the traditional institutions or outside them. This turn from objective truth to subjective authenticity brings with it a specific concern for emotions, feelings, body, individual experiences of life, personal well-being, and self-realization—all of which are not seen in contradiction or in competition with a significant relationship with the sacred." Giuseppe Giordan and Enzo Pace, eds., *Mapping Religion and Spirituality in a Postsecular World* (Leiden: Brill, 2012), 4.

23 Zwissler, "Spiritual, but Religious," 65.

24 "History: Current Operating Structure," Roman Catholic Womenpriests, accessed August 30, 2011, http://romancatholicwomenpriests.org/NEWhistory.htm. RCWP's original draft constitution read, "We are living in a time of transition: We are moving from the non-recognition and exclusion of women to service in all church ministries and to the full co-creation and co-operation of women on all levels of the Roman Catholic Church." The very first goal expressed in the constitution was this: "'RC Womenpriests' is to bring about the full equality of women in the Roman Catholic Church. At the same time we are striving for a new model of Priestly Ministry. When these goals are reached and Can. 1024 CIC has been changed, the group 'RC Womenpriests' will be dissolved."

25 Patricia Fresen, "Prophetic Obedience: The Experience and Vision of Roman Catholic Womenpriests" (speech, Southeast Pennsylvania Women's Ordination Conference, Philadelphia, Pennsylvania, March 2005), transcript, accessed July 8, 2015, http://www.womensordination.org/archive/pages/art_pages/art_Fresen2005.htm.

26 Irene Senn, "Womenpriests" survey, July 1, 2014.

27 A 1996 *National Catholic Reporter* article (reposted online in 2013) seems to best capture this "paradigm-shift spirit" that I have heard referred to in RCWP conversations and homilies. Bernard Cooke, "Winds of Change Bring a 'Paradigm Shift'; Now Faithful Must Speak Up," *National Catholic Reporter*, June 17, 2013, http://ncronline.org/news/theology/winds-change-bring-paradigm-shift-now-faithful-must-speak.

28 Philip Jenkins, *The Next Christendom: The Coming of Global Christianity* (New York: Oxford University Press, 2011), 240.

29 Jenkins, *The Next Christendom*, 243.

30 Philip Jenkins recounts that "Europe and North America have 35 percent of Catholic believers and 68 percent of priests; Latin America has 42 percent of believers but only 20 percent of the priests. In terms of the ratio of priests to faithful, the Northern world is four times better supplied with clergy than the Global South." Jenkins, *The Next Christendom*, 268.

31 Women's Ordination Worldwide conference, Philadelphia, PA, field notes, September 19, 2015.

32 Victoria Rue, "Womenpriests" survey, May 24, 2014.

33 Maureen McGill, "Womenpriests" survey, May 24, 2014; Debra Meyers, "Womenpriests" survey, May 23, 2014; Wanda Russell, "Womenpriests" survey, May 23, 2014.

34 Of course, there are exceptions, such as Mary Magdalene Apostle Catholic Community in San Diego, which is the largest RCWP community I visited and which has a robust structure of events and opportunities for congregants.

Appendix A. Interview Subjects and Primary Sources

1 Allison Delcalzo, "Waiting for Wisdom: Sophia's Response to the Roman Catholic Church's Position of Priesthood" (master's thesis, Drew Theological School, May 20¹1); Caitlin N. Gaskell, "All Are Welcome: The Roman Catholic Women's Ordination Movement and the Motivations of Participants" (undergraduate honors thesis, Washington University, March 2009).

Appendix C. Data and Interview Questions for RCWP Communities

1 My survey aimed to get a sweeping overview of RCWP community members, from all regions, all countries, and including RCWP and ARCWP; its success depended mostly on whether the womenpriests forwarded the survey link to their populations. I received twenty-eight responses with usable data. Delcalzo focused exclusively on the Sophia community in Sussex County, New Jersey, not far from the Drew campus, and she had twenty-one survey respondents. Gaskell focused exclusively on Therese of Divine Peace, in her hometown of St. Louis, and conducted in-person interviews with thirteen members.

2 I do not have specific gender data from my surveys. In what I now recognize as poor design, I put questions that would identify the respondent's gender identity at the end of the survey. As this was a lengthy questionnaire, many people did not get that far and/or chose to forgo providing any identifying information. Of the people who revealed their gender, there were fourteen women and three men.

3 "America's Changing Religious Landscape," Pew Research Center, May 12, 2015, https://www.pewforum.org/2015/05/12/americas-changing-religious-landscape/.

4 Gaskell's study included local university students and members of the St. Louis Catholic Worker—both populations that would skew young (late teens and twenties). Those populations have not been in attendance at Therese when I have been there, but this could be because when I have traveled to St. Louis—Christmas break and summers—are precisely the times when young people may be traveling as well.

5 Michael Lipka, "A Closer Look at Catholic America," Pew Research Center,

September 14, 2015, http://www.pewresearch.org/fact-tank/2015/09/14/a-closer-look-at -catholic-america/.

6 "Demographic Profiles of Religious Groups," Pew Research Center, May 12, 2015, http:// www.pewforum.org/2015/05/12/chapter-3-demographic-profiles-of-religious-groups/.

7 I did not ask about racial or ethnic identity in my survey.

8 Brian McGill, "Catholicism in the U.S.," *Wall Street Journal*, September 18, 2015, http://graphics.wsj.com/catholics-us/.

9 "Demographic Profiles of Religious Groups," Pew Research Center.

ABOUT THE AUTHOR

JILL PETERFESO is associate professor of religious studies at Guilford College.

CATHOLIC PRACTICE IN NORTH AMERICA

James T. Fisher and Margaret M. McGuinness (eds.), *The Catholic Studies Reader*

Jeremy Bonner, Christopher D. Denny, and Mary Beth Fraser Connolly (eds.),
Empowering the People of God: Catholic Action before and after Vatican II

Christine Firer Hinze and J. Patrick Hornbeck II (eds.), *More than a Monologue:
Sexual Diversity and the Catholic Church. Volume I: Voices of Our Times*

J. Patrick Hornbeck II and Michael A. Norko (eds.), *More than a Monologue: Sexual
Diversity and the Catholic Church. Volume II: Inquiry, Thought, and Expression*

Jack Lee Downey, *The Bread of the Strong: Lacouturisme and the Folly
of the Cross, 1910–1985*

Michael McGregor, *Pure Act: The Uncommon Life of Robert Lax*

Mary Dunn, *The Cruelest of All Mothers: Marie de l'Incarnation, Motherhood,
and Christian Tradition*

Dorothy Day and the Catholic Worker: The Miracle of Our Continuance.
Photographs by Vivian Cherry, Text by Dorothy Day, Edited, with an Introduction
and Additional Text by Kate Hennessy

Nicholas K. Rademacher, *Paul Hanly Furfey: Priest, Scientist, Social Reformer*

Margaret M. McGuinness and James T. Fisher (eds.), *Roman Catholicism
in the United States: A Thematic History*

Gary J. Adler Jr., Tricia C. Bruce, and Brian Starks (eds.), *American Parishes:
Remaking Local Catholicism*

Stephanie N. Brehm, *America's Most Famous Catholic (According to Himself):
Stephen Colbert and American Religion in the Twenty-First Century*

Jill Peterfeso, *Womanpriest: Tradition and Transgression In the Contemporary
Roman Catholic Church*

John C. Seitz and Christine Firer Hinze (eds.), *Working Alternatives:
American and Catholic Experiments in Work and Economy*

Matthew T. Eggemeier and Peter Joseph Fritz, *Send Lazarus:
Catholicism and the Crises of Neoliberalism*

CPSIA information can be obtained
at www.ICGtesting.com
Printed in the USA
JSHW021505170621
15996JS00003B/140